Mapping the State

New Historical Perspectives is an open access book series for early career scholars, commissioned, edited and published by the Royal Historical Society and the University of London Press in association with the Institute of Historical Research. Submissions are encouraged relating to all historical periods and subjects. Books in the series are overseen by an expert editorial board to ensure the highest standards of peer-reviewed scholarship, and extensive support and feedback for authors is provided.

The series is supported by the Economic History Society and the Past and Present Society.

Series co-editors: Professor Elizabeth Hurren (University of Leicester) and Dr Sarah Longair (University of Lincoln)

Founding co-editors: Simon Newman (University of Glasgow) and Penny Summerfield (University of Manchester)

Editorial board: Professor Charlotte Alston (Northumbria University); Professor David Andress (University of Portsmouth); Dr Christopher Bahl (Durham University); Dr Milinda Banerjee (University of St Andrews); Dr Robert Barnes (York St John University); Dr Karin Bowie (University of Glasgow); Professor Neil Fleming (University of Worcester); Professor Ian Forrest (University of Oxford); Dr Emma Gallon (University of London Press); Professor Jane Whittle (University of Exeter); Dr Charlotte Wildman (University of Manchester); Dr Nick Witham (University College London)

Recently published

Designed for Play: Children's Playgrounds and the Politics of Urban Space, 1840–2010, by Jon Winder (July 2024)

Gender, Emotions and Power, 1750–2020, edited by Hannah Parker and Josh Doble (November 2023)

ISSN 3049-5091 (print)
ISSN 3049-5105 (online)

Mapping the State

English Boundaries and the 1832 Reform Act

Martin Spychal

Available to purchase in print or download
for free at https://uolpress.co.uk

First published 2024 by
University of London Press
Senate House, Malet St, London WC1E 7HU

© Martin Spychal 2024

The right of Martin Spychal to be identified as author of this Work has been asserted in accordance with sections 77 and 78 of the Copyright, Designs and Patents Act 1988.

This book is published under a Creative Commons Attribution-NonCommercial-NoDerivatives 4.0 International (CC BY-NC-ND 4.0) license.

Please note that third-party material reproduced here may not be published under the same license as the rest of this book. If you would like to reuse any third-party material not covered by the book's Creative Commons license, you will need to obtain permission from the copyright holder.

A CIP catalogue record for this book is available from The British Library.

ISBN 978-1-914477-39-3 (hardback)
ISBN 978-1-915249-25-8 (paperback)
ISBN 978-1-915249-27-2 (.epub)
ISBN 978-1-915249-26-5 (.pdf)
ISBN 978-1-914477-75-1 (.html)

DOI https://doi.org/10.14296/mpgh8387

Cover image: Composite image of 'The Constitution of 1832',
Thomas Starling, *Geographic Annual of Family Cabinet Atlas* (1833).

Cover design for University of London Press by Nicky Borowiec.
Book design by Nigel French.
Text set by Westchester Publishing Services UK in
Meta Serif and Meta, designed by Erik Spiekermann.

For Rona and the Trawler dynasty

In memory of Kim, Freya and Craig

Contents

List of illustrations ix
Acknowledgements xiii
List of abbreviations xvii

Introduction 1

Part I Envisioning England's reformed electoral map

1. A balancing Act? Interests and parliamentary reform, 1780–1832 21
2. 'The most unpopular part of the bill throughout the country': Reintegrating boundaries into the story of reform 61
3. Towards a science of government: The 'spirit of inquiry' and the establishment of the 1831–2 boundary commission 83
4. Whipped by the beadles? Data-gathering for the boundary commission 111

Part II Redrawing England's electoral map

Chronology and voting data 151

5. 'The work we are engaged in is intended to last for a century': Redrawing England's ancient electoral map 173
6. The Droitwich dilemma: Interests, grouping and the multiple parish borough 201
7. 'All the kindred interests of the town and neighbourhood': New borough limits 233
8. Under the knife: Reconstructing the county map 263

Conclusion 301
Bibliography 313
Index 339

List of illustrations

Figures

Figure 0.1 'Captain Thomas Drummond', (1834) by Henry William Pickersgill, EU0046 © University of Edinburgh Art Collection. — xviii

Figure 1.1 Robert Seymour, 'The three years job settled', *The Looking Glass*, March 1830, RB.37.c.31. British Library. — 50

Figure 2.1 John Doyle, 'Another Sign of the Times, or Symptoms of what Modern Architects, complaisantly term–Settling', 16 September 1831. Author's collection. — 77

Figure 3.1 William Heath, 'The March of Intellect', 23 January 1828. Author's collection. — 91

Figure 8.1 Thomas McLean, 'Doctoring', *The Looking Glass*, 2 February 1835. Author's collection. — 291

Tables

Table 1.1 Recorded use of 'interests' per parliament, 1774–1868. — 31

Table 1.2 Number of parliamentarians to mention an 'interest' per parliament, 1802–32. — 33

Table 1.3 Five speakers that mentioned interests the most per parliament, 1820–32. — 34

Table 1.4 References to 'agricultural interest' by debate topic, 1802–32. — 36

Table 1.5 Discussion of major interests by category of parliamentary debate. — 39

Table 3.1 Lord John Russell's initial suggestions to Grey for boundary commissioners. — 88

Table 3.2 Proposed county and borough boundary committee, 1 September 1831. — 89

Table 3.3 Working committee of the boundary commission (by district). — 99

Table 4.1 Boroughs visited by commissioners Tancred
and Wrottesley in District G. 114

Table 4.2 Pre-1832 size range of boroughs due to retain franchise
in second reform bill. 119

Table 4.3 £10 householders in boroughs due to retain franchise
in second reform bill. 123

Table 4.4 Average maximum adult male enfranchisement levels
per category of borough franchise 1832–65. 129

Table C.1 England's reformed constituency system and its
boundary changes in 1832. 152

Table C.2 Major Commons votes and confidence divisions, 1833–68. 154

Table C.3 Support for Whig-Liberal administrations in English
boroughs according to 1832 boundary changes, 1832–68
(seat count and percentage support). 157

Table C.4 Support for Whig-Liberal administrations in English
counties and boroughs, 1832–68 (seat count and percentage
support). 158

Table C.5 Support for corn law reform in English boroughs,
1834–52 (seat count and percentage support). 162

Table C.6 Support for corn law reform in English boroughs and
counties, 1834–52. 162

Table C.7 Support for abolition of church rates in English
boroughs, 1834–66 (seat count and percentage support). 165

Table C.8 Support for abolition of church rates in English
boroughs and counties, 1834–66. 165

Table C.9 Support for the ballot in English boroughs, 1833–66
(seat count and percentage support). 168

Table C.10 Support for the ballot in English boroughs and
counties, 1833–66. 168

Table C.11 Average vote contribution of each English
constituency type, 1832–68. 168

Table C.12 Relative vote contribution of each English
constituency type, 1832–68 (if each returned 100 MPs). 168

Table 6.1 Boroughs for which grouping options were
identified prior to 20 December 1832. 209

Table 6.2 Area of boroughs extended into their parish or parishes following 1832.   218

Table 6.3 Whig-Liberal support by party label in English boroughs, 1832–68 (seat count and percentage support).   225

Table 7.1 Location of new boroughs by boundary commission district.   239

Table 8.1 Variation in population per county division for each county.   270

Table 8.2 Variation in area per county division for each county.   271

Table 8.3 Variation in registered voters per county division for each county in 1836.   273

Table 8.4 Average variation in voters per county division between 1832 and 1865.   274

Table 8.5 Election results in the twenty-seven divided counties 1832–65.   287

Table 8.6 Election results in every county, 1832–65.   287

Maps

Map 4.1 Three definitions of the modern town of Plympton Earle, PP1831-2 (20), xxxvii © National Library of Scotland; digital additions by author.   131

Map 5.1 Commissioners' original tracing for Exeter, T72/9/15 © The National Archives; digital additions by author.   177

Map 5.2 Commissioners' original map for Bridgwater with enclosed land marked, T72/8/33 © The National Archives.   180

Map 5.3 Published map of Worcester, with original proposal, PP1831 (141), xl. Author's collection; digital additions by author.   189

Map 6.1 Proposed boundaries for grouped borough of Droitwich and Bromsgrove, T72/8/36, T72/9/9 © The National Archives.   206

Map 6.2 Four-mile radius around Droitwich for identifying reformed boundary, T72/9/9 © The National Archives.   214

Map 7.1 Birmingham, Soho, its proposed and final boundary, PP1831–2 (141), xl © National Library of Scotland; digital additions by author. 245

Map 7.2 Whitby and its proposed boundaries, PP1831 (141), xl. Author's collection; digital additions by author. 248

Map 8.1 Lancashire and its proposed divisions and places of election, PP1831–2 (141), xxxix © National Library of Scotland; digital additions by author. 268

Map 8.2 Warwickshire and its proposed divisions and places of election, PP1831–2 (141), xl © National Library of Scotland; digital additions by author. 279

Graphs

Graph 1.1 Recorded use of 'interests' per parliament, 1774–1868. 32

Graph C.1 Support for Whig-Liberal administrations in English boroughs 1832–68. 155

Graph C.2 Support for Whig-Liberal administrations in English counties and boroughs, 1832–68. 156

Graph C.3 Support for corn law reform in English boroughs, 1834–52. 160

Graph C.4 Support for corn law reform in English boroughs and counties, 1834–52. 161

Graph C.5 Support for abolition of church rates in English boroughs, 1834–66. 163

Graph C.6 Support for abolition of church rates in English boroughs and counties, 1834–66. 164

Graph C.7 Support for the ballot in English boroughs, 1833–66. 166

Graph C.8 Support for the ballot in English boroughs and counties, 1833–66. 167

Graph C.9 Average vote contribution of each English constituency type, 1832–68. 169

Graph C.10 Relative vote contribution of each English constituency type, 1832–68. 170

Acknowledgements

Mapping the State has evolved from work undertaken between 2012 and 2017 for an AHRC Collaborative Doctoral Award between the Institute of Historical Research and the History of Parliament: 'Space and power in the nineteenth-century House of Commons' (1244717). The project was supervised by three incredible historians, who have provided continued enthusiasm, guidance and friendship since its completion. I am indebted to the brilliant Kathryn Rix, her consistently shrewd analysis of nineteenth-century British politics and her unparalleled eye for detail. Philip Salmon has been far too generous in sharing his peerless understanding of late Hanoverian and early Victorian parliamentary and electoral politics, and enthusiasm for the collection of nineteenth-century reform junk memorabilia. It was a joy to work with Miles Taylor, whose wise counsel, wit and breadth of expertise as my primary supervisor was invaluable in shaping this book. Tragically, two historians who were integral to *Mapping the State* died during its writing. I would not have pursued a career in history without the mentorship of Arthur Burns. I regret that we were not able to toast the book's completion in a Bloomsbury pub. Likewise, Angus Hawkins, who acted as the external examiner of my PhD, deserves special acknowledgement for his guidance during the book 'phase' of this project.

I am deeply grateful to Henry Miller and Sarah Richardson for their insightful close reading of an initial draft of *Mapping the State* (and subsequent drafts); the two anonymous peer reviewers, whose positive appraisal in 2018 led to a book contract; and Roland Quinault and Lawrence Goldman, who read early versions of this work in their capacity as internal examiners at the IHR. I would like to thank the New Historical Perspectives Series and University of London Press – particularly Jane Winters, Penelope Summerfield, Heather Shore, Elizabeth Hurren, Emma Gallon, Julie Willis, Katharine Bartlett, Neil Fleming and Philip Carter – for their support and understanding as this book has slowly neared completion. I must also acknowledge Paul Seaward and his support for my application to the History of Parliament Trust for a three-month 'collateral research project' in 2022, without which *Mapping the State* would probably never have been finished.

Since re-entering academia in 2010 I have been fortunate to be part of a spirited community of historians centred around the IHR, King's College London and UCL. Thank you to Paul Readman and Martha Vandrei for so many jubilant nights (and days) in pubs, stadiums, flats and restaurants (of which, for some reason, I have a hazy recollection); the life-affirming

Laura Forster for being the coolest historian and best pal; and John Ingram for his sartorial elegance, historical eloquence and evenings of abandon in Philadelphia, Temple and St John's Wood. My fellow class of 2012 Patriotism and National Identities conspirators – Oliver Carter-Wakefield, Christian Melby, Tuva Skjelbred Nodeland, Ian Stewart and Brian Wallace – deserve special mention for keeping the Seven Stars in business and consistently setting new historical standards to live up to. To dinners, cake, music and pets with Ann Poulson and conversation (not all about Esher) and good wine with Mike Humphries, thank you. I am beholden to my fellow historians in the Modern British History Reading Group at King's College, London, who as well as critiquing and providing advice on nearly every aspect of this book, have provided a much-needed social outlet. As well as those members already mentioned, it was a privilege to have learnt from the innovative work of Melissa Aaron, Agnes Arnold-Forster, Joel Barnes, Susanna Blomqvist, Amy Kavanagh, Naomi Lloyd-Jones, Anna Maguire, Hélène Maloigne, Anders Mikkelsen, Rebekah Moore, Grace Redhead, Fern Riddell, Maggie Scull, Matthew White and Theo Williams. I must also thank the committee members of the Alethon not already mentioned: Mark Freeman and Tim Reinke-Williams.

It has been an honour to discuss, listen to advice and receive words of encouragement about various aspect of this book at conferences, seminars (online and in-person), in classrooms and in correspondence from: Stephen Ball, Luke Blaxill, John Bryant, Jennifer Davey, Patrick Duffy, Ian Cawood, Joe Coohill, Robin Eagles, Margaret Escott, Paul Hunneyball, Margot Finn, Edward Gillin, Paul Gurowich, Amanda Goodrich, Elizabeth Hallam-Smith, Geoffrey Hicks, Boyd Hilton, Anthony Howe, Gary Hutchison, Richard Huzzey, Joanna Innes, Connie Jeffery, Lyndsey Jenkins, Thomas Jones, Charles Littleton, Simon Morgan, Colm Murphy, Katrina Navickas, Kirsty O'Rourke, Jon Parry, James Peate, Emma Peplow, Sami Pinarbasi, Robert Poole, Stephen Roberts, Matthew Roberts, Max Skjönsberg, Michael Smith, Dave Steele, Sammy Sturgess, James Smith, Mari Takayanagi, Brendan Tam, Michael Taylor, Seth Thévoz, Adam Tucker and Nigel White. Thank you to David Cannadine and Melissa FitzGerald for the props and car journeys. Thank you to the many archivists and librarians that have made researching this book such a pleasure. Thank you to my colleagues at the History of Parliament. And thank you to history and politics teachers past and present: 'Miss' Jenkins, 'Miss' Fox, Rebecca Surtees, David McKinnon-Bell, Matt Cole, John Rowley, Rob Boddice, James Sharpe and Guy Halsall.

Mum, Dad, Frankie, Lucy, James, Rob, Jeremy, Arthur and Edie and all the members of Horse Face: don't worry, I won't quiz you on boundaries, but thank you for all you do to keep me sane. To Berna, Hugh, Sophie, Jack,

Larry, Rudi and Kizzie, thank you for letting me into the clan. To more afternoons in rehearsal rooms with Dave R, Dave P, Joe, Dan, Andy, Leigh and Gaz; more festivals and cultured summer salons with Amy, Sophie, Fi, Peter, Danai, Fallon, Fran, Alice, Katie, Kev, Jess and Joanna; and many more relished days out with Ian, Julia, Ryan and Amélie (and families). Thank you to Terry and Tracy for your hospitality on a trip to the Grey papers, and my former colleagues at Tower Hamlets. Reckless, Flashback, Crazy Beat, Music & Video Exchange, Casbah, Sister Ray and Alan's Records: thank you for providing a refuge away from politics and history. I wish Kim, Freya and Craig were still here. Thank you most of all to Rona Cran and the Trawler Dynasty. You have done more for this book than anyone listed above. Here's to many more years of cities, crows, Dylan, diving, negronis, PUP and never calcifying.

List of abbreviations

BL	British Library
DSC	Durham Special Collections
EHR	*English Historical Review*
FRS	Fellow of the Royal Society
FSA	Fellow of the Society of Antiquaries
HCJ	*House of Commons Journals*
HJ	*Historical Journal*
HLJ	*House of Lords Journals*
HOP	History of Parliament
JB	*Journal of British Studies*
LB	Library of Birmingham
MOP	*Mirror of Parliament*
ODNB	*Oxford Dictionary of National Biography*
PA	Parliamentary Archives
PP	Parliamentary Papers
PRO	National Archives, Russell Papers
RA	Royal Artillery
RE	Royal Engineers
RSA	Royal Society Archives
SDUK	Society for the Diffusion of Useful Knowledge
SRO	Staffordshire Record Office
TNA	The National Archives
UCL	UCL Special Collections

Figure 0.1: 'Captain Thomas Drummond', (1834) by Henry William Pickersgill, EU0046 © University of Edinburgh Art Collection.

Introduction

On 29 June 1832 a private dinner took place at Lovegrove's Hotel, Blackwall, to celebrate the completion of the boundary commissions that redrew the United Kingdom's electoral map as part of the 1832 reform legislation.[1] Over forty commissioners were present. Each had spent the previous winter working with an even larger team of surveyors, lithographers and clerks to survey the United Kingdom's constituency system. The guest of honour was Thomas Drummond, a royal engineer, surveyor and scientist who had been in charge of the English and Welsh boundary commission and established the template for its Scottish and Irish counterparts. Drummond was congratulated by his colleagues for having undertaken a 'delicate and arduous duty, intimately connected with an important event in the history of our country'.[2] As a token of their appreciation, the commissioners arranged for Drummond to sit for his portrait with the leading artist of the day, Henry William Pickersgill. Pickersgill captured his bashful thirty-four-year-old subject with his left hand resting on a table containing the 1832 Boundary Act for England and Wales and two volumes of the boundary commissioners' extensive reports (Figure 0.1).[3] Pickersgill's intent was clear. Drummond, and by proxy his fellow commissioners, were being immortalised for their contribution to a transformative national moment.

If the 1831–2 boundary commissioners were alive today, they would be right to feel aggrieved by their invisibility in the voluminous historiography of the 1832 reform legislation and the nineteenth-century British state. They might also be bemused that the practical and theoretical questions about the United Kingdom's electoral map, which occupied their labours between August 1831 and September 1832, have been overlooked by historians and political scientists. The scale and efficiency of the commission's work surveying and reforming England's constituency system alone was startling. Drummond oversaw a commission comprising 117 members of staff, who collected reams of previously unknown electoral data from the localities and drew England's electoral map – including official plans for at least 60 of England's northern towns and cities – for the first time. The commission's recommendations transformed the geography of England's electoral system. The reform legislation of 1832 altered the boundaries of 210 (81.7 per cent) of the 257 English constituencies in the reformed Commons, created 56 newly divided counties and increased the total area of England's borough constituency system from 1,317 to 2,809 square miles.[4]

While it is not surprising that the primary narrative of a milestone political event such as the 'Great Reform Act' has focused on the moments that convulsed the nation on an almost daily basis between November 1830 and the summer of 1832, it is somewhat baffling that basic questions about how electoral reform was implemented during that time have not been the subject of sustained research. This is not for want of direction. In 1953 Norman Gash identified the 1831–2 boundary commissions as a fertile source for future enquiry, a call that was re-echoed half a century later by Philip Salmon.[5] There are three reasons for the invisibility of the commissions in our understanding of 1832. First, histories of the first Reform Act have tended to focus on *who* got the vote, not *where* people got it. This is largely a hangover from the traditional, but still influential, interpretative paradigms of British political history that prioritised franchise reform in their efforts to understand 1832 through the lens of 'democratization'.[6] Second, the 1831–2 boundary commissions have, in a sense, been tarred by their association with the controversial, and flawed, 'politics of deference' thesis of D. C. Moore.[7] As this book demonstrates, while Moore's instincts that the boundary commissions provided a key to understanding the intentions of the Grey ministry in 1832 were correct, his need to substantiate his now discredited sociological theories about the reformed electoral system caused him to misinterpret, and seriously underplay, their significance. And third, until relatively recently, the existence of the working papers of the English and Welsh boundary commission had been poorly publicised, to the extent that they were presumed destroyed.[8] Their ready availability, combined with the ongoing digitisation of official papers, parliamentary records and contemporary newspapers, has made a macro-analysis of England's reformed electoral map a much less daunting, and potentially rewarding, task than it might have been even twenty years ago.

Mapping the State aims to remedy this situation and to reignite discussion about the electoral reforms of 1832 and their significance to modern British political history. Taking England as its chief focus, this book reassesses why and how parliamentary reform was enacted in 1832, its impact on politics both at Westminster and in England's constituencies, and its significance to the expansion of the modern British state. It underlines the need to understand the reform legislation of 1832 in the long-term context of debates over the representation of interests at Westminster since the eighteenth century, and a burgeoning culture of scientists, geographers, statisticians and political economists who wanted to create a science of government during the 1820s. Parliamentary boundaries (particularly the reform of English constituencies) were a major issue in the development of the 1832 reform legislation, the national debate over its potential consequences and the parliamentary struggle to secure reform between 1830 and 1832. Importantly, a new figure emerges as central to the reform process: the royal engineer and guest of honour at Lovegrove's Hotel on 29 June 1832, Thomas Drummond. His tireless endeavours as chair of the English and Welsh boundary commission were pivotal in ensuring the passage of the 1832 reform legislation, and were significant in establishing the governing techniques and methods that underpinned the increasingly ambitious domestic social policy of the nineteenth-century British state.

Instead of viewing the 1832 reform legislation as a template for democratic enfranchisement, or minimising its legacy by stressing the continuity between pre- and post-reform electoral politics, this book reconceptualises the electoral reforms of 1832 as a set of accomplished, technical measures grounded in innovative investigative techniques and a contemporary ambition to expand the application of disinterested bureaucracy to the workings of the British state. Drawing on the previously unused working papers of the English and Welsh boundary commission, this book embraces the recent methodological shift among political historians from the more exclusively language-based approaches of the 'new political history' towards a historical model that restores the role of empirical investigation and explores the opportunities provided by new digital methods and 'big data' to answer big structural questions in modern British history.[9] In this case, how did electoral reform in 1832 change politics and political culture in the UK? In doing so, *Mapping the State* argues that the commission's ground-breaking reforms to England's electoral map in 1832 reaffirmed the centrality of community to electoral politics, shaped the political identities and electoral strongholds of the emerging Conservative and Liberal parties, and established major precedents for electoral reform that are still in use today.

The 1832 reform legislation and boundary reform

The electoral reforms of 1832 were a landmark moment in the development of modern British politics. As the first of six major packages of reform, which culminated in the establishment of a noticeably modern democracy in the United Kingdom by 1948, the legislation overhauled the country's representative system, reshaped constitutional arrangements at Westminster, reinvigorated political relationships between the centre and the provinces, and established the political structures and precedents that both shaped and hindered electoral reform over the following century. This book demonstrates that the redrawing of England's electoral map by the little-known 1831–2 boundary commission for England and Wales underpinned this turning point in the development of the British political nation.

Historical debate about the 1832 reform legislation has a long lineage, which has generally focused on explaining why the government of the second Earl Grey sought to reform the electoral system via the extension of the franchise and the redistribution of seats. Aside from some interesting early interjections from Karl Marx, the traditional Whig interpretation of the legislation, which celebrated 1832 as the first in a line of concessionary proto-democratic reforms, made in response to a nation transformed by industrial change and threatening revolution at regular intervals between 1830 and 1832, retained a position of dominance until the mid-twentieth century.[10] From the 1950s a new generation of conservative historians – inspired largely by the historical approach of Lewis Namier – sought to establish the 1832 reform legislation (primarily the 1832 Reform Act for England and Wales) as a pragmatic and conservative, rather than proto-democratic, concession intended to incorporate the intelligent middle classes into the aristocratic constitution. This debate centred less on a defence of the old Whig interpretation, than on successive, largely successful, attempts to attack the separate claims of D. C. Moore, who discounted the threat of revolution between 1830 and 1832 and portrayed the legislation as a curative measure intended to restore the electoral power of the aristocracy.[11]

Since the 1980s several distinct, but generally complementary, historical approaches have established the insufficiency of using either the concession or the cure framework for developing a coherent understanding of the 1832 reform legislation. A collective reassessment of the role of party and ideology in nineteenth-century Whiggery has led a number of historians to reframe 1832 as a concerted attempt by its framers, steeped in their own Whig conception of history, to restore the ancient representative function of the Commons within the constitution.[12] This focus on Whiggery has been accompanied by an emphasis on the influence of non-Whig and anti-reform thought on the 1832 reform legislation, and calls for a more nuanced understanding of how contemporary notions of gender, and women's political claims, influenced the reform settlement.[13] In addition, an examination of the reform legislation for Wales, Scotland and

Ireland has underlined the considerable differences in how reform was perceived and developed throughout the UK, and the unique electoral structures that were established in each of the four nations after 1832.[14] The extent to which extra-parliamentary forces influenced reform in 1832, be they structural, social or cultural, have also undergone reassessment. While the idea of a direct causal link between the industrial revolution and the 1832 reform legislation has now been severely muddied, recent research has revealed how startling anomalies in the electoral system caused by demographic growth were important in convincing legislators of the necessity of parliamentary reform by the late 1820s.[15] And, while historians remain rightly sceptical about the threat of radical revolution in 1832, recent work has stressed the significance of the French Revolution of 1830, the widespread activities of the political unions, the extra-parliamentary role of women and the religious controversy that engulfed the reform debate between 1830 and 1832 for understanding why parliament and William IV eventually assented to the Grey ministry's reform legislation.[16]

Despite its extent, this historiography has paid scant attention to the particulars of constituency reform and the boundary commissions that accompanied the reform legislation of 1832. The footnotes and occasional references in the more comprehensive histories of the Act have offered a basic indication of the key points at which boundary reform intersected with the reform process between 1830 and 1832. Michael Brock suggested that boundary changes were influential in appeasing parliamentary moderates over reform and afforded brief mention of Drummond's reorganisation of seat redistribution in December 1831 – via what became known as 'Drummond's List'.[17] Despite Gash's observation in 1953 that the activities of the 1831–2 boundary commissions represented 'an important, though neglected' aspect of the 1832 reform legislation, discussion of their activities is equally sparse.[18] In 1976, Moore briefly considered the unusual evolution of the English and Welsh commission between 1830 and 1832. Each reform bill, he observed, had made a different provision for how boundaries should be settled. He also noted the frequent changes in the commissioners' guidelines between August and December 1831, and the bestowing of extra responsibility on the commission for the redefinition of the redistribution schedules in November 1831. While Moore remained vague over its particulars, boundary reform formed an integral part of his argument that the Grey ministry had intended to create reformed county electorates, and rural boroughs, that were likely to be deferential to the interests of large landowners. As this book demonstrates, his analysis made several flawed interpretive leaps based on a selective use of the commission's published reports.[19]

More recently, Stephen Thompson and Brian Robson have re-affirmed the importance of Drummond's list to the electoral reforms of 1832. As well as drawing attention to the mass of demographic statistics produced for the purposes of parliamentary reform, Thompson has shown how Drummond's list was developed as a concession to critics, who, during 1831, had argued that the government's initial use of census data in modelling their disfranchisement schedules opened the door to the future implementation of equal electoral districts.[20] Robson has provided an instructive discussion of the use of ordnance survey and externally produced maps by the commission, and has drawn attention to how the commission identified the 'formal and functional definitions of towns' in the creation of Drummond's list.[21] This book expands on both arguments by contextualising Drummond's list as a part of the boundary commission's earlier work. In doing so, it reveals the broader significance of the surveying and statistical techniques used in Drummond's list and their importance to Drummond's 'scientific' framework for redrawing England's electoral map.

The best existing source of information relating to the issue of parliamentary boundaries, and the 1831–2 boundary commissions, is the History of Parliament's seven-volume *House of Commons 1820–1832*, which was published in 2009. The constituent parts of this study suggest that the commission and parliamentary boundaries were far more important to the processes of reform, at a central and local level, than had previously been acknowledged. Its collection of MP biographies and constituency histories are an invaluable research resource, indicating a range of reactions to individual boundary changes at a local level, and among individual MPs, that had not previously been documented.[22] Furthermore, Philip Salmon's survey of the 1832 English reform legislation for the volumes suggests that the commission and the issue of boundaries intersected with parliamentary debate over the reform bill at several key points between March 1831 and June 1832. Significantly, Salmon outlines several key research questions that defined the initial approach taken in researching this book. He identifies that very little is known about how the English borough and county boundary commissions were established, how the commissions completed their work within the localities and at Westminster, and how parliamentary and extra-parliamentary negotiations seemingly allowed for the passage of the 1832 Boundary Act with minimal opposition. He also provides some context regarding the frantic creation of Drummond's list in the days before the third reform bill was introduced to parliament, and has alluded to the extraordinary public debate sparked by its announcement – factors both Thompson and Robson omitted from their accounts.[23]

The consequences of the 1832 boundary reforms

Histories of reformed politics and the British state have paid negligible attention to the legacy of the 1831–2 boundary commissions and the striking changes that they made to England's electoral map. This book addresses these issues by emphasising the impact of the 1832 boundary reforms in three key areas. First it argues that the 1831–2 boundary commissions (rather than those on the poor laws or factory reform) were the first of the Whig-established investigative commissions of the 1830s, and that their development of a 'scientific' method of parliamentary investigation proved a significant moment in the development of the bureaucratic and legislative practices of the British state. This should not be understood as an attempt to revive the 'revolution in government' argument of the 1960s and 1970s, which viewed the rapid increase in royal commissions and the influence of Benthamite utilitarianism over policy making after 1832 as a turning point in the development of a proto-collectivist legislative approach.[24] Rather, the work of the boundary commissions is better understood in the context of a revisionist school of thought, which has outlined significant continuities between the governmental approaches of the 1830s and the preceding decades. These historians have drawn attention to the work of an active group of parliamentarians (grounded in political economy and liberal Toryism, rather than proto-collectivism), who from 1815 developed a parliamentary culture that used debate, select committees (and some royal commissions), petitions and parliamentary returns as a means of ensuring the unreformed parliament was responsive to Britain's economic and social needs.[25]

The 1831–2 boundary commissions built on these precedents, but from a different ideological and practical outlook. Significantly, many of the Whigs who constituted the Grey ministry of 1830–32 – and several of the boundary commissioners – were connected to the emerging 'useful knowledge' and social science movements and their claims that a 'science of government', which removed partiality from politics, could be discovered through 'the accumulation of simple, irrefutable facts'.[26] The boundary commission's scientific method for accumulating 'facts' relied heavily on two practices: statistics and cartography. While histories of statistics – with the exception of the work of Stephen Thompson noted above – have afforded no attention to the boundary commissions, historians of cartography have long been aware of their important role in producing the state's first official maps of England's northern towns and enlarged scale town plans for every English parliamentary borough.[27] In this regard, this book builds on the recent work of Richard Oliver, who has demonstrated that the 1831–2 boundary commissions were significant in establishing the cartographic techniques and personnel utilised by subsequent royal commissions during the 1830s, particularly those that investigated municipal corporations and tithes.[28]

By providing an empirically grounded account of a pioneering commission and its contribution to the evolution of the nineteenth-century British state, *Mapping the State* complicates Patrick Joyce's Foucauldian-inspired theory of 'liberal governmentality'. Embodied in this theory of the nineteenth-century British imperial state is the idea that the collection, and publication, of statistical and cartographic data turned previously fluid 'local' knowledge into fixed central knowledge. This knowledge, according to Joyce, allowed administrators, from India to Manchester, to 'see' the towns and cities they were governing in a rational, standardised form, while publicly reinforcing the 'empirical' nature of the institutional structures that governed these spaces.[29] As this book reveals, the work of the boundary commission represented a clear transference of knowledge from the peripheries to the centre that allowed officials to 'see' constituencies in a new light. However, following 1832 this new level of state knowledge did not result in official control, or even the peaceful governance, of electoral politics in England's reformed constituencies. In practice, the statistical and cartographic data created by the commission (as well as the official electoral data published by parliament over the following three decades) was as available to non-officials as it was to official administrators and became crucial to an array of groups and actors seeking political influence over England's reformed electoral map. In this regard, my analysis confirms the recent work of Katrina Navickas on England's northern administrative units between 1832 and 1848, which has revealed the varied impact of the codification of new administrative areas after 1832, from the vestry to the parliamentary level. As well as becoming a point of political conflict in their own regard, newly formalised poor law, municipal and parliamentary boundaries (and the data they were based on) provided radicals, in addition to governing Liberal or Conservative officials, with significant intelligence with which to organise politics and play an active role in the processes of Victorian state formation.[30]

A second theme this book considers is the impact of England's reformed electoral map on constituency politics between 1832 and 1868. While there is some overlap between the two schools of thought, historians can generally be divided between those who emphasise the transformative nature of the 1832 reform legislation, and those who do not. The work of John Phillips, Philip Salmon and Matthew Cragoe best exemplifies the first category – all three have stressed the 'modernising' nature of the electoral reforms of 1832 by focusing on local political life in the decade following reform.[31] Those who have sought to emphasise continuity following 1832, such as Frank O'Gorman, Miles Taylor, David Eastwood and Alan Heesom, have taken a longer-term view, stretching their horizons to the second Reform Act, by which time they contend that it is the similarities between pre-and post-reform electoral politics that are the most striking.[32] In reality much of the disagreement between the two groups of historians is somewhat arbitrary. It is convincing that voter registration created a very new dynamic in electoral politics following 1832, but also that this new dynamic worked alongside older electioneering cultures in the constituencies. Locality clearly remained intrinsic to constituency politics after 1832, but voter registration and the development of local party associations demonstrated how the 1832 reform legislation prompted a new national, sometimes uniform, element to constituency politics. And, it is evident that while party existed as a notion – and was definitely present within some form of national framework – politicians appropriated party in a local context, not in a 'national' post-1868, or even post-1945 'modern' two-party sense. At a constituency level, then, this book reveals how far the various English constituency types established by the 1832 reform legislation contributed to the conditions that allowed, or required, local party organisation to flourish; served to focus constituency politics around particular notions of locality and community; and introduced new uniform, national characteristics into the electoral system.

The final way this book aims to expand our understanding of the 1832 reform legislation is by exploring the impact that England's reformed electoral map had on the formation of governments, decision-making in the Commons and the evolution of party at Westminster prior to 1868. It draws from the techniques of roll-call analysis, which have been developed by political scientists and historians, in the British context at least, since the 1960s. The analysis presented here is part of my ongoing development of the massive History of Parliament and Eggers and Spirling dataset of parliamentary votes for the period 1836–1910, and is the first constituency-led analysis of voting behaviour covering the entire timespan of the reformed Commons (1832–68). Due to the vast resources required to create a comprehensive set of voting records for the period, previous roll-call analyses have generally focused on analysing individual parliaments, and usually only a specific set of votes. They have also focused primarily on measuring partisanship and party discipline at Westminster, either by comparing the voting records of MPs against party labels, using scaling methods to identify the political positions of individual MPs, or comparing MPs' votes against the activity of prototypical party whips in the Commons.[33] Eggers and Spirling's recent analysis of voting behaviour in the Commons between

1836 and 1910 applied the latter technique, and suggested that Ian Newbould's conclusions on party discipline in the Commons during the 1830s (whose work used the former technique) hold true, as do the observations of a number of qualitative studies covering the entire period. While 'party' organisation at Westminster was gradually assuming some of its twentieth-century characteristics, between 1832 and 1868 government authority continued to rely on 'cohesive, yet mutable, party connection[s]' in the Commons. These connections – a key component of the prevailing system of 'parliamentary government' – could quickly break down if an opposition identified sufficient weakness among a government's supporters to turn a policy question into an issue of confidence, a tactic that remained the general method of bringing down a government throughout the period.[34]

Comparatively less attention has been paid by roll-call analysis to the links between constituencies and voting habits in the Commons. Work completed by historians on William Aydelotte's pioneering dataset of votes for the 1841–7 parliament linked a constituency's size (according to its electorate) and socio-economic profile to the behaviour of MPs. Aydelotte, and later Cheryl Schonhardt-Bailey, observed a clear correlation between a Conservative MP's decision to support free trade or protection in 1846, and the economic interest of his constituency. They also revealed that boroughs with large electorates were more likely to favour politically and economically liberal policies between 1841 and 1847, whereas MPs returned for distinctively rural, small boroughs and counties were most zealous in their advocacy of agricultural protection.[35] These conclusions fit broadly with the work of historians who have analysed the party labels (rather than votes) of MPs between 1832 and 1868. In England, Conservative, Liberal-Conservative and Protectionist MPs are known to have prospered in the counties, boroughs with fewer than 500 voters and some larger historic boroughs where an established Anglican elite existed.[36] The variety of English Whigs, reformers, Liberals and radicals who proved willing to associate with the Whig leadership of the Commons in the 1830s, and the increasingly distinctive Liberal leadership from the late 1840s, are known to have derived considerable success from boroughs enfranchised in 1832 and ancient boroughs with large electorates.[37] My analysis expands on these arguments to explore how far the different types of constituency created by the 1832 reform legislation influenced the party identity and voting behaviour of MPs in the major votes and confidence motions that defined Westminster politics between 1832 and 1868. As the final four chapters of this book reveal, England's reformed electoral map provided a significant electoral foothold for the forces of protectionism at Westminster into the 1850s and was crucial in shaping the political identities of the emerging Conservative and Liberal parties prior to 1868.

A note on method and structure...

The 1832 reform legislation not only redrew England's electoral map, but made alterations to Welsh, Scottish and Irish boundaries. A decision was made to focus this book on the English electoral system because English boroughs and counties represented 71 per cent of the reformed electoral system (468 of 658 Commons seats), and the extent of boundary change in England was far more pronounced than in any other nation. No changes were made to the Welsh or Irish counties and only three Scottish counties underwent boundary changes in 1832. Only four of the thirty-three reformed Irish boroughs underwent substantial geographic extension, and Welsh and Scottish boroughs (of which most operated under a contributory borough system) were only updated, or defined, in order that the entire town, and space for its future growth, was included in any reformed limits.[38] In addition, the Grey ministry initially identified how to reform borough boundaries by focusing on the issue of boundary reform in England, prior to requesting that commissioners replicate these precedents in Wales, Scotland and Ireland.[39] In keeping with recent scholarship, *Mapping the State* should be viewed as the first part of a four-nation history of the boundary reform legislation of 1832.[40] It is my hope that this book prompts future investigation into the divergent research questions raised by the Irish, Scottish and Welsh boundary reforms of 1832.

The working papers of the English and Welsh borough boundary commission, which are held by the National Archives, provide the archival spine for this book. This archive has been held by the Public Record Office since 1848, when it was transferred from the custody of the then assistant tithe commissioner, and former 1831–2 boundary commissioner, Robert Kearsley Dawson.[41] Since then, the records have been stored in the records of commissions and committees division of the Treasury archive, under the catalogue number T72.[42] Despite regular publication of their availability they have never been used by historians of the 1832 reform legislation, and while historians of cartography have noted their existence they have never been subjected to historical analysis.[43] The archive consists of 260 folders of variable sizes for almost every English and Welsh borough visited by the commission, and contains the unpublished draft reports, correspondence and maps of the commission, as well as its ledger book. T72 has been used alongside the more traditional archival sources associated with 1832 – the Grey, Durham and Hatherton papers, for instance – as well as some of the less obvious personal papers related to the boundary commission, such as the Larcom papers (National Library of Ireland), Herschel papers (Royal Society), the papers of the Society for the Diffusion of Useful Knowledge (UCL) and the Boulton papers (Library of Birmingham). In addition, extensive use has been made of memoirs, parliamentary papers, newspapers (both physical and digital), and reports of parliamentary debates in *Hansard* and the *Mirror of Parliament*, as well as contemporary topographical dictionaries and maps.

Mapping the State combines what might be termed a traditional qualitative historical analysis of these sources, with several linguistic, statistical and geographical digital techniques. Methodologically, it builds on the recent work of Luke Blaxill, Naomi Lloyd-Jones, Henry Miller and James Smith, who have demonstrated how 'big data' and new digital approaches can be incorporated into political history.[44] As well as further exploring the possibilities provided by digital analysis for answering big structural historical questions (such as how did electoral reform change politics and political culture in the UK?), this digital turn in political history is part of a wider effort to reinvigorate the practices of the subject and make a case for its significance within the discipline of history, the humanities and the social sciences.[45] As Miles Taylor has suggested, this wider effort to demonstrate the relevance of political history to new audiences requires a 'new synthesis of approach', which not only embraces digital methods, but also engages with other fields of history such as intellectual history and the history of science.[46] In this regard, the book combines 'high political' methods and electoral history with big data longitudinal analysis, contributes to ongoing debates in intellectual history surrounding representation, and examines the practical application, and cultural significance, of science, statistics and cartography to nineteenth-century British parliamentary and political life. I am not claiming to have developed a new model for political history here. Rather my approach and methods have been carefully chosen as the most suitable from those available within (and without) the discipline to help answer a set of research questions that arose from trying to explain the reasons behind, and the political and electoral significance of, the work of Drummond and his fellow boundary commissioners during the autumn and winter of 1831–2.

From a digital and quantitative perspective, Chapter 1 utilises the text mining software *CasualConc* to analyse a corpus of Cobbett's and Hansard's parliamentary debates that I have created for the period 1774–1868, using digitised sources available through *Google Books*, archive.org and the UK Parliament's online *Hansard* archive.[47] The electoral statistics used throughout the book have been analysed through *Excel* and *ArcGIS* and have been compiled primarily from parliamentary returns, in particular the published papers of the boundary commission, electoral registration data for the period 1832–68 and census returns between 1821 and 1871.[48] A database of election results, party labels and parliamentary divisions also underpins the analysis of the latter two-thirds of the book.[49] My dataset of party labels and election results has been compiled from annual editions of Charles Dod's *Parliamentary Companion*, and cross referenced against the personal questionnaires completed by MPs for the *Parliamentary Companion*, rival companions, election addresses and speeches, and contemporary newspaper lists of election results.[50] In order to avoid anachronism in a process fraught with categorisation difficulties, I have only erred from Dod's party labels where clear errors occurred. My dataset of parliamentary divisions is a revised version of the History of Parliament and Eggers and Spirling's 1836–1910 dataset of parliamentary divisions, which has been updated to include parliamentary votes between 1833 and 1836, cleaned to ensure all votes are 100 per cent accurate and expanded to include 'pairs' and abstentions for each division analysed in this book. This electoral data has been geocoded to work with the shapefiles for English boundaries created by the Great Britain Historic GIS Project at the University of Portsmouth.[51]

The first half of *Mapping the State* provides the contextual backdrop to England's reformed electoral map. Chapter 1 combines qualitative and quantitative approaches to demonstrate how a fundamental shift in the 'language of interests' and attitudes towards the electoral system in the post-Napoleonic period paved the way for reform in 1832. Chapter 2 examines the implementation of the Grey ministry's theoretical plans for boundary reform from November 1830 and the public outcry over their proposals for the division of counties, which led to the government's near collapse by September 1831. Chapters 3 and 4 reveal how the lord chancellor, Lord Brougham, and the chair of the boundary commission, Thomas Drummond, established the English and Welsh boundary commission during the summer of 1831. Drummond's development of an innovative 'scientific' bureaucratic framework underpinned the redrawing of England's electoral map and the remodelling of the disfranchisement schedules in 1832, via what became known as 'Drummond's List'. The success of the commission's methods led to the collection of masses of geographic, electoral and socio-economic data. This unprecedented instance of interaction between the centre and the localities transformed the processes of electoral reform, instilled a new confidence among Whig ministers in the possibilities of domestic inquiry and established major precedents for the better-known commissions and inspectorates which continued the process of redefining the late Hanoverian and early Victorian British state.

The rest of the book analyses the boundary commission's reconstruction of England's electoral map during 1831 and 1832. The commission was characterised by its remarkable commitment to the application of Drummond's 'scientific' framework, which was only compromised by the political reality of securing parliamentary approval for the 1832 Boundary Act, and some occasional instances of naked gerrymandering by the government. Chapter 5 examines the large group of English boroughs whose boundaries were extended to include their modern town or remained unchanged in 1832. The consequences of boundary reform in these boroughs varied considerably, contrasting starkly with the 'multiple parish' boroughs discussed in Chapter 6. These extensive constituencies were created to ensure each reformed borough contained 300 voters, resulting in a significant electoral boon to the landed, agricultural interest in the reformed Commons. Chapter 7 explores the identification of boundaries for England's new boroughs in 1832, which subsequently provided the electoral foundation for the emerging Liberal party at Westminster. The final chapter investigates the work of the emerging civil servant John Shaw Lefevre in reconstructing England's county map, which contrary to Whig expectations became a long-term Conservative electoral stronghold. The enduring legacy of the boundary commission to the development of the British state, and its wide-ranging impact on England's political landscape, underline the status of the 1832 reform legislation as one of the most transformative moments in the political history of the United Kingdom.

Notes

1. I use '1832 reform legislation' to refer to the five statutes that reformed the United Kingdom's electoral system in 1832: the 1832 Reform Act (England and Wales) (2 & 3 Wm. IV, c. 45); 1832 Reform Act (Scotland) (2 & 3 Wm. IV, c. 65); 1832 Reform Act (Ireland) (2 & 3 Wm. IV, c. 88); 1832 Boundary Act (England and Wales) (2 & 3 Wm. IV, c. 64); 1832 Boundary Act (Ireland) (2 & 3 Wm. IV, c. 89).

2. SRO, Hatherton papers, D260/M/F/5/27/8, 34, commissioners to Drummond, 6 June 1832.

3. Parliamentary Papers [hereafter PP] 1831–2 (20), xxxvii. 1; PP1831–2 (141), xxxviii. 1, xxxix. 1, xl. 1, xli. 1; PP1831–2 (408), xlii. 1; PP1831–2 (519), xliii. 1.

4. In keeping with M. Cragoe, *Culture, Politics and National Identity in Wales 1832–1886* (Oxford, 2004), Monmouthshire and Monmouth Boroughs are considered part of Wales.

5. N. Gash, *Politics in the Age of Peel: A Study in the Technique of Parliamentary Representation* (London, 1971), 432–3; P. Salmon, 'The English Reform Legislation, 1831–32', in D. Fisher (ed.), *House of Commons 1820–32* (Cambridge, 2009), i, 395–401.

6. Miles Taylor, 'Parliamentary Representation in Modern Britain: Past, Present and Future', *HJ*, 65, 4 (2022), 1145-73.

7. D. C. Moore, *The Politics of Deference: A Study of the Mid-Nineteenth Century Political System* (New York, 1976), 173-83; D. C. Moore, 'Concession or Cure: The Sociological Premises of the First Reform Act', *HJ*, 9, 1 (1966), 39-59.

8. Salmon, 'English Reform Legislation', 399-400.

9. H. Miller, *A Nation of Petitioners. Petitions and Petitioning in the United Kingdom, 1780-1918* (Cambridge, 2023); L. Blaxill, *The War of Words: The Language of British Elections, 1880-1914* (London, 2020).

10. K. Marx, 'The Elections – Tories and Whigs', *New York Daily Tribune*, 21 Aug. 1852, 6; K. Marx, 'Lord Russell', *Neue Oder-Zeitung* (1855), 359; W. Molesworth, *The History of the Reform Bill of 1832* (London, 1865); J. Butler, *The Passing of the Great Reform Bill* (London, 1914); G. Trevelyan, *Lord Grey of the Reform Bill* (London, 1920).

11. Gash, *Age of Peel*, 3-33; D. C. Moore, 'The Other Face of Reform', *Victorian Studies*, 5, 1 (1961), 7-34; Moore, 'Concession'; Moore, *Deference*; E. P. Hennock and D. C. Moore, 'The First Reform Act: A Discussion', *Victorian Studies*, 14, 3 (1971), 321-37; J. Cannon, *Parliamentary Reform 1640-1832* (Cambridge, 1973); M. Brock, *The Great Reform Act* (London, 1973); A. Kriegel (ed.), *Holland House Diaries, 1831-1840* (London, 1977); J. Milton-Smith, 'Earl Grey's Cabinet and the Objects of Parliamentary Reform', *HJ*, 15,1 (1972), 55-74; R. Davis, 'Deference and Aristocracy in the Time of the Great Reform Act', *American Historical Review*, 81, 3 (1976), 532-9.

12. E. Wasson, 'The Great Whigs and Parliamentary Reform, 1809-1830', *JBS*, 24, 4 (1985), 434-64; B. Fontana, *Rethinking the Politics of Commercial Society: the Edinburgh Review 1802-1832* (Cambridge, 1985); R. Brent, *Liberal Anglican Politics: Whiggery, Religion, and Reform, 1830-1841* (Oxford, 1987); P. Mandler, *Aristocratic Government in the Age of Reform: Whigs and Liberals, 1830-1852* (Oxford, 1990); I. Newbould, *Whiggery and Reform, 1830-41: The Politics of Government* (London, 1990); L. Mitchell, 'Foxite Politics and the Great Reform Bill', *EHR*, 108, 427 (1993), 338-64; J. Parry, *The Rise and Fall of Liberal Government in Victorian Britain* (London, 1993), 72-89; B. Hilton, *A Mad, Bad, & Dangerous People?: England 1783-1846* (Oxford, 2006), 420-37.

13. Miles Taylor, 'Empire and Parliamentary Reform: The 1832 Reform Act Revisited', in A. Burns and J. Innes (eds.), *Rethinking the Age of Reform* (Cambridge, 2003), 295-311; K. Gleadle, *Borderline Citizens: Women, Gender, and Political Culture in Britain 1815-1867* (2009), 159-71; A. Hawkins, *Victorian Political Culture: Habits of Heart and Mind* (Oxford, 2015), 29-98; S. Thompson, '"Population Combined with Wealth and Taxation": Statistics Representation and the Making of the 1832 Reform Act', in T. Crook and G. O'Hara (eds.), *Statistics and the Public Sphere, Numbers and the People in Modern Britain, c. 1800-2000* (New York, 2011), 205-23; Salmon, 'English Reform Legislation', 411.

14. K. T. Hoppen, *Elections, Politics, and Society in Ireland 1832-1885* (Oxford, 1984); S. Farrell, 'Ireland', in Fisher, *Commons 1820-1832*, i. 211-16; M. Dyer, *Men of Property and Intelligence: Scottish Electoral System Prior to 1884* (Aberdeen, 1996); G. Pentland, *Radicalism, Reform and National Identity in Scotland 1820-1833* (Woodbridge, 2008); Fisher, 'Scotland', in Fisher, *Commons*, i 141-6; M. Cragoe, *Culture, Politics and National Identity*; M. Escott, 'Wales', in Fisher, *Commons*, i. 84-96.

15. R. Quinault, 'The Industrial Revolution and Parliamentary Reform', in P. O'Brien and R. Quinault (eds.), *The Industrial Revolution and British Society* (Cambridge, 1993), 183-202; D. Fisher, 'England', in Fisher, *Commons*, i, 1-62; Salmon, 'English Reform Legislation', 404-10; P. Salmon, '"Reform Should Begin at Home": English Municipal and Parliamentary Reform, 1818-32', in C. Jones, P. Salmon and R. Davis

(eds.), *Partisan Politics, Principles and Reform in Parliament and the Constituencies, 1689–1880* (Edinburgh, 2004), 93–113.

16. R. Quinault, 'The French Revolution of 1830 and Parliamentary Reform', *History*, 75, 297 (1994), 377–93; N. LoPatin, *Political Unions, Popular Politics and the Great Reform Act of 1832* (Basingstoke, 1999); R. Ertman, 'The Great Reform Act of 1832 and British Democratization', *Comparative Political Studies*, 43, 8 (2010), 1000–1022; Gleadle, *Borderline Citizens*, 171–91; R. Saunders, 'God and the Great Reform Act: Preaching against Reform, 1831–32', *JBS*, 53, 2 (2014), 378–99; T. S. Aidt and R. Franck, 'Democratization under the Threat of Revolution: Evidence from the Great Reform Act of 1832', *Econometrica*, 83 (2015), 505–47; K. Navickas, *Protest and the Politics of Space and Place 1789–1848* (Manchester, 2016), 122–9.

17. Brock, *Reform Act*, 141–2, 157–9, 247, 260–66, 269–81, 377; Kriegel, *Holland House*, xxx–xxxi, 5, 99–100, 425–6, 447.

18. Gash, *Age of Peel*, 69.

19. Moore, *Politics of Deference*, 173–83; Moore, 'Concession or Cure', 39–59.

20. Thompson, 'Population', 205–23.

21. B. Robson, 'Maps and Mathematics: Ranking the English Boroughs for the 1832 Reform Act', *Journal of Historical Geography*, 46 (2014), 66–79.

22. S. Farrell, 'Poole', in Fisher, *Commons*, ii. 334; T. Jenkins, 'Villiers, Frederick', in Fisher, *Commons*, vii. 563–64.

23. Salmon, 'English Reform Legislation', 384–88.

24. H. Clokie and J. Robinson, *Royal Commissions of Inquiry* (New York, 1937), 54–79; L. Hume, 'Jeremy Bentham and the Nineteenth-Century Revolution in Government', *HJ*, 10, 3 (1967), 361–75; W. Lubenow, *The Politics of Government Growth* (Plymouth, 1971); A. Brundage, *The Making of the New Poor Law: The Politics of Inquiry, Enactment and Implementation* (London, 1978); idem, *England's Prussian Minister: Edwin Chadwick and the Politics of Government Growth, 1832–54* (London, 1988); O. MacDonagh, *Early Victorian Government 1830–1870* (London, 1977); U. Henriques, *Before the Welfare State: Social Administration in Early Industrial Britain* (London, 1979), 18–46.

25. B. Hilton, *Corn, Cash, Commerce: Economic Policies of the Tory Governments, 1815–30* (Oxford, 1977); R. Tompson, *The Charity Commission and the Age of Reform* (London, 1979); Parry, *Rise and Fall*, 34–8; D. Eastwood, '"Amplifying the Province of the Legislature": The Flow of Information and the English State in the Early Nineteenth Century', *Historical Research*, 62, 149 (1989), 276–94; P. Mandler, 'Tories and Paupers: Christian Political Economy and the Making of the New Poor Law', *HJ*, 33, 1 (1990), 81–103; P. Jupp, *British Politics on the Eve of Reform: The Duke of Wellington's Administration, 1828–30* (Basingstoke, 1998); J. Innes, *Inferior Politics: Social Problems and Social Policies in Eighteenth-Century Britain* (Oxford, 2009).

26. T. Porter, *The Rise of Statistical Thinking, 1820–1900* (Princeton, 1986), 36; A. Rauch, *Useful Knowledge: The Victorians, Morality and the March of Intellect* (Durham, N.C., 2001); M. Cullen, *The Statistical Movement in Victorian Britain: The Foundations of Empirical Social Research* (Hassocks, 1976); S. Cannon, *Science in Culture: The Early Victorian Period* (New York, 1978); J. Morrell and A. Thackray, *Gentlemen of Science: Early Years of the British Association for the Advancement of Science* (New York, 1981); E. Higgs, *Before The Information State: The Central Collection of Information on Citizens since 1500* (Basingstoke, 2004); J. Bord, *Science and Whig Manners: Science and Political Style in Britain, c. 1790–1850* (Basingstoke, 2009); E. Gillin, *The Victorian Palace of Science: Scientific Knowledge and the Building of the Houses of Parliament* (Cambridge, 2017); L. Goldman, *Victorians & Numbers: Statistics and Society in Nineteenth Century Britain* (Oxford, 2022).

27. R. Hyde, 'Mapping Urban Britain 1831–32: The Compilation of the Reform Bill Plans', *Bulletin of the Society of University Cartographers*, 9, 2 (1978), 1–9; C. Close, *The Early Years of the Ordnance Survey* (Newton Abbot, 1969), 89, 138; C. Delano-Smith and R. Kain, *English Maps: A History* (London, 1999), 98–139; R. Hewitt, *Map of a Nation: A Biography of the Ordnance Survey* (London, 2011), 262–7.

28. R. Oliver, *The Ordnance Survey in the Nineteenth Century: Maps, Money and the Growth of Government* (London, 2014), 108–30; R. Kain and E. Baigent, *The Cadastral Map in the Service of the State* (Chicago, 1992).

29. P. Joyce, *The Rule of Freedom: Liberalism and the Modern City* (London, 2003), 35–61. Joyce draws from J. Scott, *Seeing Like a State: How Certain Schemes to Improve the Human Condition Have Failed* (Yale, 1998); J. Harley 'Deconstructing the Map', *Cartographica*, 26, 2 (1989), 1–20.

30. Navickas, *Protest and the Politics of Space*, 154–76.

31. J. Phillips, *The Great Reform Bill in the Boroughs: English Electoral Behaviour 1818–1841* (Oxford, 1992), 303; J. Phillips and C. Wetherall, 'The Great Reform Act of 1832 and the Political Modernization of England', *American Historical Review*, 100 (1995), 411–36; P. Salmon, *Electoral Reform at Work: Local Politics and National Parties 1832–1841* (Woodbridge, 2002); M. Cragoe, 'The Great Reform Act and the Modernization of British Politics: The Impact of Conservative Associations, 1835–1841', *JBS*, 47, 3 (2008), 581–603.

32. A. Heesom, '"Legitimate" versus "Illegitimate" Influences: Aristocratic Electioneering in Mid-Victorian Britain', *Parliamentary History*, 7, 2 (1988), 282–305; F. O'Gorman, *Voters, Patrons, and Parties: The Unreformed Electoral System of Hanoverian England* (Oxford, 1989); F. O'Gorman, 'Campaign Rituals and Ceremonies: The Social Meaning of Elections in England 1780–1860', *Past and Present*, 135 (1992), 79–115; D. Eastwood, 'Contesting the Politics of Deference: The Rural Electorate, 1820–60', and Miles Taylor, 'Interests, Parties and the State: the Urban Electorate in England, c. 1820–72', in J. Lawrence and Miles Taylor (eds.), *Party, State and Society: Electoral Behaviour in Britain since 1820* (Aldershot, 1997), 27–78.

33. D. Beales, 'Parliamentary Parties and the Independent Member', 1810–1860', in Robson, R. (ed.), *Ideas and Institutions of Victorian Britain* (London, 1967), 1–19; H. Berrington, 'Partisanship and Dissidence in the Nineteenth Century House of Commons', *Parliamentary Affairs*, 21 (1968), 338–74; D. Close, 'The Formation of a Two-Party Alignment in the House of Commons between 1830 and 1841', *EHR*, 84 (1969), 257–77; I. Newbould, 'The Emergence of a Two-Party System in England from 1830 to 1841: Roll Call and Reconsideration', *Parliaments, Estates and Representation*, 5, 1 (1985), 25–31; For the second technique see: W. O. Aydelotte, 'Voting Patterns in the British House of Commons in the 1840s', *Comparative Studies in Society and History*, 5 (1963), 134–63; J. Bylsma, 'Party Structure in the 1852–1857 House of Commons: A Scalogram Analysis', *Journal of Interdisciplinary History*, 7, 4 (1977), 617–35; C. Schonhardt-Bailey, *From the Corn Laws to Free Trade* (London, 2006). For the third technique see: A. C. Eggers and A. Spirling, 'Party Cohesion in Westminster Systems: Inducements, Replacement and Discipline in the House of Commons, 1836–1910', *British Journal of Political Science*, 46, 3 (2014), 567–89.

34. Hawkins, *Victorian Political Culture*, 128–31; I. Newbould, 'Whiggery and the Growth of Party 1830–1841: Organisation and the Challenge of Reform', *PH*, 4 (1985), 137–56; Parry, *Rise and Fall*; Mandler, *Aristocratic Government*, 157–99; Brent, *Liberal Anglican Politics*; Hilton, *Mad, Bad*, 513–24.

35. W. Aydelotte, 'Constituency Influence on the British House of Commons', in W. Aydelotte (ed.), *The History of Parliamentary Behaviour* (New Jersey, 1977), 225–46; Schonhardt-Bailey, *Corn Laws to Free Trade*; G. Cox, *The Efficient Secret: The Cabinet and the Development of Political Parties in Victorian England* (1987), 57–9, 148–65.

36. B. Coleman, *Conservatism and the Conservative Party in Nineteenth-Century Britain* (London, 1988), 102–5; R. Stewart, *The Foundation of the Conservative Party, 1830–1867* (London, 1978), 215–16; Parry, *Rise and Fall*, 338–41; T. Jenkins, *Sir Robert Peel* (Basingstoke, 1999), 90–91; I. McLean, 'Interests and Ideology in the United Kingdom Parliament of 1841-7: An Analysis of Roll Call Voting', *Contemporary Political Studies*, 1 (1995), 1–20; Hawkins, *Victorian Political Culture*, 181–2.

37. Parry, *Rise and Fall*, 193–4, 339.

38. M. Escott, 'Welsh Reform Legislation', D. Fisher, 'Scottish Reform Legislation', and S. Farrell, 'Irish Reform Legislation', in Fisher, *Commons*, i. 84–92, 141–6, 211–16.

39. UCL Special Collections, Brougham Papers [hereafter UCL, Brougham], 457, 'Scotch Reform Bill', fo. 24761; National Archives, T72/9/18, 'Frome', Drummond to Ansley, 20 Oct. 1831.

40. N. Lloyd-Jones and M. Scull (ed.), *Four Nations Approaches to Modern 'British' History: A (Dis)United Kingdom?* (London, 2019); J. Smith, 'Legislating for the Four Nations at Westminster in the Age of Reform, 1830–1852' (unpublished University of York thesis, 2021).

41. *Tenth Report of the Deputy Keeper of the Public Records*, C 1046 (1849), 7, 12.

42. HMSO, *Guide to the Contents of the Public Record Office: State Papers and Departmental Records* (1963), ii. 298.

43. Oliver, *Ordnance Survey*, pp. 108–9.

44. Blaxill, *War of Words*; L. Blaxill, 'Why Do Historians Ignore Digital Analysis? Bring on the Luddites', *Political Quarterly*, 94, 2 (2023), 279–89; Miller, *Nation of Petitioners*; N. Lloyd-Jones, 'A New British History of the Home Rule Crisis: Public Opinion, Representation and Organisation' (unpublished University of London PhD thesis, 2019); J. Smith, 'Legislating for the Four Nations'.

45. A. Middleton, '"High Politics" and its Intellectual Contexts', *Parliamentary History*, 40, 1 (2021), 168–91; M. Skjönsberg, 'The History of Political Thought and Parliamentary History in the Eighteenth and Nineteenth Centuries', *HJ*, 64, 2 (2021), 501–13; C. Murphy, 'The Future of British Political History', *Political Quarterly*, 94, 2 (2023), 201–7.

46. Taylor, 'Parliamentary Representation', 1173.

47. *Digging into Linked Parliamentary Data* project, https://web.archive.org/web/20230321120911/https://did3.jiscinvolve.org/wp/projects/dilipad/ [accessed 20 May 2022]; Blaxill, *War of Words*, 21–43.

48. PP1833 (189) xxxvii. 21; PP1836 (190) xliii. 363; PP1837–38 (329), xliv. 553; PP1840 (579) xxxix. 187; PP1846 (284) xxxiii. 145; PP1852 (4) xlii. 303; PP1854 (280) liii. 211; PP1859 (140) xxiii. 139; PP1862 (410) xliv. 703; PP1865 (448), xliv. 549. For census data see: PP1833 (149) xxxvi. 12–13; PP1843 (496) xxii. 8; PP1852–53 (1691) lxxxviii. 206; PP1863 (3221) liii. 278; PF1873 (872) lxxi, 12.

49. M. Spychal, 'The geography of voting behaviour: towards a roll-call analysis of England's reformed electoral map, 1832–68', https://thehistoryofparliament.files.wordpress.com/2021/03/m.spychal-geography-of-voting-ppp-seminar-16-mar-2021.pdf [accessed 5 Dec. 2022]

50. London, History of Parliament, Unpublished facsimile, 'Autobiography of five hundred members of Parliament'; J. Coohill, *Ideas of the Liberal Party: Perceptions, Agendas and Liberal Politics in the House of Commons, 1832–52* (Chichester, 2011), 19–45.

51. Great Britain Historical GIS, http://www.visionofbritain.org.uk/data/ [accessed 20 May 2022].

Part I
ENVISIONING ENGLAND'S REFORMED ELECTORAL MAP

Chapter 1

A balancing Act? Interests and parliamentary reform, 1780–1832

The United Kingdom's unreformed electoral system was a complex collection of 389, mostly multi-member, borough and county constituencies, which returned 658 MPs to the House of Commons. England returned 486 MPs, Ireland 100, Wales 27 and Scotland 45.[1] The English and Welsh counties were the most uniform set of constituencies, where those who owned a 40s. freehold, both resident and non-resident within a defined geographic space, qualified to vote. The English boroughs returned the most MPs – 402. However, each had its own unique franchise and boundary configurations, established largely by individual royal charters granted since the medieval period. Scotland's counties were closed constituencies where a handful of freeholders voted, and three paired counties alternated in electing a representative. Wales and Scotland hosted a distinctive single member grouped borough or burgh system. And, Ireland, whose constituencies had only been added to the UK electoral map in 1801, had a varied borough system as well as a county franchise that had been restricted in 1829 as part of the terms of Catholic emancipation. In addition, Oxford and Cambridge University both returned two MPs, and Dublin University returned one, via a graduate franchise.

Despite its apparent lack of logic, by the early nineteenth century successive generations of politicians and theorists had developed an extensive rationale for the unreformed electoral system. Their arguments revolved around the idea that the electoral map – particularly England's constituencies – provided for a balanced representation of the political nation's varied economic and social interests. One of the most complete formulations of this theory was provided in the Commons in March 1831 by Robert

Inglis, the anti-reform MP for Oxford University, in response to the Whig government's announcement of its reform legislation for England and Wales. For Inglis, the 'absence of symmetry' in the electoral system allowed for a *concordia discors* (a harmony of discordant elements) that provided 'the most complete representation of the interests of the people ... ever assembled in any age or country'. Inglis offered an extensive list of the various interests represented in the unreformed Commons: the landed and professional interests, as well as those of the crown, the nobility and 'the lower classes'. The interests 'of the East Indies, of the West Indies, of the colonies, of the great corporations', 'the commercial interests generally' and the 'funded debt of England' were also perfectly accounted for. It transpired that Inglis's greatest fear was that electoral reform would lead to an over-representation of 'trade and manufactures' and 'the destruction' of the nation's 'only permanent interest', namely 'the agriculture of England'.[2]

The contention that the unreformed electoral system provided for a balanced representation of the nation's interests had commanded authority at Westminster for much of the preceding century. By 1831, however, the argument stood on thin ground. This shift in opinion was best exemplified in November 1830, when the prime minister, the Duke of Wellington, was forced into a humiliating resignation, days after announcing that 'the system of [electoral] representation possessed the full and entire confidence of the country'.[3] He was replaced later that month by the second Earl Grey, who took control of a Whig government committed to the wholesale reform of the electoral system. Previous histories of the 1832 reform legislation offer little explanation as to how and why this change in attitudes over interest representation took place, or its significance in the formation of the Grey ministry in November 1830. Historians have identified the post-Napoleonic period as crucial in terms of uniting the various Whigs that comprised Grey's cabinet over the necessity for reform, but they have accorded insufficient attention to how debates over balancing the nation's interests during the 1820s helped form those connections.[4] They have also identified that one of the primary intentions of the 1832 Reform Act had been to 'remodel the representation of interests', but have overlooked the foundations of this argument in the practical politics of the post-Napoleonic era – particularly regarding parliament's need to reform cases of corruption in several English boroughs.[5]

As well as deepening our understanding of the 1832 reform legislation, this chapter builds on the work of historians in three adjacent fields. Firstly, it employs the digital techniques of corpus linguistics to analyse the evolution of the language of interests in parliament between 1774 and 1832. In extending the work of Luke Blaxill on political speeches in the late nineteenth century, this chapter seeks to demonstrate how quantitative language analysis can 'augment – and ultimately empower – traditional [historical] approaches', rather than replace them.[6] Secondly, recent research into the practices of petitioning in Britain has shown how the 'language of interest' was crucial to how different economic sectors from across England claimed political legitimacy and engaged with parliament from the late seventeenth century.[7] This chapter shows how by the 1820s, the eighteenth-century conception of interests, which previously tended to transcend party and often formed the basis of localised petitioning and policy initiatives, had evolved into a factional, prototypical language of mass politics. This new language helped contemporaries explain, and position themselves, in the increasingly divisive national debates surrounding the corn laws, economic distress and parliamentary reform. And third, this and subsequent chapters qualify and add significant political context to recent discussions in intellectual history about nineteenth-century representative theory. As well as revealing the significance of constituency geography (and not just the franchise) to contemporary legitimisations of the representative system, this chapter offers an answer to the dilemma posed by Gregory Conti. Namely, why did the final 1832 reform settlement not wholly embrace the theoretical 'mirroring' and 'variety of suffrages' models of descriptive representation advocated by contemporary Whigs?[8] In practice, while key figures in the Grey ministry were guided by representative theory, their ability to implement these theoretical 'mirroring' models was tempered by the experience of political debate during the 1820s, parliamentary negotiation over the reform legislation and the bureaucratic implementation of electoral reform between 1830 and 1832.

After exploring the rationale for the small 'c' conservative defence of the unreformed electoral map, this chapter draws from a text-mining analysis of parliamentary debates between 1780 and 1832 to explain the growth of an increasingly complex language of interests, which developed in response to debate over national economic policy and repeated bouts of distress in England's agricultural and manufacturing districts during the first three decades of the nineteenth century. During this period a rising generation of Whig politicians, most importantly, Lord John Russell, capitalised on this new language of interests to dispense with radical critiques of the electoral system and challenge the eighteenth-century defence of the unreformed electoral system on its own terms. It was the need for Westminster to reform a small number of corrupt boroughs after 1815 – either by extending their boundaries or transferring their franchises to unrepresented towns or the counties – that forced previously complacent politicians to confront the issue of whether England's ancient electoral system remained fit for purpose by 1830. As the 1820s progressed, the case for rebalancing England's electoral map appeared increasingly moderate, in contrast with those defenders of sectional interests who opposed gradualist proposals to reform corrupt boroughs. Significantly, the need to balance the nation's interests defined the approach of the government and the boundary commissioners as they reconstructed England's reformed electoral map between 1830 and 1832.

The conservative defence of the unreformed electoral system

The principal argument in favour of the unreformed electoral system had been that it provided for a balanced representation of the political nation's varied interests in the House of Commons.[9] This theory had developed from the practical realities of early eighteenth-century government for court Whigs such as Robert Walpole and Henry Pelham, who recognised that England was becoming a commercial nation, and that the profits of the landed classes – the landed interest – were dependent on the success of merchants – the commercial (or trading) interest.[10] They also accepted the need to defend the interests of legitimate financiers – the monied interest – to fund wars and preserve economic and political stability.[11] While the accepted means of affording representation to the monied interest was less clear, court Whig thought had started to rationalise the electoral system on the basis that it provided representation to landed property through knights of the shire returned by the counties, and to commercial property (and also, informally, financial property) through citizens and burgesses returned by the boroughs.[12] This rationale was contested by the country Tories and Whigs, who disputed the representative claims of the monied interest on account of the latter's dependence on the court.[13]

By the end of the eighteenth century, this practical understanding of interest representation had been incorporated into a more complex theoretical defence of the electoral system based around virtual representation. The 1765 Stamp Act – an attempt to collect direct taxes from Britain's North American colonies – provided the initial focal point for this development. The Act provoked widespread protest from American colonists, who were unwilling to consent to taxation from Westminster unless they were provided with direct representation in parliament.[14] In response, supporters of the status quo reformulated an argument made in the seventeenth century by the Whig MP Algernon Sidney. Namely that an MP was not supposed to act as a representative for the specific needs of his locality, but as a representative for the interests of the entire nation.[15] On this basis, contemporaries contended that the electoral system returned such a diverse composition of MPs – due to their varied property holdings, economic and occupational backgrounds and formal links to their constituency – that all geographic areas and economic interests were virtually represented in the Commons.[16]

As Paul Langford has demonstrated, when England's legislative interests are considered, virtual representation was reasonably faithful to the practical operation of the eighteenth-century Commons. Most of the English population lived within a few miles of property owned by an MP, and the interests of unrepresented towns were met by MPs with business or property links to those towns, as well as county MPs. Even most borough MPs who had bought their seats generally attended to their constituency's interests. For the American colonies, however, virtual representation stood on thin ground, as few MPs had any visible links to America.[17] This theory was further complicated towards the end of the century by the contention of anti-reformers that the Commons needed to ensure the stability of the mixed constitution by providing representation for the nation's three broad political interests – the monarchy, the aristocracy and the democracy. This argument developed out of a perception that the executive power of the Commons had increased at the expense of the Lords and the crown. In order to maintain cordial relations between the three branches of the constitution without formally increasing the powers of the Lords or the monarch, it was contended that the aristocracy and the crown needed to maintain some influence, through patronage, in the Commons.[18]

As virtual representation required MPs to act as representatives of the national interest, and because many MPs had links to a variety of social, economic and political interests, it was never the case that constituencies were assigned formal functions by proponents of the electoral system. As discussed above, the unreformed electoral system's 'absence of symmetry' was understood as one of its strengths.[19] Nevertheless, the need to defend the electoral system against domestic reformers from the 1770s did lead to the loose association of particular constituencies with certain socio-economic and political interests. Of the interest categories that were commonly employed during the eighteenth century, the landed interest was seen to be the most important. This was because contemporaries ascribed two meanings to the term. First, the landed interest could be used to describe MPs that represented the varied concerns of land and agriculture. In reality, as Julian Hoppit has shown, the landed interest, in this sense, should not be thought of as a coherent national interest group unless a common cause such as the land tax or the corn laws was found to unite the varied representatives of agriculture.[20] Second, the landed interest was used to describe large landowners, who, due to their property and wealth were believed to be the men best equipped to ensure that the Commons could legislate in the national interest. This idea, which had evolved from the country party ideology of the late seventeenth century, claimed that due to their property holdings and wealth, the landed interest held the greatest stake in the well-being of the country and were the only men with sufficient education, time and financial independence to ensure its disinterested governance.[21]

The counties were seen to be the natural power base for the landed interest, but as Robert Jenkinson, later the second earl of Liverpool and Tory prime minister between 1812 and 1827, explained during the debate on Charles Grey's (later the second Earl Grey) 1793 motion for reform, it was also accepted that many large boroughs returned members for the landed interest. Jenkinson attributed this to the cost and status of county and large borough elections, and the necessity for successful candidates in both to have extensive local connections as well as 'considerable property'.[22] It was also observed by the MP for Stockbridge, John Luttrell, when defending the existing electoral system against the younger Pitt's Yorkshire Association-inspired 1783 proposals to add up to 100 county members to the Commons, that additional representatives for the landed interest were not required as the wider borough system, due to its £300 a year property qualification, ensured that landowners enjoyed extensive opportunities to secure representation. By contrast, and in keeping with the activities of the Yorkshire Association over the previous four years, Pitt had urged the necessity of a massive increase in county MPs on account of their status as the class of men 'least liable to the seduction of corrupt influence', most able to act as a check on government extravagance and best placed to ensure that 'the interests of the representatives and the represented were the same'.[23] This 1783 debate also revealed a populist strain in the conservative defence of the constitution. Both Luttrell, and the former prime minister, Lord North, argued that because of its wide representation, the landed interest was already perfectly balanced against the representation of the commercial and monied interests.[24] Both warned that by increasing the representation of county members, Pitt's proposals would lead to a dangerous increase in the parliamentary influence of the aristocracy over the crown and the people (the democracy). In doing so, they equated the landed interest with the aristocracy, and the commercial interest with that of the people.[25]

The other primary interest grouping believed to require Commons representation was the commercial interest. What contemporaries meant by the commercial interest is harder to define, as some like North, were happy to delineate it from the monied and landed interest, while others like Jenkinson, provided a wider definition of commercial which incorporated merchants, bankers, colonists and manufacturers. This difficulty in definition derived from the earlier distinction drawn by the court and country party between the validity of commercial and monied men, but also from the wide eighteenth-century definition of 'merchant' and the interconnection between MPs engaged in both commerce and finance. As John Brooke has demonstrated, 'merchant' in the eighteenth-century sense could mean 'at one extreme small shopkeepers and at the other, wholesalers, exporters, bankers, and financiers'.[26] In this regard, the commercial interest might include the petitioners from the silk, woollen and linen interests (which could include manufacturers, merchants and labourers), who from the late seventeenth century had sought to capitalise on their collective identities as an 'interest' to gain influence over trade duties and tariffs.[27] This fluidity in the definition of 'commercial' was exacerbated by the fact that many of the upwards of sixty men per parliament between 1754 and 1790 who had connections with commerce, broadly defined, also had links to the landed and professional interests.[28] While no small shopkeepers were elected during the period, all other categories identified by Brooke did gain some representation in the Commons, and Gerrit Judd's separate analysis reveals that 897 MPs (or one-sixth of the total of 5,034 MPs between 1734 and 1832) were associated with some form of commercial interest. These men constituted one in nine MPs prior to 1761. By 1832 they had increased to one in four, dispersed fairly evenly between the interests of banking, domestic trade and the colonies.[29] In addition, contemporaries also started referring to the geographic and business interests of towns such as Manchester, Birmingham and Leeds when employing the term commercial interest. Manufacturers connected to these towns tended to be subsumed into the commercial interest category, and it was only towards the beginning of the nineteenth century that the 'manufacturing interest' began to be consistently employed as a separate interest category.[30]

This fluidity in definition transferred to understandings of how the commercial interest secured representation. A binary distinction of counties providing for the landed interest and boroughs providing for the commercial interest was often employed, but this did not account for the comparatively smaller number of commercial MPs. Some acknowledged that county MPs with links through property to commercial enterprise represented the commercial interest. In 1792, Jenkinson identified another, more precise means for how the commercial interest gained representation. He suggested that 'commercial towns', that is boroughs with a medium-sized electorate below that of a large town but above that of a nomination borough which tended to return the 'professional interest', were best fitted to provide representation for his wide definition of the commercial interest.[31] There was probably some truth to Jenkinson's observation, as by the end of the century provincial commercial men were regularly returned for medium-sized boroughs such as Canterbury or Cambridge, as well as the commercial ports of Bristol and Liverpool.[32]

There was another component of the commercial interest (broadly defined) that became associated with a particular type of constituency – men who had lived and made their wealth in the East or West Indies and bought their way into parliament via small boroughs with a popular franchise. During the second half of the eighteenth century these boroughs became associated with the much-vilified nabobs – men who had made their fortunes in India before buying their way into parliament.[33] Historians have observed that, in real terms, the eighteenth-century controversy surrounding nabobs entering the Commons was exaggerated, given that they only amounted to, on average, twenty MPs per parliament between 1768 and 1831.[34] Furthermore, by the 1820s MPs associated with the East India interest were outnumbered by the over thirty MPs per parliament whose wealth derived primarily from the slave plantations of the Caribbean.[35] Supporters of the electoral system argued that, while regrettable, small boroughs allowed for the commercial interests of the East and West Indies, and by extension Britain's wider imperial interests, to gain parliamentary representation. Accordingly, Francis Bassett, MP for Penryn, reasoned in 1783 that due to their long residence abroad, men associated with 'the interests of Jamaica or Bengal' required small boroughs as they did not have the necessary local connections in England to secure election without financial assistance.[36] In reality, East and West Indian merchants were supported by a much larger cast of MPs with economic interests in either the East India Company, or the West Indies as absentee landlords and slave-owners. Nicholas Draper, for instance, has recorded at least eighty MPs per parliament during the 1820s that had 'recognizable linkages with the slave economy' of the Caribbean.[37] As discussed below, parliamentary attempts to abolish the transatlantic slave trade from 1787 and the campaign to abolish slavery from 1823 meant that by the end of the eighteenth century, the pro-slavery, West India interest had supplanted the East India interest as the most vocal of these colonial lobby groups in the Commons.[38]

The final interest category requiring representation was the professional, or official interest – lawyers, naval officers and army officers. These were men of business – such as the two Pitts, Edmund Burke and Charles James Fox – that contemporaries contended were necessary to ensure the successful administration of government, but who required the patronage of a borough owner to be returned to parliament.[39] Perhaps self-interestedly then, Burke identified the need for the representation of professional interests as early as 1770, and in the same year the elder Pitt, then Lord Chatham, defended small boroughs with no discernible electorate when proposing an increase in county seats.⁴⁰ Importantly, the necessity for men of business to be returned to the Commons provided anti-reformers with a defence of the nomination borough. Again, it was Jenkinson, in 1792, who provided the most cogent rationale. Country gentlemen, or the landed interest, he contended, were too independent and busy with their estates to want to occupy themselves with the business of government, as were members for the commercial interest, who were too preoccupied with business and tended to enter parliament at too old an age to develop the expertise necessary for executive power. Furthermore, professional men acted as necessary mediators between the representatives of the landed and commercial interests. In doing so, he praised their recent influence in preventing either the landed or commercial interest from controlling corn law policy, and thus preventing 'corn from either becoming so dear as to distress the poor, or from becoming so cheap as to affect agriculture'.⁴¹

By the end of the eighteenth century these arguments had contributed to a conservative defence of the constitution that celebrated the practical efficiency of the representative system against the theoretical complaints of reformers. No other system, it was argued, could provide for as balanced a representation of the nation's varied interests in the Commons, and thus such good government. The apparent virtue of the existing representative system was underlined by the lack of extra-parliamentary petitioning from unrepresented towns such as Manchester, Birmingham and Leeds, and the general prosperity of the nation in contrast to its European neighbours.⁴² Anti-reformers continued to make this argument in defence of the ancient electoral system throughout debates on the reform bill between 1831 and 1832.⁴³ However, during the first three decades of the nineteenth century a subtle, but important shift in the categories of interest that were discussed in parliament took place. These shifts, as well as an explosion in the frequency with which the nation's interests were discussed during the 1820s, provided Whig reformers with a means of challenging the eighteenth-century defence of the electoral system on its own terms.

The shifting parliamentary language of interests, 1774–1832

This section uses a linguistic analysis of parliamentary debates to explore shifts in the types of interest discussed by parliamentarians between 1774 and 1868, with a particular focus on the period preceding the 1832 reform legislation. The primary analysis was completed using the text-mining tool *CasualConc* and is based on a new corpus of *Cobbett's Parliamentary Debates* between 1774 and 1803 and *Hansard's Parliamentary Debates* between 1803 and 1868.[44] The analysis has been supplemented with a categorisation of speakers and debate topics between 1803 and 1832, completed on a complementary dataset extracted from the Hansard at Huddersfield web resource.[45] The analysis was completed to help answer several questions about the parliamentary discussion of interests. Namely, what interest groups did parliamentarians discuss prior to the introduction of the 1832 reform legislation, how often did they discuss them and in what policy contexts? Did the meaning of interest categories, and the context in which they were debated, change over time? And finally, were 'interests' a universal aspect of political language, or was discussion about particular interests restricted to parliamentarians concerned with specific policy areas?

This analysis does not claim to provide an exact indicator as to the frequency with which individual terms were referred to in parliament: no textual analysis using the sources available to historians could. *Cobbett* and *Hansard* did not publish every parliamentary debate (particularly prior to 1803 when only major debates were recorded in *Cobbett*, a practice that only decreased gradually in *Hansard*); speeches were not required to be recorded verbatim; and short-hand techniques and the physical environments used by parliamentary reporters were still embryonic.[46] Nevertheless, steps have been taken to ensure this analysis is as accurate as possible. First, 1774 has been taken as a starting point as the coverage of debates for the preceding parliaments is not extensive enough – three volumes of *Cobbett* cover the period 1753–74, whereas the 1774–80 parliament is covered by over four volumes. Second, the smaller coverage of debates in the earlier period (the 1774 corpus contains 53,267 words per month, the 1865 corpus 682,628) has been compensated for by providing

Table 1.1: Recorded use of 'interests' per parliament, 1774–1868.

Key: frequency of 36 equates to a phrase being recorded, on average, once a day per parliament

	1774	1780	1784	1790	1796	1802	1806	1807	1812	1818
Commercial	20.65	17.53	24.35	24.31	16.09	13.06	12.43	17.07	24.36	26.78
Landed	10.33	8.22	11.77	15.47	13.74	9.33	2.49	10.97	16.36	11.08
Agricultural	0.00	0.00	0.81	1.47	0.79	2.33	1.24	8.17	31.03	13.39
Manufacturing	0.94	0.55	9.33	2.21	3.53	2.10	6.21	6.22	14.30	13.85
Shipping	0.47	0.00	0.00	0.37	1.18	6.30	13.67	4.39	3.52	0.92
West India	0.47	0.55	2.43	9.94	8.24	2.10	6.21	5.85	1.58	0.00
Colonial	0.47	0.55	0.00	1.84	3.53	1.40	2.49	1.83	3.64	0.46
East India	0.47	6.58	2.84	1.84	0.39	0.00	1.24	1.34	4.85	0.46
Monied	0.00	2.74	1.22	2.95	5.89	1.40	2.49	2.32	2.55	1.85
Church	0.94	3.84	3.65	0.00	3.53	3.96	6.21	4.27	5.94	2.77
Catholic	0.00	0.00	0.81	0.74	0.79	2.57	0.00	4.39	2.30	0.92

INTERESTS AND PARLIAMENTARY REFORM, 1780–1832   31

a relative figure for how often a term was recorded in parliament. This figure is based on the frequency that a term was used in relation to the word count of that parliament's corpus and uses the average word count per day for the period 1830–68 as a base line for the frequency of a phrase being recorded once a day.[47] Third, the data has been compiled using 'concordance', 'cluster' and 'collocation' analyses for the words 'interest' and 'interests'. This means that instead of just completing a search for the 'manufacturing interest', phrases that were commonly used together such as 'the commercial, manufacturing and landed interests' have been counted. The use of concordance and collocation techniques also ensured that variations in how reporters recorded an interest category have been taken into account. For example, this allowed phrases such as 'the interests of the West Indian colonists' or the 'interests of agriculturists' to be counted in the categories of 'West Indian interest' and 'agricultural interest' respectively. And, finally, manual checks have been completed on phrases that contained different uses of the word 'interest'. For example, when parliamentarians referred to the monetary interest rate made on a product by stating 'banking interest' or the rate of 'East Indian interest', neither were counted in the respective categories.[48]

Table 1.1 and Graph 1.1 list the eleven most discussed interest groups in each parliament between 1774 and 1868 and the changing frequency with which parliamentarians referred to each interest.[49] In order of their overall use throughout the period these interests were the: commercial interest; landed interest; agricultural interest; manufacturing interest; Church interest; shipping interest; West India interest; colonial interest; East India interest; monied interest; and Catholic interest (with discussion of the

1820	1826	1830	1831	1832	1835	1837	1841	1847	1852	1857	1859	1865
27.29	32.14	29.26	24.12	25.54	19.98	29.16	30.45	23.12	8.12	13.32	18.87	12.91
43.05	55.35	51.32	43.73	44.66	20.91	27.16	42.94	23.80	13.15	7.83	7.34	15.02
54.00	43.00	25.90	41.84	66.17	43.21	25.61	65.08	42.26	8.25	7.96	9.39	14.92
20.28	30.80	21.58	27.75	15.23	7.43	19.52	24.17	10.57	2.19	2.88	4.69	3.30
12.88	29.91	25.42	11.33	24.50	7.43	6.48	11.68	24.64	13.71	20.60	9.94	2.47
9.71	15.03	35.01	22.81	11.65	3.37	10.80	10.22	8.58	1.73	0.14	0.59	0.46
5.00	2.23	18.70	7.85	3.44	2.79	7.95	8.64	12.24	3.82	1.65	1.73	3.39
0.77	4.46	1.92	2.62	1.49	0.81	1.47	0.81	1.26	3.22	2.20	2.14	4.49
2.88	2.68	11.51	1.60	1.64	2.56	0.85	0.57	0.68	0.42	1.24	0.50	0.64
7.01	28.27	18.70	24.70	27.48	31.60	13.19	8.76	9.78	11.05	8.93	7.61	10.80
4.80	5.06	2.40	3.05	0.60	1.63	0.31	0.97	1.05	1.45	1.51	1.19	1.28

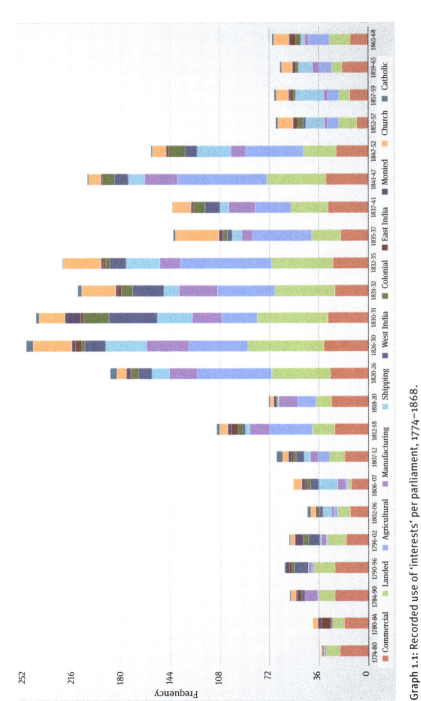

Graph 1.1: Recorded use of 'interests' per parliament, 1774–1868.
Frequency of 36 = phrase used on average once a day per parliament
Frequency of 180 = interest mentioned 5 times a day on average per parliament

latter four categories being minimal).[50] The analysis reveals a substantial growth in the parliamentary discussion of interests in the aftermath of the Napoleonic wars, particularly from 1820. This discussion peaked during the 1826 and 1830 parliaments, when MPs and peers were reported to have mentioned one of the eleven primary interest groupings, on average, between seven or eight times a day. After the 1832 Reform Act interests continued to be discussed up to four to six times a day before reducing to pre-1820 levels from 1852. To provide some perspective, the general interest phrases of the 'national interest' and the 'interest(s) of empire' were recorded around once or twice a fortnight throughout the entire period (with the latter category experiencing some notable jumps during the French Revolutionary and Napoleonic Wars).

In the three decades before the 1832 Reform Act this language of interests was employed by an increasing number of parliamentarians from across the political spectrum. Forty-nine parliamentarians (41 MPs and 8 peers) mentioned one of the main interest categories identified above during the 1802–6 parliament. During the 1820–26 parliament this had increased to 213 parliamentarians (170 MPs and 43 peers). During the much shorter 1831–2 parliament, 201 different speakers (162 MPs, 39 peers) mentioned an interest. As Table 1.2 reveals, around two to three speakers mentioned an interest for each month of the 1802, 1806, 1807 and 1812 parliaments, five to seven speakers for each month of the 1818, 1820 and 1826 parliaments, and around fifteen to seventeen speakers for each month of the 1830 and 1831 parliaments. Table 1.3, which lists the five speakers who mentioned interests most frequently during each parliament between 1820 and 1832, indicates how widespread the language of interests was. Interests were discussed by the most vocal government ministers of the period (both Whig and Tory) as well as those in charge of setting economic policy at the board of trade, but also by radical MPs such as Joseph Hume and Francis Burdett, leading members of the Whig opposition during the 1820s,

Table 1.2: Number of parliamentarians to mention an 'interest' per parliament, 1802–32.

	1802–6	1806–7	1807–12	1812–18	1818–20	1820–26	1826–30	1830–31	1831–2
MPs	41	9	72	83	56	170	138	87	162
Peers	8	5	25	14	5	43	39	18	39
Total	49	14	97	97	61	213	177	105	201
Duration of each parliament (months)	29	4.5	33	39	9	39	24	6	13
Ratio of speakers to parliament length	1.69	3.11	2.94	2.49	6.78	5.46	7.38	17.50	15.46

Table 1.3: Five speakers that mentioned interests the most per parliament, 1820–32.

1820–26	Speaker Info	Percentage of contributions
William Huskisson	Pres. Bd. of Trade 1823–7	5.67%
Joseph Hume	Radical MP, Aberdeen	3.54%
Second earl of Liverpool	PM 1812–27	3.47%
Alexander Baring	Whig MP, Taunton	3.40%
Henry Brougham	Whig MP, Winchelsea	2.83%
% of all 'interest' contributions for parliament		18.92%

1826–30	Speaker Info	Percentage of contributions
Robert Peel	Home Sec. 1822–7, 28–30	6.01%
William Huskisson	Pres. Bd. of Trade 1823–7; Leader Commons & Sec. War & Colonies 1827–8	4.76%
Francis Burdett	Radical MP, Westminster	3.74%
Joseph Hume	Radical MP, Aberdeen	3.51%
Charles Grant	Pres. Bd. of Trade 1827–8	2.72%
% of all 'interest' contributions for parliament		20.75%

1830–31	Speaker Info	Percentage of contributions
Viscount Althorp	Chancellor & Leader Commons 1830–34	8.59%
First Baron Wynford	Tory Peer	7.20%
James Mackenzie	Tory MP, Ross-shire	5.26%
George Robinson	Whig MP, Northampton	4.99%
Charles Poulett Thomson	V.Pres. Bd of Trade 1830–34	4.43%
% of all 'interest' contributions for parliament		30.47%

1831–2	Speaker Info	Percentage of contributions
Viscount Althorp	Chancellor & Leader Commons 1830–34	6.39%
First Baron Wynford	Tory Peer	3.90%
Second Earl Grey	PM 1830–34	3.30%
Edward Sugden	Tory MP, St Mawes	3.10%
Charles Poulett Thomson	V.Pres. Bd of Trade 1830–34	2.90%
% of all 'interest' contributions for parliament		19.58%

as well as some of the most vocal anti-reformers in both the Commons and the Lords between 1830 and 1832.

The two interests that remained a consistent aspect of parliamentary discussion throughout the entire period were the commercial and the landed interest. The landed interest was deployed broadly to signify the interests of those connected with the land – landowners, farmers and agricultural labourers. On a second level it was used to denote the financial interests of landed property – in contrast to financial or commercial property – and on a third, a category of parliamentarians whose financial independence and aristocratic upbringing led them to believe they were the best suited to governing the country. It was the first, broad, meaning of the term that was deployed most frequently, and from which the more factional notion of the 'agricultural interest' developed by the 1820s. The terms 'landed' and 'agricultural interest' were often interchangeable throughout the period, depending on who was speaking, and which reporter was recording them, as later sections of this chapter demonstrate. As a result, debates that led to a rise in discussion of the agricultural interest also contributed to increased discussion of the landed interest.

The first time that the agricultural interest, rather than just the landed interest, was referred to with any consistency was during debates over successive sugar distillation bills between 1808 and 1811, which proposed to afford a level of temporary tariff protection to West Indian plantation owners by placing restrictions on the use of British grain. Those opposed to the idea argued that the proposals would punish British farmers – the agricultural interest – while rewarding the speculation of West Indian planters.[51] From 1814 reference to the agricultural interest increased steadily due to the debates that preceded the passage of the 1815 Importation Act (the corn laws), during which the agricultural interest came to be defined as landowners, farmers and agricultural labourers in need of protection from cheap foreign corn, usually in contrast to consumers or workers associated with the manufacturing or commercial interests that, opponents of the bill argued, might suffer from higher bread prices. This was a debate that defined British politics over the subsequent three decades, and prompted continued reference to the agricultural and landed interest, particularly surrounding the corn law reforms of 1822 and 1828.[52] As indicated in Table 1.4, reference to the agricultural interest was compounded by agricultural distress during the winters of 1819–20, 1821–2, 1825–6 and 1829–30, when calls for some form of legislative relief – via increased protection, or currency reform – for agricultural districts hit by poor harvests were discussed, in particular, during debates over the 1819, 1822, 1826 and 1830 King's speeches and budgets.[53] Debate on distress also prompted an increased deployment of the more specific definition of the

Table 1.4: References to 'agricultural interest' by debate topic, 1802–32.

Debate topic	1802–6	1806–7	1807–12	1812–18	1818–20	1820–26	1826–30	1830–31	1831–2
Financial and monetary	80.00%	100.00%	93.55%	86.67%	73.68%	48.19%	73.08%	5.13%	14.22%
Distress	20.00%	0.00%	3.23%	1.67%	10.53%	39.82%	6.73%	69.23%	0.00%
Constitutional	0.00%	0.00%	0.00%	1.67%	5.26%	1.81%	8.65%	12.82%	82.94%
Ministerial statements	0.00%	0.00%	0.00%	6.67%	0.00%	7.24%	8.17%	5.13%	0.00%
Domestic policy	0.00%	0.00%	0.00%	1.67%	5.26%	1.13%	2.40%	0.00%	1.42%
Church/religion	0.00%	0.00%	1.61%	1.67%	0.00%	0.00%	0.48%	7.69%	0.47%
Colonial policy	0.00%	0.00%	0.00%	0.00%	0.00%	0.90%	0.48%	0.00%	0.47%
Military	0.00%	0.00%	1.61%	0.00%	0.00%	0.90%	0.00%	0.00%	0.00%
Miscellaneous	0.00%	0.00%	0.00%	0.00%	5.26%	0.00%	0.00%	0.00%	0.00%
Legal	0.00%	0.00%	0.00%	0.00%	0.00%	0.00%	0.00%	0.00%	0.47%

landed interest that denoted the wealth of landed property. This was due to complaints from landowners about the poor laws and land tax during periods of distress – the beneficiaries of which were often considered to be farmers and agricultural labourers.[54] However, it was fundholders (who were sometimes referred to as the 'funded interest' but usually the monied interest) who became the target of the landed interest's grievances in these instances, arguing that those that profited from holding funds in the national debt should be required to make payments to the poor rates.[55]

Like the landed interest, the commercial interest was often used by politicians, and recorded by reporters, interchangeably with subsidiary interest categories – the manufacturing interest, the shipping interest and sometimes the West India or East India interest, particularly when these interests could be defined against the landed or agricultural interest. However, by the 1820s these interests were being discussed frequently in their own right, as certain commercial sectors made their own legislative demands.

The issue of distress, tentative steps towards freer trade from 1819 in a range of manufacturing sectors and the corn laws were primarily responsible for the rise in the use of the term 'manufacturing interest'. The first major development in this regard came in 1812 after a winter of distress prompted a petitioning campaign from British towns for the removal of the East India Company's monopoly. The manufacturing interest in this instance was also commonly deployed alongside the shipping interest, and its wider umbrella term the commercial interest, in an array of petitions that called for the opening up of closed colonial markets as a means of increasing profits for domestic manufacturing and port towns.[56] The manufacturing interest then came to be defined in opposition to the landed and agricultural interest during debates over the corn laws from 1814, as well as tariff reform in various manufacturing sectors, and periods of urban distress in 1819–20, 1825–6 and 1829–30. Certain MPs, often prompted by petitioning, called for the government to legislate in the interests of manufacturers as they were perceived to have done for the agricultural interest in 1815 with the corn laws, either by introducing favourable protective duties for certain industries, introducing currency or banking reform, or reducing or removing protective tariffs on corn.[57]

The rise in the use of the term 'shipping interest' followed a similar trajectory, particularly surrounding the distress experienced in port towns in 1811–12, 1825–6 and 1829–30. Unlike the manufacturing interest, the shipping interest also came to be defined in reference to episodic debates over proposed alterations to the navigation laws, which since the seventeenth century had restricted British colonies from trading with other nations. These debates took place at regular intervals from 1806: first, over proposals to allow America to trade with the West Indies, then in 1821 over the timber duties, again in 1823 over the reciprocity of duties bill, and finally in 1826–8 when petitioners from various port towns called for amendments to the navigation laws to support British shipping against foreign competition.[58]

The other interest category that saw a notable rise in its use between 1820 and 1832 was the West India interest. The West India interest had been one of the few categories to appear consistently in parliamentary discussion for a period prior to the 1820s. Its use originated among those seeking to defend West Indian planters during debates over the abolition of the slave trade between 1789 and 1806.[59] After a lull in its use during the 1810s, reference to the West India interest increased gradually throughout the 1820s and during the 1830 parliament was mentioned around once a day. As a number of historians have demonstrated, the overarching issue that defined the West India 'interest' in parliament during the 1820s was the need to defend slavery.[60] Specific debates over slavery in 1824, 1826 and 1831 do account for some references to the West India interest during the period. However, the chief reason for the rise in the use of the term was discussion from 1821 of the sugar duties, which allowed West Indian planters to pay a lower duty on their slave-grown sugar than East Indian and non-colonial planters.[61] Distress in the West Indies during the early part of 1830, which was accompanied by calls for a reduction of sugar duties for West Indian exporters, then led to a proliferation in the use of the term between 1830 and 1832.

The final interest category that saw a marked increase in its use during the 1820s was the Church interest. The category was usually raised by parliamentarians discussing 'the interests of the [established] Church', primarily in opposition to the Catholic Church in Ireland (or the 'Catholic interest') but also in reaction to the provision of constitutional rights for Nonconformists. The Church interest was referred to around once a fortnight until the 1826 parliament, when its use proliferated during debates over the repeal of the Test and Corporation Acts in 1828, proposals for Catholic emancipation in 1829, and from 1830 in discussion over tithes in Ireland. Reflecting a wider trend with regard to other interest categories, by the end of the 1820s the Church interest was also being discussed in the context of debates on parliamentary reform.

A breakdown of the types of parliamentary debate where the major interests were discussed between 1802 and 1832 is provided in Table 1.5. As might be expected, between 1806 and 1830 'interests' were discussed primarily during debates on fiscal and monetary policy (particularly protective duties) and domestic distress. This peaked during the 1820 parliament, when over 80 per cent of all recorded mentions of an interest came during debate on these two topics. Between 1826 and 1832, however, the issue of parliamentary reform gradually became the main topic of debate during which 'interests' were discussed. This shift took place because increasing numbers of parliamentarians, from across the political spectrum, started to view parliamentary reform – chiefly the redistribution of seats and redrawing of boundaries – as a means of rebalancing the parliamentary representation of the nation's newly complex, and combative, interests.

Minor reform, interests and the moderate Whig case for reform

Between 1771 and 1804, the boundaries of three parliamentary boroughs were extended into their surrounding hundreds as a punishment for electoral corruption. In 1771 parliament sought to purify the electorate of New Shoreham by adding all 40S. freeholders in the surrounding rape of Bramber to the borough. In 1782 a similar reform took place in Cricklade. By the early nineteenth century contemporaries had accepted that these reforms had placed both boroughs in the control of local country gentlemen.[62] With this knowledge, in 1804 Lord Grenville and the marquess of Buckingham successfully advocated for a similar extension to the borough of Aylesbury, where they were landowners.[63] As John Cannon has suggested, by 1804, debates over Aylesbury revealed that an increasing number of country gentlemen were beginning to realise the benefits of reforming a borough by throwing it into its hundreds. As well as strengthening the representation of the landed interest, it was seen as a means of staving off radical calls for reform.[64] In 1804, failed opposition to the reform of Aylesbury was based on the argument that, as only 200 of the borough's 500 potwalloper voters had been proven corrupt, swamping the borough with 40S. freeholders threatened to deprive the innocent majority of their ancient rights.[65] In contrast with later years, no parliamentarian suggested that it was more appropriate to transfer Aylesbury's franchise to one of England's unrepresented towns.[66]

Between 1813 and 1830 debates over proposals to reform Helston, Penryn, Barnstaple, Grampound, East Retford and Evesham revealed a growing desire for an alternative means of dealing with electoral corruption, which addressed calls for the representation of populous towns and re-balanced the representation of the nation's interests. Ultimately, only two boroughs were reformed. In 1821 Grampound was disfranchised,

Table 1.5: Discussion of major interests by category of parliamentary debate.

	1802–6	1806–7	1806–12	1812–18	1818–20	1820–26	1826–30	1830–31	1831–2
Fiscal and monetary policy	33.75%	50.00%	54.71%	58.41%	37.25%	58.81%	54.82%	25.21%	16.78%
Constitutional	2.50%	0.00%	4.71%	1.77%	9.80%	1.49%	13.17%	27.98%	67.03%
Distress	2.50%	0.00%	0.72%	5.75%	23.53%	21.73%	7.24%	15.79%	0.00%
Colonial policy	16.25%	30.77%	7.61%	7.96%	0.00%	5.80%	5.94%	19.94%	4.70%
Church/religion	5.00%	0.00%	12.68%	8.41%	2.94%	3.04%	11.13%	4.43%	5.59%
Ministerial statements	0.00%	3.85%	2.54%	7.52%	0.00%	4.88%	3.90%	4.16%	0.70%
Domestic policy	0.00%	0.00%	1.45%	5.75%	7.84%	1.91%	2.13%	0.83%	2.30%
Foreign policy (non-colonial)	22.50%	15.38%	13.04%	3.54%	0.00%	1.13%	0.65%	1.11%	0.40%
Military	17.50%	0.00%	2.54%	0.44%	17.65%	0.92%	0.19%	0.00%	0.70%
Legal	0.00%	0.00%	0.00%	0.44%	0.00%	0.07%	0.83%	0.55%	1.70%
Miscellaneous	0.00%	0.00%	0.00%	0.00%	0.98%	0.21%	0.00%	0.00%	0.10%

and its seats were transferred to the county of Yorkshire, while in 1830 East Retford was extended into its surrounding hundred. Debates over both the successful and unsuccessful proposals were nonetheless significant. As well as shaping the language with which contemporaries discussed the representative system, they shifted understandings about the extent to which the borough and county constituency system needed to be amended to accommodate the demographic transformation of the previous half-century and the political and socio-economic tensions of the post-Napoleonic period.

In consecutive years between 1813 and 1816, the Commons approved bills to throw the borough of Helston into its surrounding hundreds, all of which were rejected by the Lords due to a lack of official enquiry into corruption in the borough.[67] The debates on these failed bills revealed a growing discontent with throwing a borough into its hundreds, not just among those who opposed reform, but importantly, among those in favour of reform. Thomas Brand, a Whig who had proposed his own reform schemes in 1810 and 1812, expressed agreement that Helston should be thrown into its hundreds, but called for the franchise of subsequent Cornish boroughs found guilty of corruption to be transferred to various hundreds in the under-represented Yorkshire.[68] In the same debate, several MPs also advocated the transfer of Helston's seats to Yorkshire or 'some more populous district'. In contrast to later years, however, these suggestions were not legitimised explicitly around the idea that seat redistribution could provide representation to the under-represented manufacturing or commercial interests.[69]

Debate over proposals to reform Penryn, Barnstaple and Grampound between 1819 and 1821 led to the first formal calls for the franchise of corrupt boroughs to be redistributed to England's three most populous unrepresented towns – Manchester, Birmingham and Leeds. It was here that parliamentarians started to appropriate the evolving language of interests into their arguments over minor reform. Those that supported the throwing of Barnstaple and Penryn into their surrounding hundreds started to explicitly formulate the view that minor reform provided a means of stabilising the Commons by increasing the representation of the landed or agricultural interest.[70] The 'respected country gentleman' Nicolson Calvert, MP for Hertford, supported the 1819 Barnstaple bill on this basis, arguing that it provided an opportunity to bolster the 'agricultural interest' and 'landed interest' (terms he used interchangeably), which he contended only returned twenty MPs.[71] This was because, in his opinion, 'most of the members from the agricultural counties' were returned by the influence of the 'trading interest' (as *Hansard* recorded it) or the 'trading classes' (according to *The Times*).[72] This rationale was based on two concurrent developments. First, the emerging concern among country gentlemen that the cost of county elections and the size of county electorates, which contained large unrepresented town populations, had prevented traditional, agricultural-focused landowners from standing for election in the counties.[73] And second, an increase in the number of MPs associated with commercial interests, broadly defined, from one in nine MPs during the middle of the eighteenth century, to one in four by 1818.[74]

In contrast with Calvert, several MPs objected to proposals to extend Penryn and Barnstaple into their surrounding hundreds on the basis that it would provide the landed, or agricultural interest with too much power in the Commons. Alderman Heygate, an independent reformer returned for the Tory interest in Sudbury, opposed throwing Barnstaple into its hundreds on the basis that it reflected a 'fashionable ... preference' among parliamentarians to increase the powers of the 'landed interest' (*The Times*) or the 'interests ... of agriculture' (*Hansard*) at the expense of 'the trading and commercial interest' (*Hansard*) or 'manufacturing and commercial interest' (*Morning Post*).[75] The radical MP for Colchester, Daniel Whittle Harvey, employed an alternative understanding of the landed interest when opposing the proposals, equating it with the aristocratic, rather than the agricultural interest. He argued that the addition of 800 40S. freeholders from the surrounding countryside into what had previously been a borough elected by 500 freemen was an attempt to reduce the 'democratic interest' in the Commons.[76] By extending Barnstaple into its surrounding hundreds, he contended the borough would be 'thrown into the power of some few persons of the landed proprietors in the neighbourhood', which would only serve to increase the power of 'the aristocracy and landed interest of the country'.[77] Both Heygate and Harvey opposed the extension of Barnstaple into its hundreds on the basis that it would increase the landed interest's power; however, one understood the landed interest to be agricultural (in economic competition with the manufacturing and commercial interest) and the other aristocratic (in political competition with the democratic interest).

While suggestions were made during 1819 that Penryn and Barnstaple's seats should be redistributed to an unrepresented town, these proposals did not appear in draft legislation.[78] However, in the aftermath of that summer's reform agitations and the Peterloo Massacre, in December 1819, the Whig MP for Tavistock, Lord John Russell proposed that Grampound's seats, and all future boroughs proven to be corrupt, be transferred to populous unrepresented towns, and then subsequently the country's largest counties.[79] As the Cornish hundreds surrounding Grampound were already littered with boroughs, an alternative recipient for Grampound's seats had to be identified when the borough was proven to be corrupt.[80] Russell proposed to transfer Grampound's seats to Leeds. In contrast with debates over Helston, Barnstaple and Penryn, Russell's advocacy for the reform of Grampound was structured around an embryonic Whig rationale for reform that relied on constitutional historicism, a call for the rebalancing of interests in the Commons in order that it better represented 'the people', and a wealth of statistical information revealing the extent of distortion in the electoral system.[81] Like James Mackintosh, the Whig MP for Knaresborough, who a year earlier had written a significant essay opposing the 'uniformity' that would arise from universal suffrage, Russell maintained his support for the 'mirroring tradition' of interest representation that underpinned the existing electoral system.[82] Building on Mackintosh's vague indication of support for some form of moderate reform, Russell identified how practical reform might be effected within the existing structures of the constitution – an argument designed to appeal more to supporters of the existing representative system than its radical opponents.

In doing so, Russell advised the Commons that until the reign of Charles II, the electoral system had adapted to the rise and decline of England's towns – the Crown had historically issued writs to towns as they 'rose into importance', and removed them when they fell into 'poverty and insignificance'.[83] The cessation of this practice, he continued, had led to the rise of boroughs that were bought and sold by the Treasury to the highest bidder, resulting in a Commons full of men unable, or unwilling, to engage in parliamentary discussion, and who were slavish supporters of Tory ministries and the crown.[84] Russell warned that unless the historic practice of adaptation was resumed, parliament would deteriorate further, 'like the temples of Rome in her last days of empire'.[85] The remedy, as outlined in 1821 in the first edition of his *History of the English Constitution*, was a 'new map of representation' that ensured the nation's varied interests were 'vigilantly guarded in the legislature'.[86] For Russell, to ensure continuing public confidence in the constitution:

> the representative body should be the image of the represented: not that it should represent property only, or multitude only, or farmers, or merchants or manufacturers; not that it should govern with the pride of an insulated aristocracy, or be carried to and fro by the breath of transient popularity; but it should unite somewhat of all these things, and blend these various colours into one agreeable picture.[87]

While Russell accepted that the unreformed electoral system provided each interest with some form of representation, in 1819 he warned that the interests most in need of increased representation were those associated with England's northern and midland manufacturing towns. The ongoing cases of corruption in existing boroughs provided a means of gradually remodelling England's electoral map – and for Russell, towns like Manchester, Leeds, Birmingham, Halifax and Sheffield were the most deserving recipients. According to Russell, not only had the populations of such towns risen exponentially since the late eighteenth century (for instance, Manchester had risen in population from 23,000 in 1778 to 110,000 by 1819), but more importantly, the contribution of each town's manufacturing economies to the nation was indisputable. Although these towns shared in the return of county members for Lancashire, Yorkshire or Warwickshire, Russell felt their economic significance made it inappropriate that county MPs provide their sole means of representation. In so arguing, Russell defined the manufacturing interest of a town like Manchester or Leeds. Although county MPs were skilled, they lacked the knowledge:

> for stating the grievances and the wants of manufacturers. And when we consider how many questions relating to trade, to the poor-laws, to the laws of combination, and of particular taxes, deeply affect the manufacturers, we cannot but allow the justice of their desire to be represented.[88]

Based on this rationale, Russell made the ideologically important case for the transfer of Grampound's seats to Leeds in 1819, 1820 and 1821. This argument was reiterated in the first edition of his *History* and, following the engagement of philosophic Whig thinkers such as Mackintosh, Jeffrey and Creevey, developed into the basis of the Whig rationale for reform by November 1830.[89]

Although Russell's attempts to transfer Grampound's seats to Leeds failed, his rationale convinced a number of men, from a range of political backgrounds, over the next decade, that England's manufacturing districts required representation. MPs did not necessarily have to swallow Russell's rationale entirely for it to have some impact on their thinking. In 1820 Russell's use of population data was still too radical for the Surrey MP and advocate of the agricultural interest John Holme Sumner, who argued that 'the principle of representation should rest upon … property, and not upon that of population, as the modern reformers so clamorously contended'.[90] However, Sumner conceded that Yorkshire's manufacturing interests (of which Leeds was a constituent part) required additional representation, and supported a suggestion that Grampound's seats be used to increase Yorkshire's representation to four seats. This would mean 'two members for the West Riding would be returned by the manufacturing interest, while ... the members for the other Ridings would be returned by the agricultural or landed interest'.[91]

If Sumner's view signalled a somewhat hesitant acceptance of the need for an increased representation of the manufacturing interests, then the conversion of three men – John Wilson Croker, a Tory cabinet minister who would later be one of the reform bill's most vehement opponents; the Canningite, John Ward (later the first earl of Dudley), who had hitherto been a consistent opponent of radical and moderate parliamentary reform; and the Whig Viscount Milton, who in 1812 had argued against reform on the basis that 'the great advantage of the present system was, that there could be found no description of persons in the country who were not represented' – revealed an even more marked shift in moderate opinion.[92]

In 1820 Croker, then secretary to the admiralty, sought to halt the prime minister, Liverpool's attempts to assign Grampound's seats to Yorkshire instead of Leeds. In contrast with Sumner, who favoured dividing Yorkshire into its manufacturing and agricultural ridings, Liverpool had preferred that Yorkshire, as a whole, elect four MPs. He hoped that, while this would increase the indirect representation of several manufacturing towns in the county, it would also lead to the return of more members from the landed interest.[93] According to Croker's memoirs, he almost persuaded Liverpool's cabinet to go one step further than Russell, and provide Manchester, Birmingham, Leeds and Sheffield with the seats of corrupt boroughs – a move he hoped would stave off future calls for radical reform.[94] Croker's attempts to persuade the cabinet failed, however, and Liverpool's amendment to Russell's 1821 bill transferred Grampound's seats to Yorkshire.[95]

Even though Croker supported the enfranchisement of some towns, he claimed that this stance was consistent with his position as an 'anti-reformer'.[96] This view was also held by Ward, who stood to inherit extensive coal and limestone mines in the rapidly industrialising counties of Staffordshire and Worcestershire.[97] Ward confessed his preference for transferring Grampound's seats to Leeds, but in doing so sought to disassociate himself entirely from 'giving a pledge to what was called parliamentary reform'.[98] When speaking in favour of the enfranchisement of Leeds in 1821, Ward congratulated Russell for his 'patriotic excavations'[99] of constitutional precedent and stated that 'within the last few years, many great interests had grown up in the state'.[100] As a result the 'great defect in our constitution ... [was] that our extensive manufacturing towns were not represented'.[101] At various points in this speech, and depending on which record is consulted, Ward referred to manufacturing towns as 'commercial towns', with the potential to represent 'commercial interests', as well as 'manufacturing interests'.[102] Like Russell, he maintained that while county members were the most respectable MPs, 'landed proprietors' and 'country gentlemen' were not 'the most fitted by habits and education to manage the intricate and complicated business of a manufacturing community'[103] [or 'the interests of commerce and manufacture' (*Morning Post*), or 'all those complicated but important commercial details and inquiries' (*The Times*)].[104] By framing proposed alterations to the electoral system within the established language of interest balancing, reformers like Russell had provided politicians still opposed to the idea of wholesale parliamentary reform like Ward and Croker with an acceptable means of rationalising 'practical improvement' to England's electoral map.[105]

With the case for enfranchising Leeds seemingly convincingly made, it came as a regrettable discovery to another recent convert to the cause in May 1821 that Yorkshire was to gain Grampound's seats. As Ellis Wasson has shown, the Whig Viscount Milton had remained a vehement supporter of the electoral system until at least 1817. There were multiple reasons for his conversion to reform by 1821, and Wasson has argued that the perception of despotic government policy after 1815, especially in response to Peterloo and the Queen Caroline affair, was pivotal in changing his views.[106] Another major aspect of this conversion was Milton's eventual acceptance of Russell's arguments over the need for manufacturing towns to be provided with representation – which as late as 1819, the former still dismissed as 'too theoretical'.[107] By 1821, though, Milton's stance had changed. He objected to the Liverpool government's amendments to the Grampound bill on the basis that it sent a message to the 'nation at large' that parliament could only 'legislate in a manner which operated to the benefit of one interest exclusively': the landed interest.[108] For Milton, the transfer of Grampound's seats to Yorkshire was the fourth occasion (New Shoreham, Cricklade and Aylesbury being the others) that parliament had sought to increase the representation of the landed interest, a state of affairs he considered regrettable given that the case for the enfranchisement of Leeds had become so apparent. Milton contended that it was not the duty of parliamentarians, particularly those associated with the landed interest who had historically prided themselves on their ability to legislate disinterestedly, to act in a way that gave one interest 'undue preponderance' over another.[109] In doing so, he provided a critique of Liverpool's actions as motivated by self, rather than national, interest. This foreshadowed the tenor of debate over proposals for minor reform between 1827 and 1830 and the Grey ministry's reform bill in early 1831.

The East Retford saga: turning the Canningites

Following the hijacking of his 1821 Grampound bill, Russell temporarily changed tack over his gradualist approach towards reform. This was prompted by agitation at county meetings, market dinners and country fairs from late 1821, when radical politicians like William Cobbett called for electoral reform, a reduction in taxes and a suspension in cash payments as a means of preventing future episodes of agricultural distress.[110] In response, advanced and moderate Whigs made their alternative case for parliamentary reform at county meetings across the country.[111] A rapid increase in petitioning for electoral reform followed, which gave Russell the opportunity to introduce an ambitious reform resolution to the Commons in 1822. In it he proposed to partially disfranchise one hundred boroughs, and redistribute sixty of their seats to the counties and forty to unrepresented towns – a move he repeated in 1823.[112] This more ambitious reform solution replaced his earlier gradualist proposals, but his justifications for both schemes remained the same.[113] From 1823, county activism waned following two years of agricultural prosperity, which correlated with a rapid decline in reform petitions – only five were received by parliament between January 1824 and the summer of 1827.[114] Accordingly, Russell introduced no reform motion in 1824 or 1825, and although he proposed a motion in 1826 his knowledge of its probable rejection re-kindled his focus on gradual redistribution as a means of rebalancing the representation of interests.[115] Fresh confirmation in early 1827 of bribery at Penryn and East Retford during the 1826 election provided Russell with the formal opportunity to resurrect his proposals for minor reform.[116] The ensuing parliamentary debates, which in the case of East Retford were not resolved until 1830, proved incredibly fractious. They also revealed a widespread desire among parliamentarians to rebalance England's electoral map.

As outlined above, debate over Russell's newly proposed reforms took place in a parliament that had become increasingly polarised over protective tariffs and how to respond to repeated bouts of national distress. By the mid-1820s these tensions had led to the proliferation of a newly combative language of interests, as different economic lobby groups – the manufacturing, agricultural, shipping and West India interests – made their case for preferential treatment from the legislature. Significantly, these tensions also began to surface in government as it sought a response to distress in England's manufacturing towns during the winter of 1826–7 and the accompanying agitation for the repeal of the corn laws – 'that monstrous monopoly of the landed interest' as the 'starving weavers' of Blackburn termed them in an 1827 petition.[117] The extent of distress prompted liberal

Tories within the Liverpool, and then Canning cabinet – such as Liverpool, George Canning, William Huskisson and Robert Peel – to advocate a sliding scale for corn duties in 1827.[118] With manufacturing districts calling for repeal, and liberal Tories advocating corn law reform, Wellington, then master general of the ordnance, came to be perceived as the national representative of the landed interest and the 'country Tories', who were opposed to any change in policy as well as the legislative influence of liberal political economy.[119] This perception was cemented when Wellington's intervention led to the Lords' rejection of the 1827 corn law bill – a move that also established his status as the enemy of free trade in the radical press.[120] In 1828 Wellington became prime minister. He took charge of a cabinet divided between liberal-Tory Canningites and traditional Tories. And although his ministry passed a revised corn law bill that year, the perception of a factional divide between the landed and the commercial interests (broadly defined) both outside and inside parliament increasingly came to bear on politicians' approaches to minor reform.

Following confirmation of corruption during the 1826 election, two minor reform bills relating to Penryn and East Retford were introduced late in the 1827 parliamentary session.[121] Due to the efforts of the Tory MP for Leicestershire, George Legh Keck, it was initially proposed to expand Penryn into its hundreds.[122] However, during the bill's third Commons reading, Russell secured an amendment to transfer the borough's seats to Manchester. Debate over Russell's amendment revealed a bitter jealousy between advocates of the landed and manufacturing interest, prompting a bemused William Lamb (later second Viscount Melbourne) to bemoan 'the notion of the landed interest being opposed to the manufacturing ... that had sprung up within the last three or four years'.[123] Days later, the radical MP for Bletchingley, Charles Tennyson, introduced a separate bill to transfer East Retford's seats to Birmingham, embracing the Whig rationale for the transference of seats from decayed boroughs to new centres of commerce.[124] Parliament was prorogued before either bill reached the Lords. However, at the commencement of the 1828 session, Russell and Tennyson announced their intention to reintroduce each proposal.[125]

Tensions between advocates of the landed and commercial interests were also evident in the newly formed cabinet in 1828, who were split over both proposals. Wellington and his allies preferred that both boroughs be thrown into their hundreds, while the liberal-Tory Canningites – Palmerston, Huskisson and Dudley – supported transferring their seats to Manchester and Birmingham.[126] Croker and the home secretary, Robert Peel (who while a liberal Tory was distanced from the Canningite faction by his historic relationship with Canning), were receptive to the latter option but feared a backlash from Tory electors and country gentlemen, as well as the establishment of a constitutional precedent that required the transfer of all future corrupt borough franchises to unrepresented towns.[127] A compromise was agreed which aimed to 'satisfy the agricultural and manufacturing classes' inside and outside parliament. The cabinet proposed to support the transfer of Penryn's seats to Manchester so long as East Retford was thrown into its hundred.[128]

Consequently the long-time defender of the agricultural interest, Nicolson Calvert moved an instruction to Tennyson's East Retford bill that proposed to throw the borough into the hundred of Bassetlaw, in order to provide two seats to the 'agricultural interest'.[129] The government's proposed compromise was approved by the Commons, but opposed by a large minority of Whigs and reformers following an impassioned plea from the Whig MP James Mackintosh for the Commons to seize 'one of the best opportunities that ever presented itself of sinking the constitution more deeply into the hearts of the people' by 'giving to one of our greatest trading interests [Birmingham] that protection which it requires'.[130] However, within months the government's proposed compromise was ruined, when it became clear that the Lords would not approve the transfer of Penryn's seats to Manchester. This did not stop Calvert pressing ahead with his amendment to the separate East Retford bill in a heated debate on 19 May 1828, in which he shamelessly admitted that his proposal was intended to protect the interests of agriculture against persons 'engaged in manufacture'.[131]

The prior knowledge that the Penryn bill was likely to be rejected by the Lords increased tensions in the cabinet. The Canningites confirmed their intention to vote against Calvert, arguing that if one borough was going to be disfranchised its seats had to be transferred to an unrepresented town. Wellington and his fellow traditional Tories, as well as Peel, announced their intention to support Calvert. Calvert's amendment passed by a slim majority of eighteen, but both Huskisson and Palmerston divided against it. The Canningite rump then resigned from the cabinet – Huskisson, Lamb, Palmerston, Dudley and Grant.[132] As well as prompting the County Clare by-election that would eventually lead to Catholic emancipation, it signalled that the Canningites en masse (or the 'liberal' faction as Palmerston termed them) now conceded the necessity for practical improvement to the electoral system, through the enfranchisement of unrepresented towns.[133]

In the two debates that followed, the Canningites and Whigs accused the Wellington government of disregarding the national interest, having endorsed the extension of East Retford into its hundreds to increase its electoral support among the landed and agricultural interest. Tensions were exacerbated on 2 June, when the majority in favour of throwing East Retford into its hundred received a surprise increase of 100 votes from hitherto absent government supporters. Tennyson accused the government of turning the question into a party matter, informing the Commons that 'the [Tory party] tocsin' had been 'sounded throughout the country' and that ministerial supporters had been instructed that 'the existence of a Tory government' depended on their provision of support to the bill. Palmerston, too, lamented that party affiliation had prevented the Commons from 'taking advantage of every case of delinquency, to apply a gradual remedy to the defective state of the representation'. And the moderate Whig Edward Smith Stanley (later fourteenth earl of Derby) regretted that the bill had become 'a vehicle for the expression of party feeling'. He also revealed that since the departure of the Canningites from the cabinet, he had heard 'the landed interest declare that they at last looked with confidence to a ministry from which they expected a preference to their interests over those of the manufacturing and commercial classes'.[134]

For Russell the episode established that future electoral reform must not turn the Commons into an adversarial body based around town and country factions. He was convinced that MPs would have consented to Birmingham's enfranchisement, 'if it had not been for that jealousy which had sprung up during the last two or three years between the landed and the manufacturing interests',[135] a jealousy that he felt 'originated in a great measure in the discussions on the corn bill'.[136] In doing so, Russell held out an olive branch to Peel, by suggesting that the latter too maintained a disdain for such division, and would have voted to enfranchise Birmingham if he had been allowed to vote independently of Wellington's cabinet. Russell informed MPs that agriculture and manufacturing were dependent on each other for their prosperity, and that if the Commons remained divided it would distract the lower chamber from its primary purpose of keeping a check on the power of the monarchy. He hoped that:

> the time would shortly arrive, when they should see the members of that House, whether the representatives of manufacturing or agricultural bodies, perform their duties without reference to any such distinction, and join together, as they were bound to join, in performing one of the greatest duties of that House – he meant, keeping a proper control on the expenditure of the crown.[137]

For Russell it was clear that parliamentary reform was vital, not just for ensuring the representation of the nation's interests, but in order to establish a greater disinterestedness among MPs in order that they did not get distracted from performing their wider constitutional functions.

Debate over Catholic emancipation prevented any progress on the East Retford bill during 1829, and when it was re-introduced in February 1830, the Wellington ministry pressed ahead with their support for throwing the borough into its hundred as a means of appeasing their ultra-Tory supporters following Catholic emancipation.[138] Commons majorities continued to favour the government and with the support of the Lords, East Retford was finally extended into the hundred of Bassetlaw ahead of the 1830 election, a decision that the cartoonist Robert Seymour blamed on ministerial influence in 'The three years job settled' (Figure 1.1). Throughout, the Canningites remained united with the Whigs in opposing the bill and supporting Russell's contention that the Commons no longer provided for a balanced representation of the nation's interests. In 1830 Huskisson

Figure 1.1: Robert Seymour, 'The three years job settled', *The Looking Glass*, March 1830, RB.37.c.31. British Library.

reiterated that 'every great interest of the country ought to be represented in that House [the Commons]'[139] and that it was short-sighted of the factional proponents of the landed interest not to see that their interests were tied up in the prosperity of towns like Birmingham. 'Without the manufacturing and commercial industry of Lancashire, Warwickshire, and Yorkshire', he informed MPs, 'the land of those counties would be worth comparatively little'.[140] This coalition was also united over Russell's failed February 1830 proposal to enfranchise Birmingham, Manchester and Leeds – a motion he had announced in 1829 when he realised his efforts to transfer East Retford's seats to Birmingham were futile.[141] Huskisson, Palmerston and Melbourne divided in the minority for Russell's proposal. All three conceded the case for Birmingham, Manchester and Leeds's representation without the need to wait for other boroughs to be disfranchised – a stance that would have been inconceivable even three years earlier to their erstwhile leader Canning.[142]

Conclusion: the 'three years job settled'?

Rather than settling the reform issue, the East Retford saga, as well as the debates over minor reform in the post-Napoleonic period, laid the foundations for the coalition of young Whigs, moderate Whigs, grand Whigs and liberal Tories that formed the Grey ministry in November 1830. All of them were committed on one issue: the need to rebalance England's electoral map so that it better represented the nation's interests. It was also evident that by November 1830, when he made his infamous declaration against reform, many parliamentarians who Wellington looked to for support had accepted this moderate Whig argument.

In February 1830 Peel provided his coded approval for a major redistribution of forty borough seats to the 'commercial interest', so long as it was accompanied by the provision of sixty seats to the 'landed interest' via the counties.[143] Peel's statement reflected his own awareness that the case for the representation of towns such as Manchester was now undeniable, as well as the strength of the moderate Whig case for reform. By early 1830 parliamentary reform had also become acceptable to a number of ultra-Tories to the political right of Wellington. As Moore has argued, certain ultra-Tories advocated reform because of their discontent with the passage of Catholic emancipation and the continued influence of liberal economic influence in the Wellington ministry. They also came round to reform because of the realisation of the strength of the Whig argument and the perception of an unprecedented rivalry between the nation's interests during the 1820s. Although ultra-Tory proposals varied, they accepted the need for the enfranchisement of unrepresented towns, while also seeking to increase the number of MPs independent from the influence of party and liberal political economy – which they blamed for successive bouts of distress during the previous decade. As one commentator stated in 1830, successive liberal-Tory governments had brought 'the great interests of the country into fierce contention ... expelled independence from the House of Commons, and converted it into an assembly of devoted adherents to one [liberal] faith'.[144] It was men like Peel and these ultra-Tory county members that the Grey ministry hoped to 'conciliate' by grounding their reform bill around a balance between 'town and country' in 1831.[145]

The increasingly factional post-Napoleonic domestic climate, the new language of interests it evoked and the debates over minor reform from 1819, had prompted a major shift in the majority of political opinion towards an acceptance that the unreformed electoral system, and its eighteenth-century rationale, were no longer fit for purpose. While this shift should not be conflated with support for the extensive reform proposals of the Grey ministry, it is crucial in terms of understanding why Wellington's unwillingness to countenance reform in November 1830 was perceived as a final confirmation of his inability to govern in the national interest. Unsurprisingly, the rebalancing of interests lay at the heart of the Grey ministry's reform bill and underpinned their huge redistribution of county and borough seats. However, when Russell introduced the government's initial plans in March 1831 it quickly became apparent to all sides of political opinion that certain interests – particularly the landed, agricultural and manufacturing interests – stood to profit most from reform. As a result, between 1831 and 1832, the shipping, monied, West India and East India interests all lobbied for more specific forms of representation.[146] In addition, the abolition of rotten boroughs remained a point of concern, not only for anti-reformers, but for some figures in the cabinet, who wanted to retain opportunities for the representation of the professional interest. Opposition to parliamentary reform quickly became a religious controversy in its own right, as the defenders of the Church interest both in parliament and behind the pulpit railed against the reform bill as a 'satanic' measure.[147] And as discussed in the next chapter, the perception among radicals and reformers that the landed interest stood to gain too much from proposals to divide the counties almost led to the government's downfall in September 1831.

These deficiencies in the reform legislation's interest balancing model did not escape Russell, who remained the cabinet's most faithful adherent of the interest balancing concept. He made multiple failed proposals for the introduction of additional fancy franchises (pre-existing university representation excepted) during 1831, all of which were rejected by the cabinet. In April he proposed that between twelve and twenty MPs should be chosen by stockholders who earned £100 a year from the public funds; in April, July and November, he advocated 'a limited number of members for ... colonial property'; in July he suggested that several seats might represent the specific interests of 'landed property' as distinct from the broader definition of the landed, agricultural interest; and in November, he recommended representation for the legal interest through four seats for the Inns of Court.[148] While all of these proposals failed to gain traction, Russell saw them as consistent with the cabinet's decision during debates on the second reform bill to appease the naval interest by enfranchising Chatham and the shipping interest by providing representation to Whitby.[149] Russell's willingness to rationalise seat redistribution so openly on the basis of interest representation even led to mocking from anti-reformers, who, when seeking to understand the enfranchisement of the resort towns of Cheltenham and Brighton derided the government for providing representation to the 'watering-hole' interest. This association remained with Brighton until at least the 1860s.[150] In reality, Russell's failure to make his interest balancing scheme more comprehensive meant the electoral reforms of 1832 focused primarily on providing representation to the landed and commercial interests, via agricultural and manufacturing constituencies. As this book demonstrates, the ultimate irony of the Grey ministry's rationalisation of their reform legislation as a means of balancing interests was that they created a constituency structure that accentuated, rather than pacified, the confrontation between land and commerce over the following two decades.

Notes

1. In keeping with Cragoe, *Culture, Politics and National Identity in Wales*, Monmouthshire and Monmouth Boroughs are considered part of Wales.

2. Hansard, *Parliamentary Debates*, 3rd ser., ii. (1 Mar. 1831), 1108–9.

3. Hansard, 3, i. (2 Nov. 1830), 52–3.

4. A. Mitchell, 'The Whigs and Parliamentary Reform Before 1830', *Historical Studies* (Australia and New Zealand), 12 (1965), 22–42; Wasson, 'Great Whigs', 434–64.

5. D. Eastwood, 'Parliament and Locality: Representation and Responsibility in Late-Hanoverian England', *Parliamentary History* 17, 1 (1998), 79; Parry, *Rise and Fall*, 78–87. The exception being J. F. Lively, 'Ideas of Parliamentary Representation in England, 1815–32' (unpublished University of Cambridge DPhil thesis, 1957), 109–14, 119–20, 127–34.

6. Blaxill, *War of Words*, 14.

7. P. Loft, 'Involving the Public: Parliament, Petitioning, and the Language of Interest, 1688–1720', *JBS*, 55, 1 (2016), 1–23; P. Loft, 'Petitioning and Petitioners to the Westminster Parliament, 1660–1788', *Parliamentary History*, 38, 3 (2019), 342–61;

J. Hoppit, 'Petitions, Economic Legislation and Interest Groups in Britain, 1660–1800', *Parliamentary History*, 37, 1 (2018), 52–71; Miller, *Nation of Petitioners*, 229–52.

8. G. Conti, *Parliament the Mirror of the Nation: Representation, Deliberation, and Democracy in Victorian Britain* (Cambridge, 2019), 13–30.

9. S. Collini, D. Winch and J. Burrow, *That Noble Science of Politics: A Study in Nineteenth-Century Intellectual History* (Cambridge, 1983), 105–6; Taylor, 'Interests, Parties and the State', 52–3, 65; Wahrman, *Imagining the Middle Class: The Political Representation of Class in Britain, c.1780–1840* (Cambridge, 1995), 91; Eastwood, 'Parliament and Locality', 68–81; A. Gambles, *Protection and Politics: Conservative Economic Discourse, 1815–1852* (Woodbridge, 1999), 8–9; Loft, 'Involving the Public'; Hoppit, 'Petitions, Economic Legislation and Interest Groups'.

10. H. Dickinson, *Liberty and Property: Political Ideology in Eighteenth-century Britain* (London, 1977), 85–7, 148–52, 167–72, 190–91; D. Hayton, 'The "Country" Interest in the Party System, 1689–c.1720', in C. Jones (ed.), *Party & Management in Parliament 1660–1784* (Leicester, 1984), 37–86; J. Gunn, '"Interests Will Not Lie": A Seventeenth-Century Political Maxim', *Journal of the History of Ideas*, 29, 4 (1968), 551–64.

11. Dickinson, *Liberty and Property*, 85–7.

12. G. Holmes, *British Politics in the Age of Anne* (London, 1987), 173–82.

13. E. Hargreaves, *The National Debt* (London, 1930), 73–90; M. Skjönsberg, *The Persistence of Party: Ideas of Harmonious Discord in Eighteenth-Century Britain* (Cambridge, 2021), 77–110.

14. P. Miller, *Defining the Common Good: Empire, Religion and Philosophy in Eighteenth-Century Britain* (Cambridge, 1994), 245–65; J. Brewer, *Party Ideology and Popular Politics at the Accession of George III* (Cambridge, 1976), 201–15; Dickinson, *Liberty and Property*, 217.

15. A. Birch, *Representation* (London, 1971), 37–40; Eastwood, 'Parliament and Locality', 70; Dickinson, *Liberty and Property*, 353, footnote 26.

16. Eastwood, 'Parliament and Locality'; S. Beer, 'The Representation of Interests in British Government: Historical Background', *American Political Science Review*, 51, 3 (1957), 613–50.

17. P. Langford, 'Property and "Virtual Representation" in Eighteenth-Century England', *HJ*, 31, 1 (1998), 83–115; Brewer, *Party Ideology*, 209–10; J. Pole, *Political Representation in England and the Origins of the American Republic* (London, 1966), 385–404.

18. Dickinson, *Liberty and Property*, 274–77; S. Jenyns, *Thoughts on a Parliamentary Reform* (London, 1784), 21–6.

19. Hansard, 3, ii. (1 Mar. 1831), 1108–9; Dickinson, *Liberty and Property*, 270–90.

20. J. Hoppit, 'The Landed Interest and the National Interest, 1660–1800', in J. Hoppit (ed.), *Parliaments, Nations and Identities in Britain and Ireland, 1660–1850* (Manchester, 2003), 97; J. Hoppit, 'Petitions, Economic Legislation', 68–9.

21. Hoppit 'Landed Interest', 83–102; Pole, *Political Representation*, 442–8; Hayton, '"Country" Interest', 37–86; Anonymous, *Thoughts on County Elections Addressed to the Landed Interest of the Country* (London, 1812).

22. Cobbett, *Parliamentary History*, xxx. (6 May 1792), 811–13.

23. Cobbett, xxiii. (6 May 1783), 827–35, 870–71; S. Thompson, 'Census-Taking, Political Economy and State Formation' (unpublished University of Cambridge DPhil thesis, 2010) 186–91; I. Christie, 'The Yorkshire Association, 1780–4: A Study in Political Organization', *HJ*, 3, 2 (1960), 158; M. Kilburn, 'Yorkshire Association', *ODNB*, www.oxforddnb.com [accessed 22 October 2023].

24. *Cobbett*, xxiii. (6 May 1783), 853; *Cobbett*, xxv. (18 Apr. 1785), 461.

25. *Cobbett*, xxiii. (6 May 1783), 870–71.

26. J. Brooke, 'The Members', in L. Namier and J. Brooke (eds.), *The House of Commons 1754–1790* (Cambridge, 1985), i. 131.

27. Hoppit, 'Petitions, Economic Legislation', 60–62; Loft, 'Involving the Public', 1–23; P. Gauci, 'The Clash of Interests: Commerce and the Politics of Trade in the Age of Anne', *Parliamentary History*, 28, 1 (2009), 115–25.

28. Namier and Brooke, *Commons 1754–1790*, i. 131–8.

29. G. Judd, *Members of Parliament, 1734–1832* (New Haven, 1955) 55–73.

30. *Cobbett*, xxiii. (6 May 1783), 811, 837–8; *Cobbett*, xxv. (18 Apr. 1785), 461.

31. *Cobbett*, xxx. (6 May 1793), 811–13, 863, 870–71.

32. Brooke, 'The Members', 131–8.

33. *Cobbett*, xvii. (11 Apr. 1771), 166–9; *Cobbett*, xxii. (13 Mar. 1782), 1168–70; J. Cannon, 'Cricklade', J. Brooke, 'New Shoreham', in Namier and Brooke, *Commons 1754–1790*, i, 396–9, 409–11.

34. Judd, *Members of Parliament*, 63–5; T. Nechtman, *Nabobs: Empire and Identity in Eighteenth-Century Britain* (Cambridge, 2010), 11–14, 92–40; L. Sutherland, *The East India Company in Eighteenth-Century Politics* (Oxford, 1952).

35. Judd, *Members of Parliament*, 67–9; D. Fisher (ed.), *The House of Commons, 1820–1832* (Cambridge, 2009), i., 273.

36. F. Bassett, *Free Parliaments: or a Vindication of the Parliamentary Constitution of England* (London, 1783), 68–9.

37. N. Draper, 'The Rise of a New Planter Class? Some Countercurrents from British Guiana and Trinidad, 1807–33', *Atlantic Studies*, 9, 1 (2012), 75; N. Draper, *The Price of Emancipation: Slave-Ownership, Compensation and British Society at the End of Slavery* (Cambridge, 2009), 279–302, 318–22; K. McClelland, 'Redefining the West India Interest: Politics and the Legacies of Slave-Ownership', in C. Hall et al. (eds.), *Legacies of British Slave-Ownership* (Cambridge, 2014), 127–62, 288–97.

38. Judd, *Members of Parliament*, 67–9; S. Mullen, 'Henry Dundas: A 'Great Delayer' of the Abolition of the Transatlantic Slave Trade', *Scottish Historical Review*, 100, 2 (2021), 218–48; Michael Taylor, *The Interest: How the British Establishment Resisted the Abolition of Slavery* (London, 2020); Skjönsberg, *Persistence of Party*, 247, 272.

39. Dickinson, *Liberty and Property*, 284; Pole, *Political Representation*, 451–5.

40. *Cobbett*, xvi. (22 Jan. 1770), 753–4; Dickinson, *Liberty and Property*, 150.

41. *Cobbett*, xxx. (6 May 1793), 811–13.

42. *Cobbett*, xxiii. (6 May 1783), 837–8; *Cobbett*, xxix. (30 Apr. 1792), 1321; *Cobbett*, xxx. (6 May 1793), 853; *Cobbett*, xxxiii. (26 May 1797), 681.

43. Beer, 'Representation of Interests', 613–32; Lively, 'Ideas of Parliamentary Representation', 139–45.

44. The *Hansard* corpus was compiled primarily from open-source XML files http://www.hansard-archive.parliament.uk [accessed 29 Dec. 2021]. Sixteen missing *Hansard* volumes between 1803 and 1868 and the *Cobbett* corpus were compiled from digitally available sources and made text-searchable with *FineReader*. On method see, L. Blaxill, 'Quantifying the Language of British Politics', *Historical Research*, 86 (2013), 313–41; Blaxill, *The War of Words*, 21–43.

45. Hansard at Huddersfield Project (2018). 'Hansard at Huddersfield'. University of Huddersfield https://web.archive.org/web/20230610065846/https://hansard.hud.

ac.uk/ [accessed 19 May 2022]. Session data for 1829 were added to this categorisation using *CasualConc*.

46. D. Wahrman, 'Virtual Representation: Parliamentary Reporting and Languages of Class in the 1790s', *Past and Present*, 136, 1 (1992), 83–113; K. Rix, '"Whatever Passed in Parliament Ought to be Communicated to the Public": Reporting the Proceedings of the Reformed Commons, 1833–50', *Parliamentary History*, 33, 3 (2014), 453–74.

47. For Parliament lengths from 1842: PP1852 (576), xlii. 51. Manual day counts were used between 1830 and 1841. A parliamentary week was considered to be five days.

48. Results that appeared in a debate title, appendices or indexes were excluded.

49. This 'top ten' excludes references to general interests such as the 'national interest' or 'interests of the empire'.

50. Occasional references to the 'mercantile' and 'trading' interest have been collated into the 'commercial interest'. The 'farming' interest has been collated into the 'agricultural interest'. 'Planters' interest' and 'slave owners' interest' have been collated into 'West India interest'. These additions do not affect the relative position of each category but have been collated due to their interchangeability in parliamentary reporting.

51. Hansard, xi. (23 June 1808), 998–1001.

52. B. Hilton, *Corn, Cash, Commerce: Economic Policies of the Tory Governments, 1815-30* (Oxford, 1977), 1–30, 98–169, 269–301.

53. Hansard, 1, xxxix. (25 Feb. 1819), 657; Hansard, 2, vi. (5 Feb. 1822), 3.

54. Hansard, 1, xxxx. (7 June 1819), 967; Hansard, 2, viii. (21 Feb. 1823), 233.

55. Hansard, 2, viii. (14 Feb. 1823), 120–21; Hilton, *A Mad, Bad, & Dangerous People?: England 1783–1846* (Oxford, 2006), 273–4.

56. Hansard, 1, xxii. (7 Apr. 1812), 216–21; Hansard, 1, xxii. (23 Apr. 1812), 723–7.

57. Hilton, *Corn, Cash, Commerce*, 173–201, 232–68.

58. Hansard, 1, vii. (22 May 1806), 336–47; Hansard, 2, v. (5 Apr. 1821), 50–64; Hansard, 2, viii. (6 June 1823), 795–802; Hansard, 2, xv. (17 Apr. 1826), 272–5.

59. P. Lipscomp, 'Party Politics, 1801–1802: George Canning and the Trinidad Question', *HJ*, 12, 3 (1969), 442–66; Mullen, 'Henry Dundas: A 'Great Delayer', 218–48.

60. B. Higman, 'The West India "Interest" in Parliament, 1807–1833', *Historical Studies* (Australia and New Zealand), 13, 49 (1967), 1–19; Draper, *Price of Emancipation*; McClelland, 'Redefining the West India Interest'; P. Dumas, *Proslavery Britain: Fighting for Slavery in an Era of Abolition* (New York, 2016); Michael Taylor, 'Conservative Political Economy and the Problem of Colonial Slavery, 1823–1833', *HJ*, 57, 4 (2014), 973–95; Taylor, *The Interest*.

61. McClelland, 'Redefining the West India Interest', in Hall et al. *Legacies of British Slave Ownership*, 143.

62. *Cobbett*, xvii. (11 Apr. 1771), 166–9; *Cobbett*, xvii. (13 Mar. 1772), 1168–70; J. Brooke, 'New Shoreham', in Namier and Brooke, *Commons*, i. 396–9; J. Cannon, 'Cricklade', in Namier and Brooke, *Commons*, i. 409–11.

63. D. Fisher, 'Aylesbury', in R. G. Thorne (ed.), *The House of Commons, 1790–1820* (Cambridge, 1986), ii. 19–22; R. Gibbs, *A History of Aylesbury* (Aylesbury, 1885), 254–7, 276–7.

64. J. Cannon, *Parliamentary Reform 1640–1832* (Cambridge, 1973), 148–9.

65. Hansard, 1, ii. (7 May 1804), 388–92.

66. Cannon, *Parliamentary Reform*, 149.

67. Hansard, 1, xxviii. (14 July 1814), 701; Hansard, 1, xxix. (18 Feb. 1815), 789–90; Hansard, 1, xxix. (6 Mar. 1815), 5–6; Hansard, 1, xxxiii. (15 Mar. 1816), 296–7; Hansard, 1, xxxiv. (9 May 1816), 408.

68. Hansard, 1, xvii. (10 May 1810), 134–5; Hansard, 1, xxiii. (8 May 1812), 105; Hansard, 1, xxvi. (21 June 1813, c. 805–6; Cannon, *Parliamentary Reform*, 162.

69. Hansard, 1, xxvi. (30 June 1813), 990–92; Hansard, 1, xxvi. (2 July 1813), 1082.

70. *Cobbett*, xxxiii. (26 May 1797), 689; Hansard, 1, xxx. (6 Mar. 1815), 5–6; Cannon, *Parliamentary Reform*, 131, 148, 177, 179–80.

71. Hansard, 1, xl. (17 May 1819), 464; D. Fisher, 'Calvert, Nicolson', in Fisher, *Commons*, iv. 519–24.

72. Hansard, 1, xl. (17 May 1819), 464; *Morning Post*, 3 Apr. 1819; *The Times*, 18 May 1819.

73. Anonymous, *County Elections*.

74. Judd, *Members of Parliament*, 56–7, 88–9.

75. Hansard, 1, xxxix. (2 Apr. 1819), 1392; *The Times*, 3 Apr. 1819; *Morning Chronicle*, 3 Apr. 1819; *Morning Post*, 3 Apr. 1819.

76. D. Fisher, 'Harvey, Daniel', in Fisher, *Commons*, v. 522–9.

77. Hansard, 1, xl (17 May 1819), 464; *Morning Chronicle*, 18 May 1819, 2; *Morning Post*, 18 May 1819.

78. Hansard, 1, xxxix. (26 Feb. 1819), 714, Hansard, 1, xxxix. (8 Mar. 1819), 906–24; Hansard, 1, xl (17 May 1819), 462; Hansard, 1, lxi. (7 Dec. 1819), 815.

79. Hansard, 1, xli. (14 Dec. 1819), 1102–3.

80. Cannon, *Parliamentary Reform*, 178–9.

81. Hansard, 1, xli. (14 Dec. 1819), 1096.

82. Conti, *Parliament Mirror of the Nation*, 18–22; J. Mackintosh, 'Universal Suffrage', *Edinburgh Review*, 31 (1818), 168, 175–6, 180.

83. Hansard, 1, xli. (14 Dec. 1819), 1094.

84. Hansard, 1, xli. (14 Dec. 1819), 1093–6, 1100–1101.

85. Hansard, 1, xli. (14 Dec. 1819), 1093.

86. Lord Russell, *History of the English Government and Constitution* (London, 1821), 267.

87. Russell, *History of the English Government* (1821), 251–2.

88. Hansard, 1, xli. (14 Dec. 1819), cc 1097.

89. Russell, *History of the English Government* (1821), 264–65; Hilton, *Mad, Bad*, 347; R. Smith, *The Gothic Bequest: Medieval Institutions in British Thought, 1688–1863* (Cambridge 1987), 164–70; Conti, *Parliament Mirror of the Nation*, 20–22.

90. Hansard, 2, i. (19 May 1820), 504.

91. Hansard, 2, i. (19 May 1820), 504.

92. Hansard, 1, xxiii. (8 May 1812), 148–51.

93. Cannon, *Parliamentary Reform*, 179.

94. L. Jennings (ed.), *The Correspondence and Diaries of the Late Right Honourable John Wilson Croker*, i. (London, 1885), 136–7; British Library, Liverpool Papers, Additional MS. [hereafter BL, Add. MS.] 38370, 63–7; Cannon, *Parliamentary Reform*, 179.

95. Hansard, 2, v. (21 May 1821), 857.

96. D. Fisher, 'Croker, John Wilson', in Fisher, *Commons*, iv. 798–813; Jennings, *Correspondence and Diaries*, 136–7.

97. D. Fisher, 'Ward, Hon. John', in Fisher, *Commons*, vii. 640–41.

98. *Hansard*, 2, iv. (12 Feb. 1821), 589.

99. *Hansard*, 2, iv. (12 Feb. 1821), 594.

100. *The Times*, 13 Feb. 1821.

101. *Hansard*, 2, iv. (12 Feb. 1821), 592.

102. *Hansard*, 2, iv. (12 Feb. 1821), 592; *Morning Post*, 13 Feb. 1821.

103. *Hansard*, 2, iv. (12 Feb. 1821), 592.

104. *The Times*, 13 Feb. 1821; *Morning Post*, 13 Feb. 1821.

105. P. Harling, 'Parliament, the State, and "Old Corruption": Conceptualizing Reform, c. 1790–1832', in A. Burns and J. Innes (eds.), *Rethinking the Age of Reform* (Cambridge, 2003), 98–113; D. Beales, 'The Idea of Reform in British Politics, 1829–1850', in T. Blanning and P. Wende (eds.), *Reform in Great Britain and Germany, 1750–1850* (Oxford, 1999), 159–74.

106. Wasson, 'Great Whigs', 442–50.

107. Wasson, 'Great Whigs', 449.

108. *The Times*, 31 May 1821; *Hansard*, 2, v. (30 May 1821), 1043.

109. *Hansard*, 2, v. (30 May 1821), 1043.

110. T. Crosby, *English Farmers and the Politics of Protection 1815–1852* (Hassocks, 1977), 57–60; Hilton, *Mad, Bad*, 271–2.

111. Crosby, *Politics of Protection*, 60–75; Mitchell, 'The Whigs and Parliamentary Reform', 22–42.

112. *Hansard*, 2, vii. (25 Apr. 1822), 51–139; *Hansard*, 2, viii. (17 Feb. 1823), v.8, 127; *Hansard*, 2, viii. (24 Apr. 1823), 1260–87.

113. Russell, *History of the English Government* (1821), 264–5, removed from Russell, *History of the English Government* (1823), 358.

114. D. Barnes, *A History of the English Corn Laws from 1660–1846* (London, 1930), 157–79.

115. *Hansard*, 2, xi. (17 May 1824) 756; *Hansard*, 2, xv. (7 Apr. 1826), 651–714; *Hansard*, 2, xvii. (3 May 1827), 543; Cannon, *Parliamentary Reform*, 185–6.

116. PP1826 (126) x. 63; *Hansard*, 2, xv. (28 Apr. 1826), 733; Salmon, '"Reform Should Begin at Home": English Municipal and Parliamentary Reform, 1818–32', in C. Jones, P. Salmon and R. Davis (eds.), *Partisan Politics, Principles and Reform in Parliament and the Constituencies, 1689–1880* (Edinburgh, 2004), 93–113.

117. *Hansard*, 2, xvi. (9 Feb. 1827), 412–13.

118. Gordon, *Economic Doctrine*, 52–66.

119. Jupp, *British Politics on the Eve of Reform: The Duke of Wellington's Administration, 1828–30* (Basingstoke, 1998), 391–402; Gordon, *Economic Doctrine and Tory Liberalism, 1824–1830* (London, 1979), 96–139; Barnes, *Corn Laws*, 185–219; Crosby, *Politics of Protection*, 57–75; Gambles, *Protection and Politics*, 25–55, 89–116; Hilton, *Mad, Bad*, 264–74.

120. Hilton, *Mad, Bad*, 307; Barnes, *Corn Laws*, 197–201.

121. T. Jenkins, 'Penryn', in Fisher, *Commons*, ii. 176–83.

122. *Hansard*, 2, xvii. (8 May 1827), 682–4; *Hansard*, 2, xvii. (18 May 1827), 903–23.

123. *The Times*, 29 May 1827; *Morning Post*, 29 May 1827; *Morning Chronicle*, 29 May 1827; Hansard, 2, xvii. (28 May 1827), 1047.

124. Hansard, 2, xvii. (11 June 1827), 1210–12.

125. Hansard, 2, xviii. (31 Jan. 1828), 83–6; Hansard, 2, xviii. (25 Feb. 1828), 669–76.

126. F. Bamford and Duke of Wellington (eds.), *The Journal of Mrs Arbuthnot, 1820–1832* (London, 1950), ii. 123, 173, 176, 187.

127. Bamford and Wellington, *Journal of Mrs Arbuthnot*, ii. 173; E. Ashley, *The Life and Correspondence of Henry John Temple Viscount Palmerston* (London, 1879), i. 253; Jennings, *Correspondence and Diaries*, 409–11.

128. Jennings, *Correspondence and Diaries*, 409.

129. Hansard, 2, xviii. (21 Mar. 1828), 1284.

130. Hansard, 2, xviii. (21 Mar. 1828), 1294.

131. *Morning Chronicle*, 22 Mar. 1828; *Mirror of Parliament* [hereafter *MOP*], ii. (21 Mar. 1828), 1559; Hansard, 2, xviii. (21 Mar. 1828), 1280–81.

132. Jennings, *Correspondence and Diaries*, 420–24; Lord Colchester (ed.), *A Political Diary 1820–1830, by Edward Law Lord Ellenborough*, i. (London, 1881), 106, 109; Jupp, *Eve of Reform*, 78–80; Ashley, *Life and Correspondence*, 254–79.

133. Ashley, *Life and Correspondence*, 278, 286.

134. Hansard, 2, xix. (27 June 1828), 1533–4, 1538, 1543.

135. *The Times*, 28 June 1828.

136. *Morning Post*, 28 June 1828.

137. *The Times*, 28 June 1828.

138. S. Harratt and S. Farrell, 'East Retford', in Fisher, *Commons*, ii. 800–808.

139. *Morning Post*, 6 Mar. 1830.

140. Hansard, 2, xxii. (5 Mar. 1830), 1331.

141. Hansard, 2, xxi. (5 May 1829), 1103.

142. Hansard, 2, xvii. (28 May 1827), 1049–50; Hansard, 2, xxii. (11 Feb. 1830), 350.

143. Hansard, 2, xxii. (23 Feb. 1830), 858–915; *The Times*, 24 Feb. 1830; *Morning Chronicle*, 24 Feb. 1830.

144. *Blackwood's Edinburgh Magazine* (1830), 647–48; Hansard, 2, xxii. (18 Feb. 1830), 678–726; D. C. Moore, 'The Other Face of Reform', *Victorian Studies*, 5,1 (1961)', 17–21.

145. Durham University Special Collections, Grey Papers [hereafter DSC, Grey], B50A/6/19, 1–2.

146. Miles Taylor, 'Empire and Parliamentary Reform: The 1832 Reform Act Revisited', in A. Burns and J. Innes (eds.), *Rethinking the Age of Reform* (Cambridge, 2003), 295–311.

147. R. Saunders, 'God and the Great Reform Act: Preaching against Reform, 1831–32', *Journal of British Studies*, 53, 2 (2014), 378–99.

148. National Archives, PRO [hereafter PRO] 30/22/1B, 'Memorandum on reform bill 4 Apr. 1831', 30–31; PRO, 30/22/1B, '... Russell's plan for the alteration of the Reform Bill ... Nov. 1831', 64–7; PRO, 30/22/1B, Unnamed memorandum, 193; PRO, 30/22/1B, 'Various Proposals', 240; DSC, Grey, B46/1/45, 'Memorandum on Reform Bill, by Russell, 20 Oct. 1831', 1–8; DSC, Grey, B46/1/45, Russell to Grey, 20 July 1831; B50A/6/19 1–2; Taylor, 'Empire and Parliamentary Reform', 295–311.

149. Parry, *Rise and Fall*, 83.

150. Hansard, 3, v. (22 July 1831), 215; Kriegel, *The Holland House Diaries, 1831–1840* (London, 1977), 85; DSC, Grey, B46/1/54 'Paper endorsed by Lord Althorp', 1–2; P. Salmon, 'Brighton', P. Salmon and K. Rix (eds.), *The House of Commons 1832–1868*, http://www.historyofparliamentonline.org/research/1832-1868 [accessed 19 May 2022]. For login details to access these draft articles contact psalmon@histparl.ac.uk.

Chapter 2

'The most unpopular part of the bill throughout the country': Reintegrating boundaries into the story of reform

In the summer of 1832 parliament passed legislation that overhauled the United Kingdom's electoral system. It followed one of the biggest periods of political upheaval in modern British history. Historians' efforts at telling this narrative usually commence with Wellington's declaration against reform in November 1830, the ongoing disturbances in London, the spread of the Swing Riots across England's counties and the formation of a new government under the veteran Whig reformer Earl Grey.[1] As the government's reform proposals were being drawn up in secret by a 'committee of four' during the winter of 1830–31, a major public petitioning campaign inundated Parliament. The government finally introduced their proposals in March 1831, but they proved too much for MPs who rejected the legislation. This forced a general election during April and May, which returned a sweeping Commons majority in favour of reform and was followed by one of the longest parliamentary summers on record as MPs wrangled over every detail of the government's proposals. The rejection of the reform legislation by the Lords that October sparked major riots in several English towns and the proliferation of Political Union activity across the country prior to the introduction of a third version of the government's proposals in December. After the reform legislation made its way through the Commons again, William IV's refusal to create sufficient peers to ensure its passage led to the government's resignation in May 1832. The United Kingdom was reportedly led to the brink of revolution during the 'Days of May', a state of unrest that was only curtailed by the return of the Grey government and the Lords' reluctant acceptance of reform by the summer of 1832.

This chapter begins the process of reintegrating boundary reform into this narrative, by examining the development of the boundary clauses in the government's first two reform bills and revealing their significance to political debate between March and September 1831. It explores how the Grey ministry's theoretical plans for a reformed electoral map were put into practice from November 1830, and how a campaign in the pro-reform press against the division of counties led to the government's near-collapse by September 1831. Both episodes have only received cursory attention from historians, whose narratives have instead focused on controversies concerning the franchise and the redistribution of seats. In keeping with Salmon's conceptualisation of the English reform legislation as a 'consultation', the government's proposals for boundary reform developed out of the committee of four's initial proposals, cabinet discussion, an exchange of information with local officials and parliamentary debate.[2] Following the introduction of the first reform bill in March 1831, and during the 1831 election, boundary reform provoked sustained criticism from the bill's opponents, who supposed it was a wholly unconstitutional attempt to redefine the electoral system in favour of Whig interests. After the introduction of the second reform bill in June 1831, the government was accused by its most influential supporters – most notably *The Times* – of using the division of counties as a means of increasing the influence of the aristocratic and landed interest over the reformed electoral system. While the first strand of criticism failed to alter the ambition of the government's plans, it did ensure boundary reform was underpinned by a number of constitutional checks. The government's refusal to accept the second strand of criticism forced the pro-reform press to re-evaluate the basis of its support for the bill and revealed the limits to the government's willingness to consult over the details of its reform legislation.

Developing the reform bill's boundary clauses

The first reform bill for England and Wales was introduced to the Commons on 1 March 1831. It stipulated that a privy council committee would clarify and update the parliamentary boundaries of every English and Welsh borough and extend the boundaries of every borough that contained fewer than 300 £10 householders. A second committee was to divide most double-member English counties, and the four-member county of Yorkshire was to be divided into its three ridings. Both committees were to have the power to summon witnesses, under oath, and were to complete their work within three months of the passage of the reform bill. Following this, England and Wales's new parliamentary boundaries were to be issued via royal proclamation.[3] The clauses containing these stipulations developed in a piecemeal manner between December 1830 and March 1831. They were initially the product of the committee of four, to whom Grey had delegated responsibility for drafting the reform bill. The committee met in December 1830 and submitted their proposals on 14 January 1831. These were developed further in cabinet before the parliamentary announcement of the bill in March 1831.

The division of counties was one of the few consistent features of the Grey ministry's reform scheme between December 1830 and the Reform Act's passage in June 1832. After some debate on the population threshold, the committee of four proposed to provide two additional seats to twenty-seven counties containing a population of over 150,000 and to divide these counties into two double-member electoral districts (except the four-member seat of Yorkshire, that would be divided into three double-member districts).[4] The creation of fifty-five extra county seats had served an important function in the committee's reformed electoral map. As discussed in Chapter 1, if the commercial interests of unrepresented towns were to gain forty additional Commons seats via new boroughs, the moderate Whig case for reform had established that the landed and agricultural interests were to be provided with sixty county seats. This was intended to balance the representation of interests in the electoral system, ensure the future stability of the constitution and conciliate sceptical county members over the bill. As well as assigning two additional seats to twenty-seven counties, the committee of four felt it necessary to divide these counties into double-member constituencies. This avoided the creation of four-member counties, which it was feared would force candidates to appeal to the popular, democratic vote.[5]

The committee's fears over four-member counties were based on recent experiences in Yorkshire, which had become a four-member county following the disfranchisement of Grampound in 1821. The uncontested 1826 Yorkshire election was reported to have cost upwards of £100,000. And in 1830, the populist Whig, Henry Brougham, who had no personal ties to the area, was elected following a campaign underpinned by the burgeoning liberal press that focused on winning votes in the county's unenfranchised towns through electioneering on predominantly national issues.[6] Such contests were expensive even for the largest landholders, and fears that national issues promoted by an uncontrollable press might replace the more traditional means of securing county votes suggested that the cost and size of elections had to be reduced.[7] The committee wanted men with property and historic associations with their locality to be returned for the counties, not populists like Brougham. The division of counties promised to reduce travelling, canvassing and polling costs, as well as focus electioneering on local issues. It was intended to ensure that 'men of great respectability, [and] of good family' would find it easier to stand as county candidates and represent their specific interests in the Commons.[8] The committee of four proposed that the division of counties should be decided by a privy council committee consisting of two paid secretaries, the lord chancellor (Lord Brougham), the lord president (the third marquess of Lansdowne), the lord privy seal (first earl of Durham), the speaker of the Commons (Charles Manners-Sutton) and a secretary of state, and announced via royal proclamation within six months of the reform bill's passage.[9] These plans suggest that it was hoped that a sitting committee at Westminster, rather than travelling commissioners, would be able to settle the division of counties.

The committee of four's proposals for the reform of borough boundaries underwent a series of more fundamental changes between December 1830 and March 1831. On 14 December 1830, the committee initially proposed that a royal commission of inquiry (sending travelling commissioners to collect information from the localities) should fix the boundaries of newly enfranchised boroughs.[10] This had been part of Lord John Russell's pre-committee reform proposal and suggested that the committee was aware that newly enfranchised boroughs required on-the-spot investigation. By 14 January 1831 the committee had decided that the commissioners would be unpaid and supported by one paid secretary.

Due to the receipt of parliamentary returns from individual boroughs during January 1831, the committee also proposed that the commission should clarify the boundaries of existing boroughs.[11] These returns had been requested after cabinet members raised concerns over the committee's intention to base their redistribution schedules on the 1821 census, which recorded population by parish and township, not by parliamentary borough. The returns revealed that the parliamentary limits of 101 of the 202 pre-reform English parliamentary boroughs differed from the geographical areas of the same name as defined in the 1821 census.[12] More alarmingly, five replies provided no information regarding parliamentary boundaries, and sixty-six returning officers only provided approximate information pertaining to their borough's limits.[13] This return, as well as Russell, Durham and Brougham's unsuccessful attempts at obtaining borough charters from municipal corporations during the previous decade, was also the likely cause for the clause in the first reform bill that allowed documents to be demanded from officials under oath.[14]

In February 1831, the committee's plans for a royal commission underwent further change. This followed the receipt of a second parliamentary return relating to the amount of £10, £20 and £40 householders in each existing borough, which had been provided to the cabinet by 12 February.[15] The return revealed that, of the 140 English boroughs due to retain the franchise, 87 contained fewer than 300 £10 householders.[16] As Brock has stated, the return forced the ministry's hand in terms of accepting the £10 franchise. However, even after the £10 franchise had been agreed there remained concern.[17] As the first reform bill intended to abolish many ancient borough franchise rights, the new data suggested that a £10 franchise based on existing parliamentary limits would have left 62 per cent of reformed English boroughs with fewer than 300 voters. Russell initially proposed an elaborate scheme for topping up the electorate of these boroughs, by enfranchising the wealthiest residents from the surrounding hundred until the requisite number of voters was achieved. The cabinet rejected this proposal in favour of the attorney general, Thomas Denman's suggestion that these boroughs might be thrown into their surrounding hundred, as had been done with several corrupt boroughs prior to 1830.[18] Denman's suggestion was tapered slightly in order that the boundaries of these boroughs were only proposed to be extended into their surrounding parishes until they contained 300 £10 householders. In many cases extending a borough into its surrounding hundred would have led to overlaps with other borough boundaries or created excessively large boroughs.[19]

The final alteration to the government's boundary reform proposals prior to 1 March was that a privy council committee, rather than a royal commission of inquiry, was to settle borough boundaries. It appears this change took place following the addition of the politically contentious 300 £10 householder clause, as well as the cabinet's realisation that boundary changes needed to be enacted speedily prior to reformed parliamentary elections. As constitutional precedent since the 1707 Act of Union required a separate parliamentary Act to implement the recommendations of any royal commission concerning constitutional matters, pursuing the committee of four's initial plans for a royal commission would have required that each borough boundary was subjected to the full scrutiny of a parliamentary bill.[20] If a royal commission, as planned, took six months to complete its proposals, and both houses of parliament took three months to approve these proposals, elections might not take place for a year following the passage of reform. More alarmingly, if parliament rejected a contentious boundary bill, it might invalidate a reform bill that had received royal assent. In order to avoid prolonged debate on each boundary change, the government opted to use the privy council's powers to enact laws via royal proclamation, which the committee of four had already proposed for the division of counties. This was highly unconventional in terms of domestic legislation, as by the early nineteenth century these powers were only used to issue orders in council when managing colonial affairs or deal with emergency domestic situations – as would be the case later in 1831, when a Board of Health was established to deal with a cholera outbreak.[21] Implementing both borough and county boundary reform through a privy council committee, then, provided a means of speeding up the reform process by avoiding parliamentary scrutiny. That the cabinet sought a speedy boundary settlement was re-affirmed by a reduction in the time allowed for both committees – from six months in the committee of four's original bill, to three months in the reform bill of 1 March.[22]

In contrast to the committee of four's proposals for the division of counties, boundary reform in the boroughs proved more complex. An exchange of information between the localities and Westminster, via parliamentary returns, was fundamental in shaping some of the basic principles of the Grey ministry's proposals. Furthermore, the receipt of data, by early February 1831, relating to the number of £10 householders contained in existing boroughs was highly fortuitous for the government. If the data had been received a week later, it is unlikely the proposal to extend boroughs until they contained 300 £10 householders would have been included in their first reform bill. If this had been the case, critics as well as supporters of the government would have quickly discovered that a bill, whose chief professed principle was to abolish nomination, was going to introduce a new, more numerous set of rotten boroughs into England's electoral landscape.[23] Whereas there was a clear ideological and electoral motivation behind the Grey ministry's proposals for the division of counties, their decision to propose an extensive modification to borough boundaries was taken to avoid political embarrassment. Furthermore, their subsequent decision to implement all boundary changes through the unconventional means of privy council committees indicates that a number of Whigs in the cabinet were willing to sacrifice their constitutionalist principles, and resort to the royal prerogative, to ensure reform became a reality. Such political expediency did not escape the bill's parliamentary opponents.

Anti-reform opposition to boundary reform

The good fortune experienced by the cabinet in discovering that their proposals for reform would require extensive boundary change in the boroughs did not continue. Their plans for privy council committees provided parliamentary critics with grounds for genuine constitutional concern – concerns that the government eventually conceded. Following the Commons' rejection of the reform bill in April 1831 and during the ensuing general election, criticism of the government's boundary proposals developed further in the Tory press. Alongside initial constitutional grievances, it was argued that the government's plans to expand the boundaries of some boroughs with fewer than 300 £10 householders, but disfranchise others, revealed a flagrant party motivation behind the reform bill.

During March and April 1831, parliamentary opponents of the reform bill attacked boundary reform on the grounds of constitutionality. Their main contention was that if the bill passed into law, boundary reform would escape due parliamentary process. The first reform bill provided the government with sole authority over the staffing of both privy council committees and did not allow for any parliamentary scrutiny of boundary proposals. Here, critics argued, was a blatant example of the reform bill providing the government and the crown with an unprecedented level of executive authority to effect fundamental changes to the electoral system and the power of the legislature. These fears were compounded when critics realised the borough committee would be required to alter the structure of eighty boroughs beyond recognition in order to ensure they contained 300 £10 householders. Opponents also supposed that a county committee, staffed by Whigs, would divide counties in a manner favourable to Whig landowners. With no recourse for parliament to scrutinise boundary proposals, it was argued that the Whigs would redraw the electoral map to suit their own needs. Peel, leader of the Tory opposition in the Commons, declared the government's boundary proposals unlawful, the *Quarterly Review* labelled the committees a 'most novel and unconstitutional project', and critics of the bill deployed the arguments detailed above with regularity in both houses of parliament throughout the debates on the first reform bill.[24]

During these debates, the government maintained its initial justification for their boundary reform proposals. They insisted that borough limits had to be altered in order to ensure that every reformed constituency contained a 'numerous and independent' electorate, and that the division of counties was required to increase the efficiency of county elections.[25] By contrast, the government had always accepted that their proposals to effect these changes via privy council committees were contentious. When Russell introduced the reform bill on 1 March 1831 he stated that if the opposition could suggest a more constitutional method, the government would 'have no difficulty in adopting that mode and waiving their own'. By 24 March, he was actively seeking assistance from the bill's opponents to make the committees more constitutionally agreeable.[26] The success of Gascoyne's wrecking amendment on 19 April, during the Commons committee stage of the first bill, prevented the announcement of any intended government, or opposition, amendments to the privy council committee proposals. This meant that they still formed an integral feature of the reform bill following the dissolution of parliament and during the ensuing general election. As the pro-reform press and candidates, wittingly or not, became synonymous with the electioneering slogan 'the bill, the whole bill, and nothing but the bill', their opponents focused increasingly on the issue of boundary reform.

The Tory *Morning Post* was the chief antagonist, accusing the government of attempting to nullify aristocratic and Tory power through a combination of boundary changes, borough disfranchisement and franchise alterations.[27] On 19 April, 'Zeta' argued that the boundary and disfranchisement clauses of the reform bill demonstrated how the Grey ministry had 'prostitute[d] their influence to the vile purposes of factious intrigue'. Zeta observed that through boundary changes, a number of small Whig boroughs with fewer than 300 £10 householders were to be allowed to 'make up their deficiency by a coalition with adjoining parishes'. This was in contrast to the forty Tory boroughs in schedule A that stood to be completely disfranchised. The *Morning Post* ran six editorials over the following six weeks that built on these complaints.[28] The paper's analysis of the disfranchisement and boundary clauses suggested that the reform bill was likely to lead to a 'permanent increase of [Commons] votes to the Whigs, relatively to the Tories, of about 127'.[29] The boundary clauses were proportionately more important than disfranchisement in this respect, as the paper had calculated that the Whigs would gain an advantage of fifty-one seats through disfranchisement, twenty-six through the division of counties, and fifty through the extension of borough boundaries. Subsequent editorials re-affirmed this warning, citing the inconsistencies in the 300 £10 householder boundary clause and the fact that prominent Whigs would 'whisper into the ears' of the privy council committees.[30] The *Morning Post* was not alone in its anti-boundary reform stance. The ultra-Tory *John Bull*, which supported the *Morning Post*'s sentiments, offered a further, more populist, argument against the government's plans. It warned county freeholders (who according to the first bill were to lose their county franchise if they lived within a borough, and did not qualify to vote as a £10 householder), of the potential consequences of an unconstitutional privy council committee being provided with the power to extend borough boundaries into the counties. By exercising this power, the privy council committee, *John Bull* observed, would have the power to 'deprive every freeholder they choose, of his LEGITIMATE, ENGLISH RIGHT [to vote]!'[31]

Nevertheless, efforts to rally opposition to the reform bill's boundary clauses seem to have been ineffective during the 1831 election. Colonel Jolliffe's attempts to decry the unconstitutional nature of the privy council committees were met with hissing at Petersfield.[32] Silence, rather than cheers, greeted James Freshfield's attempts to warn the electors of Penryn (which according to the first reform bill was to lose one seat and be grouped with nearby Falmouth) that the precedent set by the unconstitutional privy council committees meant that some future committee would be well within its rights to disfranchise Penryn altogether.[33] Discussion of the constitutional particulars of the reform bill was simply no match for the rallying call of 'the bill, the whole bill, and nothing but the bill'. So much so that the *Morning Post* conceded that even when candidates had expressed support for moderate reform, they had been unable to distinguish their constructive criticism of the bill's boundary clauses from a perception that they were employing anti-reform sentiment. The paper lamented: 'must a man forfeit all pretensions to the name of a genuine reformer the moment he revolts at the spectacle of [the] unjust partiality presented by the ministerial measure?'[34]

The newly formed Grey government was more disposed to listen to anti-reform argument when its second reform bill was announced on 25 June 1831. This bill stipulated that two parliamentary committees would be responsible for implementing borough and county boundary changes. In so doing, the cabinet immediately signalled that its members were eager to disassociate themselves from any electioneering pledges that may have been made for 'the whole bill' ahead of a new round of parliamentary negotiations. In practical terms, these changes appeared to have altered little, as the parliamentary committees were still required to fulfil the same role as the privy council committees. Furthermore, it was still intended that England's reformed boundaries would be issued by royal proclamation, three months after the passage of the bill. In constitutional terms, however, the amendment signalled an acceptance of parliament's right to check executive power. By allowing non-privy council committee members to sit on the committee, the crown and the government were no longer afforded complete control over setting parliamentary boundaries – a process that it was now acknowledged had the power to substantially redefine the structure of the Commons and undermine its ability to check crown and government authority.

The amendments received a cautious welcome from moderate reformers but did little to placate some anti-reformers. Edward Sugden, MP for St. Mawes, was one of the bill's most zealous detractors. He felt the changes were an empty gesture and remained unconstitutional. Over the space of two days during July 1831 he complained that three months was not long enough to redefine electoral boundaries. He feared that the government would fill the committee with its friends and complained that it had neither offered any indication of the criteria for redefining boundaries nor provided any opportunity for parliament to scrutinise boundary proposals.[35] In reply to Sugden, Edward Stanley (who had offered his support for moderate reform during the recent election) welcomed the government's changes and stated that he was 'content to let the matter rest until the names of the ... commissioners were laid before the house'. He lambasted Sugden's obstinacy and welcomed the government's concessions as a sign that they had realised the futility of pushing for 'the whole bill'.[36]

The changes were also appreciated by government supporters, who, freed from the fear of being labelled an anti-reformer (or perhaps just desirous of toeing the ministerial line), were now able to express that they had found plans for a privy council committee unconstitutional all along. John Campbell, who during the 1831 election had called the reform bill 'a great measure', expressed his support for the amendment, confessing that he had always thought the proposed privy council committees were 'highly unconstitutional'.[37] As well as remedying a widely accepted constitutional defect in their first bill, the government's amendments served to increase the chances of the bill's success by appeasing moderates and marginalising die-hard anti-reformers. This encouraged cross-party co-operation over the issue of boundary committees during July, following which the government also agreed to set limits on the extent to which borough boundaries could be extended, and granted parliament the right to vote on boundary proposals prior to their issue via royal proclamation.[38] What the government did not foresee was that sustained criticism from the pro-reform public would soon develop in response to the division of counties.

The Times and the 'county-mongering clause'

Aside from an editorial campaign during March in the *Norwich Mercury*, and some localised discontent in Wiltshire and Leicestershire during May, there had been little pro-reform opposition to the government's proposals for the division of counties prior to July 1831.[39] The government's modifications to their plans for privy council committees in their second reform bill, however, inadvertently drew attention to the boundary clauses of their bill. By August the majority of the pro-reform press, most notably *The Times*, was engaged in a bitter campaign on the issue. *The Times*, under the editorial supervision of Thomas Barnes, had by 1831 become Britain's largest circulating newspaper, shifting 14,000 copies a day – almost double that of its nearest competitors.[40] Since November 1830, Barnes's editorials had called for a respectable measure of reform, warning consistently against radical clamour for the ballot and universal suffrage.

The reform crisis had provided Westminster with a stark reminder of his power. In December 1830 *The Times* called for mass petitioning and meetings in favour of reform. By March 1831, over 600 petitions supporting reform had been sent to Westminster, and the number of English political unions had increased from 13 to 29.[41] Barnes was well on his way to earning Wellington's later recognition as 'the most powerful man in the country'.[42]

The first major pro-reform expression of discontent with the division of counties came on 28 June, when the Birmingham Political Union (BPU) declared its opposition to the government's proposals. Curiously, this opposition, and the subsequent outcry, developed from a misreading of the bill, which had supposed that the government intended to divide counties into four single-member districts. Based on this misinterpretation, the BPU publicly accused the government of attempting to create closed county constituencies, 'each under the patronage of some wealthy and influential peer or commoner'. Grey replied immediately, informing Thomas Attwood, the BPU's chairman, that he had been mistaken and that no alteration had been made to this aspect of the bill.[43] Grey's reply had been published in the press by 2 July, but did little to prevent an increasing perception among reformers that the division of counties had been intended as a means of creating closed county districts.[44] On 6 July, the newly elected pro-reform MP for Yorkshire, George Strickland, informed the Commons that the division of counties would allow for 'noblemen and men of property' to drive up 'herds of tenants to [county] hustings' and that the country 'would soon hear as much of nomination counties, as they now heard of nomination boroughs'.[45] Significantly, on 9 July, *The Times* took up the cause, following the publication of a letter from an anonymous Worcestershire resident, which re-affirmed the BPU's original complaint. Barnes announced in the same edition that he shared these concerns and congratulated Strickland for raising the issue in the Commons.[46]

Barnes, who it seems had not read Grey's rebuke to Attwood, warned his massive readership that some counties 'might really be cut into three close boroughs, in each of which a great family might return its own man'.[47] A letter published in *The Times* two days later corrected Barnes, informing him that the second reform bill did not intend to divide counties into single-member electoral districts. Barnes, however, re-iterated his opposition to the proposals knowing that a meeting of 200 pro-reform MPs was scheduled for the same day.[48] Two further letters were published in *The Times* during July, but in order to not distract public attention from debate over the reform bill's disfranchisement schedules, Barnes refrained from any further editorials until the issue was discussed in parliament.[49]

Parliamentary criticism continued to mount, however, and on 24 July the Whig MP for Staffordshire, Edward Littleton, informed the cabinet that it might be defeated on the matter.[50] The next day, the eccentric country reformer, William Hughes Hughes, announced his intention to move in committee to erase the division of counties.[51] On 11 August, when Hughes Hughes's motion was scheduled for discussion, *The Times* implored MPs to reject the clause. In addition, the Birmingham-based radical, Joseph Parkes, published an editorial in the pro-reform *Morning Chronicle*, announcing the paper's opposition to the issue.[52]

Barnes and Parkes's opposition rested on the notion that the geographic extent of undivided counties acted as a legitimate curb on aristocratic influence in the unreformed electoral system. Although large landowners were able to influence voters in one part of a county, they contended, a candidate's need to appeal to public opinion across a whole county diminished their electoral power. As one correspondent to *The Times* had put it, 'distant voters form a check to the overpowering weight of local influence'.[53] Barnes and Parkes feared that dividing counties into smaller districts would nullify the power of public opinion to rein in aristocratic influence, turning counties into nomination counties. Their solution was that counties should return four members but remain undivided. This had been the intended outcome of Hughes Hughes's proposed amendment on 11 August, and during the debate on his motion, the MP accepted Barnes's theory that division would lead to nomination. Unlike Barnes, however, Hughes Hughes did not see nomination, in its own right, as a negative. Instead, his main contention was that nomination counties would legitimise radical demands for the ballot. After terming the division of counties 'the most unpopular part of the bill throughout the country' he also warned that division would diminish the status of county MPs, that it required a still unconstitutional boundary committee and was unlikely to necessitate cheaper elections. This could be avoided, he argued, if undivided counties returned four MPs – a system that had proved practicable in the four-member constituencies of Yorkshire, the City of London and Weymouth, and had been partially sanctioned by the government following their separate plans in the second reform bill for seven, three-member counties, without division.[54]

The ministerial response was provided by the chancellor of the exchequer and the leader of the Commons, Viscount Althorp. He argued that the fears of both Hughes Hughes and *The Times* were unfounded due to a flaw in their theory that the division of counties would create electoral districts under the control of large landowners. Property, he argued, would always influence the nomination of county candidates, this 'was neither to be wondered at, nor objected to'. He also accepted that in some counties, division might make it easier for large landowners to influence nomination. However, in contrast with nomination boroughs, where a proprietor was able to apply pressure to a small group of voters, a nominated candidate in a divided county would still have to rely on popular election by a large electorate. Even following division county electorates would be too large to allow landowners to influence voter choice.[55]

Althorp might have rested his argument there. However, his subsequent remarks provoked a massive rift between the government, Barnes and the pro-reform press over the following weeks. He went on to explain that in the unlikely event of the nomination county theory being correct, the 'framers of the bill' would not have objected to it. It had always been their intention to preserve aristocratic and landed influence by providing extra county seats as compensation for an increase in the democratic share of the representation provided by the enfranchisement of large towns. In contrast with Barnes, who felt that large electorates and popular elections were the greatest asset of the county system, Althorp stated that an 'evil of the present system' was 'that mere popularity could return a county member'. Division, he revealed, had been intended all along as a means of redressing the power balance between democracy and aristocracy in the counties. If plans for division inadvertently tipped the balance of interests in the counties even further towards the aristocracy, so be it, appeared to be Althorp's message.[56]

While the government had previously alluded to their aristocratic aims for the division of counties, they had never done so quite so emphatically and in direct defiance of Barnes and *The Times*.[57] The government defeated Hughes Hughes's amendment by a majority of 109, but only after many government supporters were heavily whipped.[58] Still, forty-nine pro-reform MPs rebelled and the government majority was helped by the votes of at least sixteen anti-reform MPs and the abstention of several high-profile Tories, including Peel, Croker and Henry Goulburn. All three had signalled their support for the division of counties during the debate.[59] Peel welcomed it on the basis that it would allow 'gentlemen of landed property' to retain a 'fair share of influence' in the electoral system, and the moderate reformer and MP for Cirencester, Joseph Cripps, reasoned that if division was 'properly arranged' it 'would be advantageous to the agricultural interest'.[60]

Althorp's statement, the support it received from moderates and anti-reformers, and the failure of Hughes Hughes's proposed amendment, rather predictably, angered Barnes. In stark contrast to his conciliatory tone of days earlier, and *The Times*'s wider coverage of reform since November 1830, Barnes published a series of ferocious editorials opposing the government and the reform bill. On 15 August, he expressed his disgust at being 'let behind the curtain by his lordship [Althorp]', calling the division of counties an 'abominable clause'. His tirade continued:

> What was the professed object of the bill? ... Why, the national grievance was, aristocratic power, – more properly speaking, oligarchic power, and to talk of 'mere popularity' having too much weight in the county representation under the present system, is a direct insult to the common sense of the country.

The only means, Barnes proposed, of saving the country from the 'rotten county system' would be to introduce the ballot.[61] He continued his onslaught the next day, calling for popular meetings to pressure the government over the division of counties, which Barnes suggested revealed the reform bill to be 'corrupted in its core'.[62] Barnes, albeit briefly, sought to revive his status as an organiser of mass reform agitation. On the following day, in an attempt to demonstrate popular anger against the clause, he explained that *The Times* 'continue[d] to receive innumerable letters on the reform bill'. He also celebrated Hughes Hughes's intention to move for a 'rejection of the county-mongering clause' during the Commons report stage.[63]

Within days of Barnes's outburst the pro-reform *Morning Herald* offered its support to *The Times*, as did the *Leeds Mercury* and the influential radical-Whig periodical the *Examiner*.[64] Added to the *Morning Chronicle*'s opposition, for a brief period the highest selling and most respected organs of the pro-reform press opposed the government. The Tory press rejoiced at this apparent break in the pro-reform consensus. The *Morning Post* commented, 'the darling bill ... has suddenly lost all credit among those who have hitherto been its most furious supporters' and *John Bull* remarked, 'it seems that the bubble is bursting – the framers and supporters of the thing are at loggerheads'.[65]

The ferocity of Barnes's campaign shocked Westminster. Viscount Duncannon asked Brougham (known for his close links to Barnes), 'why is *The Times* writing so violently against us?'[66] Althorp labelled Barnes a 'villain' and stated that 'he might do his worst', before threatening to abolish stamp duty in order to remove *The Times*'s competitive advantage over its rivals. By 18 August *The Times*'s hostility had reportedly 'been the general subject of conversation in the Commons for three nights'.[67] Aside from an ideological opposition to the division of counties, the ferocity of *The Times*'s attack can also be attributed to an ongoing dispute between Barnes and the foreign office over the recent Dutch invasion of Belgium, and the publication of a letter in the *Globe* in late July, which contained what Barnes believed was a defamatory statement against *The Times*'s Lisbon correspondent written by the foreign secretary, Viscount Palmerston.[68]

In response, the cabinet stepped up its public relations efforts. On 17 August a letter, evidently written by someone connected to the cabinet, was printed in the *Morning Chronicle*.[69] It criticised *The Times* for not raising concerns over the division of counties earlier, and warned the paper that the only beneficiaries of continued dissent would be the enemies of reform.[70] On the same day, Thomas Young, Lord Melbourne's private secretary, was sent to appease Barnes, prompting a public apology for the latter's 'angry' language over the division of counties. However, Young's visit did not affect *The Times*'s opposition to the issue, as Barnes still trusted that public opinion was on his side.[71] Althorp, desirous of avoiding Barnes, then appealed directly to the public by responding to correspondence objecting to the division of counties from the recently formed Northern Political Union. In a letter published widely across the national and provincial press, Althorp explained that the division of counties would not give 'undue influence to the aristocracy', since the 'great landed proprietor[s]' would only be able to secure at least one seat per county division. Only rarely, he stated, would 'any one man's influence [be] so overwhelming' that he might secure both seats.[72]

The government was dealt an additional blow in its attempts to appease Barnes on 18 August, when it was defeated over the Chandos clause. Combined with the division of counties, the enfranchisement of £50 tenants-at-will in the counties (whom he had termed 'a numerous body of dependent vassals'), seemed proof to Barnes that the vested interests of the aristocracy had hijacked the reform bill.[73] In response, Barnes called for the borough franchise to be reduced to £5 or £6 in order to prevent the extension of borough boundaries. He argued that this would counteract the effects of the division of counties and the Chandos clause, by ensuring a sufficient number of independent urban voters in divided counties.[74] Over the following fortnight Barnes continued to print critical editorials and letters, and by the end of August the Tory press had started to speculate that the government was close to resignation.[75] Then, without warning on 3 September Barnes called a ceasefire. He told his readers that he still objected to the division of counties, but informed them that 'the point is ... settled against us'.[76]

This sudden about-turn can be explained by a number of factors. The increased efforts of the government to reach out to Barnes and increasing Tory speculation about a government resignation had clearly moderated his mood – did he really want the reform bill to be lost because of *The Times*? Furthermore, reports by the end of August had provided contradictory impressions as to the success of Barnes's attempts to rally public opinion. Leicestershire and Derbyshire were apparently sufficiently agitated, but Kent, Nottinghamshire and 'one or two other counties' had reportedly not expressed much alarm.[77] Finally, on 1 September the government announced the names of the commissioners who would be responsible for redefining England's parliamentary boundaries. As the following chapter will explore, the majority of these men were active members of the Society for the Diffusion of Useful Knowledge and had been recruited at the behest of the society's president, Lord Brougham. As well as being a frequent breakfast partner, Brougham was Barnes's closest ally in the Grey cabinet.[78] The division of counties, Barnes was surely assured, was now in safe hands.

Conclusion

The Times's retreat signalled the end of a concerted pro-reform opposition to the division of counties, which remained a key component of the third version of the government's reform bill when it was reintroduced in December 1831. Crucially, by the time the issue was debated again in January 1832, the government had been able to secure the approval of sitting county MPs for the recently completed proposals of the boundary commission. *The Times* still opposed the division of counties, but by early 1832 Barnes had accepted that a parliamentary rebellion was off the cards and declined to initiate a second campaign on the issue.[79] Although *The Times* was unable to influence the government to abandon the division of counties, the episode remains important. It reveals that between 1831 and 1832 respectable reformers could differ wildly from the government as to the potential impact of the reform legislation, a notion that existing historiography usually fails to acknowledge.[80] The government hoped divided counties would rejuvenate structures of aristocratic and localised influence in the counties, but for Barnes, the policy was a direct attack on the influence a liberal press might have exerted over undivided county electorates. By backing down, Barnes and the pro-reform public accepted that while less than ideal, the bill was the best reformers could hope for. This argument was re-affirmed by the political unions as they attempted to position themselves as national peacekeepers during November and December 1831.[81]

Privileging the issue of English boundaries in the initial development of the reform legislation has also revealed the extent to which different parliamentarians, local officials, the press and the public could engage and influence the reform process within the 'consultation' model posited by Salmon.[82] The government was willing to listen to local officials and anti-reform parliamentary opinion to make practical and procedural adjustments to their proposals. The amendments to the boundary,

Figure 2.1: John Doyle, 'Another Sign of the Times, or Symptoms of what Modern Architects, complaisantly term – Settling', 16 September 1831. Author's collection.

redistribution and franchise clauses in the reform legislation that took place following the receipt of parliamentary returns in early 1831, and the government's eventual agreement to allow parliamentary scrutiny of boundaries (rather than use privy council committees) revealed where consultation did lead to change. When it came to extra-parliamentary forces the government was much more cautious. As this and subsequent chapters demonstrate, the public were allowed to engage with the reform process through formal channels such as parliamentary returns, official engagement with boundary commissioners and local petitions highlighting issues with data or proposed boundaries. However, while the government was perfectly happy to co-opt the power of 'public opinion' to urge the necessity of reform at multiple points between 1830 and 1832, it was not willing to yield to newspaper editors, such as Barnes at *The Times*, who sought to use the weight of 'public opinion' to make demands for substantial radical, or reactionary, amendments to the reform legislation.

Maintaining such a stance with the press was a delicate balancing act. The dispute with *The Times* during the summer of 1831 provided an important wake-up call to those Whigs who after sixty years in opposition had not immediately understood the need to institute a public relations strategy. Through their junior secretaries and their new parliamentary solicitor from 1833, Joseph Parkes, a concerted effort was made to institute better relationships with Fleet Street, and insulate the details of the government's reform agenda, as far as was possible, from the pressure of public opinion.[83] The short-term fallout from the episode, however, could not be controlled. Significantly, the ferocity of *The Times*'s disagreement with the government over the division of counties underpinned a wider perception in parliament of a shift in popular support for the reform legislation by September 1831.[84] This has never been fully appreciated in histories of the reform legislation, and explains why by mid-September, the political cartoonist John Doyle (Figure 2.1) was able to note the irony of the Grey ministry trying to rebuild crumbling popular backing for the bill, by recourse nonetheless to a newly supportive *Times*. Such perceptions proved vital in terms of persuading the Lords to divide against the bill in October 1831.[85]

Notes

1. For recent popular histories see E. Pearce, *Reform!: The Fight for the 1832 Reform Act* (London, 2004); A. Fraser, *Perilous Question: The Drama of the Great Reform Bill 1832* (London, 2014).

2. Salmon, 'The English Reform Legislation, 1831–32', in D. Fisher (ed.), *The House of Commons, 1820–32*, i. (Cambridge, 2009), 411.

3. PP1830–31 (247), ii. 200–203.

4. C. W. New, *Lord Durham*, 128; DSC, Grey, B46/1/36, 'Appendix No. 5', 1–2.

5. Hansard, 3, ii. (3 Mar. 1831), 1329; Hansard, 3, iii. (18 Apr. 1831), 1519–20; C. W. New, *Lord Durham* (Oxford, 1929), 113; Lord Russell, *An Essay on the History of the English Government and Constitution from the Reign of Henry VII to the Present Time* (London, 1821), 183; Salmon, 'English Reform Legislation', 407–10; D. C. Moore, 'The Other Face of Reform', *Victorian Studies*, 5,1 (1961), 31–4.

6. Hansard, 3, ii. (1 Mar. 1831), 1074; M. Casey, 'Yorkshire', in D. Fisher (ed.), *The House of Commons, 1820–1832* (Cambridge, 2009), iii. 245–53.

7. Lord Colchester, *A Political Diary 1820–1830* (London, 1881), ii. 329.

8. Hansard, 3, ii. (1 Mar 1831), 1074–5; Hansard, 3, v. (11 Aug. 1831), 1226–8; New, *Lord Durham*, 128.

9. DSC, Grey, B46/1/38, 'Reform Bill for England and Wales', 1–10.

10. DSC, Grey, B46/1/27, 'Reform Committee Minutes ... Dec. 11 & 14 1830', 1–2; DSC, Grey, B46/1/27, B46/1/33, 'England, reform bill ... based on Lord J. Russell's plan of reform', 1–10.

11. DSC, Grey, B46/1/38, 'Reform Bill for England and Wales', 1–10.

12. H. Brougham, *The Life and Times of Henry Lord Brougham* (London, 1871), iii. 92–3.

13. PP1830–31 (338), x, 1–62.

14. P. Salmon, '"Reform Should Begin at Home": English Municipal and Parliamentary Reform, 1818–32', in C. Jones, P. Salmon and R. Davis (eds.), *Partisan Politics, Principles and Reform in Parliament and the Constituencies, 1689–1880* (Edinburgh, 2004), 93–113.

15. DSC, Grey, B46/2/36, Russell to Durham, 13 Feb. 1831, 5; Hansard, 3, ii. (21 Dec. 1830), 6–26.

16. PP1830–31 (202), x. 1–13.

17. M. Brock, *The Great Reform Act* (London, 1973), 142–3, F. T. Baring, *Journals and Correspondence of Sir Francis Thornhill Baring* (London, 1905), 83; D. Le Marchant (ed.), *Memoir of John Charles Viscount Althorp* (London, 1876), 294–6; Brougham, *Life and Times*, iii. 92–3.

18. DSC, Grey, B46/2/36, Russell to Durham, 13 Feb. 1831, 1–5.

19. Brock, *Reform Act*, 142–3.

20. H. Clokie and J. Robinson, *Royal Commissions of Inquiry* (New York, 1937), 46–8; DSC, Grey, B46/1/55, 'Printed paper endorsed by Lord Howick, 4 April 1832', 1–16.

21. F. Brockington, 'Public Health at the Privy Council 1831–34', *Journal of the History of Medicine and Allied Sciences*, 16, 2 (1961), 161–85; National Archives, Privy Council, 2/211A, 213.

22. PP1830–31 (247), ii. 200–203.

23. Hansard, 3, ii. (1 Mar. 1831), 1075.

24. Anonymous, 'Reform in Parliament', *Quarterly Review*, 45 (1831), 323; Hansard, 3, iii. (21 Mar. 1831), 687–8; Hansard, 3, iii. (22 Mar. 1831), 764–800; Hansard, 3, iii. (24 Mar. 1831), 901; Hansard, 3, iii. (28 Mar. 1831), 983–99; Hansard, 3, iii. (14 Apr. 1831), 1327–8; Hansard, 3, iii. (18 Apr. 1831), 1550; Hansard, 3, iii. (21 Apr. 1831), 1742–7.

25. Hansard, 3, iii. (28 Mar. 1831), 1030.

26. Hansard, 3, ii. (1 Mar. 1831), 1076; Hansard, 3, iii. (22 Mar. 1831), 800.

27. *Morning Post*, 9 Apr. 1831, 19 Apr. 1831.

28. *Morning Post*, 23 Apr., 12, 20, 21, 26 May, 13 June 1831.

29. *Morning Post*, 23 Apr. 1831.

30. *Morning Post*, 21 May 1831.

31. *John Bull*, 25 Apr. 1831.

32. *The Times*, 2 May 1831.

33. *Morning Chronicle*, 7 May 1831.

34. *Morning Post*, 12 May 1831.

35. Hansard, 3, iv. (12 July 1831), 1117; Hansard, 3, iv. (13 July 1831), 1200, 1215–16; D. Fisher, 'Sugden, Edward', in Fisher, *Commons*, vii. 352–6.

36. Hansard, 3, iv. (13 July 1831), 1227; S. Farrell, 'Stanley, Edward', in Fisher, *Commons*, vii. 257–59.

37. Hansard, 3, iv. (6 July 1831), 819; D. Fisher, 'Campbell, John', in Fisher, *Commons*, iv. 532–8.

38. Hansard, 3, iv. (13 July 1831), 1200; PP1831 (232), iii. 10–14.

39. *Leicester Chronicle*, 14 May 1831; S. Farrell, 'Bennett, John', in Fisher, *Commons*, iv. 238–40; M. Escott, 'Norfolk', Fisher, *Commons*, ii. 717.

40. A. Wadsworth, 'Newspaper Circulations 1800–1954', *Transactions Manchester Statistical Society*, 122 (1954–5), 9; PP1831-2 (290), xxxiv. 119.

41. The petitions data come from the Leverhulme project 'Petitions and Parliament in the Long Nineteenth Century' (RPG-2016-097) led by Richard Huzzey and Henry Miller; PP1831 (263), iii. 421. *The Times*, 1 Dec. 1830; N. D. LoPatin, *Political Unions, Popular Politics and the Great Reform Act of 1832* (Basingstoke, 1999), 174–9.

42. Anonymous, *History of The Times: "The Thunderer" in the Making 1785–1841* (London, 1935), 338.

43. *Cobbett's Political Register*, 9 July 1831.

44. *Birmingham Journal*, 2 July 1831.

45. Hansard, 3, iv. (6 July 1831), 851.

46. *The Times*, 9 July 1831.

47. *The Times*, 9 July 1831.

48. *The Times*, 11 July 1831; SRO, Hatherton, D260/M/F/5/26/7, 11 July 1831, 62.

49. *The Times*, 15, 23 July, 18 Aug. 1831.

50. SRO, Hatherton, D260/M/F/5/26/7, 24–25 July 1831, 81–4.

51. *Morning Post*, 25 July 1831.

52. History of Parliament, Unpublished Parkes Transcripts, Parkes to Tennyson, 14 Aug. 1831; *The Times*, 11 Aug. 1831; *Morning Chronicle*, 11 Aug. 1831.

53. *The Times*, 15 July 1831.

54. Hansard, 3, v. (11 Aug. 1831), 1225–6.

55. Hansard, 3, v. (11 Aug. 1831), 1226–9.

56. Hansard, 3, v. (11 Aug. 1831), 1226–9.

57. Hansard, 3, iii. (28 Mar. 1831), 998.

58. SRO, Hatherton, D260/M/F/5/26/7, 11 Aug. 1831, 114.

59. *The Times*, 12, 13 Aug. 1831.

60. Hansard, 3, v. (11 Aug. 1831), 1230, 1236–7; *Morning Post*, 12 Aug. 1831.

61. *The Times*, 15 Aug. 1831.

62. *The Times*, 16 Aug. 1831.

63. *The Times*, 17 Aug. 1831.

64. *The Examiner*, 14 Aug. 1831; *Leeds Mercury*, 20 Aug. 1831; *Standard*, 3 Sept. 1831.

65. *Morning Post*, 16 Aug. 1831; *Standard*, 16 Aug. 1831.

66. A. Aspinall, *Politics and the Press* (London, 1949), 251; A. Aspinall, *Three Early Nineteenth Century Diaries* (London, 1952), 116–28.

67. Aspinall, *Three Diaries*, 117–18; A. Kriegel, *The Holland House Diaries, 1831–1840* (London, 1977), 29.

68. News International Archives, Barnes Papers, T/ED/BAR/1, Barnes to Lord Brougham, 27 July 1831, 13; Aspinall, *Politics and the Press*, 251; *Weekly Dispatch*, 21 Aug. 1831.

69. Aspinall, *Politics and the Press*, 243.

70. *Morning Chronicle*, 17 Aug. 1831.

71. *The Times*, 18 Aug. 1831.

72. *Evening Mail*, 2 Sept. 1831; *Monmouthshire Merlin*, 3 Sept. 1831; *Sheffield Independent*, 3 Sept. 1831; *Cambridge and Hertford Independent Press*, 10 Sept. 1831; LoPatin, *Political Unions*, 175.

73. *The Times*, 20 Aug. 1831.

74. *The Times*, 22, 23 Aug. 1831.

75. *The Times*, 25 Aug., 1 Sept. 1831; Aspinall, *Three Diaries*, 121–8; HOP, Parkes Transcripts, Parkes to Tennyson, 24 Aug. 1831.

76. *The Times*, 3 Sept. 1831.

77. *The Times*, 22 Aug. 1831, 6, 25 Aug. 1831; *Examiner*, 21 Aug. 1831.

78. Anonymous, *History of The Times*, 457–61.

79. *The Times*, 26 Jan. 1832.

80. The exception being, N. Lopatin-Lummis, 'The 1832 Reform Act Debate: Should the Suffrage be Based on Property or Taxpaying?', *JBS*, 46 (2007), 320–45.

81. LoPatin, *Political Unions*, 87–130.

82. Salmon, 'English Reform Legislation', 411.

83. E. Wasson, 'The Whigs and the Press, 1800–50', *Parliamentary History*, 25, 1 (2006), 68–87.

84. Brock, *Reform Act*, 223; Moore, 'Other Face', 29–30.

85. Brock, *Reform Act*, 240; Duke of Wellington (ed.), *Despatches, Correspondence, and Memoranda of Field Marshall Arthur Duke Wellington* (1878), vii. 531–2; Aspinall, *Three Diaries*, 121–8.

Chapter 3

Towards a science of government: The 'spirit of inquiry' and the establishment of the 1831–2 boundary commission

During the 1830s the Whig governments of the second Earl Grey and Viscount Melbourne oversaw extensive reforms to the electoral system, the Church, the poor laws, factory employment, local government, tithes, public health and policing. In 1836, Lord John Russell, then home secretary, explained the philosophy of the Whig reform agenda to the poor law commissioner, Edwin Chadwick. 'We are endeavouring to improve our institutions', Russell informed Chadwick, by introducing 'system, method, science, economy, regularity, and discipline'.[1] As Boyd Hilton has argued, Russell's statement encapsulated the ethos behind a formative decade in the development of the British liberal state. During the 1830s, Whig governments – flanked by a new bureaucratic cast of commissioners and inspectors – discarded traditional localised solutions to social problems in favour of complex legislative solutions applied to 'the whole country on a one-size-fits-all basis'. This legislative agenda reflected a subtle shift in the 'mechanical imagination' of British governance. In contrast to their more cynical Newtonian-inspired liberal-Tory predecessors, men like Russell maintained a Scottish enlightenment-infused confidence in the potential for civilisational progress and the possibility of a new inductive legislative approach, which rejected 'hypothesis and deduction' in favour of the contemporary scientific trend for 'observation and experiment'.[2]

The first major public indication that the Grey ministry intended to apply science, method and discipline to domestic reform was made during the debates over their proposals for electoral reform. On 1 September 1831, the chancellor of the exchequer, Viscount Althorp, announced the thirty-one boundary commissioners who had been identified to redraw England and Wales's electoral map. He revealed that each commissioner had been chosen based on their 'character, knowledge, and science' and formed 'a class of men as little biased as possible, either by politics or party feelings'.[3] He claimed that these 'gentlemen of intelligence and science'[4] would act with 'perfect and uniform impartiality' to redesign the electoral system 'according to principles of strict justice' and without any recourse to the '[political] influence which may be prevalent' in a constituency.[5] Given the widespread opposition to the government's proposed boundary reforms discussed in the previous chapter, Althorp's resort to a rhetoric of science and impartiality was clearly an attempt at deflecting accusations that the government intended to skew the electoral system in their favour. However, his rhetoric was also grounded in political experience. As this chapter demonstrates, it reflected a flurry of activity and exchange of ideas behind the scenes at Whitehall over the previous month, as key figures in the government had started planning for a boundary commission.

Existing histories of the 1832 reform legislation provide little information about the formation of this boundary commission or its activities, and have offered no insight into the government's desire, or intentions, for a boundary commission on disinterested, scientific terms.[6] Furthermore, histories of the British state and parliamentary investigation – which place great stead on the 1830s as a decade of transformation in terms of legislative inquiry and the evolution of the 'information state' – rarely acknowledge that a boundary commission accompanied the 1832 reform legislation.[7] Without seeking to revive now-disregarded notions of a post-1832 proto-collectivist state, this chapter adds several key pieces to the 'intriguing puzzle' that beguiled a previous generation of historians concerned with the nineteenth-century 'revolution in government'.[8] Namely, where did the personnel and bureaucratic methods that dominated later commissions and inspectorates of the 1830s and 1840s, such as those concerning the poor law, factories and public health, emanate from? Additionally, this chapter begins the process of widening the chronological and intellectual margins of a subsequent body of work on the nineteenth-century British liberal state, which has sought to explain the reasons, both 'principled or pragmatic', behind the Whig 'embrace of programmes of social and economic regulation' following 1832.[9] The 'scientific' methods and ideas developed by those involved in redrawing England's electoral map between 1831 and 1832 were significant in this regard. Borne out of a combination of necessity, the engineering and scientific expertise of its chairman, Thomas Drummond, and a willingness among members of the Grey ministry to embrace new governing practices, the boundary commission established a pioneering bureaucratic model that paved the way for the better-known commissions of the 1830s and 1840s.

This chapter begins by exploring how and why the 1831–2 boundary commission for England and Wales was established, placing the government's scientific claims and their boundary commissioners in their intellectual and institutional context. It contrasts Russell's initial proposals for a traditional cross-party committee with the innovative plans for a commission put in place by the lord chancellor, Lord Brougham, and the royal engineer and scientist, Thomas Drummond. Brougham was a leading light of the Scottish Enlightenment who had been frustrated with his limited influence over state administration over the previous two decades. From August 1831 he seized his opportunity to staff the first of the Whig-established commissions of the 1830s with a clique of progressives associated with the Society for the Diffusion of Useful Knowledge and London University. Drummond had recently joined Brougham's set in 'godless' Bloomsbury. Guided by a genuine belief in scientific disinterestedness, he created a novel inductive framework for redrawing England's electoral map that drew on the emerging discipline of social statistics and the techniques of surveying and cartography associated with the ordnance survey.[10] In doing so, Brougham and Drummond established a framework for legislative investigation whose influence was felt for decades to come.

Commissions of inquiry and Russell's initial cross-party proposals

The 1831–2 boundary commission for England and Wales belongs to a group of investigative bodies of the British state called commissions of inquiry. Commissions of inquiry have a long lineage, originating in the Domesday Inquiry of 1086.[11] Having fallen into abeyance by the mid-eighteenth century, they were resurrected during the 1780s as part of the governmental drive for economic reform and increased in frequency from 1806 as part of a further push to streamline legal and military institutions, as well as the national finances.[12] Commissions of inquiry were also used as a tool for investigating episodic domestic and colonial issues that could not be solved by select committees at Westminster. An important forerunner of the boundary commission was the 1818 charity commission, which established a template for roving assistant commissioners, whose reports from across the country were overseen by a central cross-party committee of parliamentarians.[13] In keeping with the push for economic reform, the vast majority of commissioners since 1780 had been unpaid parliamentarians, with assistant commissioners and clerks receiving remuneration. The majority of non-parliamentary appointments were usually barristers, but depending on the expertise required, financiers, engineers, chemists and physicists occasionally served as commissioners – such as on the 1819 investigation into the forgery of bank notes and the 1827 commission into London's water supply.[14]

It is important to acknowledge that the 1831–2 boundary commissions (Irish and Scottish commissions were established on the template of the English and Welsh commission discussed here) inhabited a legal grey area. While referred to by contemporaries and in official reports as commissions, they were never accorded the formal status of a royal commission or commission of inquiry as their commissioners were never appointed by parliament or the crown. Instead, they worked from August 1831 on the somewhat dubious authority of the home secretary's capacity to gather parliamentary returns from the localities. At the time, the government insisted it was necessary to exercise this legal loophole on the basis that reformed boundaries needed to be identified (and approved by parliament) as soon as possible prior to new elections taking place.[15] If the government's second reform bill had not been rejected in October 1831, the boundary commission's preliminary reports would have been formally approved by a formal commission of inquiry (which would have included the commissioners entrusted with completing preliminary reports). However, by the time the government introduced its third reform bill in December 1831 the commission's reports were almost complete. Instead of using the reform bill to establish a commission of inquiry, as had been intended in their second bill, the government opted to expedite the process by publishing the boundary commission's reports as a parliamentary return and submitting their recommendations to parliamentary scrutiny via a separate boundary bill.[16] This backstory helps, in part, to explain why the boundary commission has not been noticed by historians of public administration, as their analysis of commissions of inquiry has been rooted in parliamentary returns that list official commissions.[17] It is also a reflection of the Grey government's legal inexperience and initial lack of preparation over the fine details of reform from November 1830, the exigencies of parliamentary debate about reform throughout 1831 and the emergence of an increasingly bullish attitude among cabinet members towards implementing boundary reform from August 1831.

The government started planning for a boundary commission in May 1831, when it became clear that the ongoing general election would return a majority in favour of reform. On 22 May, Grey asked Russell to propose modifications to the reform bill that might make it more amenable to its opponents.[18] In doing so, Russell mooted a cross-party committee of seven to oversee boundary reform. He also urged Grey to:

> think of the [boundary] commissioners to be named. I should say that some of the ejected members, such as Knatchbull, Cartwright and Dickinson would do very well. With three friends, and one such man as Lord Rosslyn, who is neither Lib Tory, nor new Whig.[19]

Edward Knatchbull, William Cartwright and William Dickinson had all voted against the reform bill in April and lost their seats at the ensuing general election.[20] Lord Rosslyn had been lord privy seal under the previous administration, was an 'old-Tory' and a close friend of Wellington.[21] By proposing a cross-party committee, Russell sought to address Tory and ultra-Tory complaints, which, as discussed in the previous chapter, had perceived boundary reform as an unconstitutional attempt to redefine the electoral system in favour of Whig interests. Russell's suggestions also maintained the trend for cross-party parliamentary committees, containing active 'committee men' – Knatchbull and Rosslyn in this instance – that had been characteristic of the Wellington administration between 1828 and 1830.[22]

Grey approved the suggestion for conventional, cross-party committees, prompting Russell's submission of an extended list of commissioners to the cabinet by 17 July.[23] It identified nine potential county commissioners and eight borough commissioners (Table 3.1) – Knatchbull being the only surviving name from his original suggestions. These seventeen men comprised a combination of twelve former and current parliamentarians representing a broad spectrum of views over reform, as well as five parliamentary and legal officials. Both committees contained a combination of three Whig and three Tory committee men, and eleven of the proposed members had experience of sitting on, or providing evidence to, royal commissions of inquiry or select committees. Russell's proposals suggested he was aware that some combination of scientific, parliamentary and legal expertise would be essential to the work of both commissions. Seven of his candidates were fellows of the Royal Society; four were privy counsellors; one was sergeant in arms to the Lords; and one was clerk assistant to the Lords. It was hoped that the scientific backgrounds of four of the Royal Society fellows – William Sturges Bourne, Knatchbull, Thomas Frankland Lewis and the marquess of Lansdowne (a member of the cabinet) – would counterbalance their moderate views respecting reform.[24] Aside from this, there is little evidence that Russell completed any planning for how the commissions would work in practice. It is likely that the legal experts and the less senior, retired or former parliamentarians were envisaged as active

Table 3.1: Lord John Russell's initial suggestions to Grey for boundary commissioners.

Key: PC: Privy Councillor; FRS: Fellow of the Royal Society; FSA: Fellow of the Society of Antiquaries; CM: 'committee man'; SC: select committee; RC: royal commission.

For boroughs	PC	FRS	FSA	CM	SC/RC
Lord George Seymour					
William Courtenay					X
Edward Littleton				X	X
Daniel Sykes					
Richard Sharp		X	X		
Thomas Frankland Lewis	X	X		X	X
3rd marquess of Lansdowne		X		X	X
Sir William Herries					

For counties	PC	FRS	FSA	CM	SC/RC exp
20th Baron Dacre				X	X
William Sturges Bourne	X	X		X	X
Edward Knatchbull		X		X	X
Henry Hobhouse	X				X
Henry Martin					X
Francis Beaufort		X			
Sir Anthony Hart	X				X
John George Shaw Lefevre		X			
John Currie					X

travelling commissioners, while the senior parliamentarians would have been based in London.[25] Edward Littleton's remark upon being asked to be a commissioner on 22 July, 'I accepted – so no Penkridge shooting this year', suggests that Russell had only told potential commissioners to clear a considerable time in their autumn and winter schedules.[26]

Ultimately, only four of Russell's July suggestions appeared on the final list of thirty-one commissioners announced in parliament on 1 September 1831 – Francis Beaufort, Littleton, Henry Martin and William Courtenay (Table 3.2).[27] In a number of cases the candidates put forward by Russell were agreed to in cabinet on 17 July, but due to unavailability or unwillingness did not accept.[28] In keeping with Russell's reasoning that the committee needed to appear politically bi-partisan, replacements were identified for the four moderate, but scientifically minded, reformers who had either turned down the opportunity to sit on the committee, or had been rejected in cabinet.[29] Notably, Davies Gilbert, Tory MP and president of the Royal Society, Henry Hallam, a fellow of the Royal Society and Whig historian known to be at odds with his party towards reform, and Sir James

Table 3.2: Proposed county and borough boundary committee, 1 September 1831.
Key: PC: Privy Councillor; FRS: Fellow of the Royal Society; FRA: Fellow of the Society of Antiquaries; SC/RC: select committee/royal commission; SDUK: Society for the Diffusion of Useful Knowledge; RE/RA: Royal Engineer/Artillery

Name	PC	FRS	FSA	SC/RC	SDUK Cttee	SDUK Map Cttee	SDUK Contact	RE/RA
James Abercromby (Chair)	X				X			
Edward John Littleton				X				
Davies Gilbert		X	X	X				
William Courtenay				X				
Henry Martin				X				
William Wingfield								
Sir James Willoughby Gordon		X						
Henry Hallam		X	X	X	X			
Francis Beaufort		X			X	X		
Launcelot Baugh Allen							X	
Henry Gawler							X	
Thomas Birch								
William Martin Leake		X						X (RA)
Benjamin Ansley			X					
Henry Rowland Brandreth								X (RE)
John James Chapman								X (RA)
Robert K. Dawson								X (RE)
Thomas Drummond					X	X		X (RE)
John Elliot Drinkwater							X	
Thomas Flower Ellis					X	X		
Henry Bellenden Ker				X	X	X		
George Barrett Lennard								
William Ord					X			
John Romilly							X	
Robert John Saunders								X (RA)
Richard Sheepshanks		X					X	
William Edward Tallents								
Henry William Tancred					X		X	
John Wrottesley					X	X		
William Wylde								X (RA)
Francis Martin			X					
Richard Scott								X (RA)

Willoughby Gordon, fellow of the Royal Society and MP who had to absent himself from the first reform bill debates due to his opposition to the bill.[30] Gordon's selection, at least, was probably Grey's handiwork.[31] The identification of three further commissioners can also be attributed to the personal recommendations of cabinet ministers: Thomas Birch, Melbourne's former private secretary; James Abercromby, chief baron of Scotland, who had asked Brougham to nominate him; and William Tallents, a bi-partisan political agent and returning officer for the borough of Newark, whom Brougham also recommended.[32] The principal difference between Russell's July committees and those announced in parliament on 1 September was that they contained fourteen men associated with the reform-minded mass education institution, the Society for the Diffusion of Useful Knowledge, and seven officers from the royal engineers or royal artillery with close ties to the ongoing ordnance survey.

The march of Brougham, Drummond and the SDUK

Born and raised in Edinburgh and heir to a 'modest paternal estate' near Penrith, Henry Brougham was educated at the University of Edinburgh. As a member of the 'Edinburgh Literati' of the 1790s he attended classes on moral philosophy under Dugald Stewart, mathematics under John Playfair, chemistry under Joseph Black and law under John Millar and David Hume.[33] His 'complex mind and indomitable ego' were evident from an early age, publishing two articles on optics and light in the *Transactions* of the Royal Society by 1797. A prolific polymath, over the following decade he wrote with unabashed self-assuredness on mathematics, physical and natural sciences, political economy and the law, particularly in the *Edinburgh Review* that he helped launch in 1802 with his friends Francis Jeffrey, Francis Horner and Sydney Smith.[34] He trained as a barrister in London from 1803 and secured a seat in the Commons in 1810, where he associated initially with the radical Whigs. He was noted for his debating talent but also skill at fuelling the mistrust of Tory ministerialists and much of the Whig aristocracy. Having acted as the high-profile attorney general to Queen Caroline during 1820, his election for Yorkshire in 1830 affirmed his position as one of the country's most popular politicians. On the formation of the Grey ministry in November 1830, he eventually accepted the post of lord chancellor, when he was elevated to the peerage as first Baron Brougham and Vaux. Importantly, for many Whigs who distrusted him, Brougham's appointment removed him from the Commons.[35]

As a reformer, Brougham's most enduring efforts prior to 1830 were made in the cause of popular education. He was closely involved in the British and Foreign School Society during the 1810s and established the 1816 select committee on education that ultimately prompted the formation of the 1818 charity commission. He was closely involved with Birkbeck London Mechanics Institute from 1824 and founded the London University (now University College London) in 1826. The most innovative outlet for Brougham's educational reform ambitions was the Society for the Diffusion of Useful Knowledge (SDUK). He established the society in 1826 with a number of reform-minded lawyers, educators and politicians (including the future cabinet members Russell, Althorp and Denman) to use new printing and distribution technologies to mass-publish affordable educational material. By 1831 the Society comprised an extensive national network of progressive intellectuals and reformers, who contributed to its considerable publishing output of cheap treatises respecting science, history, art, ancient scholarship and modern literature.[36]

The SDUK professed to be operating above party politics but was frequently linked in contemporary Tory discourse with the recently established London University (which shared many founding members). Both institutions were seen by reactionaries as part of a secular, radical movement responsible for the oft-mocked 'march of intellect' – which allowed satirists such as William Heath to envision a Brougham-inspired dystopian future of literate street sellers, chess-playing butchers, steam-powered flying ships and bridges across the Channel (Figure 3.1).[37] In reality the politically active members of the SDUK varied in their ideological outlook. Its council represented a mixture of Benthamites, philosophic Whigs and radicals associated with the *Edinburgh Review*, young Whigs with a more 'rural' outlook such as Althorp, and some moderate Canningites or liberal Tories more frequently associated with the Political Economy Club.[38] What the SDUK, under Brougham's active supervision, and its

Figure 3.1: William Heath, 'The March of Intellect', 23 January 1828. Author's collection.

association with the avowedly secular London University did represent, however, was an active challenge to the established Anglican institutional order. As Rosemary Ashton has demonstrated, the SDUK's geographic association with the progressive or 'godless' area of Bloomsbury in north London further encouraged this perception, by physically distancing itself from London's traditional power base of Westminster, as well as England's ancient Anglican universities of Oxford and Cambridge.[39]

Russell was also an active member of the SDUK, but, probably conscious of the society's political reputation, had made little recourse to its members when nominating his original committee.[40] Francis Beaufort, hydrographer of the navy since 1829, and John George Shaw Lefevre, a member of the Political Economy Club as well as Althorp's land conveyancer, were the only SDUK members on Russell's original list – and Lefevre, who later chaired the county commission, was removed from the list of commissioners announced on 1 September.[41] The selection of Beaufort does indicate that Russell was aware any boundary commission would require geographic expertise. As well as co-ordinating the mapping of the world's oceans, Beaufort was an active member of the Royal Society, Royal Geographical Society, Royal Astronomical Society and the SDUK's map committee.[42] His biographer has suggested that Sir James Graham, first lord of the admiralty, secured his nomination to the boundary commission.[43] However, it seems probable that Russell would have known of Beaufort through the SDUK, and that Beaufort's multiple professional affiliations meant that Russell saw him as the perfect apolitical 'scientific' expert required for the commission.

It was Brougham and his discussions with his friend Charles Henry Bellenden Ker that initiated the major changes in the commission's personnel by September 1831. Ker was a conveyancing barrister and active SDUK member who had established the SDUK map committee with Beaufort in 1828 – an ambitious project to print an affordable world atlas, that Ker hoped would 'find its way into every house in the empire'.[44] In contrast with Beaufort, Ker was an active philosophic-Whig reformer, closely associated with Brougham in Westminster's reforming circles since his 1819 publication of a pamphlet highlighting the deficiencies of the 1818 charity commission. He had provided evidence to the select committees on property law during the 1820s and was Brougham's nominee for the 1828 real property commission, but was rejected by Peel.[45] He had stood unsuccessfully as a reformer at St. Mawes in 1831.[46] In July 1831, Ker reportedly recommended that Brougham discuss the boundary commission with their SDUK colleague Thomas Drummond.[47]

Thomas Drummond was born in Edinburgh, one of four siblings in a debt-laden Whig family. He grew up in Musselburgh under the care of his mother and attended a local grammar school where he received private tutoring during the summers from George Jardine, professor of logic and rhetoric at the University of Glasgow. Following a resettlement of the family's debts, Drummond commenced the study of mathematics, natural philosophy and chemistry at Edinburgh University, aged thirteen, under John Leslie and Brougham's favourite mathematics tutor, John Playfair. Drummond left Scotland, aged fifteen, following his appointment to a cadetship at the Royal Military Academy, Woolwich. A gifted mathematician, he quickly worked his way through the academy's ranks, and by July 1815 had secured a position with the royal engineers. Over the next five years he assumed various roles before joining the board of ordnance's survey of Scotland and England in 1820.[48] Drummond remained with the board of ordnance when the survey of Ireland commenced in 1824, working closely with Thomas Colby, superintendent of the ordnance, until 1829. While in Ireland, Drummond rose to prominence after combining his inventive mind, engineering skills and scientific knowledge to modify the heliostat, compensation bars and limelight for the specific purposes of surveying in Ireland's treacherous conditions.[49] His modifications to Gurney's limelight, which became known as 'the Drummond light', brought him to London by 1829, where he was commissioned by the Trinity House Corporation with developing limelight for use in lighthouses. His demonstrations of the light at Trinity House and in Purfleet excited considerable public attention during 1830. These experiments also brought him to the attention of scientific society. He became a fellow of the Royal Astronomical Society in May 1830, gave a lecture on limelight to the Royal Society in June 1830 and dined with William IV at the Royal Pavilion in January 1831.[50]

Brougham's desire to see Drummond's light led to their meeting at Ker's house in March 1831. Drummond recorded that during his demonstration of the light in Ker's greenhouse:

> the chancellor [Brougham] seemed greatly afraid of his eye, and could hardly be persuaded to look at it [Drummond's light]. I spied him, however, peeping at a corner, and immediately turned the reflector full upon him, but he fled *instanter*. He [Brougham] started immediately afterwards, at eleven o'clock, for Lord Grey's.[51]

This demonstration was sufficient for Drummond to be welcomed into the SDUK. In April 1831, he dined with the SDUK council and started attending meetings of the map committee with Ker and Beaufort. Later that year he was formally proposed as an SDUK council member by Brougham and Ker.[52] Brougham met Drummond several times during July 1831 to discuss the potential scope of a boundary commission. The latter's experience working for the ordnance survey impressed Brougham sufficiently for him to recommend in cabinet that Drummond should supervise a preliminary working committee of the commission.[53] Following this, cabinet responsibility for organising the boundary commission shifted from Russell to Brougham.

From the first week of August 1831, Brougham, Ker and Drummond started contacting a network of friends, SDUK associates and engineers with sufficient time and finances to take up a non-salaried role on a working committee of the boundary commission (see Tables 3.2 and 3.3). John Wrottesley and Thomas Flower Ellis, two further members of the SDUK map committee, were appointed. Ker's uncle, Henry Gawler, a barrister who had recently written an article on the operation of the poor laws for the SDUK, was nominated, as were George Barrett-Lennard and Benjamin Ansley, who along with Wrottesley had previously been directors of the Metropolitan Loan and Investment Company, for which Ker had acted as a legal counsel.[54] SDUK committee attendee William Ord, regular SDUK contributor John Elliot Drinkwater, and SDUK correspondent and reform pamphleteer Henry Tancred, also agreed to work for the commission.[55] John Romilly, council member of the London University and committee member alongside Ord on the 'Loyal and Patriotic Fund for Assisting Reform', was also appointed.[56]

Brougham had also encouraged Drummond to nominate 'gentlemen who would perhaps make an active and useful member of the reform commission'. This resulted in Richard Sheepshanks, astronomer and fellow of Trinity College, Cambridge, Francis Baily, president of the Royal Astronomical Society, Colonel Frederick Page, who had recently written a treatise on the poor law, and John Chapman, royal artillery officer, being contacted. Sheepshanks accepted, but Page and Baily declined as they were 'much occupied with their own private business'.[57] Chapman became one of seven royal artillery or royal engineers officers (including Drummond) recruited to the working committee. Chapman was working for the ordnance survey of Ireland when contacted by Drummond, as was Robert Kearsley Dawson, who Drummond enlisted to manage a separate team of surveyors who were to work alongside the commissioners.[58] The manner in which the four other officers were appointed remains unclear. It is likely that the SDUK map committee were aware of Henry Rowland Brandreth, a royal engineer who had completed a survey and report of the Ascension Islands for the navy during 1830.[59] However, the whereabouts of William Wylde, Robert Saunders and Richard Scott during 1830 and 1831 are uncertain. The SDUK map committee would have known of Scott, as he had recently published a topographical account of Hayling Island, and Wylde's large private collection of maps makes it likely that the map committee also knew him. Saunders was a Waterloo veteran and retired royal artillery officer, who was later derided as a 'poor aristocrat' when serving as a factory inspector between 1833 until his death in 1852.[60]

These recruits, along with Tallents and Birch (whom Brougham and Melbourne had already identified), formed the twenty-one-man working committee of the English and Welsh boundary commission that commenced operations by the end of August 1831. The close affiliation that most of these commissioners had with Brougham, the SDUK, and to a lesser extent the London University represented a distinct departure from Russell's original intention that the boundary commissions be established on a conventional, cross-party basis. Furthermore, in comparison to Russell's original nominations, the working committee had very little official government experience. The only member to have worked for the government at Westminster was Thomas Birch, Melbourne's private secretary from 1827 to 1828.[61] The only member with any experience attending parliamentary committees or commissions of inquiry was Ker. Four of the committee's members – Wrottesley, Barrett-Lennard, Romilly and Ord – were linked to prominent Whig families. However, the political fortunes of their fathers had meant their legal expertise, and reforming ambitions, had only previously been put to use in the extra-parliamentary domain. And, while the royal engineers and royal artillery officers had experience working in an official capacity for the state, their work had never previously been directly linked to the legislative process. What these seven officers (including Drummond), and the four SDUK map committee members, did introduce to the committee was a considerable core of surveying and cartographical expertise. In contrast with the primarily legalistic outlook of Russell's original nominations for commissioners, the working committee now contained a broad amalgam of legal and geographic experts. This synthesis of knowledge was crucial in terms of defining how the committee sought to reconstruct England's electoral map.

Science, statistics and cartography: Drummond's inductive method for boundary reform

The Grey government's proposals for boundary reform had caused considerable controversy since their introduction in March 1831. As discussed in the previous chapter, one of the chief concerns of both anti-reformers and reformers had been that the Grey ministry would gerrymander the electoral system in favour of Whig or aristocratic electoral interests. The government needed to navigate boundary reform carefully, particularly if their proposals were to secure parliamentary approval. During June and

July 1831, they provided repeated assurances and worked with opposition parliamentarians to identify some form of mutually agreeable framework for setting boundaries. By July these efforts had focused on securing a traditional cross-party commission to formulate proposals. However, once Brougham and Drummond took over planning for the commission by August 1831 this cross-party framework stood on thin ground. Instead, under Brougham and Drummond's influence, focus was placed on the scientific personnel and methods of the commission as a means of assuring parliamentarians that boundaries could be proposed in an impartial manner.

In the early nineteenth century, 'science' was often used as a catch-all expression to denote knowledge that in one way or another had been reduced to a system. Contemporaries happily spoke of military science, the science of law, politics, finance and even religion, alongside what we would think of today as the natural sciences.[62] By 1830 science as a practice and idea was also increasingly associated with the politics of reform. This was thanks largely to the rise of gentlemanly scientific society culture from the later 1790s, which promoted such disciplines as chemistry, geology and natural history; the influence of political economy on liberal-Tory ministries during the 1820s; and the establishment of mechanics' institutes and the SDUK in the 1820s, which sought to expand scientific learning to the masses. For many Whigs in the Grey ministry, 'the all conquering science', as Lansdowne had termed it in 1824, and its proliferation and widespread application across society, explained their sense of a march of progress, and Britain's continuing journey to a higher plane of civilisation, since the Napoleonic wars.[63]

Science lay at the root of Whig identity and their ambitions for reform. As Joe Bord has demonstrated, experience of inter-partisan cooperation at scientific societies from the 1810s led to the belief among a new generation of Whigs that similar cooperation might be engendered in the political sphere.[64] For cabinet ministers such as Brougham this conviction was underpinned by a commitment to an 'enlightenment ideal' that believed 'science was not confined to chemistry and optics' but offered 'a universally applicable method of arriving at knowledge'.[65] In particular, this marked out the 1820s as a period of growing enthusiasm for statistics among Whiggish and reforming legislators and helped give rise to the emerging social science movement. In September 1831, as the boundary commission commenced its work, the Whig MP for Northamptonshire and close friend of the cabinet Viscount Milton, presided over a 'Festival of Science' at York that led to the formation of the British Association for the Advancement of Science (BAAS).[66] In his opening speech Milton spoke of 'impressing on the government of this country ... the necessity of affording it [science] due encouragement, and of giving every proper stimulus to its advancement'.[67]

Within two years the BAAS had established a statistical section, whose secretary John Elliot Drinkwater had acted as a boundary commissioner, and whose leading advocates were the polymath William Whewell, the physicist and astronomer John Herschel, the mathematician Charles Babbage, and the political economist and future tithe commissioner Richard Jones. They had spent the previous decade at the University of Cambridge taking formative steps towards developing an inductive method of 'social economy' that embraced the statistical approaches of the Belgian astronomer and mathematician Adolphe Quetelet. Importantly, they rejected the 'rigidly deductive' approach of political economists such as David Ricardo in favour of 'measuring, collecting, tabulating, and calculating ... [and] reasoning on the basis of data collected'. By 1830, even the most cautious of this set, Herschel, was able to look forward to a time when 'legislation and politics become gradually regarded as experimental sciences'.[68] In 1834 these figures were the driving force behind the foundation of the Statistical Society of London and were influential in the formation of the Manchester Statistical Society. As Theodore Porter has argued, both societies advocated the creation of a 'science of government' through 'the accumulation of simple, irrefutable facts'.[69]

It was in this intellectual context that Drummond worked with cabinet ministers to establish 'general principles' for identifying parliamentary boundaries.[70] The home secretary, Viscount Melbourne, provided Drummond with formal authorisation to commence making arrangements for a commission on 8 August, providing a skeletal outline of the government's initial expectations for the commission.[71] With the support of two draftsmen, Drummond began making technical arrangements for the boundary commission at its Westminster headquarters in the robing room in the privy council office on Whitehall.[72] A typical working day lasted between 10:00 and 19:00, and during August consisted of 'frequent communications and interviews' with Brougham, Althorp and Russell, who acted as intermediaries between Drummond and the cabinet.[73] These meetings allowed Drummond to develop his more detailed 23 August guidelines, intended to standardise the commissioners' approach to boundary setting across every English and Welsh borough.[74]

Drummond sought to establish an inductive method for defining electoral communities based on observation and fact, which avoided partisan politics and allowed for boundaries to be defined with 'as much uniformity, as the very irregular and occasionally difficult nature of the subject will admit'.[75] He proposed that the commission should complete an up-to-date cartographical survey of every English and Welsh borough and its surrounding areas, ascertain its ancient parliamentary and extra-parliamentary boundaries, and identify, from a variety of local sources, the number of £10 householders in the borough and surrounding areas. This data was to be complemented with a statistical and socio-economic survey of each borough that considered 'the employment of the surrounding population, their connection with the town or with the country, [and] their municipal or rural character'. Each borough survey was required to evaluate 'the direction in which a town is increasing' in order that 'the boundary determined to-day may not require alteration tomorrow'.[76]

He established a strict set of criteria for identifying a borough's future electoral community. No recourse to public opinion regarding local preference for, or the political implications of, potential boundaries was to be made. If a borough contained fewer than 300 £10 householders, the most suitable area with comparable social and economic interests within seven miles was to be found with which to increase the borough's electorate. If a borough contained more than 300 £10 householders, reformed boundaries were to encompass the modern extent of the borough and allow for a century's worth of town expansion.[77] Drummond organised the working committee around nine teams of two commissioners. Each team was assigned a district in England or Wales containing twenty to thirty boroughs – seven teams were assigned to England (Table 3.3).[78] The commissioners were to be supported by a centrally organised team of mostly locally based surveyors and draftsmen under the supervision of Dawson. The commissioners were to be provided with expenses only, while the surveyors and draftsmen were paid on an hourly basis. Drummond was authorised by the treasury to open an account with Greenwood, Cox & Co., banking agents, who financed the commission's daily operations.[79]

As well as containing 'men of science' associated with the ordnance survey and the SDUK, the substantive scientific claims of the boundary commission revolved around its mechanical application of cartographic and statistical data to arrive at a set of apparently disinterested proposals. Creating a map of each constituency was an integral aspect of the commission's work, and Drummond enlisted a considerable body of surveying expertise from the ordnance survey, to ensure that accurate, up-to-date maps provided the foundation for reformed boundaries. When the commission started its work in August 1831 it did not have access to official maps containing town plans of each parliamentary borough or their existing boundaries. The ordnance survey of Britain – which had started in 1791 – was still incomplete and had ground to a halt by 1825. In that year, work began on the ordnance survey of Ireland, which was still underway in 1831. In 1831 official trigonometrical surveying remained to be completed on the north of England and Scotland. For areas where surveying had

Table 3.3: Working committee of the boundary commission (by district).[1]

Chair of the working committee		Thomas Drummond
Supervisor of the surveyors		Robert K. Dawson
District	Boroughs	Primary commissioners
District A (south-east England)	39	John Elliot Drinkwater
		Robert John Saunders
District B (south England)	48	Benjamin Ansley
		Henry Gawler
District C (south-west England)	40	Thomas Birch
		Henry Rowland Brandreth
District D (east England)	31	Richard Sheepshanks
		William Edward Tallents
District E (west England)	34	John James Chapman
		William Ord
District F (south Wales)	11	Thomas Flower Ellis
		William Wylde
District G (north-east England)	25	Henry William Tancred
		John Wrottesley
District H (north-west England)	24	Launcelot Baugh Allen
		John Romilly
District I (north Wales & north-west England)	5	Henry Bellenden Ker
		George Barrett-Lennard
Not assigned a specific district		Richard Scott

[1] Compiled from TNA, T72.

been completed by the ordnance survey, English and Welsh town plans were at best six years out of date. In some cases – such as for constituencies in Kent – the ordnance survey reflected the state of urban development prior to the Napoleonic wars. The unavailability of basic official maps was resolved by making use of commercially available maps produced by independent surveyors such as Christopher Greenwood and Andrew Bryant. By 1831 both had completed their own detailed triangulations of the north of England. Their maps of England's southern counties also contained the most up-to-date basic town plans of most English boroughs.

To ensure that the boundary commissioners could complete their work, Drummond oversaw the creation of enlarged, up-to-date plans of every English and Welsh borough using official and unofficial maps at a scale of two inches to one mile. This was undertaken by a team of seventy surveyors, nine lithographers and ten colourers, that Drummond recruited to work in London, or locally with the commissioners in each borough. From late August 1831 the team of London-based surveyors completed at least one enlarged tracing of every constituency for England and

Wales. These tracings were sent to the boundary commissioners ahead of their arrival in each constituency, who were accompanied by at least one or two surveyors. In each locality the commissioners and their surveyors refined and updated their basic town plans, documented local legal boundaries (many known only to local officials) and recorded their proposed parliamentary boundary. By creating an accurate bird's eye view of a constituency, Drummond created the first building block with which a disinterested bureaucrat might be able to identify a parliamentary boundary.

Statistical inquiry was the second technique applied by the commission. Prior to the commission's commencement, the reform bill had prompted the creation of a plethora of electoral statistics that revealed that the demographic data contained in the 1821 and 1831 census was lacking in sufficient detail for boundary reform. This information included what was known centrally about the limits of existing parliamentary boroughs; data relating to recent elections and the specific franchise of each borough; copies of memorials and petitions submitted by individual boroughs relating to the reform bill; 1821 and 1831 census returns for each borough and its surrounds; the number of houses in each borough and their value according to the inhabited house duty; and the annual amount of assessed taxes contributed by each borough during the previous decade.[80]

The commissioners were to build on these statistics and develop a body of personally verified electoral data, focused on population, household valuations and taxation data. To collect this information, Drummond instructed the commissioners to liaise with local officials in every borough – such as overseers of the poor, surveyors of taxes and clerks of the peace – as well as 'intelligent men' in each locality. If officials were not forthcoming with information, letters from the home office demanding information could be provided. Drummond warned the commissioners to be wary of local officials, and advised cross-referencing multiple data sources in each borough and, if necessary, a personal valuation of houses. Drummond was to complete a personal review of this data in London, demanding amendments and further investigation where inconsistencies appeared. As every step in the commissioners' data collection process was to be completed by personal investigation, Drummond claimed that all boundaries would bypass the 'ignorance and insolence' of local officials, and the 'deception' of parties motivated to provide information for political ends.[81]

The commissioners met Drummond either in groups or individually in London during late August and early September 1831. At these meetings he advised each commissioner to keep a journal detailing every interaction in each borough, in order that they could substantiate their proposals in front of a planned parliamentary committee.[82] The first commissioners to commence their work were Tallents and Sheepshanks, who had submitted their first report to Drummond by 31 August – a day before the government announced its boundary commissioners to parliament.[83] Unsurprisingly, the government's claim to have identified an impartial scientific means of redrawing constituency boundaries was met with scepticism. The additional revelation that a secret committee of boundary commissioners had started work without parliamentary permission only further angered the reform bill's opponents.

'What in the world has science to do here?'

When the names of the commissioners were announced in parliament on 1 September 1831, MPs only recognised those of a few Whig sons – Ord, Wrottesley, Romilly and Barrett-Lennard – as well as that of Ker, who had achieved a degree of infamy in Westminster during the previous decade due to his links with Brougham.[84] Given the SDUK's partisan reputation, anti-reformers missed an opportunity to embarrass the government by failing to connect the commissioners with the society. Although the *Standard* termed the commissioners 'abject creatures of the cabinet', the ultra-Tory *John Bull* conceded they were 'wholly unexceptionable, for ... they never were heard of before'.[85] It was Althorp's wider claims regarding the impartial and scientific character of the commission that provoked most fury. For traditional Tories Althorp's use of a language of science revealed the government's desire to assimilate a new generation of liberal political economists into the administration of the British state.[86]

The *Morning Post* led this charge, dismissing the commissioners as a new breed of 'political architects' trained on the mathematical teachings of 'Cocker and a slate pencil'[87] and the trigonometrical techniques of 'Colonel Colby and the Irish [ordnance] survey'.[88] It lamented that 'England shall be squared and parcelled like a harlequin's jacket' and mocked the idea that Althorp had been 'studying the rudiments of mathematical policy, and learning how to rule kingdoms by compasses and the quadrant'. Preferring any boundary commission to rely on the knowledge and oversight of local officials, it mockingly asked:

> What in the world has science to do here? Is the division [of counties] to be geological according to minerals or strata? Or is it to be astronomical, by latitudes and transits? If not we had rather trust [boundary reform] to the fattest justice of the peace, who had grown old upon his

district, than to the thinnest geometrician who ever measured the habitable globe.[89]

Whether the announcement of the commissioners helped to convince more liberally minded Tories, such as Peel, is difficult to say, as he did not respond during the debate. It is unlikely, however, that his 'strenuous opposition' to 'riding commissioners' had changed. A month earlier he had reasoned that parliament had 'details enough before them' to decide on new boundaries, either during debate or in select committee, and that enfranchising 40s. freeholders in their respective boroughs, rather than counties, would remove the need for any significant changes to England's borough constituencies.[90]

The reform bill's supporters were more positive. *The Times* (which had spent the previous three weeks violently criticising the government over their plans to divide the counties) welcomed the naming of commissioners on the basis that it made the bill's passage 'more certain'.[91] The paper also signalled its approval of Althorp, Drummond and Brougham's scientific ambitions for the commission. It viewed the commission's task in grandiose terms, expressing hope that the commissioners would bring 'order out of confusion' to the electoral system, as the Court of Fire had done following the Great Fire of London, 'when all boundaries of premises were obliterated, and all local rights and jurisdictions confounded'. While *The Times* acknowledged that the commission had 'a difficult work to perform', it expressed its full confidence that through effective management, 'uniformity will undoubtedly be attained, and all anomalies made to disappear'.[92] Such a glowing appraisal, in comparison to the paper's editorial stance over the previous weeks is best explained by Brougham's close relationship with the paper's editor, Barnes.[93] As a further sign of Brougham's influence, in the same editorial, *The Times* defended Brougham's close friend and boundary commissioner, Ker, against the recriminations of the MP for Guildford, Charles Baring Wall. Wall had objected to Ker's nomination on the basis that he was an 'unaccommodating and unquiet individual'.[94]

The Times's endorsement did little to prevent mounting opposition anger over subsequent days, when reports of the commissioners' activities trickled in from the localities. On 3 September the *Standard* reported that 'the commissioners who were appointed, or rather named, on Thursday night ... have already (whether prematurely or not remains to be proved) commenced their labours. They assemble with a great number of clerks every day at the council office'.[95] On 5 September opposition MPs sought to halt the commission, on the basis that it had commenced operations without statutory approval. Baring Wall shared some correspondence from a constituent with the Commons, which he had initially read with 'unfeigned astonishment'.[96] It transpired that commissioners Drinkwater and Saunders together with Dawson, had been collecting information in Guildford since 26 August. Most alarmingly, they had compelled parish overseers and churchwardens to provide information under the authority of the home secretary. Opposition MPs were outraged – Baring Wall informed a political confidant he was 'mad about this part of the bill', and Charles Wetherell announced that it was a 'monstrous infringement of the privileges of parliament'. Accordingly, Wetherell proposed a parliamentary motion to prevent the commissioners from completing any further work on the grounds of their illegality.[97]

Opposition MPs were correct to point out that in contrast to a royal commission of inquiry, the working committee had not received the prior authorisation of an act of parliament. As a check on executive power, since 1688, non-emergency, administrative royal commissions had required statutory approval.[98] Althorp defended the government's actions by arguing that the committee's work represented an extension of the home secretary's authority to demand legal documents from parishes or corporations.[99] He also tried to reassure the Commons that the working committee were only compiling preliminary reports, which were to be considered by a full commission of thirty-one after the reform bill had passed into law. He apologised for the fact that the committee had started their work prior to the naming of the commissioners but stated this had only occurred due to the unforeseen length of the reform bill's committee stage. Decisively, the pro-reform majority in the Commons indicated that, while imperfect, they were willing to accept the government's rationale. As well as putting an end to Wetherell's proposed wrecking motion, this de facto parliamentary approval of the working committee was sufficient for Drummond to proceed at pace in implementing his scientific plans for redrawing England's electoral map.

Conclusion

The 1831–2 boundary commission for England and Wales established a pioneering bureaucratic model for the personnel, methods and ideas used to reform the British state during the 1830s and 1840s. Studies of state formation in the late Hanoverian and early Victorian period, which have not acknowledged the boundary commission, instead suggest that this transformative period of legislative inquiry commenced with the royal commissions on the poor laws (established in 1832), factories and municipal corporations (both established in 1833).[100] The detailed study of recruitment and planning for the 1831–2 boundary commission provided here revises this historiography, establishing Drummond (and to a lesser extent Brougham) as a major intellectual and practical influence for subsequent commissions and inspectorates. Importantly, instead of viewing the 1832 Reform Act as a convenient chronological marker for the social reforms that followed, the practical need to implement electoral reform during 1831 and 1832 needs to be understood as crucial in establishing a template for subsequent domestic inquiries and legislation. In this regard, the boundary commission was a key moment in the 'slow and fitful process' of British state growth during the nineteenth century, a process that historians have generally agreed owed more to individual impetus than any consistent strategy – let alone governing consensus – for how administrative reform should take place.[101] If Drummond's experiments with limelight had not brought him to Brougham's attention during the early months of 1831, the future of electoral reform, and the wider evolution of the British state, might have looked very different.

As it transpired, the example set by Drummond and Brougham in establishing the boundary commission initiated a major shift in the governing attitudes of the Grey ministry during the summer of 1831. The experience was crucial in demonstrating to politicians like Russell – who was central to the Whig reform agenda for the next two decades – that 'system, method, [and] science' were practicable as a governmental strategy.[102] In this regard, the difference in bureaucratic aspiration between Russell's initial plans for a 'cross-party' committee in May 1831 and Drummond's meticulously organised commission of August 1831 are startling. Having discarded a traditional cross-party approach, the government and Drummond resorted to science as a methodological and rhetorical device to assure opponents, and themselves, that England's electoral map could be redrawn in a politically objective manner. To an extent this reflected a genuine belief among a number of leading Whigs in the virtues of science and its potential to underpin a new era of disinterested bureaucracy. As this and subsequent chapters demonstrate, this belief was best embodied by Drummond, who drew on his experience on the ordnance survey, and as a mathematician and chemist, to create an innovative, inductive framework for the identification of reformed parliamentary boundaries. The resort to a political rhetoric of science, as exemplified by Althorp's announcement of the commissioners to the Commons in September 1831, was also in keeping with a wider cultural enthusiasm for science in Whig and progressive intellectual circles by the early 1830s. This enthusiasm – particularly that for the legislative possibility of statistics – encapsulated an emerging view that bureaucracy and political decision-making might be transformed into an apparently disinterested, mechanical model.

That said, Drummond's bureaucratic model and its scientific trappings (both practical and rhetorical) afforded several clear political benefits to the Grey ministry. And, any claims that the boundary commission (and subsequent commissions and inspectorates) represented a form of literal bureaucratic impartiality have to be treated with scepticism. In terms of recruitment, the fears of anti-reformers during 1831 (see Chapter 2) proved well founded. Discarding a cross-party framework, and justifying their appointments on the basis of their status as men of science, allowed the Grey ministry to enlist a boundary commission staffed largely by their political allies. Second, the process of establishing boundaries was anything but transparent. The methods employed by Drummond remained shrouded in secrecy for several months, and as the next chapter will discuss, maintaining secrecy about the commission's activities became an increasingly important aspect of Drummond's scientific framework. And third, while Drummond established a mechanical model with which to consistently identify boundaries, the broader basis for what a borough constituency was supposed to encompass (either its modern town population or a town and its surrounding parishes), as well as authority for how the commission's cartographic, statistical and qualitative data were to be applied, still rested with the government. If the data collected by Drummond led to a politically questionable boundary settlement, the government still had the power to change how that data was used. It is to Drummond and the commission's attempts to collect data from the localities that this book turns next.

Notes

1. B. Hilton, *A Mad, Bad, & Dangerous People?: England 1783–1846* (Oxford, 2006), 589.
2. Hilton, *Mad, Bad*, 599–602, 608–9.
3. Hansard, 3, vi. (1 Sept. 1831), 982–6; *Morning Herald*, 2 Sept. 1831.
4. *The Times*, 2 Sept. 1831; *Globe*, 2 Sept. 1831.
5. *Mirror of Parliament*, i. (1 Sept. 1831), 1863; *Stamford Mercury*, 9 Sept. 1831.
6. P. Salmon, 'The English Reform Legislation, 1831–32', in D. Fisher (ed.), *The House of Commons, 1820–32*, i. (Cambridge, 2009), 400.
7. H. Clokie and J. Robinson, *Royal Commissions of Inquiry* (New York, 1937); A. Brundage, *Making of the New Poor Law: The Politics of Inquiry, Enactment and Implementation* (London, 1978); E. Higgs, *Before The Information State: The Central Collection of Information on Citizens since 1500* (Basingstoke, 2004). The exception is Hilton, *Mad, Bad*, 603.
8. U. R. W. Henriques, *Before the Welfare State: Social Administration in Early Industrial Britain* (London, 1979), 251; O. MacDonagh, *Early Victorian Government 1830–1870* (London, 1977), 1–21, 197–205; Lubenow, *The Politics of Government Growth* (Plymouth, 1971), 15–29.

9. P. Mandler (ed.), *Liberty and Authority in Victorian Britain* (Oxford, 2006), 10; P. Mandler, *Aristocratic Government in the Age of Reform: Whigs and Liberals 1830–1852* (Oxford, 1990); R. Brent, *Liberal Anglican Politics: Whiggery, Religion, and Reform, 1830–1841* (Oxford, 1987); I. Newbould, *Whiggery and Reform, 1830–41: The Politics of Government* (London, 1990).

10. R. Ashton, *Victorian Bloomsbury* (London, 2012), 1–81.

11. Clokie and Robinson, *Royal Commissions*, 26–53.

12. R. Tompson, *The Charity Commission and the Age of Reform* (London, 1979), 50–54.

13. Tompson, *Charity Commission*, 116–56.

14. PP1819–20 (64), ii. 399; PP1828 (267), ix. 65.

15. Hansard, 3, vi. (1 Sept. 1831), 982–6.

16. Hansard, 3, ix. (12 Dec. 1831) 151.

17. PP1834 (291), xli. 349; PP1836 (528), xxxvii. 492; PP1837 (290), xxxix. 205; PP1837–38 (346), xxxvi. 191; PP1847–48 (669), xxxix. 295. The exception is Hilton, *Mad, Bad*, 603.

18. DSC, Grey, B6/3B/9, Durham to Grey, 25 Aug. 1831, 24.

19. DSC, Grey, B50A/6/18, Russell to Grey, 23 May 1831, 1.

20. T. Jenkins, 'Dickinson, William', in D. Fisher (ed.), *The House of Commons, 1820–32* (Cambridge, 2009), iv. 919–22; S. Farrell, 'Knatchbull, Sir Edward', in Fisher, *Commons*, v. 922–33; M. Casey and P. Salmon, 'Cartwright, William Ralph', in Fisher, *Commons*, iv. 592–5.

21. H. Stephens and J. Sweetman, 'Erskine, James St Clair (1762–1837)', *Oxford Dictionary of National Biography* [hereafter *ODNB*], www.oxforddnb.com [accessed 6 Jun. 2022].

22. P. Jupp, *British Politics on the Eve of Reform: The Duke of Wellington's Administration, 1828–30* (Basingstoke, 1998), 210–16, 233.

23. TNA, PRO 30/22/1B, 'Russell to Grey', undated, 157–8; A. Kriegel (ed.), *The Holland House Diaries, 1831–1840* (London, 1977), 5; UCL, Brougham, 3, Abercromby to Brougham, undated, 39,600.

24. Kriegel, *Holland House*, 6.

25. Tompson, *Charity Commission*, 116–30; J. M. Collinge, *Office Holders in Modern Britain, Volume 9, Officials of Royal Commissions of Inquiry 1815–1870* (London, 1984), 9–16.

26. SRO, Hatherton, D260/M/F/5/26/7, 22 July 1831, 78.

27. Hansard, 3, vi. (1 Sept. 1831), 982–6.

28. Kriegel, *Holland House*, 5–6, 42; SRO, Hatherton, D260/M/F/5/26/7, 21–22 July 1831, 78–80.

29. Hansard, 3, vi. (13 Sept. 1831), 1399–403; Kriegel, *Holland House*, 5–6.

30. T. Lang, 'Hallam, Henry (1777–1859)', *ODNB*, www.oxforddnb.com [accessed 6 June 2022]; D. Miller, 'Gilbert, Davies (1767–1839)', *ODNB*, www.oxforddnb.com [accessed 6 June 2022]; T. Jenkins, 'Gordon, Sir James Willougby', in Fisher, *Commons*, v. 308–11.

31. T. Jenkins, 'Gordon, Sir James Willougby', in Fisher, *Commons*, v. 311.

32. PP1830–31 (338) x. 36; 'Thomas Bernard Birch', *Legacies of British Slavery*, https://www.ucl.ac.uk/lbs/person/view/15128 [accessed 6 June 2022]; UCL, Brougham, 3, Abercromby to Brougham, undated, 39,600; Kriegel, *Holland House*, 6; R. Gaunt and P. O'Malley, 'Tallents, William Edward (1780–1837)', *ODNB*, www

.oxforddnb.com [accessed 6 June 2022]; R. Gaunt, *Politics, Law and Society in Nottinghamshire: The Diaries of Godfrey Tallents of Newark 1829–1839* (Nottingham, 2010), 26; E. Smith, 'The Election Agent in English Politics, 1734–1832', *EHR*, 134 (1969), 12–35.

33. H. Brougham, *The Life and Times of Henry Lord Brougham* (London, 1871), i. 47, 56–7.

34. Brougham, *Life and Times*, 59; A. Aspinall, *Lord Brougham and the Whig Party* (Stroud, 2005), 16; W. D. Stockwell, 'Contributions of Henry Brougham to Classical Political Economy', *History of Political Economy*, 23, 4 (1991), 645–73.

35. M. Lobban, 'Brougham, Henry Peter, first Baron Brougham and Vaux', *ODNB*, www.oxforddnb.com [accessed 6 June 2022]

36. C. Knight, *Passages of a Working Life during Half a Century* (London, 1864), 113; M. J. Cullen, *The Statistical Movement in Victorian Britain* (Hassocks, 1976), 21, 80.

37. R. Ashton, 'Society for the Diffusion of Useful Knowledge (*act.* 1826–1846)', *ODNB*, www.oxforddnb.com [accessed 6 June 2022]; M. C. Grobel, 'The Society for the Diffusion of Useful Knowledge, 1826–1846' (unpublished University of London MA thesis, 1933).

38. P. Mandler, 'Tories and Paupers: Christian Political Economy and the Making of the New Poor Law', *Historical Journal*, 33, 1 (1990), 94; Mandler, *Aristocratic Government*, 91, 100, 113; Anonymous, *Political Economy Club, Names of Members 1821–1860* (London, 1860); Ashton, *Victorian Bloomsbury*, 58–81.

39. Ashton, *Victorian Bloomsbury*, 1–81; A. Rauch, *Useful Knowledge: The Victorians, Morality and the March of Intellect* (Durham, N.C., 2001); V. Gray, *Charles Knight: Educator, Publisher and Writer* (Aldershot, 2006).

40. Kriegel, *Holland House*, 5–6,

41. M. Curthoys, 'Lefevre, Sir John George Shaw (1797–1879)', *ODNB*, www.oxforddnb.com [accessed 6 June 2022].

42. J. Laughton and N. Rodger, 'Beaufort, Sir Francis (1774–1857)', *ODNB*, www.oxforddnb.com [accessed 6 June 2022].

43. A. Friendly, *Beaufort of the Admiralty* (London, 1977), 267.

44. M. Cain, 'The Maps of the Society of the Diffusion of Useful Knowledge: A Publishing History', *Imago Mundi*, 46 (1994), 151; M. Brown, 'How Not to "Regain Paradise": Henry Bellenden Ker, F.R.S. from 1819 to 1831', *Notes and Records of the Royal Society of London*, l (1996), 211–15; C. Carr, *A Victorian Law Reformers Correspondence* (London, 1955).

45. J. Vaizey, 'No. 67 "Charles Henry Bellenden Ker"', *The Institute: A Club of Conveyancing Counsel. Memoirs of Former Members*, i. (London, 1907), 218–42.

46. D. Fisher, 'St Mawes', in Fisher, *Commons*, ii. 192–3.

47. National Library of Ireland, Drummond Papers, Ker to Dawson, 9 Nov. 1840, 75–6; Captain Larcom, 'Memoir of the Professional Life of the late Captain Drummond', *Royal Engineers Professional Papers*, 4 (1841), xviii–xxii; J. Mclennan, *Memoir of Thomas Drummond* (Edinburgh, 1867), 142; Brougham, *Life and Times*, iii. 379.

48. McLennan, *Thomas Drummond*, 1–36; R. B. O'Brien, *Thomas Drummond: Under-Secretary in Ireland 1835–40: Life and Letters* (London, 1889), 3–20.

49. C. Close, *The Early Years of the Ordnance Survey* (Newton Abbot, 1969), 71–6.

50. T. Drummond, 'On the Illumination of Lighthouses', *Philosophical Trans. Royal Soc. London*, 120 (1830), 383–98; McLennan, *Thomas Drummond*, 113–37; Close, *Ordnance Survey*, 74.

51. Mclennan, *Thomas Drummond*, 135–7.

52. UCL Special Collections, Papers of the SDUK [hereafter UCL, SDUK], In-papers, 24, Drummond to Coates, 27 Apr. 1831; UCL, SDUK Map Committee minutes, 6, 16 Apr. 1831; Knight, *Passages of a Working Life*, 118; Grobel, 'SDUK', iv. Appendix, 'SDUK Committee list'.

53. Larcom, 'Captain Drummond', xviii–xxii; Brougham, *Life and Times*, iii. 379; Mclennan, *Thomas Drummond*, 142; PP1831–32 (141), xxxviii. 5.

54. UCL, SDUK, In-papers, 29, Gawler to Coates, 25 May 1831; *The Times*, 14 Apr. 1824, 2.

55. UCL, SDUK, Out-papers 1830–1833, 19, Coates to Ord, 12 Nov. 1831; SDUK, In-papers 24, Drinkwater, John Elliot, 1828–1835; M. Spychal, 'Tancred, Henry William (1782–1860)', in P. Salmon and K. Rix (eds.), *The House of Commons 1832–1868* (forthcoming).

56. *The Times*, 31 May, 21 June 1830.

57. UCL, Brougham, 225, Drummond to Brougham, 5 Aug. 1831, 33,076, Drummond to Brougham, 12 Aug. 1831, 39468; *The Times*, 11 Mar. 1830, 10 Oct. 1863; F. Page, *The Principle of the English Poor Laws* (London, 1830); Hansard, 3, i. (11 Nov. 1830), 417; W. Ashworth, 'Baily, Francis (1774–1844)', *ODNB*, www.oxforddnb.com [accessed 6 June 2022].

58. McLennan, *Thomas Drummond*, 143; Close, *Early Years*, 73, 82.

59. G. Lewis, 'Memoir of Henry Rowland Brandreth', *Papers on Subjects Connected with the Duties of the Corps of Royal Engineers*, 10 (1849), 1–36; M. Brandreth, *Some Family and Friendly Recollections of 70 Years, of Mary Elizabeth Brandreth* (1888, privately printed), 10–13; L. Dawson, *Memoirs of Hydrography Part One 1750–1830* (Eastbourne, 1883), 101–4; Cain, 'The Maps of the Society of the Diffusion of Useful Knowledge', 151–67.

60. I. Cawood 'Corruption and the Public Service Ethos in Mid-Victorian Administration: The Case of Leonard Horner and the Factory Office', *EHR*, 135 (2020), 869; P. Clamp, 'Robert J. Saunders, Factory Inspector, and his National Factory Schools Experiment 1841–1843', *Journal of Educational Administration and History*, 18, 1 (1986), 23–33; Close, *Early Years*, 99–118; R. Scott, *A Topographical and Historical Account of Hayling Island* (Skelton, 1826); TNA, T72/43, 'Ledger of the commission', 65–6; 'Wylde Family', *Durham University Special Collections Catalogue*, http://reed.dur.ac.uk/xtf/view?docId=ead/pol/wylde.xml [accessed 6 June 2022].

61. C. Dod, *The Parliamentary Companion* (London, 1848), 131.

62. Hansard, 1, xiv. (2 June 1809), 876; Hansard, 2, xix. (7 July 1828), 1638; *Morning Advertiser*, 4 Nov. 1829; *Morning Post*, 4 Nov. 1829; H. Brougham, *The Objects, Advantages, and Pleasures of Science* (London, 1827).

63. Hansard, 3, ii. (15 Mar. 1824), 991; Hilton, *Mad, Bad*, 169–74.

64. J. Bord, *Science and Whig Manners: Science and Political Style in Britain, c. 1790–1850* (Basingstoke, 2009), 64–72.

65. J. A. Dwyer, 'An Enlightened Scot and English Reform: A Study of Henry Brougham' (unpublished PhD thesis, Univ. British Columbia, 1975), 18–22.

66. *York Herald*, 1 Oct. 1831.

67. Anonymous, *Report of the First and Second Meetings of the British Association for the Advancement of Science* (London, 1833), 16.

68. L. Goldman, *Victorians and Numbers: Statistics and Society in Nineteenth Century Britain* (Oxford, 2022), 36–9.

69. T. Porter, *The Rise of Statistical Thinking, 1820–1900* (Princeton, 1986), 36.

70. PP1831–32 (141), xxxviii, 6.

71. PP1831–32 (141), xxxviii. 5; Collinge, *Office Holders*, 1–8; UCL, Brougham, 457, Brougham to Lamb, 8 Aug. 1831, 24761.

72. UCL, SDUK, In-papers 19, Coates to Parrat, 9 or 10 Sept. 1831; TNA, T72/8/56, 'Christchurch', Ansley to Drummond, 16 Nov. 1831.

73. UCL, Brougham, 39,468, Drummond to Brougham, 5 Aug. 1831, 12 Aug. 1831; Brougham, *Life and Times*, iii, 379; McLennan, *Thomas Drummond*, 143.

74. PP1831–32 (141), xxxviii. 6–10.

75. PP1831–32 (141), xxxviii. 6.

76. PP1831–32 (141), xxxviii. 7.

77. TNA, T72/11/25, 'Stamford', 'Observations on Stamford Report', Drummond to Tallents and Sheepshanks, 6 Sept. 1831.

78. Hereford was assigned to District F (south Wales).

79. TNA, T72/43, 'Ledger of the commissioners', 1–2; McLennan, *Thomas Drummond*, 143.

80. S. J. Thompson, '"Population Combined with Wealth and Taxation": Statistics Representation and the Making of the 1832 Reform Act', in Tom Crook and Glen O'Hara (eds.), *Statistics and the Public Sphere, Numbers and the People in Modern Britain, c. 1800–2000* (New York, 2011), 205–23.

81. PP1831–32 (141), xxxviii, 9.

82. I have not located these journals. TNA, T72/10/68, 'Preston', Drummond to Romilly and Allen, 24 Sept. 1831; T72/11/46, 'Truro', Drummond to Birch, 27 Sept. 1831; T72/11/49, 'Wakefield', Drummond to Wrottesley, undated; T72/11/34 'Sudbury', Drummond to Tallents, 30 Sept. 1831.

83. TNA, T72/10/43, 'Newark', Drummond to Sheepshanks and Tallents, 1 Sept. 1831.

84. Hansard, 3, vi. (1 Sept. 1831), 982–1017; Vaizey, 'Bellenden Ker', 218–42.

85. *Standard*, 14 Sept. 1831; *John Bull*, 5 Sept. 1831.

86. B. Hilton, 'The Political Arts of Lord Liverpool', *TRHS*, 38 (1998), 147–70; B. Hilton, 'Peel: A Reappraisal' *HJ*, 22 (1979), 585–614; D. Eastwood, 'Robert Southey and the Intellectual Origins of Romantic Conservatism', *EHR*, 104, 411 (1989), 308–31.

87. A reference to *Cocker's Arithmetick*, first published in 1677.

88. *Morning Post*, 3 Sept. 1831.

89. *Morning Post*, 5 Sept. 1831.

90. Hansard, 3, v. (11 Aug. 1831), 1232–6.

91. *The Times*, 3 Sept. 1831.

92. *The Times*, 3 Sept. 1831.

93. Anonymous, *The History of The Times: "The Thunderer" in the Making 1785–1841* (London, 1935), 271–2; D. Maclise, *The Editor of "The Times"* (1830), British Museum, London.

94. Hansard, 3, vi. (1 Sept. 1831), 1007.

95. *Standard*, 3 Sept. 1831, 3; *Morning Post*, 5 Sept. 1831, 3; *John Bull*, 5 Sept. 1831, 3.

96. Hansard, 3, vi. (5 Sept. 1831), 1147–9.

97. H. Spencer, 'Wall, Charles Baring', in Fisher, *Commons*, vii. 613; Hansard, 3, vi. (5 Sept. 1831), 1150.

98. Clokie and Robinson, *Royal Commissions*, 82–3.

99. Hansard, 3, vi. (5 Sept. 1831), 1149–50.

100. Henriques, *Before the Welfare State*, 26, 83–4; Mandler, *Aristocratic Government*, 135–6; Cawood 'Corruption and the Public Service Ethos', 867–8; Collinge, *Office Holders*, ix. 16–28.

101. P. Harling, 'The Powers of the Victorian State', in P. Mandler (ed.), *Liberty and Authority in Victorian Britain* (Oxford, 2006), 25–50; Mandler, *Liberty and Authority*, 26; Lubenow, *Government Growth*, 26–7; MacDonagh, *Early Victorian Government*, 5, 9–10; Cawood, 'Corruption and the Public Service Ethos', 889–90; Goldman, *Victorians and Numbers*, 24–5, 99–100.

102. Mandler, *Aristocratic Government*, 123–282.

Chapter 4

Whipped by the beadles? Data-gathering for the boundary commission

In October 1831, the Whig MP for Calne, Thomas Macaulay, contacted his friend and fellow barrister Thomas Flower Ellis who had been working as a boundary commissioner in the west midlands and Wales for the previous six weeks. When asking Ellis how his 'work of numbering the gates and telling the towers of boroughs' was progressing, Macaulay intimated that a joke had been doing the rounds in London society. 'Is it true', he asked, 'that the [boundary] commissioners are whipped on the boundaries of the boroughs by the beadles, in order that they may not forget the precise line they have drawn'?[1] The quip was a reference to the tradition of 'beating the bounds', a ceremony still in operation today, where inhabitants perambulate their parish boundary to commit it to collective memory. Contemporary custom held that as a perambulation reached each boundary stone, a boy would either be whipped, or pushed over a stone, in 'order to impress' the local parish boundaries 'abidingly on their young memories'.[2]

The correspondence offers a revealing insight into contemporary Whig opinion about the nature of central-local relationships in the British state. For Macaulay, and his metropolitan counterparts, it had become a point of ridicule to hear that commissioners had been sent across the country to gather local records and statistical data from provincial officials such as the bumbling, whip-yielding beadle. The chair of the boundary commission, Thomas Drummond, held similar fears. When establishing the commission in August 1831 he expressed concern that its work would be restricted by provincial parochialism, obstruction and the distrust with which local bureaucrats held the intrusive activities of central officials.

These reservations were supported by the experiences of Brougham, Russell and Durham during the previous decade, when seeking to effect franchise and local government reform in England's closed municipal corporations by obtaining, and challenging, their clandestine ancient governing charters. All three had experienced limited success in securing even a fragment of the data required by the commission.[3] Such experiences figured heavily in Grey's assessment in August 1831 that the commission might take three years to complete its work.[4]

Building on the analysis of the personnel and 'scientific' methods of the commission in Chapter 3, this chapter examines the reality of central-local interactions during the boundary commission, revealing that the Whig characterisation of the inept and untrustworthy parish official was far from the truth. In keeping with historians who have stressed the development of a 'patchy' but still 'relatively high base' of governance in the localities by the beginning of the nineteenth century, local officials proved generally co-operative and produced accurate electoral data for the boundary commission with relative ease.[5] As a result, the commission was able to complete the vast majority of its investigatory work in a matter of months. This co-operation was encouraged by the commission's attempts to foster a sense of political neutrality by gathering data from a wide cross-section of officials and dignitaries in each constituency – be they parish officials, local tax collectors, municipal officers or surveyors. It was also aided by the commission's low public profile during its visits to each borough, and Drummond's acceptance that the process of proposing boundaries had to avoid any consideration of local political opinion – the subject of the first part of this chapter.

The chapter continues by exploring the commission's unexpected success in obtaining parliamentary boundary and £10 householder data in England's unreformed boroughs during its first weeks of operation. The ease with which this data had been collected led to a major shift in the government's ambition for the commission. Following the rejection of the second reform bill by the Lords in October 1831, the commission was asked to gather additional information about £10 householders in the new boroughs to help refine the borough franchise clauses in the government's reform legislation. The government then requested that Drummond extend the commission's survey to England's rotten boroughs. This substantial new inquiry – explored in the chapter's final two sections – was used to redesign the reform bill's controversial disfranchisement schedules and placed the boundary commission and its scientific approach at the centre of national discussion about parliamentary reform.

Due to its prominence, 'Drummond's list', as it became known, is one of the few instances where the work of the commission has attracted historical attention.⁶ Unlike other accounts, however, this chapter is the first to contextualise Drummond's list within the wider work of the commission, underscoring its contingence on the surveying and data-gathering techniques already developed by the commission. As well as confirming the centrality of the commission to the wider process of reform and reaffirming the validity of the 'consultation' interpretation of the 1832 reform legislation, this chapter establishes the commission's activities during the autumn and winter of 1831–2 as a formative moment in the development of the British state.⁷ Unacknowledged in previous accounts of nineteenth-century governance, the boundary commission instilled a new confidence in the minds of Whig legislators, not only in their ability to collect social data from the localities, but also in using this data as the basis for an increasingly ambitious domestic reform agenda over the subsequent decade.⁸

The boundary commission and local opinion

The English borough boundary commission was established in August 1831 under the auspices of Lord Brougham and the royal engineer, Thomas Drummond. By early September, seven teams containing two commissioners and at least one surveyor had been assigned to different regions across England to report on, and propose boundaries for, every parliamentary borough due to return MPs under the government's reform bill. A separate team of mapmakers and clerks based at the privy council office in Westminster assisted Drummond in co-ordinating this work from London. Table 4.1 provides an itinerary of the initial visits completed to each borough in District G (Yorkshire, Durham and Northumberland) by commissioners Tancred and Wrottesley between 12 September and 1 November 1831. Each team of commissioners maintained a similar schedule between September and November 1831, usually spending no more than three days in each borough. The commissioners continued their work following the rejection of the second reform bill by the Lords on 7 October, and by January 1832 boundaries had been proposed for all 186 boroughs that the Grey ministry intended to constitute England's reformed electoral map.

Contrary to initial expectations, the boundary commission completed its work in little over four months. As discussed in Chapter 3, Drummond's 'scientific' framework for the commission deliberately eschewed a consideration of local opinion in the boundary setting process, relying instead on a 'disinterested' survey of a borough's geographic, demographic and socio-economic circumstances. There were no public forums for the discussion

114 MAPPING THE STATE

Table 4.1: Boroughs visited by commissioners Tancred and Wrottesley in District G.

Constituency	Schedule[1]	County	Date in borough (if known)[2]
Leeds	C	Yorkshire	12/09/1831
Wakefield	D	Yorkshire	14/09/1831
Pontefract	N/A	Yorkshire	
Kingston upon Hull	E	Yorkshire	19/09/1831
Beverley	N/A	Yorkshire	22/09/1831
Scarborough	N/A	Yorkshire	
Malton	N/A	Yorkshire	27/09/1831
Whitby	D	Yorkshire	
Sunderland	C	Durham	01/10/1831
Newcastle upon Tyne	N/A	Northumberland	
Gateshead	D	Durham	
South Shields	D	Durham	07/10/1831
Tynemouth	D	Northumberland	09/10/1831
Morpeth	B	Northumberland	
Berwick-upon-Tweed	N/A	Northumberland	
Durham City	N/A	Durham	
Richmond	B	Yorkshire	
Northallerton	N/A	Yorkshire	17/10/1831
Thirsk	B	Yorkshire	20/10/1831
Ripon	N/A	Yorkshire	22/10/1831
Knaresborough	N/A	Yorkshire	24/10/1831
Aldborough	B	Yorkshire	27/10/1831
Boroughbridge	A	Yorkshire	27/10/1831
York	N/A	Yorkshire	01/11/1831

[1] Status in PP1831 (22), iii. 9.
[2] Compiled from newspaper reports and TNA, T72

of boundary proposals, and the commissioners arrived in each borough without any warning to the press or local officials. As well as being a key element in Drummond's strategy of bureaucratic impartiality, keeping a low public profile increased the feasibility that the commissioners might gather the requisite data required to propose boundaries within the brief time allotted to visit each borough. It was also intended as a means of preventing local officials from evading the commissioners or preparing embellished returns.

This is not to say that the public was not kept abreast of the commission's work. Coverage of the commissioners' activities did appear in some provincial and national newspapers, following information sharing between local officials and newspaper editors. Reports could take the form of a single sentence, such as the following from the *Hampshire Telegraph*: 'Henry Gawler, Esq. and Colonel Ansley, the commissioners under the reform bill, arrived at Lymington on Wednesday last, and have this day departed for Christchurch'.[9] Some extended to a lengthier paragraph that detailed the commissioners and their activities, provided some speculation as to their proposed boundaries and offered an indication of their itinerary.[10] One of the most extensive concerned commissioners Ord and Chapman's visit to Birmingham. On 26 September the *Birmingham Gazette* reported that:

> The commissioners [Ord and Chapman] are acting under instructions from the home office, and have official letters requesting all overseers, churchwardens, and municipal officers to furnish them with any necessary information for the purposes of the commission. The above two gentlemen we believe have completed their labours in Gloucester, Worcester, Droitwich, Warwick, Coventry, and other places in their circuit. They will finish their inquiries in this town in the course of a day or two, and proceed to Bridgnorth, Kidderminster, Walsall, Dudley, Wolverhampton, and other towns in Worcestershire and Staffordshire on which the elective franchise is conferred by the bill. The commissioners are at the Hen and Chickens, attended by a government surveyor, with the ordnance survey, &c. They have been in communication with the high and low bailiffs, the town surveyor, Mr Kempson, the steward of the manor, and other official persons of the several districts added to Birmingham in the [reform] bill.[11]

Most reports were somewhere between the two in length and were initially published in the local news sections of provincial papers, before sometimes being reprinted by the national press.

Editorial comment about the commissioners' activities was rare and tended to be made in the anti-reform press. On 10 September the Tory *Leeds Intelligencer* commented that: 'we really think there is no necessity to saddle the country with the expenses of these commissioners before the reform bill becomes the law of the land.'[12] Similar concerns about the cost of an unsanctioned commission were raised in the ultra-Tory *John Bull* following the news that the commission had continued its work after the Lords' rejection of the second reform bill.[13] The Tory *Essex Standard* expressed a more localised concern following the commissioners' visit to Colchester, which they warned might lead to an increase in taxation. It transpired that the commissioners had discovered 1,200 £10 householders in the borough, but that only 630 houses were rated at £10 or above for the inhabited house duty. This signalled a potential increase, the paper argued, in assessed rates for undervalued houses when the surveyor of taxes next visited the borough.[14] The only actively supportive comments about the commissioners tended to refer to the thoroughness of their work. The pro-reform *Worcester Herald* congratulated commissioners Ord and Chapman for being 'fully competent to the important task assigned to them' and 'indefatigable in their exertions' at Tewkesbury.[15] The rare occurrence of negative editorial comment among pro-reform editors indicates that they did not necessarily see the commission's arrival in a borough as an intrusion. Rather, their presence was probably seen as a welcome indication of the progress of the reform bill – a stance taken by *The Times* when the commission commenced its work.[16]

The commissioners' low public profile reflected the disinterested attitude towards local opinion that they had been advised to assume when commencing their work. However, in contradiction to his initial framework for setting boundaries, and the government's Commons announcement in September 1831 that the commission would pay no attention to local opinion, Drummond briefly explored establishing covert methods for gauging local reception. This followed informal advice from cabinet members in mid-September that a full commission in London might want to consider the likely public response to boundary proposals when evaluating borderline, or less straightforward cases.[17] Following this advice, Drummond surprised commissioners Ord and Chapman by informing them it would be 'very desirable to know the opinion of the most respectable of the inhabitants [of Worcester]' regarding their boundary recommendation for the borough (the full details of which are discussed in the following chapter). Drummond, at the behest of ministers, also offered to procure 'an introduction to some of the inhabitants, whose opinions it might be desirable to ascertain'.[18]

The commissioners' guarded response reaffirmed to Drummond that any attempt to obtain local opinion was fraught with danger. Ord argued that even if a convenient means of deducing local opinion were available, which he doubted, the process would prove futile. He warned Drummond that:

> It is hardly necessary to observe upon the great variety ... of views and interests which must exist, not only among classes, but amongst individuals, upon the subject of these boundaries ... the discordance of those opinions, and wishes would make it utterly impossible to draw any boundary.

Ord quoted a local official who had observed that if the commissioners quizzed inhabitants over their proposed boundaries they 'would never have had any peace in Worcester'. He also questioned the propriety of Drummond's proposal that the state of local opinion should be ascertained by questioning a few individuals through private introductions. Ord argued that it was important that the commissioners 'keep up the appearance as well as the reality of judging [future boundaries] for ourselves'. It was inevitable, he stated that 'one or two will probably coincide with us as in the boundary we propose' and 'immediately be taken to have influenced our decision'. Those that did not agree with their proposals, Ord argued, would claim their opinions had been disregarded for partisan reasons. The easiest way to avoid charges of political favouritism, Ord contended, was to propose boundaries, as Drummond had initially requested, with no recourse to local opinion.[19]

This stance was supported by the subsequent discovery that in order to appease local opinion, in some boroughs, the commissioners would have had to propose boundaries in contravention to their scientific principles for establishing boundaries in other boroughs. In Banbury the commissioners discovered a strong feeling among the town's inhabitants that the borough should not be extended to encompass an area of the town owned by the marquess of Bute. In cases such as Banbury, which contained more than 300 £10 householders, the commissioners had not been instructed to design boundaries that neutralised any single political influence. Rather, they were required to propose limits that encompassed the modern town settlement, even if this potentially led to an increase in the power of a particular landowner. Drummond conceded that given their wider instructions, satisfying local opinion was outside the commission's remit. When discussing the case of Banbury he recognised that 'we have no business in our present work with politics, no matter to whom the ground belongs, if the houses belong properly to the town they should be included even though by so doing it becomes a close borough'.[20]

The experiences of Banbury and Worcester confirmed to Drummond that seeking local opinion over boundaries raised questions of an inherently political nature; questions that the commission had not been entrusted with answering. If the government, or a full commission subsequently wanted to ascertain such information to inform decision making they would have to do so via a separate process. The benefit of such a position was that when the commission's reports were published, they were able to argue with conviction that their proposals were based on a set of disinterested principles that paid no attention to local opinion. This was in line with Drummond's original 'scientific' framework for proposing boundaries, which was seen as the best means of avoiding charges of partiality on a borough-by-borough basis and increased the likelihood of parliament's future approval of their proposals. As subsequent chapters demonstrate, the commission found it impossible to maintain complete ignorance of local opinion in their day-to-day work, but by early October 1831 any pretence that it should be actively courted had been dismissed. Fortuitously, this guarded approach towards the public did little to restrict the commission's work.

Collecting boundary data

The first task of the commissioners when they arrived in a borough was to ascertain its parliamentary boundary. As no central repository containing this information existed, constituency responses to a parliamentary return, requested in December 1830, provided the only preliminary indication as to the extent of each borough. The responses to this return provided by seventy-seven constituencies stated that their parliamentary limits were coextensive with the definition of the town or borough provided in the 1821 census. Sixty-three boroughs reported that their parliamentary limits were different to those recorded in the 1821 census and provided a brief description of the parishes or townships thought to be within their boundaries. Five boroughs did not provide any information as to their boundaries.[21] The data afforded by the 1821 census and the December 1830 returns offered no cartographic illustration of a borough's boundaries, only a list of the parishes or townships that were supposed to be contained in each constituency. To supplement this preliminary boundary data, the commissioners liaised with either borough officials (usually town clerks, overseers of the poor, bailiffs and collectors of taxes), persons deemed of intelligence within each locality (usually local surveyors or solicitors) and occasionally local patrons. In order to facilitate the sharing of information, the commissioners arrived in each locality armed with letters signed by the home secretary and addressed to known local officials.[22] Once the commissioners had demonstrated they were acting in an official capacity, they verified the legal areas already known to be within each constituency. They then confirmed the geographic extent of each parliamentary boundary by reference to official documents, boundary stones or collective local knowledge maintained by the custom of perambulation.

Once agreement as to the parliamentary limits of a borough had been ascertained, a borough's boundary was drawn onto the traced town plan of the constituency that Drummond's team of mapmakers in London had prepared and distributed to the commissioners. For most boroughs south of the midlands these maps were usually enlarged tracings at a 2:1 scale of published or unpublished ordnance survey maps (Map 5.1). For the midland boroughs northwards, these tracings tended to be made from maps published by independent mapmakers. The commission discovered that in 116 of the 145 existing boroughs they visited, the parliamentary boundary was either well known or undisputed within the locality, or had been accurately defined in the December 1830 parliamentary return.[23] In a few cases it was found that a map of the town with the boundary detailed on it was in the possession either of officials or a local resident. In

Tewkesbury, for instance, perambulation to ascertain the exact limits of the parliamentary borough was not required as 'an exceedingly good parish map [was] kept in the parish work house'.[24] Where no map existed, a written description of the borough's boundaries combined with local memory and convention (developed through 'beating the bounds' and the placing of boundary stones) had to be relied on.

In most boroughs the commissioners and their surveyors were required to confirm a boundary, or parts of it, through perambulation with local officials. A sizeable majority could be perambulated – 92 of the 145 boroughs (Table 4.2) were less than three square miles in size, and 60 of these were less than one square mile. The following letter from Robison Wright, a surveyor on the commission, detailed how the boundaries of five boroughs in Wiltshire had been confirmed with local officials – Calne being the largest of these at 1.6 square miles:

Table 4.2: Pre-1832 size range of boroughs due to retain franchise in second reform bill.

Size of borough	Number of boroughs
Over 10 square miles	7
7–9.9 square miles	8
4–6.9 square miles	13
3–3.9 square miles	19
2–2.9 square miles	19
1–1.9 square miles	13
0–0.9 square miles	60
Not known	6

> **Calne** – An excellent map of the borough in the possession of the vestry clerk – also partially proved by perambulation.
>
> **Marlborough** – Perambulated and sketched with a guide, and others.
>
> **Devizes** – an old engraved map of the town; other M.S. maps in the possession of the town clerk – and perambulation.
>
> **Shaftesbury** – an engraved map of the town, and perambulation with an overseer.
>
> **Wilton** – perambulation with two overseers.[25]

Likewise, in Gloucester, which was 0.5 square miles, after consulting with local officials, commissioners Chapman and Ord reported that the boundaries of the ancient borough drawn onto the map by their surveyor were 'very well and accurately defined; [and that] boundary stones are placed at intervals and a perambulation is made every year'.[26] In the larger boroughs, the commissioners relied on maps and resorted to partial perambulation – as was the case in Colchester, which consisted of sixteen parishes and had a 68.8-mile perimeter.[27] In this instance Drummond proposed that the commissioners and their surveyors build a composite boundary based on the individual parish boundaries of Colchester detailed in Greenwood's county plan of Essex.[28]

In twenty-nine boroughs the commissioners discovered that there were either local disputes over parliamentary boundaries, or that the limits of a constituency were unknown. In a number of these cases it was eventually found that some boroughs did not possess a parliamentary boundary. At Banbury, Winchester, Leominster, Hertford and Taunton, the commissioners discovered that minor disputes had arisen during recent elections due to the development of walls or gardens that overlapped the borough's parliamentary boundaries.[29] Aside from the extra time expended in recording these disputes, they had little impact on the commissioners' decision-making process – their power to propose future boundaries, including what they regarded as the modern limits of the town, allowed them to circumvent such disagreements. At Plymouth, Weymouth, Cirencester, Andover, Canterbury, Sandwich and Lincoln issues arose as to whether geographically anomalous areas of local government formed part of the parliamentary borough. After consulting with the town clerk, the assessor of the taxes, the overseers of the poor and a local surveyor in Andover, for instance, the commissioners discovered that two areas contained within the parish limits existed under distinct corporate jurisdictions. In order to remove confusion over the borough's boundaries, Drummond and the commissioners agreed to move forward on the basis that the entire geographical area contained within the parish of Andover had to be included within the constituency's future limits.[30] In seven cases the commissioners were unable to discover any officially recorded confirmation of a constituency boundary. The commissioners reported that they could not rely on the information of local officials in Bridgwater, Honiton and the City of London.[31] And in Ashburton, Lyme Regis, York and Westbury, the commissioners discovered that due to poor record keeping and a lack of recent perambulation the parliamentary boundary had been erased from local collective memory.[32]

In the remaining ten cases the commissioners were unable to define a borough's existing boundary because its ancient franchise had never required fixed geographical limits. Durham was found to possess a unique elastic boundary. Local custom granted all apprentices in the borough the freedom of the city (and thus the franchise) if they served their master 'in the suburbs of the city, as well as in the city itself'. This meant that the parliamentary boundary of Durham had expanded as new streets and houses were added to the city.[33] The remaining nine boroughs found not to possess a boundary (Truro, Liskeard, Ludlow, East Grinstead, Ripon, Thirsk, Northallerton, Richmond and Wells) were all burgage boroughs, where voting rights had been granted to tenants of specific burgage tenure properties that had historically provided certain services to the monarch.[34] In these cases the experience of commissioners Drinkwater and Saunders in East Grinstead, which had originally stood in Schedule B but was later disfranchised completely, was broadly representative. The commissioners consulted the parish officers, the current and historic bailiffs and 'the agent for the noblemen, to whom the town chiefly belong[ed]'. To their disbelief, they discovered that each person 'agreed in disclaiming all knowledge of any line round the borough'.[35] This confusion had resulted from the fact that the parliamentary borough of East Grinstead had always been defined by its thirty-two burgage tenure properties, rather than a boundary. Given the political reputation of burgage boroughs, the commissioners had originally viewed the information provided by their officials with suspicion. But, after being informed by Drummond that several similar cases had been discovered, their evidence was accepted. In these ten cases, and the seven where the borough's boundary was unknown, the commissioners used their discretion to define the town's existing geographical extent.

Collecting £10 householder data

After collecting the requisite boundary data, the commissioners were required to identify how many potential £10 householders lived within a borough's existing limits. As with boundaries, the commissioners were afforded a preliminary indication of these figures by a parliamentary return. This was the parliamentary return detailing the £10, £20 and £40 houses assessed to the inhabited house duty in each existing borough (discussed in Chapter 2), which had forced the government to raise their proposed borough franchise to £10 in February 1831.[36] The return proved a flawed dataset, however, as houses worth £10 throughout England were frequently assessed and exempted from paying the inhabited house duty by being rated below £10. Commissioner Tallents suggested to Drummond that if the assessed tax return recorded 300 £10 householders within a borough it was 'a pretty sure sign that there were twice the number of £10 houses'.[37] Furthermore, the boundary information already gathered by the commissioners had confirmed that the geographical areas referred to in the February 1831 return could not be relied on to correspond with parliamentary boroughs of the same name. For these reasons, Drummond reprimanded any team of commissioners who relied solely on these figures in their reports.[38]

As with boundaries, specific data relating to £10 householders had to be collected from local officials. The primary means of doing this was through interviews with overseers of the poor. Although the poor law system was implemented in a heavily localised manner, every parish in the country could be relied on to levy a poor rate based on some form of locally agreed property valuation and maintain records relating to the value of each property within their jurisdiction. This meant that when a parliamentary boundary was found to include only parts of a parish, the commissioners could request returns specific to the parliamentary borough. Most parishes assessed their houses at a proportion of their actual value and then collected a percentage of this annual value from each householder, which constituted the poor rate. In a few cases, parishes based their rates on regular revaluations. In South Lynn (which formed part of King's Lynn) a committee of fifteen examined the poor rates every three months. Property was recorded at one-third of its actual value, which meant that all houses assessed at £2 10s. 9d. in the rate books had an actual annual rental value of £10.[39] In the majority of England's parishes, however, such as the three contained in Evesham (St Lawrence, All Saints, and St. Peter's), parish rates were based on outdated valuations that had to be adjusted by local officials. All houses in Evesham were recorded in the poor rate books at seven-tenths of their 1811 value (a house with an annual value of £10 in 1811 was still recorded at £7 in 1831). Despite only 201 houses being recorded at £7 in the rate books, the overseers of Evesham's three separate parishes advised the commissioners that, according to contemporary valuations, 318 houses within the borough had an annual value of £10.[40]

Over time the commissioners developed strategies for either verifying or increasing the reliability of returns provided by parish officials. If available, local records of assessed taxes broken down by individual householder could be consulted in the same manner as the poor rate returns. Some boroughs had also been granted powers under permissive legislation to levy paving, watch and lighting rates for municipal purposes. The local collectors of these taxes had been required to make their own valuation of property, and as most Paving, Watching and Lighting Acts had been passed during the 1820s these valuations were relatively up to date. Evesham and Arundel were cases in point, and in both boroughs this data was used to verify the overseers' estimates of £10 householders.[41]

The interview process was also used as a means of verifying information. Commissioners Tancred and Wrottesley described their method for consulting overseers and their rate books:

> We have always recommended the parish officers to make their estimates such, that, if hereafter called upon they could verify them upon oath; and we have required them to sign certificates of the numbers of houses and of houses with land attached; and this has been done by

them openly, and usually in the presence of the churchwardens and overseers of the other parishes interested.[42]

If the threat of being questioned by a neighbouring official was not sufficient, the commissioners could personally inspect houses, or consult with local inhabitants regarding the houses that parish officials had reported stood on the margin of being worth £10 a year. This was the case in Calne where Ansley and Gawler (along with their surveyors) personally inspected each household reported to be of £10 value, before ensuring that their lists were 'confirmed by other inhabitants of the parish'.[43]

During the first few weeks of the commission, the extent to which the commissioners were required to verify data relating to £10 householders was dictated by an ancient borough's proximity to the 300 £10 householder threshold. If it was clear that a borough contained over 300 £10 householders, the commissioners moved straight on to the task of identifying a future parliamentary boundary that encompassed the modern town.[44] Following the rejection of the second reform bill on 7 October 1831, the commissioners were placed under increasing pressure by Drummond, at the behest of the government, to obtain precise data relating to £10 householders in these boroughs.[45] In reply to his initial report on Hull (which contained 2,136 houses assessed to the house duty at £10) Drummond informed Tancred on 13 October that it was:

> much regretted that you have not entered into the question of the number of qualifying houses ... the present enquiry furnishes the only means of obtaining this information for towns as they are recommended to be now defined ... [this] has now become essential.[46]

Sixty of the 145 ancient boroughs (Table 4.3) were found to contain over 500 £10 householders, and by October 1831 a more thorough approach to valuing houses within these boroughs was expected by Drummond.

In the remaining eighty-five boroughs more initial care had been taken to ensure parish returns were accurate. This was because the number of £10 householders contained within the existing borough determined the extent to which it would have to be extended into its neighbouring towns or parishes. In these cases, Drummond was aware that £10 householder data formed the basis of potentially controversial boundary proposals and was

Table 4.3: £10 householders in boroughs due to retain franchise in second reform bill.[1]

£10 Householders within ancient boroughs	Number of boroughs
0–99	7
100–299	43
300–499	35
500–999	25
Over 1000	35

[1] Compiled from PP1831–2 (141), xxxviii–xli and T72.

scrupulous in demanding the commissioners' figures could withstand future parliamentary scrutiny. He was also wary that local officials might embellish data to prevent the increase of a borough's boundary. From the outset, in these boroughs the commissioners were instructed to cross-reference £10 householder data from as many sources as possible, data that Drummond reviewed closely. If Drummond was not satisfied with the commissioners' initial reports, he requested that they either correspond with local officials, or complete additional visits to a borough to verify their information.

In several cases (Horsham, Christchurch, Shaftesbury, Malmesbury, Tavistock, Calne, Tamworth and Northallerton) the commissioners, or Drummond, suspected deception by local officials. However, it was usually found that incompetence rather than malicious intent was the cause of misinformation.[47] In Malmesbury, for instance, an illiterate alderman was found to be the cause of a suspicious parish return.[48] When clear discrepancies in £10 householder data did arise Drummond usually laid the blame on the commissioners. After receiving a report that contained a range of estimates as to the number of £10 householders in Northallerton, Drummond cautioned Tancred:

> Amidst conflicting statements, amidst returns irreconcilable with each other and inconsistent with those from other places, if the government cannot rely with implicit confidence on the numbers given by the commissioners, upon whom can they depend?[49]

In November 1831 the government requested that the commission gather additional data to redesign the disfranchisement schedules. This provided Drummond with another opportunity to enforce diligence in boroughs that either stood close to the 300 £10 householder mark, or had been on the cusp of disfranchisement or partial disfranchisement in the first two reform bills.[50] He also used the authority of the sitting committee of the commission, which from late October 1831 commenced a review of every borough report ahead of its publication, to request that where initial £10 household data was still unsatisfactory it was rechecked.[51]

Drummond's insistence that the commissioners personally cross-referenced multiple data sources had the positive effect of suggesting to officials in factious parliamentary boroughs that information had been gathered impartially. Importantly, this helped to ensure the commissioners' visits, in general, sparked little local controversy. The consequence of not maintaining a judicious approach was underlined when commissioner Ansley visited Wallingford in late November 1831. Ansley outsourced his data collection to a local solicitor, who, it transpired was the election agent for both of the borough's Whig MPs.[52] When the local Tory corporation discovered Ansley had not consulted them, they immediately aired their grievances with Westminster, questioning the authenticity of the boundary and £10 householder information provided to the commission.[53] These complaints found their way from the cabinet to Drummond and the sitting committee, who reprimanded Ansley and demanded he return to the borough to gather additional data.[54] Fortunately for the commissioners, Ansley's experience in Wallingford was an exception. That similar disputes had not flared elsewhere revealed that Drummond's diligence since August had paid dividends in terms of presenting the work of the commission in an independent, impartial light. In general, the commissioners tended to meet Drummond's requirements. In doing so they discovered that local officials across England were, on the whole, compliant with their requests for reliable data.

The £10 householder in the new boroughs

The commissioners' visits to the new boroughs provided the government with the opportunity to gain clarity over one of the most contentious aspects of its reform legislation – the £10 householder franchise. While the government had hoped the £10 franchise would enfranchise the respectable and intelligent portion of the political nation, since March 1831 anti-reformers had warned of its democratic tendencies, advanced reformers had argued it was not radical enough and politicians from across the spectrum had repeatedly identified pitfalls in the legal phrasing of the qualification.[55] As the commissioners travelled from borough to borough, their reports revealed a wide discrepancy in who was likely to qualify for a vote in the new boroughs. Commissioners Ord and Chapman, for instance, were taken aback by how few householders were likely to qualify for a vote in the west midlands. They found that Kidderminster's population of 16,000 was unlikely to return more than 500 voters due to the 'unusually large proportion of the labouring class amongst the other inhabitants'.[56] The likely enfranchisement rate was even lower in Stoke-on-Trent, whose population of 53,000 was predicted to return an electorate of around 1,500. This was not due to a scarcity of respectable voters. Rather, the commissioners discovered that an abundance of space, and the ready availability of inexpensive materials for house building, had led to very low property valuations in the locality. As a result, they reported that the 'respectable ... small capitalists' of Stoke 'such as retail tradesmen, workmen in possession of some stocks or machinery and employing apprentices, or clerks, foreman, [and] overseers', who generally met the £10 franchise requirements elsewhere in England, were unlikely to qualify to vote.[57] Even fewer 'small capitalists' were found to qualify for a £10 vote in Blackburn, where the commissioners discovered that 2.3 per cent of the population (or 9.75 per cent of adult males) occupied houses worth £10 per annum.[58] According to the commissioners' predictions, Blackburn had the lowest ratio of population to £10 electors of all the new boroughs, whereas the London borough of Finsbury, at 18.64 per cent (or 79.01 per cent of the adult male population) had the highest. For the majority of new boroughs this figure fell within a range of 3.5–6 per cent (or 15–25 per cent of the adult male population).[59]

The government was also aware that it was not just the annual rental value of a house, but the manner in which a tenant paid his rent that would determine his ability to vote. This had led to extensive, and often highly confused, parliamentary debate over the £10 franchise since March 1831, particularly over the issues of how long prospective £10 voters needed to have been resident, how frequently they were required to pay rent, the valuation system that was to be used to identify £10 houses and whether tenants should qualify if they 'compounded' (i.e. their landlords assumed responsibility for paying their rates).[60] The final draft of the second reform bill that was rejected by the Lords in October 1831 had stipulated that all male householders whose house had an annual rental value of £10 according to the house duty, poor rate or landlord rental would qualify, so long as they had paid their rent and rates for an entire year, not received any parochial relief in the previous year and did not compound their rates.[61]

The commission provided the government with the opportunity to clarify who it was that these clauses would include within, and exclude from, the £10 franchise. Following the October 1831 rejection of the second reform bill, and due to the success of the commission's data-gathering efforts thus far, the cabinet requested that Drummond organise an extensive survey of rental practice in Manchester, Salford, London and the existing borough of Liverpool. In Manchester, commissioner Romilly submitted questionnaires to parish overseers in every township in his proposed borough boundary. He inquired as to the type of families that were exempt from the payment of rates, the usual length of residence for tenants that paid rates and those who did not, and the extent to which landlords compounded with tenants.[62]

Romilly discovered that those exempt from the payment of rates in the more industrial areas of Manchester had generally been exempted on account of 'age, disease and accident', whereas those in the more agricultural areas, consisting of 'principally hand loom weavers', were exempt on account of unemployment. He reported that across the 'Lancashire manufacturing districts' tenants who paid their rent weekly were usually factory operatives whose landlord was their employer, and who also paid their rates. These tenants, who 'seem to move about very much' dependent on 'fluctuations in trade', generally lived in a house divided into two flats, with two families paying separate rents to the same landlord. This meant that the annual rental value of houses with a weekly rental charge was almost double that of a similar sized house with a tenant who paid his rent annually, occupied the entire house and paid his own rates. Romilly provided Drummond with the following example:

> [two] tenants [each] paid 7s 6p a week which amounts to 18l 18s per annum: while I saw many houses near which seemed to me to be as good, where the [single] tenant paid between 10l 7s and 11l per annum.

While both houses were worth £10 a year, only the property with a single tenant was likely to qualify for a vote. Neither tenant in the house which had an annual rental income for the landlord of almost £20 would qualify, because the rates were paid by the landlord.

In London, commissioner Drinkwater discovered that tenants who lived in houses of up to £20 rental value generally compounded their rates with their landlord (aside from in St. Giles in the Field and St. George's, Bloomsbury where houses of up to £30 annual value usually compounded). These tenants had the right to demand to pay their own rates if they wanted to, but for most it was financially beneficial to compound.[63] Returns obtained from the three parishes that were proposed to be included in Marylebone suggested that tenants in up to 22.5 per cent of the borough's 24,236 £10 houses did not pay their own rates, and in the parish of St. Luke in Finsbury this figure was 40 per cent.[64] Even before a tenant's record of rental and rate payment was taken into account, as well as the question of whether he had been in receipt of parochial relief, the £10 franchise requirements, as they stood, were likely to prevent the enfranchisement of a significant number of householders whose annual rent was £10.

The cabinet was informed of these reports prior to the introduction of their third reform bill, leading to the simplification of their proposed £10 householder clause (which now made it necessary that householders rated to the poor rate, who lived in a house 'of clear yearly value' were entitled to be considered for the franchise). However, the government did not alter the provision requiring compound householders to 'demand to be rated' in order that they could be registered to vote.[65] They also showed no inclination to lower the franchise in new boroughs, such as Blackburn or Stoke, to account for the lower house valuations discovered by the commissioners.[66] In fact, when discussing the reform bill in April 1832, Earl Grey revelled in informing the Lords that the commission had confirmed anti-reformers' democratic prognostications over the £10 franchise to be a 'fallacy'.[67] He suggested that the low numbers of £10 houses discovered by the commissioners, combined with female householders, non-resident electors, those claiming relief, tardy ratepayers, compounders and the registration fee, would reduce the commissioners' £10 predictions by at least 25 per cent.

This assessment proved remarkably accurate. In the new boroughs in 1832 on average 63.74 per cent of the £10 householders counted by the commissioners found their way on to the electoral register. This figure had risen to 78.78 per cent by 1836, which as Salmon has demonstrated was the most efficient annual registration year in the immediate aftermath of reform.[68] A lack of ancient franchise rights, and the large number of midland and northern boroughs enfranchised in 1832 (31 of 42), meant the new boroughs, as a group, had the lowest enfranchisement rates in England (Table 4.4). At the 1832 election on average, around 13.3 per cent of adult males qualified to vote in the new boroughs. This figure had increased to 16.8 per cent by the 1865 election. These figures mask considerable regional variations caused by house valuations. In 1832 a maximum of only 7.3 per cent (around one in fourteen) adult males qualified to vote in Halifax, while 30.6 per cent (over one in four) qualified to vote in Finsbury. On average between 1832 and 1865 around 20 per cent of adult males were enfranchised in new boroughs in the south-east, 17 per cent in the south-west and between 12 and 13 per cent in the north and the midlands. The average maximum rate of adult male enfranchisement in the new boroughs between 1832 and 1865 was around 15 per cent, the equivalent figure for boroughs with an ancient restrictive franchise was around 20 per cent, and for those with a popular franchise it was around 30 per cent. However, the latter figure, which masked a decline from around 35 per cent to 25 per cent between 1832 and 1865 needs to be understood as a maximum possible rate due to the prevalence of non-resident voters.

Drummond's list

The efficiency of the boundary commission during the autumn of 1831 prompted one final extension of its data-gathering responsibilities. In November the government held secret negotiations with a number of Tory peers, known as 'the Waverers', to secure their support for their reform legislation. While the cabinet refused the Waverers' request to send the commissioners back to every borough to 'hear whether any well-founded objections' existed to their boundary proposals, they did offer to reconsider the controversial use of census data as the basis for disfranchisement.[69] On 15 November, Grey, Althorp and Russell met Drummond to discuss the feasibility of compiling accurate tax and household data for every borough

Table 4.4: Average maximum adult male enfranchisement levels per category of borough franchise 1832–65.[1]

	Oct-32 %	Oct-34 %	Oct-36 %	Oct-40 %	Oct-46 %	Oct-51 %	Oct-56 %	Oct-58 %	Oct-64 %
New Boroughs (£10)	13.30	13.02	14.84	15.05	14.54	14.87	15.19	15.65	16.78
Burgage	20.00	20.56	21.63	22.41	21.37	20.81	22.12	22.82	24.49
Corporation	19.93	21.21	21.87	22.55	21.12	20.40	20.04	20.88	21.12
Freeholder	23.95	24.32	24.87	25.48	21.53	21.40	21.03	21.77	22.77
Freeman	33.10	33.00	34.24	34.46	31.70	29.39	27.76	27.86	27.28
Householder	55.29	44.95	41.36	37.09	30.75	25.99	23.50	25.12	24.48
Scot and Lot	38.32	34.26	33.60	32.29	28.22	25.69	23.87	23.83	23.25
All English Boroughs	27.45	26.68	27.55	27.52	25.16	23.67	22.82	23.14	23.25

[1] For sources see Introduction.

scheduled to be fully disfranchised, partially disfranchised, or that had stood on the margins of disfranchisement in the first two versions of the government's reform bill.[70] Nine days later, on 24 November, the government issued Drummond with a formal instruction, requesting that he collect this data for all ninety-seven boroughs then in Schedules A and B, as well as 'the ten or fifteen immediately above them in size and importance'.[71] Drummond assumed the upper limit of the government's formal request, and made immediate preparations to collect data for the 112 double-member boroughs with the lowest population according to the 1831 census.[72]

The government also requested that Drummond 'make a scale' ranking each of these boroughs in order of their 'relative importance'.[73] Instead of just adding or multiplying together the number of houses and assessed taxes paid by each borough and compiling a list, Drummond developed a scaling method intended to afford 'equal weight' to the number of houses in, and the amount of assessed taxes (the house and window taxes) paid by, the modern town settlement of England's smallest boroughs.[74] His method proposed to provide a score for each borough, by dividing the amount of assessed taxes paid by a borough against the total number of assessed taxes paid by every borough in the list, and likewise for the number of houses. These two figures were then to be added to each other for each borough and multiplied by

1,000 to give every borough a non-fractional ranking score.[75] For a mathematician like Drummond, developing this scaling method was easy. The 'arduous part' of his new responsibilities he complained, 'consisted in obtaining correct data' that would allow him to redesign the reform bill's disfranchisement schedules with 'certainty and with justice'.[76]

Much to Drummond's despair, the government proposed to announce these new disfranchisement schedules on 12 December, giving the commission three weeks to gather the requisite data. Even with his experience overseeing the commission's operations thus far, this was a tall order. In the knowledge of his probable new responsibilities, on 21 November Drummond requested 'as many surveyors as could be spared' from the board of ordnance to help with compiling new reports.[77] On 24 November he issued an urgent circular to every boundary commissioner still at work in the vicinity of boroughs that 'bordered upon partial or total disfranchisement'. He asked that they replicate his 'scientific' framework for defining a borough's modern town settlement (see Chapter 5), before clarifying the tax and household data relative to this area.[78] On the same day he issued a questionnaire to every returning officer in every borough selected for the list.[79] The questionnaire asked officers whether the town associated with their borough had outgrown its parliamentary boundary, how many houses associated with the town were outside and inside its boundary, and the amount of assessed taxes paid by these houses. As with existing and new boroughs, Drummond's team of surveyors at the council office prepared tracings of town plans from ordnance survey or privately available maps for twenty-four Schedule A boroughs (boroughs to be fully disfranchised) with the highest number of houses and tax receipts in order that the replies to Drummond's questionnaire could be verified on the spot. As time and resources were thin, Drummond made the decision not to send commissioners to the thirty-two Schedule A boroughs with the lowest population, as it was felt that even slight discrepancies in their data would do little to save them from disfranchisement.[80] In addition, tracings of town plans were submitted to the commissioners, who ultimately re-visited a further forty-one Schedule B boroughs (boroughs to be partially disfranchised) and fifteen boroughs on the margins of partial disfranchisement.[81]

The Schedule A borough of Plympton Earle (Map 4.1) in Devon is illustrative of how complex this process proved. The local returning officers' questionnaire was received in London in late November. It stated there were 313 houses in the modern town of Plympton Earle, paying £485 4s. 3d. in annual assessed taxes. On visiting the borough in early December, commissioners Birch and Dawson reported that the returning officers had overstated the extent of the modern town by including the adjoining

DATA-GATHERING FOR THE BOUNDARY COMMISSION   131

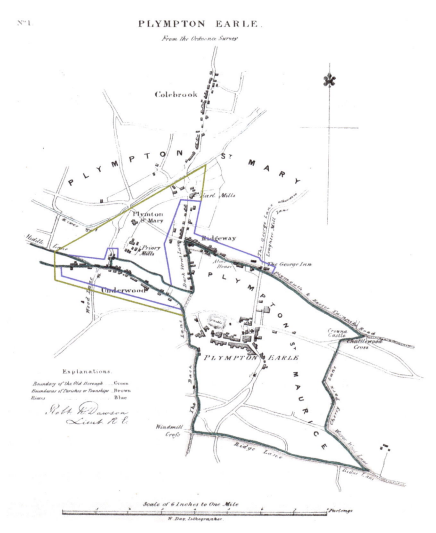

Map 4.1: Three definitions of the modern town of Plympton Earle, PP1831–2 (20), xxxvii © National Library of Scotland; digital additions by author.
Key: Existing boundary used by commission (green line). Boundary including Ridgeway and Underwood, ranking Plympton 55 in Drummond's List (blue line) [digital addition]; Rendel's original definition, ranking Plympton 60 on Drummond's list, disfranchising Petersfield (yellow line) [digital addition].

villages of Ridgeway, Underwood and Colebrook. The commissioners discovered a detailed map of the borough's boundaries, signed by a 'numerous body of persons' at the previous perambulation of the constituency in July 1817, which they contended included everything that could be considered the modern settlement of Plympton Earle. While several houses in the villages of Ridgeway and Underwood had been built within the limits of Plympton Earle's parliamentary boundary, the commissioners contended that both were distinct villages 'not to be considered part of the town'. While the commissioners were required to count those houses within the borough's boundary, they refused to extend the definition of Plympton's modern town to include any part of Ridgeway and Underwood that did not form 'continuous portions of streets' with Plympton's central town settlement.[82] Their definition of Plympton's modern town (which consisted of every house within the borough's ancient boundary) contained 182 houses worth £322 10s. 10d. in annual assessed taxes.

For Drummond the case was not as clear-cut. His concern was that as over time the villages of Ridgeway and Underwood had crossed into Plympton's parliamentary boundary, an equally valid case could be made that they formed part of the 'modern town'. To provide parliament with the ability to make a final decision, the commission contacted a local Plymouth surveyor, James Meadows Rendel. On 6 December Rendel was asked to complete an additional survey of Ridgeway, Underwood and Colebrook. On 10 December, two days before the government intended to introduce its third reform bill, Rendel submitted his report. With time being of the essence Rendel advised the commission that his survey had been hampered by the death of a local official. He recorded that he had:

> laid down all additional houses, and corrected those that were wrong in the [original map] sketch. I have also crossed out such roads as are now stopped up, adding the new ones. We have had more difficulty than usual in this enquiry, from the circumstances of the parish officer having died the day I received your letter.

Rendel eventually obtained the data from another official, and after consulting local tax records confirmed that if Plympton Earle's 'modern town' was assumed to include Ridgeway, Underwood, Earl Mills, Plympton St. Mary and Priory Mills it would lead to an additional 158 houses assessed at £178 4s. 8d.[83]

Given that it took twenty-four hours of continuous travel for the mail coach to deliver a letter from Plymouth to London, it is likely that Rendel's report was one of nine that reached London on the morning of 12 December. Later that evening the government introduced the third version of its reform bill containing Drummond's revised disfranchisement schedules. The introduction of the bill was delayed by 45 minutes, while Drummond and his clerks recalculated which boroughs were to be disfranchised at the privy council office. The Staffordshire MP, Edward Littleton, who had been supporting Drummond, recorded the bureaucratic frenzy in his diary:

Lord John Russell introduced his reform bill for the third time this year. He was to have begun at 5 o' clock, and the house waited for him, from that hour till 1/4 before 6 – some of the opposition began to laugh, to cry adjourn. They little suspected the real cause of Lord John's absence, which was that he had not been able to settle which of the boroughs should be placed in the [disfranchisement] schedules – nine reports respecting as many different places came to town only this morning, and their contents altered the relative position of so many places on the list or scale that was made – in which each place [is] marked by a figure representing its exact importance – that it was all but impossible to complete the calculation in time for the debate.[84]

Ultimately, Drummond decided to use the commissioners' initial house and tax figures to identify Plympton Earle's placement in his scale.[85] Given the last-minute nature of the data he was concerned that Rendel's new definition of Plympton Earle had been too liberal, as no parts of Priory Mills, Earl Mills or Plympton St. Mary had spilt over into the borough's existing boundary. Furthermore, while it was clearly one of the most borderline cases, Rendel's last-minute definition of Plympton Earle was inconsistent with those of Brackley, Buckingham, Evesham, Eye, Huntingdon, Leominster, Lostwithiel, Malmesbury, Midhurst, Newton (Lancashire), Pontefract, Wallingford, Wareham and Wilton where nearby villages close to an existing boundary had not been taken into the 'modern town' simply as a matter of course.

With his figures for the 12 December draft of the reform bill agreed, Drummond placed Plympton Earle in his scale by dividing 182 (the number of houses in the borough) by the average number of houses for all boroughs in the list, which was 452. This gave a figure of 0.4027. He then divided 322 (the amount of assessed taxes paid by the borough) by the average amount of assessed taxes paid by all boroughs in the list, which was 545. This gave a figure of 0.5908. He added both of those figures together (0.9935) and multiplied the total by 1,000. This gave Plympton Earle a ranking number of 993, which placed it at number 40 in his list.[86] If Rendel's last-minute figures for Plympton had been used, the borough would have been ranked at number 60, placing it in Schedule B and relegating Petersfield to Schedule A. This made it even more important that Plympton's 'modern town' was defined as accurately as possible. In the knowledge that the 12 December version of the list would not be final, Drummond requested that Rendel provide a further assessment of the borough's houses and taxes that excluded Plympton St. Mary, Earl Mills and Priory Mills, in order that the Commons could be given as many options as possible if they were required to make a final decision as to what constituted the borough's 'modern town'.[87]

Ultimately, all boroughs placed either 56 or below in Drummond's list – which included Plympton Earle – were marked for total disfranchisement. All boroughs between 57 and 86 were scheduled to be partially disfranchised and return one MP. Drummond's list and the reduction in Schedule B from forty-one to thirty boroughs in the third reform bill, transferred five boroughs from Schedule B to A; five from Schedule A to B; placed seven boroughs in Schedule B that had not previously been scheduled to lose any seats; and spared eighteen boroughs from partial disfranchisement.[88]

The response to Drummond's list

When Russell announced Drummond's list on 12 December Peel and John Croker welcomed the government's concession that census data was unsuitable for settling the question of disfranchisement. However, these supportive opposition comments proved short-lived. After repeated requests from Croker in the days that followed, the initial data, workings and rationale for Drummond's list were published on 17 December.[89] This opened several new avenues of complaint for anti-reformers, who over the next two months developed an increasingly wide-ranging, if at times specious, critique of the methods and data behind Drummond's list. Drummond's method for ranking the boroughs was the first aspect to come under fire. Croker claimed in the Commons that simply adding together the number of houses and amount of assessed taxes for each borough offered a simpler and more effective way of ranking England's smallest boroughs. His complaint was supported by the Tory *Morning Post* but immediately dismissed by Russell who suggested that 'no schoolmaster of any science' would accept Croker's method.[90] *The Times* agreed with Russell, considering Drummond's formula 'true in principle, and therefore just in application'.[91] Drummond, who from a mathematical point of view had assumed his methods would be accepted, was taken aback. After watching Croker dismiss his methods in the Commons, Drummond rode straight to Woolwich to meet his former mathematics master at the royal military academy, Peter Barlow, who offered his 'authoritative approval' to his methods prior to parliament breaking up for Christmas.[92]

During the recess the pro-reform *Courier* surprised the government and the commissioners by publishing a letter in support of Croker's alternative method.[93] This prompted the boundary commissioner, Francis Beaufort, to contact the Cambridge mathematician (and his and Drummond's friend), John Herschel, asking for his views on Drummond's methods 'purely as a mathematical question'. Beaufort advised Herschel that his response would be used to inform peers and MPs over the merits of Drummond's methods as 'ninety-nine out of every hundred of its [parliament's] members have no means of deciding such a question'.[94] Herschel approved of Drummond's 'rules of computation' but raised issue with the decision to only rank 110 boroughs, instead of every English borough, as well as the exclusion of Welsh boroughs. As the list was for boroughs susceptible to total and partial disfranchisement, it only included double-member boroughs, which was why Welsh boroughs (which all returned a single member) had been excluded.[95] The decision to only rank 110 boroughs had been made partly due to time constraints, and partly because Drummond had estimated that the house and tax data already collected for every other borough as part of the commission's primary work would place them 'beyond the limits of the schedules [A & B]'.[96]

Herschel conceded the final point, stating that even if every borough was placed in Drummond's list it would require house and tax data containing 'violently improbable suppositions' to alter the order of those close to the disfranchisement schedules. Herschel also proposed that the government redraft their request to Drummond in more mathematically accurate terms. He stated that Drummond's method was the most accurate means of identifying:

> the relative importance of a borough – weighted to the houses which it contains and to the assessed taxes which it pays, proportional to their respective numbers – and such that the whole weight of all the houses shall be equal to the whole weight of all the taxes in the mass of boroughs considered.

On this basis, Herschel admitted that 'every algebraist will at once admit' to 'conclusions identical with those which follow from Lieutenant Drummond's rules'.[97] In addition, the government approached the Cambridge mathematician and astronomer George Biddell Airy, who rejected any alternative method that used simple addition or multiplication and accepted that Drummond's 'method alone, or one equivalent to it, is the only one that can be used'.[98] The chair of mathematics at Edinburgh University, William Wallace, also endorsed Drummond's formula, stating that if houses and taxes were to be considered of equal importance, 'so simple a question' could be answered in 'no other way'.[99]

When parliament resumed on 17 January anti-reformers continued to question Drummond's formula, but also started to challenge the data underpinning his list. The government had previously offered MPs private assurances that '400 sets of explanatory documents' of maps and reports for each borough in Drummond's list would be published by 26 December.[100]

By mid-January these reports had still not appeared, prompting Croker to demand that debate on the entire reform bill be postponed until all documentary evidence relating to Drummond's list was published.[101] Opposition MPs were given further cause to question the commission's data when a revised version of Drummond's list was published on 20 January, the day the government proposed to go into committee on the reform bill. This new document contained revised house and tax data for several boroughs whose returns had been incomplete when the government initially announced Drummond's list. It also contained an explanation of the data sources used in each borough, that Drummond hoped would help parliamentarians 'account for certain differences in the returns received from different authorities'.[102] Much to the opposition's surprise, the document directed readers at several points to the still unpublished '[boundary] commissioners' report'.[103]

Although Drummond's revised list led to no changes in the proposed disfranchisement schedules, the government's acknowledgement that its original list had been based on tentative data, and its apparent unwillingness to publish the commission's reports caused Peel to accuse the cabinet of seeking to effect constitutional reform via 'blind and hurried legislation' and Croker to accuse the ministry of a 'premeditated design to delude, perplex, and insult the house [of Commons]'. It was not just anti-reformers complaining about a lack of information. The radical MP for Preston, Henry Hunt, called it a matter of 'common decency' that the commission's reports were published prior to debate progressing any further. Although Croker failed to delay discussion on the entire reform bill, the lack of published data caused the government to postpone the committee debate on whether Schedules A and B had been 'properly made' until the full report on Drummond's list had been published.[104]

The first copies of the report began publication on 10 February 1832. The report included the returning officers' questionnaire for every borough, and a commissioners' report and map for sixty-eight boroughs where questions had arisen surrounding house and tax data.[105] In the interim, editorials and pamphleteers continued to offer their opinion on Drummond's methods. The *Scotsman* deemed Drummond's list 'perfectly fair and unobjectionable', mocking Croker for failing to grasp a problem of 'common arithmetic, which every boy can solve' and defending Drummond's reputation as a 'man of science' and a 'mathematician of no mean rank' who was 'equally skilled in surveying and calculating'.[106] The anonymous mathematician, 'Spoon', of Sidney Sussex College, Cambridge, called for a 'stop to the nonsense which is nightly uttered in a certain assembly whenever the principle of Mr Drummond's list of boroughs is alluded to', and the pro-reform *Globe* and *Sun* confirmed their support for Drummond's methods.[107]

By contrast, the anti-reform *Standard* and *St James's Chronicle* railed against Drummond's 'abstruse algebraic calculus', and an anonymous pamphlet on the *Classification of Boroughs to Lord John Russell* published on 9 February complained that by giving equal weight to houses and taxes Drummond's formula unfairly rewarded boroughs whose wealth was distributed widely among a large population, over more deserving boroughs where the same amount of wealth was distributed among fewer, more respectable inhabitants.[108] Following the lead of this pamphlet, a Hackney lawyer and amateur mathematician, Dr Eneas McIntyre, proposed an alternative method that entailed dividing the product of a borough's houses and assessed taxes by the total number of houses and assessed taxes in the list. Doing so would have saved Amersham from complete disfranchisement at the expense of Westbury, and saved Helston from partial disfranchisement at the expense of Totnes.[109] This method enjoyed the support of Croker, who introduced a petition to the Commons from McIntyre complaining that Drummond's list was based on 'an erroneous principle'.[110] Having had a chance to examine the returns in full, on 20 February Croker also raised concern with inconsistencies in the tax data in Drummond's list. In some cases, he had discovered that returns omitted tax exemptions enjoyed by certain boroughs for stabling cavalry horses, and in others failed to include some boroughs' tax contributions under the game duties. The government conceded these errors and promised to recalculate Drummond's list using revised figures, but correctly assured Croker that any changes would be so minor that they would not affect the disfranchisement schedules.[111]

When the disfranchisement schedules were eventually debated in committee on 20 February, opposition to Drummond's list was led by the MP for Huntingdon and former senior wrangler at Cambridge University, Frederick Pollock. He reiterated the complaints of McIntyre, Croker and the anonymous pamphleteer, but instead proposed to recalculate Drummond's list by simply multiplying the number of assessed taxes and houses in each borough. He claimed that doing so would be consistent with how a merchant would calculate the relative value of 'a large number of bales of merchandise' by 'multiply[ing] the quantity of each bale by the price' to 'bring out their relative value'. This method was simpler than McIntyre's proposed alternative, and according to Pollock's own calculations would have saved Amersham from total disfranchisement and Helston from partial disfranchisement.[112] Pollock recommended that Schedule A be reduced to 55 boroughs, which was where the greatest 'chasm' in the scores assigned to each borough by his and Drummond's lists existed. In Drummond's list, Lostwithiel ranked 54 with a score of 1,339, Brackley ranked number 55 with a score of 1,389, Amersham ranked 56 with a score of 1,585 and Petersfield ranked 57 with a score of 1,611. According to Drummond's calculations, Pollock argued, Amersham was closer in terms of importance to Petersfield, which was to return a single MP, than Brackley, which was to be fully disfranchised.

The government dismissed Pollock's reasoning on both fronts, citing the mathematicians who had vouched for Drummond's method and insisting that the number of Schedule A boroughs had to remain at 56 as this had been accepted by the Commons during debate over the second reform bill. Pollock was further embarrassed by the Tory president of the Royal Society, Davies Gilbert, who maintained that Drummond's methods were 'perfectly correct' and the radical MP for Bridport and amateur scientist, Henry Warburton, who forced Pollock to admit that he had forgotten to apply the square root when calculating the relative scores assigned to each borough in his version of the list. Sensing that Pollock had ruined anti-reformers' chances of leading a successful division to replace Drummond's formula, Croker sought instead to delay discussion on the disfranchisement schedules by calling for every borough in England to be included in the list.

This prolonged debate appears to have bemused and baffled most MPs, one of whom complained that the Commons was 'involved in a maze of figures, which appeared to puzzle the heads of the wisest among them'.[113] For the ardent anti-reformer, Charles Wetherell, it was all too much. He interjected 'away with the mathematicians, away with speculative arguments ... let us look at the question [of disfranchisement] as members of parliament'. In doing so he reiterated the traditional Tory complaint about science and reform, discussed in the previous chapter, namely that MPs needed to dispense with their algebra and data and discuss the relative merits of each borough on a case-by-case basis as gentlemen legislators.[114] Pollock and Croker's efforts at forcing a recalculation of Drummond's list via a different method ended later that day when the Commons approved each Schedule A borough in the order assigned to them in the reform bill. Drummond who watched the debate with several other commissioners from 'under the [Commons] gallery' viewed proceedings as 'a complete triumph' and 'vindication from all the previous attacks' on his method.[115]

Once his formula had been accepted by parliament, anti-reformers turned to critiquing the data that placed individual boroughs in either schedule A or B as each was debated. MPs used a close reading of the commissioners' recently published reports to raise apparent inconsistencies in the methods by which the modern town of several boroughs had been defined, or their assessed taxes counted. Complaints were raised that the primarily anti-reform Tory boroughs of Minehead, Appleby, Plympton, Lostwithiel, Amersham, Petersfield, Helston and Dartmouth had been unfairly ascribed confined modern limits, either by erroneous assumptions about the borough's associated town settlements or its ancient boundaries. The methods in these boroughs were contrasted with those employed in the largely pro-reform Whig Schedule B boroughs of Westbury, Midhurst and Morpeth, as well as Tavistock and Ripon, which were due to escape total disfranchisement.

These boroughs, anti-reformers argued, appeared to have been afforded a more liberal treatment in terms of how their modern town had been defined or their taxes counted. In response, ministers pursued a blanket tactic of defending every proposal of the commissioners, reiterating the inherent difficulty of the task and the lengths the commission had gone to in borderline cases to verify inconsistent data, investigate the particularities of local charters and boundaries, and define a borough's modern town settlement.[116] Opposition MPs forced a vote over the cases of Appleby, Amersham, Helston and Dartmouth but the government secured comfortable majorities in every instance. Once the disfranchisement schedules had been approved in committee, Drummond's list faced little serious challenge. Significantly, in the Lords during May 1832, a motion in favour of maintaining Schedule A in its entirety by key opposition peer Lord Ellenborough distanced moderates from hard-liners, reducing considerably the chance of a successful Tory-led administration during the 'days of May'.[117] National debate about Drummond's list also quickly subsided, as what was left to discuss about the rights and wrongs of his formula played out in scientific journals rather than the national press.[118]

In the individual boroughs in which anti-reformers had complained about partisan figures, the government was justified in arguing that the commission had acted with consistency. Ministers were also justified in arguing that the commissioners had gone to considerable lengths to verify their geographic, house and tax data, which in many instances was completed via several return visits to a borough. As will be seen in the following chapters, this work ethic was thanks largely to Drummond's meticulous oversight of the commission and his efforts to ensure it adhered to his 'scientific' framework. In the borderline cases of Plympton Earle, Appleby and Midhurst, Drummond and his commissioners acknowledged the inevitability that their framework for establishing what constituted a modern town settlement still left some room for interpretation. In this knowledge they provided parliament with sufficient data to overturn their recommendations.[119]

It is evident, however, that electoral considerations influenced decision-making once discussion over the disfranchisement schedules and individual cases moved from the commission to the cabinet. As subsequent chapters discuss, this also proved to be the case with a handful of boundary proposals. The clearest case of gerrymandering with regard to the boroughs in Drummond's list was Appleby. In late May 1832 the government was close to reconsidering Appleby's case, after new tax returns and a local petition suggested there were genuine grounds to move it from Schedule A to B. Nevertheless, ministers decided against granting an extended definition of Appleby's modern town and thus saving it from disfranchisement. They did so after advice from local agents that any reformed borough (however its boundaries were defined) would probably fall into Tory hands, while also removing Whig voters from the county constituency of Westmorland. Interestingly, Appleby is one of the few boroughs for which draft reports and notes from cabinet ministers have not survived in the boundary commission's archive.[120]

Conclusion

The 1831–2 boundary commission for England and Wales was a formative Whig experiment in the collection and legislative application of local data, which had an enduring impact on the practices of the nineteenth-century British state. Given the scepticism that surrounded the commission at its commencement, its compilation of cartographic and demographic data relating to England's parliamentary boroughs between August 1831 and February 1832 was remarkable. The only occasion on which the commissioners were unable to obtain information from local officials was when they visited Bristol during the reform disturbances there in late October 1831. However, with corporation and parish officials occupied with restoring public order the commission acquired the requisite information about Bristol's boundaries and £10 householders from a local surveyor.[121] The government, it transpired, had underestimated the competence of local officials and their willingness to co-operate with the boundary commission. The receipt of conflicting statements and irreconcilable returns, as Drummond had feared, did not characterise the commissioners' experiences. And in no cases, as Macaulay had joked, did beadles resort to their whips.

If anything, the sheer volume of locally held information relating to boundaries and house valuations typified the commissioners' day-to-day operations – which was compounded by Drummond's eye for detail and the Grey ministry's increased desire for data from October 1831. Throughout, the level of co-operation experienced from the localities defied Westminster's expectations, with any difficulties tending to stem from oversights on behalf of the commissioners rather than local officials. This stood in stark contrast to the efforts of anti-corporation reformers during the 1820s, who had failed to secure the voluntary engagement of local officials when seeking similar data. Their efforts, however, had lacked official authority and targeted closed corporations, which were resistant to the idea of reforming themselves.[122] By contrast, the 1831–2 boundary commission enjoyed government backing, had the support of the public, was incredibly diligent in its approach and developed a framework for its work that sought out, but did not rely on, the co-operation of local officials. The army of commissioners and surveyors that Drummond was able to mobilise was also significant, as they represented a marked difference to anything that had come before, in terms of the resources and tactics used to interrogate England's unreformed electoral system. This entire process was prototypical of the subsequent collection and use of public health data in England throughout the nineteenth century, which Crook has observed 'empowered all kinds of agents much beyond a central core of officials' and reflected a British state whose 'statistical eyes were many and multiperspectival, gazing bottom-up as much as top-down'.[123]

The level of data collected by the commission, the national network of information sharing that it relied on and the increasing extent to which this data was used to reconstitute, and legitimise, the government's reform legislation underlines the importance of conceptualising the electoral reforms of 1832 as a 'consultation' between the centre and the localities.[124] The benefits of this consultative model were made plain during November and December 1831, when the Grey ministry took a bold step in using Drummond's data-gathering machine, and his personal mathematical expertise, to redefine its disfranchisement schedules. Until then, disfranchisement had proven one of the most controversial aspects of reform. As well as answering a year's worth of parliamentary criticism over the inaccuracy of census data, Drummond's list redefined the terms of debate over the issue. By placing disfranchisement in the hands of a supposedly disinterested bureaucrat, who had deployed mathematics and surveying to rationalise the issue, and using the secondary opinion of experts to legitimise Drummond's work, the government effectively neutralised one of the most controversial aspects of its reform bill.

Discussion was no longer about whether disfranchisement should take place, but the manner in which disfranchisement should be calculated. Drummond's response – his tireless efforts to ensure the commission gathered accurate data for every borough and his systematic attempts to verify his formula once it was questioned in parliament – revealed the extent to which he personally aspired to his principles for bureaucratic disinterestedness. The complexity of Drummond's list, the volume of data that went into it and the government's rationale for its use both impressed, and sidestepped, parliamentarians in equal measure, proving crucial to securing moderate parliamentary support for the reform bill. As discussed in the following chapters, the government's strategy of forcing MPs to approve the general principles that underpinned Drummond's list, and their relentless defence of the data that underpinned it, was replicated on a much larger scale when they sought parliamentary approval for the commission's boundary proposals.

Most significantly, the experience of the boundary commission instilled a new confidence within the Grey ministry in the potential of parliamentary investigation. In February 1832, as the boundary commission's reports were being prepared and Drummond's list was being debated, planning for a poor law commission commenced. By July that year, twenty-six assistant commissioners had been dispatched to 3,000 of England and Wales's 15,000 parishes, with the expectation that their extensive questionnaires regarding poor law administration be completed in a timely manner.[125] By 1839 this process had culminated in permanent poor law commissioners reporting on the local specifics of crime, education, sanitary conditions, the causes of epidemics and employment conditions.[126]

The poor law commission and its fellow commissions of inquiry and inspectorates of the 1830s and 1840s were built on the example set by Drummond and the boundary commission. All were supplied with reforming bureaucrats from the same networks; infused with a confidence (if not always the same rigour in application) in the merits of data collection as a basis and defence for reform; were highly ambitious in terms of what types of information they tried to extract from the localities; were characterised by strict instructions and oversight by centrally based commissioners; and were reliant on an increasing willingness among Whig legislators to place the oversight of investigation outside parliamentary control.[127] For every Joseph Parkes or Edwin Chadwick, who demonstrated how such a framework might be adapted, or provide a foil, for achieving personal or political ends, there were commissioners and assistant commissioners who ascribed to Drummond's belief in the possibility, and benefits, of aspiring to a form of bureaucratic objectivity.[128] This might be seen in the example of Drummond's 'intimate friend',[129] the diligent factory inspector Leonard Horner, or the 'dogged persistence' of a generation of assistant poor law commissioners who carefully navigated the limited terrain of their powers to effect 'a higher standard of bureaucratic efficiency'.[130] While the commissions and commissioners that followed in his stead might not all have endorsed such principles, this should not detract from the innovative nature of Drummond's bureaucratic approach, or diminish from the boundary commission's influence over the ideas and practices of the late Hanoverian and early Victorian British state.

Notes

1. G. O. Trevelyan, *The Life and Letters of Lord Macaulay* (London, 1876), 247–8.

2. *Bell's New Weekly Messenger*, 28 May 1843.

3. P. Salmon, '"Reform Should Begin at Home": English Municipal and Parliamentary Reform, 1818–32', in C. Jones, P. Salmon and R. Davis (eds.), *Partisan Politics, Principles and Reform in Parliament and the Constituencies, 1689–1880* (Edinburgh, 2004), 93–113.

4. H. Brougham, *The Life and Times of Henry Lord Brougham* (London, 1871), iii. 379.

5. J. Innes, 'Forms of "Government Growth", 1780–1830', in D. Feldman and J. Lawrence (eds.), *Structures and Transformations in Modern British History* (Cambridge, 2011), 90–92; J. Innes, 'Seeing Like a Surveyor: Imagining Rural Reform in the Early Nineteenth-Century UK', in B. Kinzer, M. Kramer and R. Trainor (eds.), *Reform and Its Complexities in Modern Britain: Essays Inspired by Sir Brian Harrison* (Oxford, 2022), 57–76.

6. M. Brock, *The Great Reform Act* (London, 1973), 265; S. J. Thompson, '"Population Combined with Wealth and Taxation": Statistics Representation and the Making of the 1832 Reform Act', in Tom Crook and Glen O'Hara (eds.), *Statistics and the Public Sphere, Numbers and the People in Modern Britain, c. 1800–2000* (New York, 2011), 205–23; B. Robson, 'Maps and Mathematics: Ranking the English boroughs for the 1832 Reform Act', *Journal of Historical Geography*, 46 (2014), 66–79; P. Salmon, 'The English Reform Legislation, 1831–32', in D. Fisher (ed.), *The House of Commons, 1820–32*, i. (Cambridge, 2009), 384–88.

7. Salmon, 'English Reform Legislation', 411.

8. D. Eastwood, '"Amplifying the Province of the Legislature": The Flow of Information and the English State in the Early Nineteenth Century', *Historical Research*, 62, 149 (1989), 276–94; P. Harling, 'The Power of Persuasion: Central Authority, Local Bureaucracy and the New Poor Law', *EHR*, 107, 422 (1992), 30–53; P. Mandler; *Aristocratic Government in the Age of Reform: Whigs and Liberals 1830–1852* (Oxford, 1990), 157–99; C. Hamlin, *Public Health and Social Justice in the Age of Chadwick* (Cambridge, 1998), 121–55.

9. *Hampshire Telegraph*, 26 Sept. 1831.

10. *Cheltenham Chronicle*, 15 Sept. 1831; *Liverpool Mercury*, 16 Sept. 1831.

11. *Birmingham Gazette*, 26 Sept. 1831.

12. *Leeds Intelligencer*, 15 Sept. 1831.

13. *John Bull*, 10 Oct. 1831.

14. *Essex Standard*, 1 Oct. 1831.

15. *Worcester Herald*, 24 Sept. 1831.

16. See Chapter 3.

17. TNA, T72/11/66, 'Winchester', Drummond to Gawler, 13 Sept. 1831; T72/10/46, 'Newport', Drummond to Ansley, 22 Sept. 1831; T72/10/63, 'Plymouth', Drummond to

Birch and Brandreth, 23 Sept. 1831; T72/10/68, 'Preston', Drummond to Allen and Romilly, 24 Sept. 1831; T72/11/72, 'Worcester', Drummond to Chapman, 24 Sept. 1831; T72/11/49, 'Wakefield', Drummond to Wrottesley, undated but before 27 Sept. 1831; T72/11/34, 'Sudbury', Drummond to Sheepshanks, 30 Sept. 1831.

18. TNA, T72/11/72, 'Worcester', Drummond to Ord and Chapman, 24 Sept. 1831.
19. TNA, T72/11/72, 'Worcester', Drummond to Ord and Chapman, Ord to Drummond, 25 Sept. 1831.
20. TNA, T72/8/52, 'Cheltenham', Drummond to Chapman, 14 Sept. 1831.
21. PP1830–31 (202), x. 9.
22. *Northampton Mercury*, 1 Oct. 1831; *Leamington Spa Courier*, 1 Oct. 1831; *Leeds Intelligencer*, 15 Sept. 1831; *The Times*, 16 Sept. 1831; *Hampshire Telegraph*, 19 Sept. 1831; *Newcastle Courant*, 1 Oct. 1831; PP1831–2 (141), xxxviii. 7.
23. Compiled from PP1831–2 (141), xxxviii–xli. and TNA, T72.
24. TNA, T72/11/41, 'Tewkesbury', Ord to Drummond, 15 Sept. 1831.
25. TNA, T72/8/41, 'Calne', Robison Wright to Lieutenant Dawson, 31 Jan. 1832.
26. TNA, T72/9/20, 'Gloucester', Ord and Chapman to Drummond, 9 Sept. 1831.
27. TNA, T72/9/31, 'Hereford', Ellis and Wylde to Drummond, 9 Sept. 1831.
28. TNA, T72/8/61, 'Colchester', Report on Colchester received before 27 Sept. 1831; T72/11/34, 'Sudbury', Drummond to Tallents, 30 Sept. 1831.
29. TNA, T72/8/15, 'Banbury', Chapman to Drummond, 23 Nov. 1831.
30. TNA, T72/8/9, 'Andover, Ansley and Gawler to Drummond, 8 Sept. 1831.
31. TNA, T72/8/33, 'Bridgewater', undated note by Littleton and Beaufort; PP1831 (141), xxxix. 141, xl. 116.
32. TNA, T72/10/20, 'Lyme Regis', and PP1831–2 (141), xxxviii, 113–14; xxxix. 141, xl. 117, 171.
33. PP1831–2 (141), xxxix. 161; T72/9/11, 'Durham', Drummond to Tancred and Wrottesley, 17 Oct. 1831.
34. C. Seymour, *Electoral Reform in England and Wales* (Oxford, 1970), 26–8.
35. TNA, T72/9/24, 'East Grinstead', Drinkwater and Saunders to Drummond, 12 Oct. 1831; T72/11/43, 'Thirsk'; T72/10/51, 'Northallerton'.
36. PP1830–31 (202), x. 9.
37. TNA, T72/10/43, 'Newark', Tallents to Drummond, 3 Nov. 1831.
38. TNA, T72/10/63, 'Plymouth', Drummond to Birch & Brandreth, 7 Nov. 1831.
39. TNA, T72/10/20, 'King's Lynn', Sheepshanks and Tallents to Drummond, 26 Dec. 1831.
40. PP1831–2 (141), xl. 133.
41. T72/8/10, 'Arundel', Drinkwater and Saunders to Drummond, 29 Sept. 1831.
42. TNA, T72/8/21, 'Beverley', Tancred to Drummond, 17 Oct. 1831.
43. TNA, T72/8/41, 'Calne', Ansley and Gawler to Drummond, 19 Nov. 1831.
44. TNA, T72/9/40, 'Kingston upon Hull', Wrottesley and Tancred to Drummond, 24 Sept. 1831.
45. TNA, T72/9/11, 'Durham', Drummond to Wrottesley and Tancred, 17 Oct. 1831.
46. TNA, T72/9/11, 'Durham', Drummond to Tancred, 13 Oct. 1831.

47. See respective TNA, T72 folders, also T72/10/21, 'Lymington', undated note by Drummond.

48. TNA, T72/10/27, 'Malmesbury', Drummond to Ansley, 14 Nov. 1831, Ansley to Drummond, 16 Nov. 1831; T72/9/38, 'Horsham', Drinkwater to Drummond, 2 Nov. 1831.

49. TNA, T72/10/51, 'Northallerton', Drummond to Tancred, undated but between 24 Oct. and 2 Nov. 1831.

50. PP1831–2 (141), xxxviii. 11.

51. TNA, T72/8/41, 'Calne', Beaufort to Ansley and Gawler, Nov. 1831; T72/11/39, 'Tavistock', map drawn 17 Sept. 1831; SRO, Hatherton, D260/M/F/5/26/7, 28 Nov. 1831, 241; PP1831–2 (141), xxxviii. 129–30.

52. TNA, T72/11/50, 'Wallingford', Ansley to Drummond, 24 Nov. 1831, 'Report', undated.

53. TNA, T72/11/50, John Joseph Allnatt to Russell, 28 Nov. 1831, Thomas Greenwood to Melbourne, 29 Nov. 1831.

54. TNA, T72/11/50, note on Wallingford by Beaufort, Littleton and Ansley.

55. Brock, *Reform Act*, 137–45; Salmon, 'English Reform Legislation', 374–81; R. W. Davis, 'Deference and Aristocracy in the Time of the Great Reform Act', *American Historical Review*, 81, 3 (1976), 532–9; N. Lopatin-Lummis, 'The 1832 Reform Act Debate: Should the Suffrage Be Based on Property or Taxpaying?', *JBS*, 46, 2 (2007), 320–45.

56. TNA, T72/9/47, 'Kidderminster', 'Report'.

57. TNA, T72/11/31, 'Stoke-upon-Trent', 'Report', undated.

58. TNA, T72/8/24, 'Blackburn', Allen to Drummond, 1 Nov. 1831.

59. Compiled from PP1831–2 (141), xxxviii–xli. and T72.

60. Salmon, 'English Reform Legislation', 374–81; P. Salmon, *Electoral Reform at Work: Local Politics and National Parties, 1832–1841* (Woodbridge, 2002) 186–8; R. Saunders, *Democracy and the Vote in British Politics, 1848–1867* (Farnham, 2011), 120, 243–58.

61. PP1831 (244), iii. 139–40.

62. TNA, T72/10/9, 'Manchester'.

63. PP1831–2 (141), xxxix. 111–12.

64. PP1831–2 (141), xxxix. 130.

65. PP1831 (244), iii. 7–8; 2 Gul. IV, c.45 (7 June 1832); *Hansard*, 3, ix. (12 Dec. 1831), 166–8.

66. Lopatin, 'Property or Taxpaying?'.

67. Hansard, 3, xii. (9 Apr. 1832), 18–22; PP1831 (68) xvi. 58–9.

68. Salmon, *Reform at Work*, 27–42.

69. BL, Add MS. 79717, 67; A. Kriegel, *The Holland House Diaries, 1831–1840* (London, 1977), 81, 445; H. Taylor (ed.), *The Reform Act, 1832: The Correspondence of the Late Earl Grey* (1867), i. 473; Brock, *Reform Act*, 260–65; Salmon, 'English Reform Legislation', 381–88; Thompson, 'Population'; S. Thompson, 'Census-Taking, Political Economy and State Formation in Britain, c. 1790–1840', PhD diss. Cambridge (2010), 206–21; Robson, 'Maps and Mathematics'; Brock, *Reform Act*, 264–65.

70. PP1831–2 (20), xxxvii. 2–5; SRO, Hatherton, D260/M/F/5/26/7, 15 Nov. 1831, 209.

71. PP1831–32 (17), xxxvi. 1.

72. Aylesbury was excluded as its boundaries had been reformed prior to 1832.

73. PP1831–32 (17), xxxvi, 1–3.

74. Hansard, 3, x. (20 Feb. 1832), 533.

75. PP1831–2 (20), xxxvii, 4; PP1831–2 (17), xxxvi, 1–3.

76. PP1831–2 (17), xxxvi, 1.

77. National Archives, War Office, 47/1555, Board of Ordnance Minute Book, 21 Nov. 1831, 10435–7; PP1831–2 (20), xxxvii, 1.

78. See TNA, T72/10/33 'Midhurst'; T72/10/35 'Minehead'; T72/10/49, Newton, Lancashire'; T72/8/43 'Camelford'.

79. PP1831 (208), xvi, 237; PP1831–2 (69), xxxvi, 205; Hansard, 3, ix. (17 Jan. 1832), 570–71.

80. PP1831–2 (19), xxxvi, 95.

81. Compiled from TNA, T72 and PP1831–2 (19) xxxvi. 95.

82. PP1831–2 (20), xxxvii, 5.

83. TNA, T72/10/64, 'Plympton Earle', Rendel to Dawson, 10 Dec. 1831, Rendel to Dawson, 11 Jan. 1832; PP1831–2 (222), xxxvi, 203.

84. SRO, Hatherton, D260/M/F/5/26/7, 12 Dec. 1831, 263.

85. PP1831–2 (19), xxxvi, 95.

86. PP1831–2 (17), xxxvi, 24; PP1831–2 (18), xxxvi, 27.

87. TNA, T72/10/64, 'Plympton Earle', Rendel to Dawson, 11 Jan. 1832; PP1831–2 (222), xxxvi, 203.

88. PP1831 (244), iii, 133; 2 Gul. IV, c.45 (7 June 1832).

89. Hansard, 3, ix. (12 Dec 1831), 178–84, (15 Dec. 1831), 257–8, (16 Dec. 1831), 392–419, (17 Dec. 1831), 429–547.

90. *Morning Advertiser*, 17 Dec. 1831; Morning Post, 17, 19 Dec. 1831.

91. *The Times*, 20 Dec. 1831.

92. J. Mclennan, *Memoir of Thomas Drummond* (Edinburgh, 1867), 148; National Library of Ireland, Larcom papers, MS. 7511, Barlow to Larcom, 17 May 1840, 31–4.

93. Mclennan, *Thomas Drummond*, 148; *Globe*, 24 Jan. 1832.

94. RSA, Herschel papers, box 3, 326, Beaufort to Herschel, 10 Jan. 1832.

95. RSA, Herschel papers, box 21, 100, Herschel to Beaufort, 12 Jan. 1832.

96. PP1831–2 (19), xxxvi, 101.

97. RSA, Herschel papers, box 21, 100, Herschel to Beaufort, 12 Jan. 1832.

98. Hansard, 3, x. (20 Feb. 1832), 555.

99. *The Philosophical Magazine* (London, 1832), xi. 218–23.

100. Hansard, 3, ix. (17 Jan. 1832), 564.

101. Hansard, 3, ix. (20 Jan. 1832), 657.

102. PP1831–2 (44), xxxvi, 185.

103. PP1831–2 (44), xxxvi, 189–6.

104. Hansard, 3, ix. (20 Jan. 1832), 657, 660, 661, 675.

105. Salmon, 'Reform Legislation', 399; *Leeds Mercury*, 11 Feb. 1832.

106. *Scotsman*, 21 Dec. 1831.

107. *Globe*, 24 Jan. 1832; *Sun*, 31 Jan. 1832.

108. Anonymous, *Two Letters to the Right Hon. Lord John Russell on the Classification of Boroughs* (London, 1832); *Standard*, 25 Jan. 1832; *St James's Chronicle*, 26 Jan. 1832.

109. *HCJ* (1831–2), lxxxvii. 126; *The Philosophical Magazine* (London, 1832), xi. 360–62.

110. *Morning Chronicle*, 21 Feb. 1832; *HCJ* (1831–2), lxxxvii. 126.

111. Hansard, 3, x. (20 Feb. 1832), 536–39; PP1831–2 (222), xxxvi, 201–3; PP1831–2 (184), xxxvi. 267.

112. Hansard, 3, x. (20 Feb. 1832), 545–53.

113. Hansard, 3, x. (20 Feb. 1832), 553–64.

114. Hansard, 3, x. (20 Feb. 1832), 566–7.

115. McLennan, *Thomas Drummond*, 151.

116. Hansard, 3, x. (20 Feb. 1832), 567–70, (21 Feb. 1832), 592–632, (23 Feb. 1832), 693–721, (2 Mar. 1832), 1098–103.

117. Hansard, 3, xii. (7 May 1832), 729–30; Brock, *Reform Act*, 291.

118. *The Philosophical Magazine* (London, 1832), xi. 360–62; *London and Edinburgh Philosophical Magazine and Journal of Science* (1832), i. 26–30; Mclennan, *Thomas Drummond*, 154–60.

119. PP1831–2 (222), xxxvi, 203.

120. M. Escott, 'Appleby', in D. Fisher, *House of Commons, 1820–1832* (Cambridge, 2009), iii. 154–6; *HLJ* (1831–2), lxiv. 114, 221, 255.

121. TNA, T72/8/35, 'Bristol', Gawler to Drummond, 5 Nov. 1831.

122. Salmon, 'Reform Should Begin at Home', 93–113.

123. T. Crook, *Governing Systems: Modernity and the Making of Public Health in England, 1830–1910* (Oakland, CA, 2020), 67.

124. Salmon, 'English Reform Legislation', 411.

125. U. R. W. Henriques, *Before the Welfare State: Social Administration in Early Industrial Britain* (London, 1979), 26; Mandler, *Aristocratic Government*, 35–6.

126. J. Parry, *The Rise and Fall of Liberal Government in Victorian Britain* (London, 1993), 113–26.

127. Henriques, *Before the Welfare State*, 246–55; O. Macdonagh, *Early Victorian Government 1830–1870* (London, 1977); Eastwood, 'Amplifying the Province'; Mandler, *Aristocratic Government*, 123–274; Hamlin, *Public Health*, 84–334; Crook, *Governing Systems*, 23–147.

128. P. Salmon, 'Parkes, Joseph (1796–1865)', *Oxford Dictionary of National Biography* https://doi-org/10.1093/ref:odnb/21356 [accessed 13 Nov. 2023]; P. Mandler, 'Chadwick, Edwin (1800–1890)', *ODNB* https://doi-org/10.1093/ref:odnb/5013 [accessed 13 Nov. 2023].

129. I. Cawood, 'Corruption and Public Service Ethos in Mid-Victorian Administration: The Case of Leonard Horner and the Factory Office', *English Historical Review*, 135 (2020), 860–91.

130. Harling, 'Power of Persuasion', 50–51.

Part II
REDRAWING ENGLAND'S ELECTORAL MAP

Chronology and voting data

The rest of this book examines the redrawing of England's electoral map in 1832 and its electoral and political consequences. It identifies six types of constituency in England's reformed electoral system (Table C.1). Chapter 5 focuses on two constituency types: ancient boroughs whose boundaries were extended to include their modern town and space for its future growth (modern town), and those whose parliamentary limits remained unchanged (unchanged borough). Chapter 6 explores a group of boroughs extended into their surrounding parish, or parishes, to ensure they contained 300 £10 householder voters after 1832 (multiple parish).[1] Chapter 7 discusses England's new boroughs (new borough), and the final chapter assesses the construction of England's reformed county map – where most counties were divided into two new geographic entities (divided county) and a small number remained unchanged (unchanged county). Each chapter scrutinises the consistency with which the boundary commission employed Drummond's 'scientific' framework for establishing boundaries (see Chapters 3 and 4), and the role of the cabinet, parliamentarians and the public in effecting changes to these proposals once they were published. The chapters then provide a broad analysis of the electoral and political impact of England's reformed electoral map between the first and second Reform Acts. This analysis draws from a newly developed dataset of electoral statistics, party labels and Commons voting records between 1832 and 1868, pre-existing constituency histories – including draft articles in the History of Parliament's forthcoming *Commons 1832–1868* – and newly completed case studies of constituencies that have not received historical treatment elsewhere.[2] Due to its complexity, and because it informs the analysis of all four chapters, the voting data is presented in

Table C.1: England's reformed constituency system and its boundary changes in 1832.

	Single member	Double member	Three member	Four member	Total seats
County	1	60	7		142
Unchanged county		5	7		31
Divided county	1	55			111
Borough	52	133		1	322
Multiple parish	30	24			78
Unchanged borough	2	30		1	66
Modern town	1	57			115
New borough	19	22			63
University borough		4			4
Total	53	195	7	1	468

this preliminary section to the second half of this book with a contextual explanation and guide to reading it.

It is important to note that the local surveys, boundary proposals and policy decisions discussed in the following chapters were made between late August 1831, when the first visits to England's boroughs were completed by the boundary commission, and the enactment of the 1832 Boundary Act for England and Wales on 11 July 1832. This work of electoral reform took place in three phases. The first was the compilation of initial proposals for England's reformed constituency system between August and December 1831 outlined in the previous two chapters. The second was the preparation of boundary proposals for parliamentary review, which took place between late October 1831 and February 1832. The government had initially proposed that this work would be completed by a parliamentary commission. However, after the rejection of the second reform bill by the Lords in October 1831, and because of the unexpected speed with which the commission had completed its initial work, their proposals were subjected to full legislative review via a boundary bill. This coincided with the establishment of a small 'sitting committee' of the commission on 28 October in London, which consisted of Drummond, the Whig MP for Staffordshire, Edward Littleton, and the hydrographer of the navy, Francis Beaufort.[3] This sitting committee reviewed every boundary proposal and maintained communication with the cabinet, who approved, or in a handful of cases, overrode individual proposals. The decisions of the sitting committee were published in the first draft of the boundary bill for England and Wales, introduced in the Commons on 16 February 1832. The final phase consisted of a parliamentary and public review of the commission's proposals and their enactment by July 1832 via the 1832 Boundary Act for England and Wales and several clauses of the 1832 Reform Act for England and Wales. As the government had deliberately rejected the idea of public hearings to discuss boundary reform, parliamentary debate, local petitioning and private discussions between parliamentarians provided a means of ensuring that England's reformed electoral map was agreed to, at least in part, via negotiated settlement.

The voting data used in this book draw from an analysis of over fifty votes in the Commons between 1833 and 1868 including twenty-four major divisions, and thirty-four votes on three policy issues: the corn laws, the ballot and the abolition of the compulsory church rate in England and Wales.[4] The first and largest group of votes is a set of divisions and confidence votes that made, and broke, the fifteen different ministries that governed the UK between the passage of the 1832 reform legislation and the dissolution of parliament in 1868.[5] These votes are detailed in Table C.2, which provides attendance records for each division; the UK and English percentage of support for Whig-Liberal administrations (or opposition to Conservative administrations) in each vote; and the numeric size of the pro-Whig-Liberal majority (or minority) for each vote.

Graphs C.1 and C.2 and their accompanying data tables (Tables C.3–C.4) provide a breakdown of these votes according to the type of boundary change that took place in England's constituencies after 1832. Graph C.1 and Table C.3 compare the votes of MPs representing the four different types of borough (multiple parish, modern town, unchanged borough and new borough) in the reformed electoral system. Graph C.2 and Table C.4 compare the votes of MPs representing divided counties with those for unchanged counties and the English boroughs as a whole. The bars in each graph indicate the number of seats each type of constituency contributed to the overall vote in each division. A positive bar reflects a Whig-Liberal majority in any vote, and a negative bar reflects a Conservative majority. The lines indicate the percentage of Whig-Liberal support in each division for all MPs in attendance.

It will be useful to take Peel's successful no confidence motion in the Whig Melbourne administration of 4 June 1841 as an example of how to read this data. Table C.2 confirms the vote had a 98.7 per cent attendance rate, with 49.9 per cent of UK MPs present (a minority of 1) and 45.8 per cent of English MPs present (a minority of 39) supporting Melbourne. Graph C.1 and Table C.3 reveal that among new borough MPs (denoted by a yellow bar) a majority of twenty-five supported the Melbourne administration. This amounted to 70.5 per cent of new borough MPs attending the division (denoted by a yellow line). By contrast only 45.5 per cent of MPs in attendance who represented multiple parish boroughs (denoted by a green line) were willing to support the Melbourne administration, meaning that this group of boroughs contributed a minority of seven votes to the overall total (denoted by a green bar).

Table C.2: Major Commons votes and confidence divisions 1833–68.

Date	Division	Govt	Attendance*	W-L % (UK)	W-L % (E)	W-L Maj (UK)	W-L Maj (E)
21/04/34	Church rates	W-L	63.5%	63.5%	66.9%	109	100
02/04/35	Irish Church	C	95.3%	52.5%	50.2%	31	2
04/02/36	Address	W-L	90.0%	54.7%	53.2%	52	25
15/05/38	Irish tithes	W-L	96.6%	51.5%	47.1%	19	−26
06/05/39	Jamaican constitution	W-L	97.9%	50.4%	46.9%	5	−28
31/01/40	No confidence	W-L	97.4%	51.6%	47.2%	20	−25
04/06/41	No confidence	W-L	98.7%	49.9%	45.8%	−1	−39
27/08/41	Address	W-L	97.7%	42.9%	39.0%	−91	−100
13/04/42	Income tax	C	92.5%	41.0%	37.1%	−106	−111
23/02/44	Ireland	C	95.1%	42.1%	37.4%	−98	−111
25/06/46	Irish coercion	C	86.3%	56.6%	57.3%	74	58
28/06/50	Foreign policy	W-L	92.0%	53.8%	52.1%	46	18
20/02/51	County franchise	W-L	27.1%	35.7%	35.7%	−48	−36
20/02/52	Militia bill	W-L	49.9%	48.3%	47.0%	−11	−14
16/12/52	Budget	C	95.9%	51.6%	49.1%	20	−8
29/01/55	Crimean war	W-L	85.5%	34.5%	32.6%	−158	−138
03/03/57	Canton censure	W-L	87.3%	48.3%	47.5%	−19	−20
19/02/58	Orsini Affair	W-L	78.2%	48.2%	45.9%	−18	−30
31/03/59	Reform bill	C	96.3%	53.1%	54.5%	39	40
10/06/59	Address	C	98.8%	51.0%	52.0%	13	18
08/07/64	Denmark & Germany	W-L	96.8%	51.5%	53.5%	19	31
18/06/66	Reform bill	W-L	95.7%	49.1%	47.1%	−11	−27
12/04/67	Reform bill	C	95.9%	48.2%	47.5%	−22	−22
03/04/68	Irish Church	C	95.9%	54.8%	52.6%	61	23

* These attendance figures include recorded pairs.

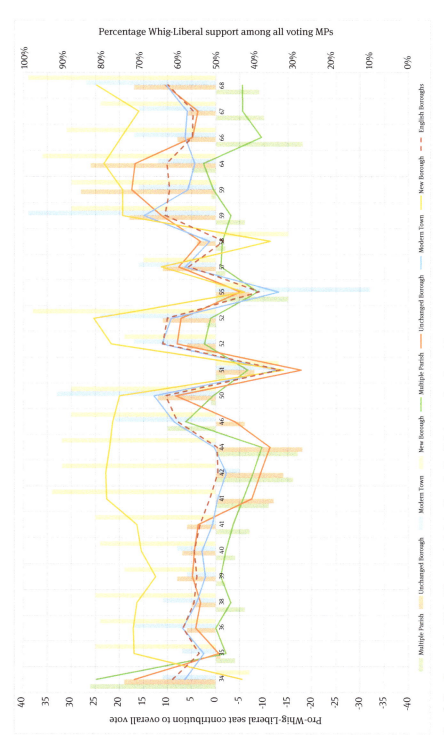

Graph C.1: Support for Whig-Liberal administrations in English boroughs 1832–68.

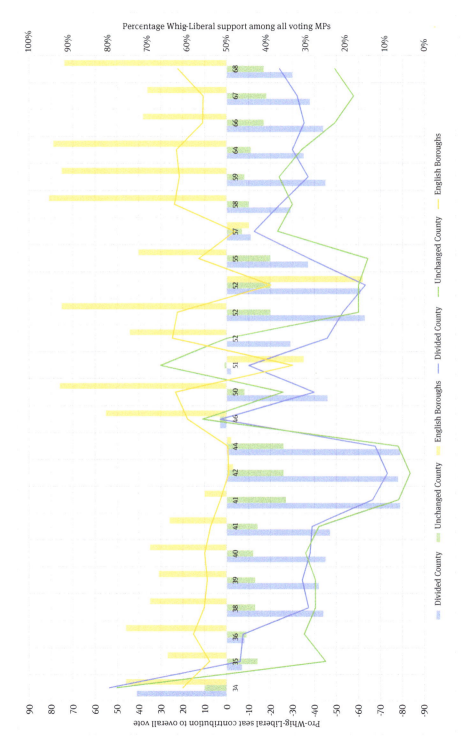

Graph C.2: Support for Whig-Liberal administrations in English counties and boroughs, 1832–68.

Table C.3: Support for Whig-Liberal administrations in English boroughs according to 1832 boundary changes, 1832–68. (seat count and percentage support).

	1834	1835	1836	1838	1839	1840	1841 (1)	1841 (2)	1842	1844	1846	1850
Multiple parish	26	−4	0	−6	−2	−4	−7	−11	−16	−17	10	1
Unchanged borough	19	−1	6	5	8	7	6	−12	−14	−18	−6	12
Modern town	11	7	17	11	6	8	2	−1	−5	1	21	33
New borough	−7	25	24	25	19	24	25	34	32	32	30	30
Multiple parish	81.0%	47.3%	50.0%	46.1%	48.7%	47.4%	45.5%	42.9%	40.3%	38.0%	57.8%	50.7%
Unchanged borough	71.1%	49.2%	55.2%	54.0%	56.1%	55.6%	54.5%	40.6%	38.3%	35.9%	45.0%	60.3%
Modern town	58.0%	53.1%	58.6%	55.0%	52.7%	53.6%	50.9%	49.6%	47.2%	50.5%	60.8%	66.0%
New borough	43.1%	71.2%	71.4%	70.5%	65.6%	69.4%	70.5%	78.3%	78.6%	77.6%	76.8%	75.0%

	1851	1852	1852	1855	1857	1858	1859 (1)	1859 (2)	1864	1866	1867	1868
Multiple parish	−2	2	2	−15	−2	−2	−6	1	5	−18	−10	−9
Unchanged borough	−8	6	11	−7	11	4	18	28	26	8	6	17
Modern town	−12	17	24	−32	16	3	39	16	12	17	16	27
New borough	−13	19	38	−8	15	−15	30	30	36	31	24	39
Multiple parish	41.7%	52.9%	51.4%	39.1%	48.6%	48.3%	46.1%	50.6%	53.2%	38.2%	43.1%	43.1%
Unchanged borough	27.8%	60.0%	59.0%	43.6%	59.6%	54.0%	64.1%	71.9%	71.0%	56.1%	54.7%	63.1%
Modern town	34.2%	63.9%	61.5%	33.7%	58.0%	51.6%	68.6%	57.3%	55.5%	57.9%	57.4%	62.9%
New borough	32.4%	77.1%	81.7%	42.6%	64.2%	35.8%	74.2%	74.2%	79.0%	74.6%	70.0%	81.0%

Table C.4: Support for Whig-Liberal administrations in English counties and boroughs, 1832–68 (seat count and percentage support).

	1834	1835	1836	1838	1839	1840	1841 (1)	1841 (2)	1842	1844	1846	1850
Divided county	41	−7	−8	−44	−42	−45	−47	−79	−78	−79	3	−46
Unchanged county	10	−14	−9	−13	−13	−12	−14	−27	−26	−26	3	−8
English boroughs	46	27	46	35	31	35	26	10	−3	−2	55	76
Divided county	79.7%	46.6%	45.8%	29.2%	30.9%	29.0%	28.4%	13.1%	9.4%	12.4%	51.6%	27.9%
Unchanged county	77.8%	25.0%	30.4%	27.6%	27.6%	30.0%	26.7%	6.5%	3.6%	6.7%	56.0%	35.7%
English boroughs	61.2%	54.3%	58.5%	55.6%	54.9%	55.6%	54.1%	51.6%	49.5%	49.7%	59.9%	63.0%

	1851	1852	1852	1855	1857	1858	1859 (1)	1859 (2)	1864	1866	1867	1868
Divided county	−2	−29	−63	−61	−37	−11	−29	−45	−35	−44	−38	−30
Unchanged county	1	0	−20	−20	−20	−7	−10	−8	−11	−17	−18	−17
English boroughs	−35	44	75	−62	40	−10	81	75	79	38	36	74
Divided county	44.4%	24.6%	20.6%	14.9%	29.2%	43.0%	36.4%	29.4%	33.3%	30.4%	32.1%	36.6%
Unchanged county	66.7%	50.0%	16.7%	16.7%	14.3%	37.0%	33.3%	36.7%	31.0%	22.6%	17.9%	22.6%
English boroughs	33.3%	63.8%	62.5%	38.8%	57.0%	48.0%	63.2%	62.0%	62.7%	56.1%	55.9%	62.4%

Graphs C.3–C.8 use the same template to provide a breakdown of voting by boundary change type between 1832 and 1868 in three specific policy areas – free trade in corn, the ballot and the abolition of English and Welsh church rates. These votes were chosen as they offer a basic indicator as to the economic, political and religious fault-lines in the Commons between 1832 and 1868, and because they were discussed and voted on consistently across successive parliaments. All three policy demands started the period as radical causes but experienced differing fortunes.

Initially a demand of radicals, most reformers and some Whigs during the 1830s, the corn laws were repealed by Peel's Conservative ministry in 1846, following several years of extra-parliamentary campaigning by the Anti-Corn Law League, and counter-campaigning by protectionist societies, as well as famine in Ireland (Graphs C.3 and C.4 and Tables C.5 and C.6). Following repeal, protectionist MPs, seeking the reinstatement of the corn laws, were returned in large numbers at the 1847 and 1852 elections, but the primacy of free trade as a commercial policy was ultimately established by a series of votes during November and December 1852, which contributed to the eventual resignation of the protectionist-backed Derby ministry.

The Nonconformist demand for the abolition of compulsory church rates (Graphs C.5 and C.6 and Tables C.7 and C.8) in England and Wales was another issue that was voted on regularly throughout the entire period. Although Commons majorities could generally be secured for the abolition of church rates from 1856, a successful Conservative rearguard campaign in favour of their retention (and opposition to their abolition in the House of Lords), meant the compulsory church rate remained in place until 1868. While local custom meant that the enforcement of a compulsory church rate in England and Wales was effectively abolished in many areas prior to 1868, the church rate issue became a defining cause for most Whig-Liberals who saw abolition as a core requirement of religious freedom in a future, secular liberal state. For most Conservatives (and many moderate Whigs even until 1868) the defence of the church rate was seen as essential to warding off future disestablishment and maintaining the Anglican state.[6]

The introduction of the ballot (Graphs C.7 and C.8 and Tables C.9 and C.10), or secret voting, at parliamentary elections (eventually introduced in 1872) was a consistent demand of radicals, most reformers and some Whigs and Liberals throughout the period. As a public campaign (which held that secret voting would eliminate corrupt practices and illegitimate influence in elections), the ballot probably reached its popular zenith in the aftermath of the 1837 election. Fading as a popular single-issue during the 1840s, it was revived as a demand of radicals and some Liberals in

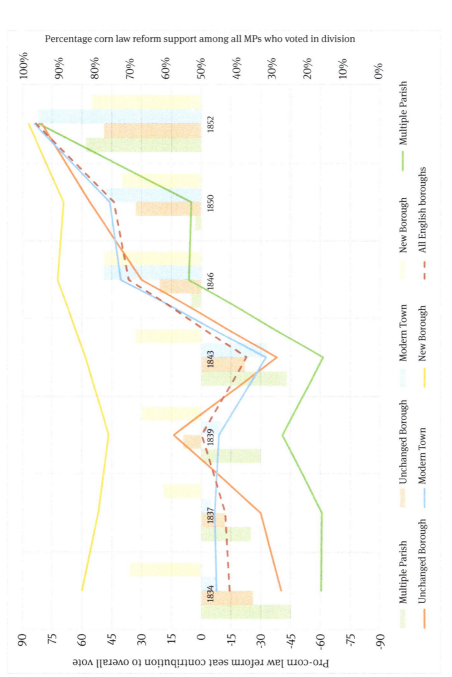

Graph C.3: Support for corn law reform in English boroughs, 1834–52.

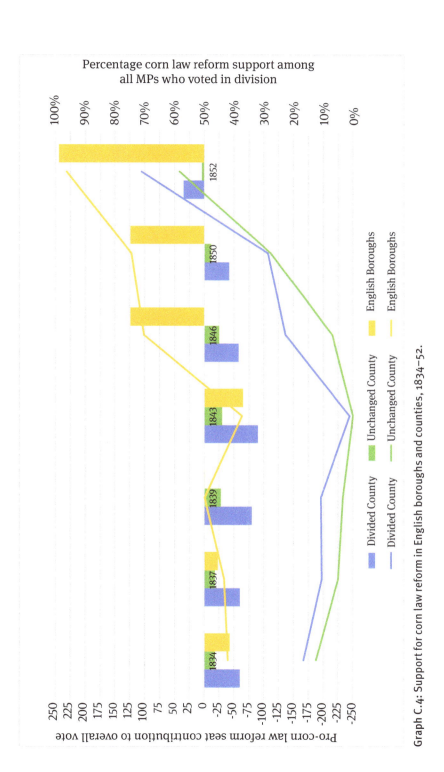

Graph C.4: Support for corn law reform in English boroughs and counties, 1834–52.

Table C.5: Support for corn law reform in English boroughs, 1834–52 (seat count and percentage support).

	1834	1837	1839	1843	1846	1850	1852
Multiple parish	−45	−25	−30	−43	5	3	58
Unchanged borough	−26	−12	9	−22	21	33	49
Modern town	−8	−5	−10	−33	49	48	82
New borough	36	19	30	33	49	40	55
Multiple parish	16.42%	16.22%	27.27%	15.87%	53.42%	52.73%	95.31%
Unchanged borough	27.59%	33.33%	57.63%	28.85%	66.67%	81.13%	94.55%
Modern town	45.65%	46.15%	45.00%	31.87%	72.48%	75.53%	96.59%
New borough	83.33%	78.79%	75.86%	82.35%	90.16%	88.46%	98.25%

Table C.6: Support for corn law reform in English boroughs and counties, 1834–52.

Constituency type	1834	1837	1839	1843	1846	1850	1852
Divided county	−60	−60	−80	−90	−58	−42	35
Unchanged county	−18	−18	−28	−30	−25	−12	4
English boroughs	−43	−23	−1	−65	124	124	244
Divided county	16.67%	10.53%	10.78%	1.09%	22.64%	28.57%	71.08%
Unchanged county	12.50%	5.00%	3.33%	0.00%	6.90%	27.59%	58.33%
English boroughs	42.07%	43.27%	49.82%	37.35%	70.26%	74.41%	96.21%

the 1850s. However, as one historian has stated, by the 1860s the campaign for the ballot appeared to have 'succumbed to the forces of neglect and indifference', as well as the general acceptance (even among some advanced Liberals) that voting was a public rather than a private act.[7]

Each of these confidence and policy votes has been used to compile two final graphs that provide a general indication of the partisanship of each type of constituency between 1832 and 1868. Graph C.9 and Table C.11 offer an overview of the average vote contribution of each type of English constituency in major confidence and policy divisions during the period.[8] While the graph does not reflect how voting habits of MPs representing these constituencies changed over time, for most categories of constituency it offers a fairly accurate indicator as to how their MPs would have voted in a division on each issue during the period. It reveals that the counties and multiple parish boroughs, for instance, provided the primary source of support for Conservative governments and the policy status quo throughout the period, while new borough MPs were the most important sources of support for Whig-Liberal governments and small 'l' liberal policy reforms.

Graph C.10 and Table C.12 indicate the average vote contribution that each English constituency type would have delivered on all four policy

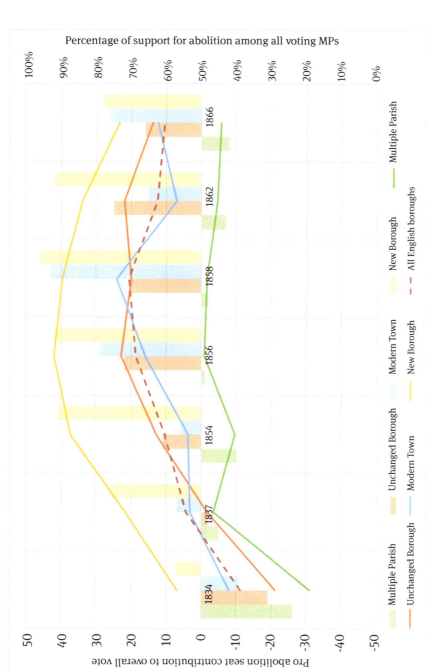

Graph C.5: Support for abolition of church rates in English boroughs, 1834–66.

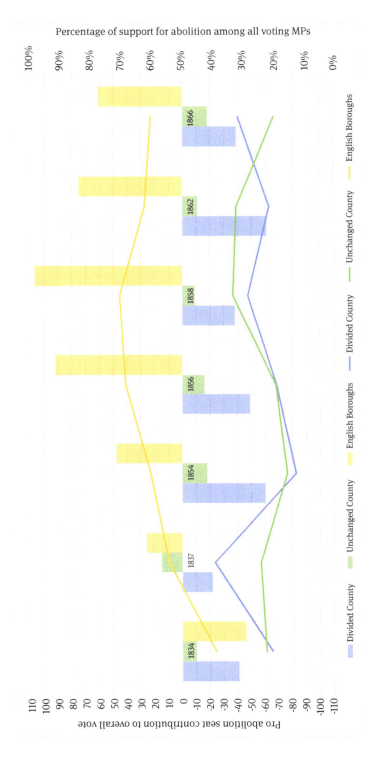

Graph C.6: Support for abolition of church rates in English boroughs and counties, 1834–66.

areas, if each type of constituency had returned 100 members to Parliament. This data is useful for comparing how partisan each constituency type was. While the university seats only returned four members, these MPs were by far the most conservative (with a small 'c') type of MP. MPs for unchanged counties were fractionally more conservative than those for the divided counties, and those that represented multiple parish boroughs were moderately conservative. New boroughs returned by far the most liberal members, while all other ancient borough MPs as a cohort were moderately liberal.

Table C.7: Support for the abolition of church rates in English boroughs, 1834–66 (seat count and percentage support).

	1834	1837	1854	1856	1858	1862	1866
Multiple parish	−26	−5	−10	−1	−2	−7	−8
Unchanged borough	−19	−2	11	22	20	25	16
Modern town	−11	7	6	29	43	15	26
New borough	7	26	41	42	46	42	28
Multiple parish	19.05%	46.48%	40.38%	49.12%	48.39%	45.33%	44.29%
Unchanged borough	28.89%	48.33%	62.79%	72.92%	70.00%	71.93%	63.79%
Modern town	42.03%	53.21%	53.75%	65.93%	74.16%	57.01%	62.26%
New borough	56.86%	71.67%	87.27%	92.00%	89.66%	83.87%	73.33%

Table C.8: Support for abolition of church rates in English boroughs and counties, 1834–66.

Constituency type	1834	1837	1854	1856	1858	1862	1866
Divided county	−41	−22	−60	−49	−38	−61	−39
Unchanged county	−10	15	−18	−16	−9	−11	−18
English boroughs	−46	26	48	92	107	75	61
Divided county	20.29%	39.22%	12.50%	18.99%	28.41%	21.50%	31.78%
Unchanged county	22.22%	24.14%	15.38%	19.23%	33.33%	32.26%	20.00%
English boroughs	38.83%	54.33%	60.43%	68.70%	70.66%	62.46%	60.41%

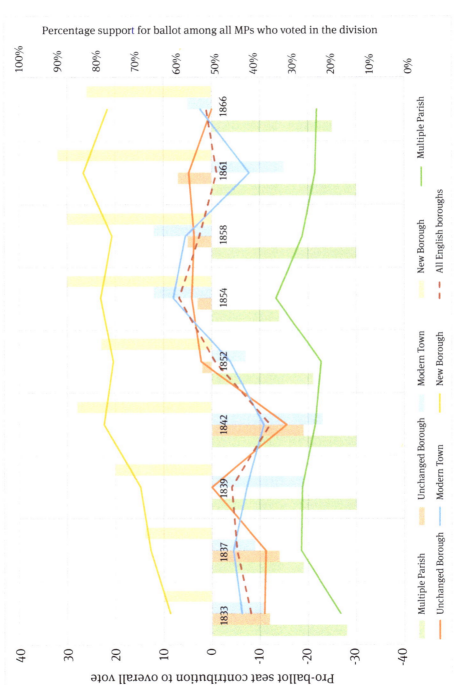
Graph C.7: Support for the ballot in English boroughs, 1833–66.

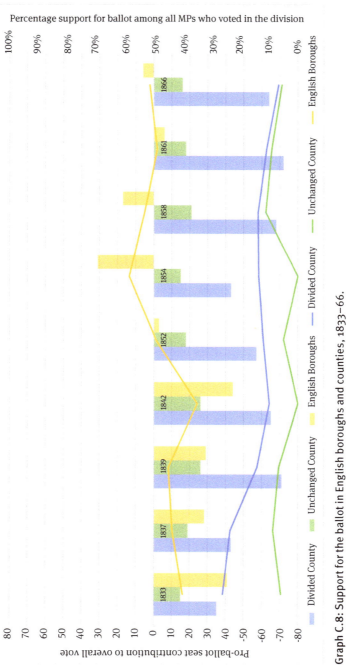

Graph C.8: Support for the ballot in English boroughs and counties, 1833–66.

Table C.9: Support for the ballot in English boroughs, 1833–66 (seat count and percentage support).

	1833	1837	1839	1842	1852	1854	1858	1861	1866
Multiple parish	−28	−19	−30	−30	−21	−14	−30	−30	−25
Unchanged borough	−12	−14	0	−19	2	3	5	7	0
Modern town	−11	−9	−19	−23	−7	12	12	−15	5
New borough	10	14	20	28	23	30	30	32	26
Multiple parish	16.67%	26.83%	26.56%	23.21%	21.62%	33.33%	26.56%	23.21%	22.73%
Unchanged borough	36.36%	36.00%	50.00%	30.61%	52.78%	55.17%	54.55%	55.93%	50.00%
Modern town	42.25%	44.44%	40.95%	36.47%	45.21%	60.00%	56.82%	40.26%	52.94%
New borough	60.87%	65.91%	68.52%	78.00%	75.56%	78.85%	75.86%	83.33%	77.08%

Table C.10: Support for the ballot in English boroughs and counties, 1833–66.

Constituency type	1833	1837	1839	1842	1852	1854	1858	1861	1866
Divided county	−35	−43	−71	−65	−57	−43	−68	−72	−64
Unchanged county	−15	−19	−26	−26	−18	−15	−21	−18	−16
English boroughs	−41	−28	−29	−44	−3	31	17	−6	6
Divided county	26.03%	23.46%	14.14%	9.88%	12.00%	13.56%	13.83%	10.87%	6.76%
Unchanged county	5.88%	8.70%	6.67%	0.00%	5.00%	0.00%	11.11%	9.09%	5.56%
English boroughs	39.90%	43.52%	44.84%	34.88%	49.21%	58.47%	53.21%	48.75%	51.43%

Table C.11: Average vote contribution of each English constituency type, 1832–68.

	Whig-Lib govt support	Free trade	Ballot	Church rates (abolition)
University borough (4 seats)	−3	−1	−3	−3
Unchanged county (32 seats)	−13	−18	−19	−12
Divided county (110 seats)	−33	−51	−58	−40
Multiple parish (78 seats)	−3	−11	−26	−8
Unchanged borough (66 Seats)	11	7	−4	7
Modern town (115 seats)	25	18	−7	10
New borough (63 seats)	32	37	24	27

Table C.12: Relative vote contribution of each English constituency type, 1832–68 (if each returned 100 MPs).

	Whig-Lib govt support	Free trade	Ballot	Church rates (abolition)
University borough	−84	−34	−82	−86
Unchanged county	−42	−60	−64	−40
Divided county	−32	−46	−54	−38
Multiple parish	−4	−16	−34	−10
Unchanged borough	18	12	−8	12
Modern town	22	16	−6	10
New borough	52	60	38	44

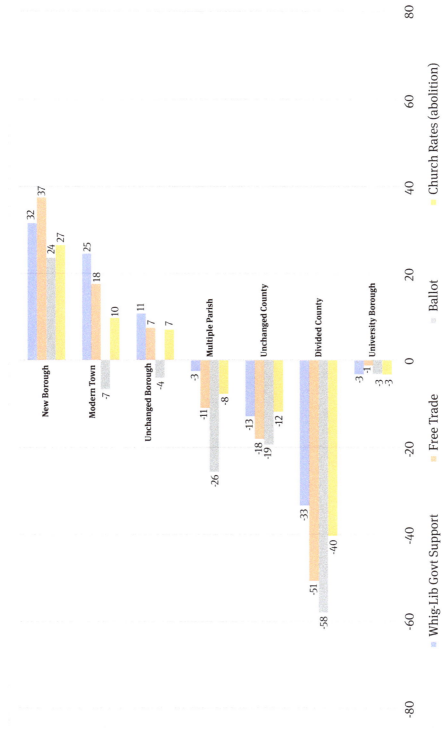

Graph C.9: Average vote contribution of each English constituency type, 1832–68.

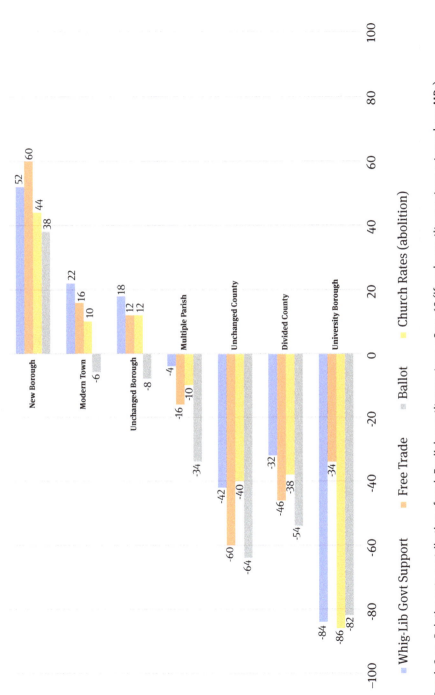

Graph C.10: Relative vote contribution of each English constituency type, 1832–68 (if each constituency type returned 100 MPs).

Notes

1. The four 'Clause 5' boroughs (New Shoreham, Cricklade, Aylesbury and East Retford) reformed prior to 1832 have been included in the 'multiple parish' category.
2. P. Salmon and K. Rix, *The House of Commons 1832–68* (forthcoming).
3. SRO, Hatherton, D260/M/F/5/27/7, Russell to Littleton, 18 Oct. 1831, fo. 70, 23 Oct. 1831, 60, D260/M/F/5/26/7, 27 Oct. 1831, 190.
4. For a detailed explanation of this data see, M. Spychal, 'The geography of voting behaviour: Towards a roll-call analysis of England's reformed electoral map, 1832–68', *History of Parliament Blog* (February, 2021) https://thehistoryofparliament.wordpress.com/2021/03/09/the-geography-of-voting-behaviour-towards-a-roll-call-analysis-of-englands-reformed-electoral-map-1832-68/ [accessed 5 Feb. 2024].
5. This includes the Wellington caretaker ministry of Nov.–Dec. 1834.
6. J. P. Ellens, *Religious Routes to Gladstonian Liberalism* (University Park, PA, 1994); Coohill, *Ideas of the Liberal Party*, 131–53.
7. B. Kinzer, *The Ballot Question in Nineteenth-Century English Politics* (1982), 1.
8. The Whig-Liberal government confidence score uses 1832 party labels, and a major division from each of the subsequent parliaments that had very low dissent and very high turnout. Party labels have been used in 1832 as no 'straight' partisan division took place during the parliament.

Chapter 5

'The work we are engaged in is intended to last for a century': Redrawing England's ancient electoral map

As the English borough boundary commission commenced its work in September 1831, its chair, Thomas Drummond, reminded his commissioners that 'the work we are engaged in is intended to last for a century'.[1] His advice was not hyperbole. Rather, it reflected Drummond's genuine belief that redrawing England's electoral map in a methodical, 'scientific' manner was vital to ensuring the long-term stability of the reformed electoral system. To achieve this, Drummond devised an investigative framework for his commissioners that was to be deployed indiscriminately in every constituency they visited. The chief aim of this framework was to ensure that the boundaries of every reformed English borough encompassed their entire modern community, while also providing sufficient space for the constituency's future demographic growth. This chapter discusses the fifty-eight English boroughs whose boundaries were expanded in 1832 according to this method, as well as the thirty-three boroughs whose limits remained unchanged as they already met these requirements.[2]

Historians have acknowledged that such principles governed the majority of English borough boundary changes in 1832, however, no in-depth consideration of how they were identified and the consistency with which they were implemented has taken place.[3] D. C. Moore has provided the only extended speculation as to why the majority of England's borough map was reformed in this manner. He suggested that it reflected a wider 'community principle' at the heart of the 1832 reform legislation, which sought 'to separate the two major types of social community in the kingdom, the urban and the rural' in order to create electoral communities that were deferent to the interests of local elites.[4] While a community principle, as Moore has suggested, underpinned the commission's work, it was not intended to spread deference. Rather, as this and previous chapters demonstrate, it was established to provide a framework for defining an electoral community in a disinterested, scientific manner and to ensure the longevity of the reform settlement. It was also in keeping with the 'ideal of constituency communities' that, Hawkins has argued, 'underlay the Whigs' legislative intentions' for reform in 1832. This Whig desire to ensure that the reformed constituency system 'engaged the whole local community, voters, and non-electors alike' relied to a great extent on the continuation of open canvassing and voting, multi-member seats and pre-reform electoral customs after 1832.[5] At its most basic level, however, this Whig ideal also required that the geographic definition of each constituency encompassed its legitimate electoral community and associated interests.

In order to define each constituency's legitimate electoral community, the boundary commissioners were required by Drummond's 'scientific' framework to consider the legal, economic and social conditions of a borough in order to define its modern population. With the assistance of their surveyors, the commissioners then completed a survey of each borough's likely future economic and geographic growth. For some commissioners, implementing this framework proved complex. Others questioned its validity. Despite these challenges, by February 1832, Drummond and the sitting committee's supervision of the commission's work led to the publication of a remarkably consistent set of boundary proposals, the vast majority of which were enacted by the 1832 Boundary Act.

As well as providing the basis for England's reformed electoral map, this redrawing and formalisation of parliamentary boundaries was an early part of the wider process by which England's various local 'administrative geographies' were redefined and expanded during the first half of the nineteenth century. As Navickas has shown, this process encompassed the creation of new geographic limits across England's localities for the administration of municipal politics, the poor law, the police and improvement commissions, all of which sat alongside more established parish jurisdictions and led to a multiplicity of contested political spaces within any single locality.[6] The interplay of these contested political spaces proved of concern to several commissioners as they considered the potential implications of their work, concerns that proved prescient when the long-term effects of boundary reform are considered. While a remarkably uniform method was used to define each borough discussed here, the political and electoral impact of doing so varied considerably.

In a minority of constituencies boundary reform proved largely inconsequential; in others, particularly those with a restricted ancient franchise, defining a constituency by a geographic space created an entirely new set of electoral conditions. In most boroughs, subtle boundary changes led to equally subtle shifts in electoral power, the consequences of which often took decades to emerge.

Defining a borough's modern town

Defining the modern town or city associated with a parliamentary borough was a core requirement of Drummond's disinterested technique for defining English borough boundaries. For the commissioners this process began as a map-based exercise that utilised their updated town plans for each borough. As discussed in the previous chapter, these plans had been completed in conjunction with the commissioners' surveyors during their initial work in each constituency. The commissioners were advised to use their town plans to identify every grouping of houses within one mile of a borough's ancient boundaries – an arbitrary limit that had been agreed in cross-party talks over the reform legislation.[7] In order to decide whether a grouping of houses formed part of the modern borough the commissioners were asked to evaluate the legal, economic and social connections between an ancient borough and its nearby houses.[8] Each borough provided the commissioners with an array of particular conditions to consider, and all but two pairs of commissioners were consistent in terms of fulfilling this brief.

Drummond advised his commissioners that legal conventions binding a borough with a nearby population should take precedent over any economic or social connections. The discovery that a small part of Strood formed part of the liberties of Rochester meant commissioners Drinkwater and Saunders were compelled to add the entire town to the borough, even though they were not connected by trade or custom. Once the commissioners had concluded that Strood was required to form part of Rochester, they had to define the modern limits of Strood and identify its likely direction of future expansion.[9] Similarly, commissioner Ker was compelled to include the Herefordshire township of Ludford in the parliamentary borough of Ludlow (located in Shropshire), because a person living in Ludford had been allowed to bring a case to the King's Bench as a resident of Ludlow.[10]

Economic links between a borough and a nearby settlement presented the most convincing reason for redefining the extent of a borough. Drinkwater and Saunders recommended the addition of Fordington to the borough of Dorchester on this basis. Although they found Fordington to be 'extremely wretched', at least 700 of the village's 2,000 inhabitants were employed in Dorchester.[11] By contrast, the conflicting economic circumstances of two nearby towns could present as a justification for not extending an ancient borough. After surveying the area surrounding the ancient borough of Leominster, commissioners Ellis and Wylde reported that the only settlement within close proximity was the town of Kingsland. Kingsland, however, was deemed unsuitable for boundary extension as Leominster's inhabitants were primarily 'tradesmen and handicraftsmen', while Kingsland's population was 'entirely agricultural'.[12]

Social connections between boroughs and their nearby settlements were more difficult to evaluate. Despite initially opposing such an expansion, commissioners Birch and Brandreth were convinced by Drummond to recommend that the village of Heavitree form part of Exeter. Drummond persuaded the commissioners that Heavitree's social connection with Exeter, as a resort for its retired and wealthy inhabitants, meant that it was legitimate to consider it as part of the modern borough.[13] The expansive boundary that Birch and Brandreth then recommended was justified on the basis of the 'connections in trade, interests ... [and] ... intercourse' between Exeter, its inner suburbs and Heavitree (Map 5.1).[14]

Attempting to define a modern borough by judging its economic, social and legal circumstances was a complex task. The alternative method was to quiz local inhabitants. As discussed in the previous chapter, this was a method that Drummond and the government had been wary of utilising for fear that politicised local opinion might influence boundary proposals. Nevertheless, Drummond accepted that defining a modern borough was challenging, and in his informal discussions with the commissioners he agreed that while proposals could not be led by local opinion, cautious questioning of inhabitants when difficulties arose could take place. Such guidance was provided to commissioners Allen and Romilly when they could not decide whether the township of Fishwick should be considered as part of the modern borough of Preston. Drummond advised them that it would be beneficial in such borderline cases to embark on a guarded survey of local inhabitants in order that the sitting committee of the commission could be fully informed on the matter when they made their final decision over the borough. If the commissioners deemed it necessary to survey inhabitants, Drummond informed them that they had to 'record minutely the information received – the names of the persons – their occupation and respectability'. He explained that local opinion should only be used as a springboard for further careful investigation, stating that when proposing a boundary:

Map 5.1: Commissioners' original tracing for Exeter, T72/9/15 © The National Archives; digital additions by author.
Key: Proposed boundary excluding Heavitree (green). Proposed boundary including Heavitree (red) [digital addition].

We may not follow the wish of the inhabitants but we ought to know it. Where that wish is to extend and include it is entitled to great attention. Where it is to retain and exclude it should be rigidly and jealously examined, and that examination will furnish us with the means of justification if required.[15]

Two pairs of commissioners, less confident in their investigative abilities, relied heavily on this method. Commissioners Ansley and Gawler advised Drummond that they had relied upon the opinion of local inhabitants when trying to settle whether the village of St. Cross was part of Winchester. Although conscious that local political leanings might have influenced their report, they informed Drummond that discussing the issue with locals had been the only way to decide.[16] While Ansley and Gawler generally managed to keep such discussions discreet, commissioners Tancred and Wrottesley's eagerness to gauge local opinion realised the fears of those who had earlier warned that doing so would compromise the commission's impartiality. When visiting Durham, Wrottesley became embroiled in hostile correspondence with local officials after it was discovered that he had relied heavily on information provided by a town clerk. The town clerk, it transpired, had sought to play on Durham's peculiar elastic boundary (see Chapter 4) to convince the commissioners to include certain areas that would have been favourable to local Tory electoral interests in Durham's reformed boundary.[17] If Wrottesley had simply taken the town clerk's information in Durham as a starting point for further investigation, as the commissioners had been instructed to do, it is unlikely he would have become involved in such a dispute.

In their published reports, Tancred and Wrottesley also exhibited no caution in terms of referring to the fact that they had based their recommendations on the wishes of local inhabitants. In their report on Berwick-upon-Tweed (in which they had recommended the addition of Tweedmouth and Spittal townships to the borough) they qualified their recommendation by stating that the 'respectable classes' of both townships and Berwick's corporation agreed with their recommendation. During debate over the boundary bill, the discovery of this statement allowed John Wilson Croker, one of parliament's most vehement antireformers, to accuse the commission of failing to consistently base their recommendations on disinterested principles. Instead, Croker argued, Berwick's proposal demonstrated that the commission had been poorly supervised and that individual commissioners had been more than willing to defer to the politically motivated wishes of local inhabitants when they saw fit.[18]

The examples of Durham and Berwick revealed the dangers of resorting to local opinion, and the case of Berwick caused particular embarrassment to the commission when discussed in parliament.[19] However, given the extent of the commissioners' investigations in each borough, and the inescapable fact that they had to converse with local inhabitants to gather even basic information, it seems unlikely that they would have been able to avoid forming an idea as to the potential reception of their proposed boundaries. The commissioners were well aware that they had to distance themselves from their knowledge of local opinion when attempting to define a modern town, by focusing primarily on the legal, economic and social connections that existed between an ancient borough and its surrounding population. The inability of Ansley and Gawler, and Tancred and Wrottesley, to fully adhere to this approach was the exception, rather than the rule. Given the experience of Durham as well as Croker's later criticism, it was prudent that the commissioners, in the main, were discreet about any questioning of local inhabitants and avoided making any reference to the potential public response to their boundary proposals in their published reports. Doing so ensured that the commission could complete its work within a short timescale, and helped to maintain the public appearance, if not always the actual realisation, of bureaucratic impartiality.

Proposing boundaries to last for a century?

As well as ensuring that their boundaries encompassed the modern extent of a borough, Drummond had instructed the commissioners to provide a 'liberal allowance' for each borough's likely future growth in order that the 'boundary determined today may not require alteration tomorrow'.[20] He clarified the timescale implied by 'tomorrow', as well as the rationale for this instruction in correspondence with commissioners Sheepshanks and Tallents, informing them that:

> the work we [the commissioners] are engaged in is intended to last for a century ... if we draw our lines too close [to a borough] we shall presently have houses extending beyond them – and then petitions to parliament to send commissioners to draw new boundaries.[21]

The commissioners had been entrusted with the complex task of designing boundaries that allowed for the long-term future growth of a parliamentary borough, primarily in order that the question of parliamentary boundaries did not burden the legislature over the following century. Most of the commissioners embraced this instruction, and in many cases a comprehensive survey of each borough's geography and economy was completed in order to identify planned and likely sites for future development. The accuracy with which this work was completed was dependent on the engineering and surveying skill available to each set of commissioners. Furthermore, the contrast between most southern boroughs and northern England's rapidly expanding manufacturing towns and cities meant that the room allowed for a century of population growth varied considerably from borough to borough, and region to region.

Commissioners Birch and Brandreth in District C, with the assistance of their primary surveyors George Dobson and Edward Harris, completed some of the most detailed predictive work in the twenty-four boroughs that they visited in Cornwall, Devon and Somerset.[22] In Bridgwater they proposed a fairly wide boundary on the basis of the town's position as a well-connected inland commercial port, and its high current and future capacity to manufacture a particular type of brick based on silt deposits left by the tides of the River Parrett. They discovered that the river deposited this silt for a mile either side of the developed town and that a number of brick building yards and housing developments had been built or were in the process of being established for a mile to the north and south of the borough. They also found that the land to the west and east of the borough was liable to flooding and thus unsuitable for building.[23] Accordingly they proposed a boundary that extended the borough to the north and south but remained close to the existing town settlement to the east and west. As Bridgwater was not surrounded by many rivers or canals, and contained very few roads or high objects such as trees and windmills, the commissioners utilised the drains and hedges that separated the various plots of land surrounding Bridgwater, details of which had been obtained from an enclosure map of the area acquired by their surveyors, to mark out a new boundary for the borough (Map 5.2).[24] A similarly comprehensive approach to surveying a borough's local conditions could also prompt commissioners to recommend that ancient boundaries be retained when it was discovered that no building land was available near to a town's limits. In Maidstone, for instance, commissioners Drinkwater and Saunders recommended that there should be no extension to the borough's eastern boundary as an expanse of land adjacent to the borough's boundary had been purchased by a local paper-manufacturing proprietor, James Whatman, to ensure greater privacy for his family's grounds in the nearby Vinters Park estate.[25]

Map 5.2: Commissioners' original map for Bridgwater with enclosed land marked, T72/8/33 © The National Archives.

BRIDGEWATER

Wembdon

Allins Farm
Chilton moor Lane
Reed moor
Three Elms
Three Pennic Reach
Bristol
Saltlands
Escott cottage
Brick
Crow Pill
Russel Place
Kidsbury Lane
Malt Shovel Inn
WEMB[DON PARISH]
East Street
Kelyms Cross
East Street
East [Street]
Mathew's Field
Town Mill Leat
Hamp Brook
Hamp Ward
Hamp Mill Leat
Hamp Lane
Hamp F.
Brickiln
West Road
Row Lane
Brick Yards
Hamp
Barland Clize
Barland Lane Bridge
R. Parret

The extent to which the commissioners could complete such predictive work was often contingent on their surveying team. Although assigned primarily to Wales, commissioners Ker and Barrett-Lennard visited four ancient boroughs in England, and highly detailed maps marking out all identified areas for future building accompanied their original reports.[26] Their town plan for Liverpool included houses that were in the process of being constructed as well as individually marked plots of land that had been sold for building. Given the extent of the townships that comprised Liverpool's suburbs this must have been a sizeable surveying task, and if Ker and Barrett-Lennard had not been able to make use of the expertise of Manchester-based surveyors Robert Thornton and Thomas Smith, it is doubtful that they would have been able to present such a compelling proposal for Liverpool's extension.[27] By contrast, a lack of expertise in District B meant that commissioners Ansley and Gawler found it challenging to get to grips with predicting future growth – even with the assistance of their primary surveyor George Carrington.[28] This made their work particularly difficult in the larger boroughs they visited, where they only paid lip service to issues such as land suitable, or already set aside, for building.[29] In their initial correspondence with Drummond over Bristol and Bath, Ansley and Gawler reported 'difficulty' in terms of knowing how far to extend both boroughs, initially opting to extend both into nearby parishes that contained a considerable amount of countryside unsuited for building.[30] With the support of Drummond reviewing and amending their reports in London, however, they were eventually able to propose boundaries that met the minimum standard expected of the commissioners.[31]

Perhaps unsurprisingly, the commissioners who visited England's northern boroughs allowed much more space for a borough's future expansion, particularly if a borough they visited showed any signs of industry and manufacturing. In District H, commissioners Allen and Romilly visited seven ancient boroughs and eleven new boroughs, including Manchester and Sheffield. As a mark of their confidence in the north-west of England's capacity for manufacturing growth, even though they saw fit to describe the borough of Lancaster as a 'decaying place', the discovery that a large factory had been built in the adjacent township of Bulk was felt to be a sufficient reason to propose a large extension to the borough (even though in its present state Bulk only contained five houses worth £10 a year). While Allen and Romilly disagreed as to how far this extension should be carried (Allen proposed to allow over one square mile for future developments, Romilly about half a square mile), even Romilly's conservative estimation as to the likely future urban growth based around a single factory was unprecedented in comparison to elsewhere. Ultimately,

Allen's wider boundary was adopted, suggesting that Drummond and the sitting committee shared the same expectations for the future growth of England's northern manufacturing towns.[32] Similarly, Tancred and Wrottesley, who visited the north-east of England, allowed considerable room for population growth in Hull and Newcastle upon Tyne, whose local manufacturing and commercial economies were found to be flourishing.[33]

Not every large borough in northern England was found to be thriving, however, and when signs of economic prosperity were not present, Drummond had to remind the commissioners to limit their boundary extensions. Following discussions with Drummond, Tancred and Wrottesley's initial boundary for Durham (a large and respectable city, but due to its economic state 'unlikely according to all accounts to increase'[34]) was reduced towards the west, and additional geographic reasons were provided to justify its extension to the east.[35] Tancred and Wrottesley took on board Drummond's advice with regard to Durham in future reports, and as a result recommended a conservative extension to York's boundary that accommodated the modern town, but allowed less space for future development than elsewhere. The decision was based on their prediction that although York was not in decline, it was unlikely to expand. York's status as 'a northern metropolis', they reported, had been supplanted by cities such as Newcastle upon Tyne, Manchester and Leeds due to a transformation in the 'habits and manners which have taken place throughout the kingdom in the last half century'.[36] The general propensity for wider boundaries in the northern manufacturing towns was reflected in the fact that on average, northern boroughs extended to include their modern town tended to experience a greater increase in area than their southern counterparts – the median increase of these boroughs in the north being 2.34 square miles, in the midlands 1.77 square miles, and in the south of England 1.22 square miles.[37]

Rebellion and standardisation

Despite some challenges in the implementation of their guidance, seven of the nine teams of commissioners consistently applied the methods outlined above. Two pairs of commissioners, for differing reasons, proved less co-operative. A consideration of their dissent reveals that Drummond's method for disinterestedly defining an electoral community was contested even within the commission. It also provides an insight into the processes by which the sitting committee of the boundary commission (consisting of Drummond, the Whig MP for Staffordshire, Edward Littleton, and the hydrographer of the navy, Francis Beaufort) standardised the commissioners' work from late October 1831. Although the committee ensured the vast majority of boundary proposals were consistent with Drummond's 'scientific' principles, a handful of inconsistent proposals were published. This was due to the influence of Littleton, who like one pair of commissioners feared the electoral impact of too rigid an application of Drummond's principles on large borough electorates in the midlands.

To Drummond's exasperation, throughout their visits to boroughs in the east of England, commissioners Sheepshanks and Tallents proved reluctant to revise ancient boundaries to allow room for future growth. This was prompted in part by their personal and professional backgrounds, which were distinct from those of the majority of their colleagues associated with the SDUK and the ordnance survey (see Chapter 3). Sheepshanks had a tempestuous character and his willingness to challenge authority while in official positions (particularly as secretary of the Royal Astronomical Society from 1829) has been well documented by historians.[38] Furthermore, his close personal ties with Drummond (he had been Drummond's personal nomination for the commission), gave him little impetus to temper this brazen attitude.[39] Tallents was a prominent election agent in the east midlands and the east of England, and was well known for his role supporting candidates on behalf of the Tory Duke of Newcastle in Newark and the Whig Lord Yarborough in Great Grimsby.[40] Aside from the clear conflict of interests presented by the fact that he had been assigned to define boundaries for both boroughs, Tallents's experience as an election agent in the unreformed electoral system meant that he, better than any other commissioner, understood the subtle historic interplay between parliamentary and local jurisdictions.[41] On one level he was aware that maintaining ancient boundaries provided one less change of electoral circumstances for him to deal with in post-reform politics. On another, he was wary of provoking unforeseen changes in a borough's future local administration by altering its parliamentary boundaries. Sheepshanks's outspoken nature proved the perfect conduit for Tallents's conservatism.

Sheepshanks and Tallents legitimised their stance by ascribing considerable importance to a statement in their preliminary instructions of 8 August 1831, that 'little or no portion of country' should be added to boroughs that contained over 300 £10 householders – an instruction that was invalidated by a secondary instruction of 23 August granting them permission to extend boroughs for up to one mile into their surrounding countryside to allow for population growth.[42] They also used their personal interpretation of the government's conservative intentions for the reform bill to challenge what they perceived to be Drummond's zealousness for redrawing ancient boundaries. After being questioned over several proposals that failed to allow for a borough's future growth, Sheepshanks explained:

> We differ certainly a good deal from you [Drummond] and probably the rest of the commissioners as to the value of legal boundaries ... where an old rule is broken ... the public feeling, especially in England, demands a strong case. I do not read the [reform] bill as you do, if it be thought to encourage change, it only permits change for sufficient cause and ... gives large powers [to the commissioners] to be used discreetly and even timidly.

He acknowledged that their choice as to whether to propose new boundaries, or not, 'depend[ed] upon a sort of tact and feeling made up of a number of unaccording principles' – namely, the geographic, legal, economic and social circumstances that existed between a borough and its surrounding population. It was only when a consideration of all of these factors provided an overwhelming case for extension, he continued, that he and Tallents would consider altering ancient boundaries.[43]

In Stamford, this led to a proposal that only allowed a slight extension of the borough so that it included a few houses in an adjoining parish, but no room for the town's future growth in that direction. On reading this report Drummond expressed 'great regret' that a wider boundary had not been proposed, prompting his reminder to both commissioners that 'the work we are engaged in is intended to last for a century'.[44] Even following a subsequent warning from Drummond that they demonstrated 'a great disposition to cut close to the town', they continued to defy his advice.[45] In some cases, Sheepshanks and Tallents's conservatism had merit. For example, they identified several reasons for not extending the boundary of Cambridge, despite discovering that the city was expanding and that six houses, which backed onto Magdalene College, stood outside the borough's ancient limits.[46] These houses, they reported, stood on the other side of a turnpike from the rest of Cambridge, and had been purposefully built outside Cambridge's parliamentary boundary due to a peculiarity in local jurisdictions. Furthermore, they were reluctant to alter a well-known legal boundary just to add six voters to a constituency that already contained 1,600 £10 householders.[47] Differing legal jurisdictions, as well as Cambridge's already ample constituency, also led to their refusal to consider whether the nearby village of Chesterton should form part of the future borough. For Sheepshanks and Tallents, their work required an acute knowledge of local circumstances, and although parliamentary boundary changes would formally have no technical impact on existing local legal frameworks, they believed that informally they would. For instance, if in the future the inhabitants of Chesterton were to share the privilege of electing MPs with Cambridge, they contended it was not unreasonable that the inhabitants of the latter might demand the inhabitants of the former also shared their legal burdens. Such thinking also provided the basis for their recommendations that Northampton, Peterborough, Boston and King's Lynn should not be extended. This was despite the fact that each borough contained a population grouping outside its existing parliamentary limits, which in Drummond's view had a tenable association with the existing borough and was likely to experience future expansion.[48]

Rather than amending these boundaries to suit Drummond's wishes, Sheepshanks and Tallents insisted on defending their proposals in front of the sitting committee. Ultimately, the committee accepted their arguments for not extending Cambridge and Northampton, but overruled their initial proposals for Stamford, Peterborough, Boston and Great Yarmouth. Accordingly, Drummond redesigned Stamford's boundary, to ensure it conformed with the commissioners' recommendations elsewhere.[49] Likewise, their proposed arbitrary boundary for Great Yarmouth, which cut very close to the town, was overruled in favour of a more expansive boundary.[50] The sitting committee utilised their 20 December instructions for boroughs with fewer than, or near to, 300 £10 householders (discussed in the following chapter) to extend Peterborough (which contained 348 £10 householders) into an adjoining parish. This avoided sending another commissioner to the borough to draw an arbitrary boundary that included the entire town.[51] Finally, Sheepshanks was sent back to Boston in January 1832, at the behest of the sitting committee as well as the chancellor of the exchequer, Viscount Althorp, who had received a petition from the inhabitants of the parish of Skirbeck requesting they be included in the borough.[52] This prompted a revised proposal for Boston that added some houses not previously included, which the sitting committee expanded to include the entire parish of Skirbeck.[53]

Commissioners Ord and Chapman in District E (west England/midlands) offered a different, more overtly partisan, challenge to their instructions. When reporting on large boroughs they were reluctant to propose boundary extensions that removed town voters from the counties. Ord was a member of a prominent Whig family in Northumberland. His father had been a long-standing Whig MP, and Ord, himself a self-professed radical, would become an MP in 1832.[54] While Ord and Chapman's correspondence never demonstrated directly that party bias lay behind their reluctance to extend large borough boundaries, it was certainly the case that a growing number of reformers and Whigs had come to the realisation during 1831 that it would enhance their own electoral prospects if reformed counties retained an influential urban electorate.[55] This notion had become particularly apparent following the passage of the Chandos clause as part of the reform bill in August 1831, enfranchising £50 tenants at will in the counties, which threatened to reduce the influence of borough freeholders by providing rural, agricultural voters with a preponderating influence over England's reformed counties.[56] When Ord and Chapman were presented with a borough that contained a small voting population, such as Tewkesbury (318 £10 householders under ancient boundaries), they showed no hesitancy in proposing boundaries that encompassed the modern borough and allowed for its future growth.[57] However, when presented with a more densely populated borough, such as Worcester, they proposed a boundary which appeared to cut off a considerable number of houses in the city and provided very limited room for future expansion (Figure 5.3).[58]

When questioned by Drummond over their contradictory recommendations, Ord explained that he and Chapman had proposed their boundaries after evaluating their likely impact on county electorates. In Tewkesbury, he explained, the transference of around fifty to one hundred county voters to this small borough from the county was not only important in terms of increasing the borough's respectability, but also because in relative terms this redistribution of voters was unlikely to make much difference to Gloucestershire's electorate of 10,000. Furthermore, the £10 householders transferred to Tewkesbury from the county, he reasoned, were likely to welcome the increased weight of their two votes in a small borough electorate of 400, in comparison to their previously minimal influence in Gloucestershire. By contrast, they felt that in Worcester the extension of the borough to encompass every house associated with the city was likely to have a detrimental impact on Worcestershire's electorate. The ancient limits of Worcester contained between 1,300 and 1,400 £10 householders and the entire city was thought to include around 2,000 £10 householders – potentially removing 700 voters from a county of 8,000 that was also due to be divided. Ord explained that he and Chapman had sought to reduce the number of transferred voters by excluding particular suburbs from Worcester's borough boundary. These suburbs, they had discovered, contained primarily long-term freehold properties that either conferred the county franchise, or were the county residences of voters who also owned a property in the borough. Their proposed boundary, they contended, would be welcomed by these voters as their houses 'properly belonged' to the county, and because no-one would be deprived of the franchise. Furthermore, they argued, residents with two properties would be allowed to keep their county and borough votes.[59]

Such considerations were clearly outside the commissioners' remit, as they had not been asked to consider the redistributive impact of their boundary changes. Accordingly, Drummond ensured a redesigned boundary for Worcester in line with the commissioners' instructions (Map 5.3).[60] Despite this, Ord and Chapman continued to allow the redistributive impact of boundary reform to influence their work. Their proposals for Gloucester and Derby purposefully avoided the addition of a number of houses associated with both cities, and in Coventry and Nottingham they explicitly avoided boundary expansion on the basis that it would remove town-based voters from the counties of Warwickshire and Nottinghamshire respectively.[61] Drummond's ability to amend Ord and Chapman's final reports was compromised by the presence on the sitting committee of Littleton, who shared their reluctance to remove town influence from county electorates. When considering their proposal for Coventry, which had mooted adding the village of Stoke to the borough, Littleton expressed a wish that if the Chandos clause was to stand in the third reform bill, the electoral influence of Stoke's weavers might be more useful to Whig interests if they voted in Warwickshire. In a note on the borough, Littleton stated that the addition of Stoke to Coventry 'should depend very much on the question [of] whether £50 tenants at will should be admitted to the franchise in the new bill. If they shall be admitted, will it be prudent to take manufacturing influence ... out of the counties?'[62] Littleton got his way and Coventry's boundary was not extended. Furthermore, no amendment was made to Ord and Chapman's boundary proposals for Derby or Gloucester. And, while a slight amendment was initially proposed to Nottingham, Littleton ensured the recommendation was overturned ahead of the Commons committee stage of the boundary bill. This decision was aided by a deputation of local inhabitants who had contacted Littleton separately, calling for no change to take place to the borough's boundaries.[63]

To justify these decisions, the commissioners' published reports were amended to minimise any social connections that existed between populations that lived in, or owned second residences on, the outskirts of these midland cities, instead emphasising the more natural connection they shared with the county franchise.[64] These four boroughs provided the only instances among the existing boroughs where the sitting committee actively sidestepped Drummond's disinterested principles. Unsurprisingly, these inconsistencies were seized on by anti-reformers in parliament, and Derby and Nottingham, in particular,

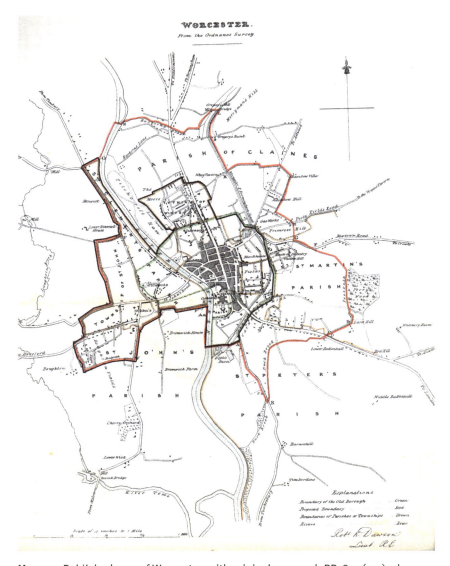

Map 5.3: Published map of Worcester, with original proposal, PP1831 (141), xl. Author's collection; digital additions by author.
Key: Existing boundary (green). Original proposal (black) [digital addition]. Final boundary (red).

prompted charges of gerrymandering against the government and the commission. Littleton shamelessly, but successfully, defended these cases, arguing that they were anomalous in comparison to other large boroughs such as Exeter, which had been extended to include its nearby associated population.[65]

Parliamentary approval and political impact

The consistency with which the boundary commission redrew England's electoral map meant that only nine of the ninety-one proposals discussed in this chapter underwent any amendment between their publication in February 1832 and the passage of the Boundary Act in July 1832.[66] Of these, Boston and Nottingham have already been discussed, and Arundel, which the commission initially proposed to extend into its surrounding parishes, is discussed in the following chapter. Two cases, Bridport and Pontefract, were amended by the government to demonstrate to parliamentarians that they were willing to address any slight inconsistencies in the commissioners' proposals if identified. Bridport's boundary, for instance, was amended following Tory complaints that the commissioners had been too quick to dismiss the inclusion of the town's harbour in their proposal.[67] The commissioners' recommendations for the remaining four boroughs were amended following local petitioning and lobbying. In Barnstaple local inhabitants from two neighbouring villages made the successful case for their inclusion in the reformed borough on the basis that the commissioners had underappreciated their socio-economic connection with the borough.[68] The government agreed to amend Stamford and Poole following complaints that the commission's proposals would inadvertently turn both into closed boroughs under the influence of Tory and Whig patrons respectively.[69] Amending Stamford also served to appease the borough's radical MP, Charles Tennyson, and the electoral agent, Joseph Parkes, who the government had been unwilling to conciliate over their demands for a reduced borough franchise qualification.[70] And in Abingdon fierce local reaction against a very minor boundary change prompted the government to maintain the borough's ancient boundary to avoid any further controversy.[71]

This pragmatic approach to the management of the boundary bill ensured its passage through parliament after only a few hours of debate – a remarkable feat given the level of parliamentary and public dissent over the government's boundary reform plans since March 1831. The speed with which local dissent was mobilised in a few cases reveals how difficult the recommendations of a poorly managed commission might have been to enact. That so few complaints were made about the boroughs discussed here attests to the wisdom of the government's decision to revise England's electoral communities via Drummond's 'scientific' framework. In addition, the government's ability to address specific local complaints as the boundary bill proceeded through parliament helped to ensure that boundaries remained one of the most enduring aspects of the 1832 reform settlement at Westminster, and in the localities. Although Drummond's ambition that the commission's proposals should last for a century was overly ambitious, the long-term legacy of the commission's work was striking. Within a year of the 1832 Boundary Act reformers in Hertford and Warwick sought to negate the Conservative advantage of the 1832 boundary settlement in their constituencies by extending the limits of their respective boroughs.[72] Both efforts were rejected by Parliament, meaning that every parliamentary boundary enacted by the 1832 Boundary Act remained in place until the 1868 Boundary Act. Two thirds (sixty-one) of the ninety-one boundaries discussed in this chapter remained in place until the 1885 Redistribution of Seats Act, and of these, eighteen remained in place until 1918.[73]

Of the ninety-one boroughs discussed in this chapter, eighty-five eventually became municipal boroughs under the terms of the 1835 Municipal Corporations Act, and a remarkably high number of these, sixty-seven (79 per cent), were assigned their 1832 parliamentary boundaries. In one sense, this is not surprising, given that the 1833–5 municipal corporations commission shared many of the same personnel and approaches as the boundary commission.[74] However, the fact that the geographic definitions provided to many boroughs by the commissioners during the winter of 1831 were adopted at municipal level for most of the nineteenth century is significant on three levels. First, shared boundaries in parliamentary and municipal politics helped to cement the levels of shared political partisanship among constituents that flourished in parliamentary and local elections after 1832.[75] Second, the limits identified by the commissioners in 1832 provided the future physical boundaries within which many Victorian urban planners developed their modern towns and cities.[76] And third, during the 1830s the leadership and organisation of constituency politics became part of an increasingly enmeshed web of local administrative geographies overseeing parish, municipal, poor law, improvement and police administration. As 'training ground[s] for political talents' these interconnected polities were integral to the operation of reformed constituency politics, ensuring that electoral organisation continued to be defined as much by the local, as it was the national.[77]

When considered as a voting block at Westminster between 1832 and 1868 the ninety-one boroughs discussed in this chapter usually provided moderate levels of support to Whig-Liberal governments and became increasingly supportive of free trade, the abolition of church rates and the ballot by the 1850s (Graphs C.9–C.10 and Tables C.11–C.12). Unlike in the new boroughs and multiple parish boroughs, the boroughs under consideration here demonstrated higher levels of fluctuation in terms of party and government support across parliaments and were remarkably consistent in tracking the average voting behaviour of English borough MPs throughout the period (Graphs C.1, C.3, C.5 and C.7 and Tables C.3, C.5, C.7 and C.9). Both types of borough provided a small, but declining, Whig-Liberal majority in major confidence divisions in the Commons between 1832 and 1841, and aside from the radical-led rebellions of 1851 and 1855, continued to provide a reliable source of support for Whig-Liberal governments between the 1847 election and the passage of the 1867–8 reform legislation. The 1841 parliament proved the exception, when MPs representing boroughs with unchanged boundaries, in particular, swung markedly behind the Conservatives – specifically at Bedford, Cambridge, Harwich, London, Newark, Reading, Thetford, Westminster and Wigan.

On policy matters, modern town and unchanged borough MPs tracked each other quite consistently across the entire period, both switching to support for free trade in 1846, the ballot by 1852 and the abolition of church rates by 1854. However, the 1859 election led to a notable decline in the willingness of MPs who represented boroughs extended to include their modern town to support Whig-Liberal administrations, the ballot and the abolition of church rates. This was due primarily to an influx of candidates using the Liberal Conservative label, such as the MP for Truro, Montagu Smith, who had been able to use the ambiguity inherent in the label to capitalise on divisions within local Liberal ranks and secure moderate Liberal and Conservative votes.[78] Boroughs whose boundaries had remained unchanged witnessed a similar swing towards the Conservatives at the 1865 election, particularly in Lichfield, Derby, Coventry, Thetford, Bury St. Edmunds, Tiverton and Hastings. However, even with this gradual shift in parliamentary and constituency opinion towards the Conservatives from 1859, by the end of the 1865 parliament 60 per cent of MPs representing the boroughs discussed in this chapter proved willing to support Gladstone's Irish Church resolutions in April 1868. As had been the case throughout the period Whig and Liberal MPs generally fared better than Conservatives in ancient boroughs whose boundaries were extended, or clarified, in order that they encompassed their modern electoral community and space for its future growth.

While there is an observable correlation in the voting patterns of MPs representing these constituencies, the extent to which boundary reform in 1832 can be said to have caused these patterns should not be overstated. In contrast to the constituencies considered in subsequent chapters, where a particular type of boundary change caused clearer partisan shifts at Westminster, the impact of boundary changes in these boroughs evades any neat description and needs to be evaluated subtly, on a case-by-case basis. In reality, the electoral and political legacy of defining ancient boroughs according to their modern geographic communities was contingent on the continuation of ancient franchise rights after 1832, the operation of the £10 householder franchise, electorate sizes, voter registration and the evolution of localised political culture in each constituency.[79]

The decision to extend a borough's boundaries to include its modern town, or the clarification of existing boundaries, had its clearest impact in the twenty-one boroughs discussed here that had operated under a restricted corporation, burgage or freeman franchise prior to 1832. While these boroughs had technically had boundaries prior to 1832, the politics of those living within these limits had never been put through the political scrutiny of canvassing and voter registration, or publicised via poll books following elections. Whether it was a small town like Andover – whose electorate was extended from 24 to 246 – or a large city such as Bath – whose electorate expanded from 30 to 2,853 – the politics of the parishes, streets and individuals that constituted these boroughs became public knowledge for the first time after 1832, a process of politicisation that was consolidated by the 1835 Municipal Corporations Act.[80]

The political impact of this opening up of restricted boroughs into new spaces was far from straightforward. In some boroughs – such as Dartmouth and Tiverton – the pre-1832 hopes of reformers were confirmed as either government or Tory influence shifted almost immediately to local reforming landowners or manufacturers previously excluded from the representation.[81] But in other boroughs – such as Devizes, Winchester, Portsmouth or Ripon – established networks of Whig, Tory or government patronage were able to retain influence so long as they spent time and resources cultivating the new electorates within their borough's boundaries. Such cultivation was usually achieved via attention to registration, developing local party structures, the creation of votes or the generous funding of electioneering.[82] However, if established patrons did not adapt, or were unwilling to provide financial backing for the new types of local party organisation that were required to thrive in the registration courts after 1832 – as happened at Knaresborough or Scarborough – very new electoral dynamics and spaces for influence within a borough's existing, or new, geographic limits quickly developed.[83]

In the seventy boroughs discussed in this chapter that had previously enjoyed either a more extensive freeman, ratepayer or householder franchise prior to 1832 the impact of boundary extension, or clarification, was equally varied. In some cases, boundary reform proved largely inconsequential. It is difficult to suggest that the legal identification of borough boundaries, or their minor extension, via the 1832 Boundary Act caused any significant shift in political dynamics in the old inhabitant ratepayer electorates of Abingdon, Reading, Westminster, Windsor or the freeman borough of York.[84] That said, cases where boundary reform had no meaningful observable impact after 1832 are in the minority. This was because the extension of ancient boundaries into new areas of a town or city frequently led to the growth of new pockets of political influence in individual constituencies, particularly as the influence of ancient franchise voters declined in the decades after 1832, and urban (and suburban) growth extended borough settlements to the edge of their revised limits. By the 1860s, Conservatives in Exeter had derived real electoral benefit from the extension of the borough's boundaries into its surrounding suburbs in 1832, and a similarly prototypical 'villa-Toryism' was detectable in Liverpool's reformed boundary throughout the period.[85] The opposite proved to be the case in Leicester, where the borough's extended boundaries proved beneficial to local Liberals, who by the 1850s outnumbered the predominantly Anglican Conservative voter base in the centre of the city.[86] Similarly, in Northampton the shift from a potwalloper to a more elite £10 franchise within the borough's unchanged boundaries proved crucial in cementing Liberal control over the borough by the 1860s.[87]

As well as the creation of new pockets of electoral power, one of the most intriguing effects of the 1832 Boundary Act was its unforeseen impact on the evolution of electoral corruption. The extension and clarification of boundaries in 1832 combined with the enfranchisement of £10 householders and the disfranchisement of non-resident freeman 'out-voters' (those who lived more than seven miles from a borough's boundaries) to allow new cultures of electoral corruption to develop in many of England's ancient boroughs. In the freeman borough of Gloucester, for example, the resources that local parties had previously spent on transporting out-voters from London were transferred to new and existing voters within the borough's more formalised post-1832 geography. By 1849 this had led to a massive expansion in the 'agencies, bands, banners, open houses, ribbons, and all the tawdry paraphernalia of corruption' at election time, and the rise of a group of 200 'notoriously corrupt' voters who charged up to £10 for their votes.[88] In other boroughs the electoral traditions and practices of the unreformed system simply expanded, or were adapted, within new borough boundaries. In Totnes, with its previously exclusive franchise, the new £10 voters within the borough's extended boundaries quickly embraced cultures of treating and bribery, and local parties made use of the borough's extended boundaries to create fictitious voters.[89] And where thriving cultures of bribery and treating had been prevalent prior to 1832, election agents spared little resources (and faced little resistance) in extending the benefits of flagrant corrupt practices to the newly expanded areas and voters of reformed Great Yarmouth, Stafford, Sudbury and St. Albans – the details of which were widely publicised by successive election committees at Westminster and led to the disfranchisement of the latter two boroughs in 1844 and 1852.[90] That boundary extensions intended to revitalise electoral politics around a constituency's legitimate community encouraged the illegitimate aspects of electoral politics to flourish in the reformed political landscape had not been foreseen by Drummond or the Grey ministry in 1832. Their fears over the continuation of the more corrupt elements of the unreformed electoral system, as discussed in the next chapter, had instead focused on a set of boroughs whose unreformed boundaries contained far fewer electors.

Notes

1. TNA, T72/11/25, 'Stamford', Drummond to Tallents and Sheepshanks, 6 Sept. 1831.

2. The Clause 5 boroughs of Aylesbury, Cricklade, East Retford and New Shoreham, whose boundaries were reformed prior to 1832, are considered in Chapter 6.

3. N. Gash, *Politics in the Age of Peel: A Study in the Technique of Parliamentary Representation* (London, 1971), 69; P. Salmon, 'The English Reform Legislation, 1831–32', in D. Fisher (ed.), *The House of Commons, 1820–32*, i. (Cambridge, 2009), 395–401.

4. D. C. Moore, 'Concession or Cure: The Sociological Premises of the First Reform Act', *Historical Journal*, 9, 1 (1966), 52–5; D. C. Moore, *The Politics of Deference: A Study of the Mid-Nineteenth Century Political System* (New York, 1976), 173–83.

5. A. Hawkins, *Victorian Political Culture: Habits of Heart and Mind* (Oxford, 2015), 163.

6. K. Navickas, *Protest and the Politics of Space and Place 1789–1848* (Manchester, 2016), 154–76.

7. Hansard, 3, vi. (1 Sept. 1831), 1010–17.

8. PP1831–2 (141), xxxxviii. 7.

9. TNA, T72/11/9, 'Rochester'; PP1831–2 (141), xl. 29.

10. PP1831–32 (141), xl. 207; TNA, T72/10/19, 'Ludlow', pencil marking on Charles Evans's map.

11. TNA, T72/9/5, 'Dorchester'; PP1831–2 (141), xxxxviii. 194.

12. TNA, T72/10/5, 'Leominster'; Leominster was subsequently extended into its parish, Hansard, 3, xiii. (7 June 1832), 513–33; *HCJ*, lxxxvii. (8 June 1832), 390.

13. TNA, T72/9/15, 'Exeter'; *Morning Post*, 1 Dec. 1831.

14. PP1831–2 (141), xxxxviii. 122.

15. TNA, T72/10/68, 'Preston', Drummond to Allen and Romilly, 24 Sept. 1831.

16. TNA, T72/11/66, 'Winchester', Ansley and Gawler to Drummond, 16 Sept.1831.

17. M. Escott, 'Durham City', Fisher, *Commons*, ii. 369; TNA, T72/9/11, 'Durham', Drummond to Tancred and Wrottesley, 17 Oct. 1831.

18. Hansard, 3, xiii. (7 June 1832), 519–20.

19. SRO, Hatherton, D260/M/F/5/27/8, Sheepshanks to Littleton, undated (early June 1832).

20. PP1831–2 (141), xxxxviii. 7.

21. TNA, T72/11/25, 'Stamford', Drummond to Tallents and Sheepshanks, 6 Sept. 1831.

22. TNA, T72/43, 'Ledger of the Commissioners', 44, 142, 148. Four other surveyors (Rendel, Thomas, Smith and Vicars) supported this work.

23. TNA, T72/8/33, 'Bridgwater', 'Report on Bridgwater', by Birch and Brandreth.

24. TNA, T72/8/33, 'Bridgwater', 'Reference to the names and fields in the Bridgwater Plan'; PP1831–2 (141), xl. 230–31; Probably the 1802 enclosure map of Bridgwater, R. Kain et al., *The Enclosure Maps of England and Wales 1595–1918* (Cambridge, 2004), 313.

25. TNA, T72/10/25, 'Maidstone', Drinkwater and Saunders, Initial report on Maidstone, undated.

26. TNA, T72/11/22 'Shrewsbury'; TNA, T72/10/10, 'Liverpool'; TNA, T72/10/19, TNA, 'Ludlow'; PP1831–2 (141), xl. 207.

27. TNA, T72/10/10, 'Liverpool', Thornton to Drummond, 6 Jan. 1832, 15 Jan. 1832.

28. TNA, T72/43, 'Ledger of the Commissioners', 136.

29. TNA, T72/10/46, 'Newport'; TNA, T72/11/66, 'Winchester' and TNA, T72/8/18, 'Bath'.

30. TNA, T72/8/18, 'Bath'; TNA, T72/8/35, 'Bristol'.

31. TNA, T72/8/35, 'Bristol'; TNA, T72/11/66, 'Winchester'; TNA, T72/9/4, 'Devizes', Drummond to Ansley, undated (likely 13 Nov. 1831), Ansley to Drummond, 14 Nov. 1831.

32. TNA, T72/10/2, 'Lancaster'.

33. TNA, T72/9/40, 'Hull', Report on Hull by Tancred and Wrottesley, 24 Sept. 1831; TNA, T72/10/45, 'Newcastle-upon-Tyne', Report on Newcastle-upon-Tyne by Tancred and Wrottesley, 6 Oct. 1831.

34. TNA, T72/9/11, 'Durham', Drummond to Tancred and Wrottesley, 17 Oct. 1831.

35. TNA, T72/9/11, 'Durham', Drummond to Tancred and Wrottesley, 17 Oct. 1831; PP1831–2 (141), xxxxviii. 161–2.

36. PP1831–2 (141), xl. 171–2.

37. The median has been used instead of the mean to exclude outliers and account for the smaller sample set in the north and the midlands.

38. A. M. Clarke, rev. M. Hoskin, 'Sheepshanks, Richard (1794–1855)', *ODNB*, https://doi.org/10.1093/ref:odnb/25290 [accessed 9 Dec. 2022]; M. Hoskin, 'Astronomers at War: South v. Sheepshanks', *Journal for the History of Astronomy*, 20 (1989), 175–212; M. Hoskin et al., 'More on "South v. Sheepshanks"', *Journal for the History of Astronomy*, 22, 2 (1991), 174–9.

39. TNA, T72/8/42, 'Cambridge', Sheepshanks to Drummond, numbered D.32; TNA, T72/11/76, 'Great Yarmouth', Sheepshanks to Drummond ending 'Great Yarmouth, Friday night'.

40. R. Gaunt and P. O'Malley, 'Tallents, William Edwards', *ODNB*, https://doi.org/10.1093/ref:odnb/68173 [accessed 6 Aug. 2022]; R. Gaunt, *Politics, Law and Society in Nottinghamshire: The Diaries of Godfrey Tallents of Newark 1829–1839* (Nottingham, 2010), 26; R. Gaunt, *Unhappy Reactionary: The Diaries of the Fourth Duke of Newcastle-under-Lyne* (Nottingham, 2003), 64, 80, 83–4.

41. On local jurisdictions see, P. Salmon, '"Reform Should Begin at Home": English Municipal and Parliamentary Reform, 1818–32', in C. Jones, P. Salmon and R. Davis (eds.), *Partisan Politics, Principles and Reform in Parliament and the Constituencies, 1689–1880* (Edinburgh, 2004), 93–113.

42. PP1831–2 (141), xxxxviii. 5–7.

43. TNA, T72/8/42, 'Cambridge', Sheepshanks to Drummond, received 30 Sept. 1831.

44. TNA, T72/11/25, 'Stamford', numbered 'D.3', 'Observations on Stamford Report', Drummond to Tallents and Sheepshanks, 6 Sept. 1831.

45. TNA, T72/10/61, 'Peterborough', Drummond to Sheepshanks and Tallents, 8 Sept. 1831.

46. TNA, T72/8/42, 'Cambridge', Report on Cambridge received 23 Sept. 1831.

47. TNA, T72/8/42, Sheepshanks to Drummond, received 30 Sept. 1831.

48. TNA, T72/8/42, Sheepshanks to Drummond, received 30 Sept. 1831; TNA, T72/10/52, 'Northampton'; TNA, T72/10/61, 'Peterborough'; TNA, T72/10/52, 'Northampton'; TNA, T72/8/27, 'Boston'; TNA, T72/10/22, 'Lynn Regis'.

49. TNA, T72/11/25, 'Stamford', Drummond to Tallents and Sheepshanks, 6 Sept. 1831; PP1831-2 (141), xxxxix. 105-8.

50. TNA, T72/11/75, 'Great Yarmouth'.

51. TNA, T72/10/61, 'Peterborough', Tallents to Drummond, 9 Sept. 1831.

52. *Stamford Mercury*, 13 Jan. 1832, 4.

53. TNA, T72/8/27, 'Boston'; PP1831-2 (488), iii. 52; Hansard, 3, lxxxvii. (25 May 1832), 343.

54. M. Escott, 'Ord, William', in D. Fisher (ed.), *The House of Commons, 1820-1832* (Cambridge, 2009), vi. 570-82; S. Lees, 'Ord, William. H', in P. Salmon and K. Rix, *The House of Commons, 1832-1868*, (forthcoming).

55. *The Times*, 12 Aug. 1831; Moore, 'Concession or Cure', 53-4.

56. After 1832 a person could not qualify for the county franchise in respect of any property they owned, rented or leased that would qualify them to vote as a resident £10 borough householder: P. Salmon, *Electoral Reform at Work: Local Politics and National Parties, 1832-1841* (Woodbridge, 2002), 134-5, 174-5; Salmon, 'English Reform Legislation', 401-4; 2 & 3 Wm. IV, c. 45.

57. TNA, T72/11/41, 'Tewkesbury'. Tewkesbury was later thrown into its parish, see Chapter 6.

58. TNA, T72/11/72, 'Worcester'.

59. TNA, T72/11/72, 'Worcester', Report on Worcester, received 20 Sept. 1831, Ord and Chapman to Drummond, 25 Sept. 1831.

60. PP1831 (141), xl. 143.

61. TNA T72/8/62, 'Coventry', Chapman to Drummond, 1 Oct. 1831; T72/9/3, 'Derby'; T72/9/20, 'Gloucester'; T72/10/52, 'Nottingham'.

62. TNA, T72/8/62, 'Coventry', undated note by Littleton.

63. PP1831 (141), xxxix. 184; PP1831-2 (488), iii. 56; TNA, T72/10/52, 'Nottingham', B. Fryman to Littleton, 20 Dec. 1831.

64. TNA, T72/9/3, 'Derby'; PP1831 (141), xxxviii. 105.

65. Hansard, 3, xiii. (7 June 1832), 519-21, 526, 534-5, (3 July 1832), 1264, xiv. (9 July 1832), 170-2; *HLJ*, lxiv. (3 July 1832), 347-8.

66. The text of three cases (Hertford, St. Albans and Hastings) was amended due to slight descriptive errors.

67. Hansard, 3, xiii. (7 June 1832), 518-19, 531.

68. *North Devon Journal*, 14 June 1832; D. Fisher, 'Barnstaple', in Fisher, *Commons*, ii. 261-2.

69. *Hampshire Advertiser*, 3 Mar. 1832; *HCJ*, lxxxvii. (8 Mar. 1832), 176; S. Farrell, 'Poole', in Fisher, *Commons*, ii. 329; *Examiner*, 24 June 1832; *Stamford Mercury*,

24 Feb. 1832; M. Casey and P. Salmon, 'Stamford', in Fisher, *Commons*, ii. 660-61.

70. History of Parliament, Unpublished Parkes Transcripts, Parkes to Northouse, 23 June 1832; Hansard, 3, xi. (19 Mar. 1832), 406-12.

71. *Berkshire Chronicle*, 3 Mar., 14, 28 July 1832; *Oxford Journal*, 16 June 1832; D. Fisher, 'Abingdon', in Fisher, *Commons*, ii. 34.

72. Hansard, 3, xxii. (21 Apr. 1834), 1060-77; H. Miller, 'Warwick', in Salmon and Rix, *Commons 1832-1868*.

73. 2 & 3 Will. 4. c. 64 (11 July 1832); 30 & 31 Vict. c.46 (13 July 1868); 48 & 49 Vict. c.23 (25 June 1885); 8 Geo. V. c.64 (6 Feb. 1918).

74. Compiled from PP1867-8 (3972), xx. i.

75. P. Salmon, 'Local Politics and Partisanship: The Electoral Impact of Municipal Reform, 1835', *Parliamentary History*, 19, 3 (2000), 357-76.

76. A. Briggs, *Victorian Cities* (London, 1990); D. Fraser, *Urban Politics in Victorian England* (Leicester, 1976), 154-75; S. Gunn, *The Public Culture of the Victorian Middle Class* (Manchester, 2000), 36-59; P. Joyce, *The Rule of Freedom: Liberalism and the Modern City* (London, 2003), 144-82.

77. Navickas, *Politics of Space*, 165.

78. M. Spychal, 'Smith, Montagu Edward (1806-1891)', and J. Owen, 'Thetford', in Salmon and Rix, *Commons 1832-1868*.

79. Salmon, *Electoral Reform*, 254-5.

80. Salmon, *Electoral Reform*, 185-237; J. Phillips, *The Great Reform Bill in the Boroughs: English Electoral Behaviour 1818-1841* (Oxford, 1992), 211-39; Fraser, *Urban Politics in Victorian England*, 115-236.

81. *Daily News*, 8 Sept. 1868; T. Jenkins, 'Dartmouth', and 'Tiverton', in Fisher, *Commons*, ii. 267-8, 299-300.

82. *Daily News*, 17 Sept. 1849, 16 May 1857, 31 Aug., 3 Sept. 1868; *The Times*, 13, 18 Feb. 1852; P. Salmon and H. Spencer, 'Portsmouth', and 'Winchester', in Fisher, *Commons*, ii. 446, 450-61; S. Farrell, 'Wiltshire', in Fisher, *Commons*, iii. 184-5; M. Casey, 'Ripon', in Fisher, *Commons*, iii. 284; K. Rix, 'Ripon', in Salmon and Rix, *Commons 1832-1868*; Gash, *Age of Peel*, 220-23, 327, 336.

83. *Daily News*, 7 Feb., 29 Mar. 1849; M. Casey, 'Knaresborough', and 'Scarborough', in Fisher, *Commons*, iii. 272-3, 284; K. Rix, 'Knaresborough', and 'Scarborough', in Salmon and Rix, *Commons 1832-1868*; Gash, *Age of Peel*, 209-11.

84. *Daily News*, 21 Apr. 1849; D. Fisher, 'Abingdon', 'New Windsor', 'Reading', and 'Westminster', in Fisher, *Commons*, ii. 34, 38, 48, 694; M. Casey, 'York', in Fisher, *Commons*, iii. 294; K. Rix, 'York', in Salmon and Rix, *Commons 1832-1868*; Gash, *Age of Peel*, 284-300, 376-84; P. Tillott (ed.), *A History of the County of York: The City of York* (London), 268-9.

85. M. Spychal, 'The power of returning our members will henceforth be in our own hands': parliamentary reform and its impact on Exeter, 1820-1868', *Victorian Commons*, http://victoriancommons.wordpress.com [accessed 1 Aug. 2022]; Fraser, *Urban Politics in Victorian England*, 214-33; T. Jenkins, 'Exeter', in Fisher, *Commons*, ii. 267; M. Escott, 'Liverpool', in Fisher, *Commons*, ii. 592; C. Harvie, and H. C. G. Matthew, '"Villa Tories": The Conservative Resurgence', *Nineteenth-Century Britain: A Very Short Introduction* (Oxford, 2008), 107-17.

86. *Leicestershire Mercury*, 7 May 1859; H. Miller, 'Leicester', in Salmon and Rix, *Commons 1832-1868*; Fraser, *Urban Politics*, 49-51.

87. M. Spychal, 'Northampton', in Salmon and Rix, *Commons 1832-1868*.

88. *Daily News*, 3 Aug. 1849; T. Jenkins, 'Gloucester', in Fisher, *Commons*, ii. 413.

89. *The Times*, 13 Feb. 1868; T. Jenkins, 'Totnes', in Fisher, *Commons*, ii., 302-3; Gash, *Age of Peel*, 164.

90. *Norfolk News*, 29 April 1848; *Manchester Times*, 20 October 1866; *The Times*, 20 Aug. 1866; *Tavistock Gazette*, 24 Aug. 1866; M. Escott, 'Sudbury', and 'Great Yarmouth', in Fisher, *Commons*, ii. 66-7, 726-7; D. Fisher, 'St. Albans', in Fisher, *Commons*, ii. 508; P. Salmon, 'Stafford', in Fisher, *Commons*, iii. 25; H. Miller, 'Stafford', M. Spychal, 'Grote, George (1794-1871), in Salmon and Rix, *Commons 1832-1868*; M. Baer, *The Rise and Fall of Radical Westminster, 1780-1890* (Basingstoke, 2012), 30, 34-9; Gash, *Age of Peel*, 159-60.

Chapter 6

The Droitwich dilemma: Interests, grouping and the multiple parish borough

In 1832 a drastic expansion of the boundaries of the Worcestershire constituency of Droitwich increased the area of the parliamentary borough from 2.7 to 34.7 square miles. It was one of fifty constituencies extended into their surrounding parish, or parishes, by the 1832 Boundary Act, in order to ensure that every English parliamentary borough contained three hundred voters under the new £10 householder qualification. From a geographic perspective, the extension of these boroughs represented one of the most startling changes to England's reformed electoral landscape. Prior to 1832, the combined area of these constituencies had been 73.4 square miles. After 1832 it was 1,008 square miles. Norman Gash was the first historian to draw attention to the 'drastic enlargement' of this 'large class of bastard constituency', which he suggested had been intended to operate electorally like thinly 'veiled rural districts'.[1] More recently, Philip Salmon has suggested that these 'miniature counties' were established to appease wavering parliamentarians during negotiations over the English reform legislation, and were highly significant in terms of mitigating 'political divisions between town and country' at Westminster after 1832.[2] These boroughs also formed part of D. C. Moore's contention that the Grey ministry had used boundary reform to transform England's constituencies into a series of deferential electoral communities. The fifty boroughs discussed in this chapter, Moore contended, had been designed around a 'rural-agricultural-aristocratic complex' intended to create electorates deferential to the local gentry.[3]

This chapter builds on Gash and Salmon's observations, and challenges Moore's suggestion that the creation of deferential electoral communities motivated the boundary commission. The story behind these constituencies is more intricate than previously supposed. Until October 1831, the commission had proposed an alternate method of boundary reform in these boroughs – the introduction of grouped town electorates similar to those in use in Wales and Scotland. However, as the sitting committee reviewed the commissioners' reports in London from November, they became increasingly wary, for different reasons, of sanctioning such proposals. By late December, the cabinet had settled on an alternative solution of extending these boroughs into their rural surrounds, in the hope that increasing the electoral influence of the landed, agricultural interest would appease wavering and anti-reform parliamentarians over their reform legislation. Following the 1830 and 1831 elections, which witnessed an increase in support for the Whigs in England's agricultural counties, some cabinet ministers also entertained notions that such reforms might prove electorally beneficial to the government. However, as with the Grey ministry's 'spectacular own goal' of increasing the number of county seats in 1832, this Whig assessment of a long-term shift in the political opinion of the landed interest proved somewhat hasty.[4] As a result the creation of this group of fifty rural boroughs in 1832 provided a significant electoral foothold for protectionism and the emerging Conservative party over the following three decades.

Finding 300 £10 householders

In February 1831 the Grey ministry discovered that 87 English boroughs due to survive reform contained fewer than 300 houses assessed to the inhabited house duty at over £10 per annum. In order to ensure that each reformed English borough contained 300 £10 householders, the government proposed to extend these boroughs into their surrounding, or adjoining, parish. This proposal was conceived as a watered-down version of the boundary reforms that had taken place in the boroughs of New Shoreham, Cricklade, Aylesbury and East Retford since the late eighteenth century. These boroughs had been thrown into their surrounding hundred or hundreds – an administrative unit between the size of a parish and a county – as a means of purifying their corrupt electorates by adding 40s. freeholders from the surrounding county. As discussed in Chapter 1, during the 1820s this method of electoral reform became associated with the partisan advocates of the corn laws, who realised its electoral benefit for increasing the representation of MPs associated with the agricultural and landed interests.

When the government announced its reform legislation in March 1831 it did not go so far as to recommend the extension of over eighty English boroughs into their surrounding hundreds. Doing so would have been impractical, given that most boroughs only required an addition of around 100 voters, and that such extensive boundary reform would have removed large swathes of voters from the counties. It was also unpalatable to the more progressive cabinet members, two of whom – Durham and Russell – had already sought to disfranchise Shoreham, Cricklade, Aylesbury and East Retford when drafting the reform legislation. The association of these boroughs with the landed interest made them politically contentious, and their untraditional form as half-borough, half-county was inconsistent with Russell's notion of reform as a means of constitutional restoration.[5] Creating a new set of Shorehams and Cricklades also threatened to disturb the 60:40 balance for the redistribution of seats between the landed and commercial interests that the cabinet hoped might secure parliamentary approval.[6]

The compromise solution of extending each of these boroughs into their parish remained in place until August 1831, when Drummond commenced planning for the boundary commission. After preliminary investigations in London, he advised the cabinet that the parishes surrounding most of these boroughs contained very few potential £10 voters, and that an alternate means of boundary extension was required to satisfy the 300 £10 householder requirement. In response, the cabinet set an upper geographical threshold for boundary extension in these boroughs of seven miles from existing borough limits. On 1 September, the government advised the Commons that other than this seven-mile limit, the commissioners were to 'be left at full liberty to draw up instructions' for how to extend the boundaries of these boroughs.[7]

In keeping with his desire to identify a means of redrawing England's electoral map in a uniform, disinterested manner through socio-economic investigation, Drummond established several principles to guide the commissioners in these boroughs. It was hoped that some boroughs with fewer than 300 £10 householders would contain a sufficient electorate if their boundaries were extended to encompass their modern town (see Chapter 5). If this did not work the commissioners were advised to identify the most appropriate population grouping with which to enlarge a borough within seven miles of its existing limits. First, the commissioners were to consider the 'principal lines of communication' that existed between a borough and its surrounding country as well as the direction in which a borough's population was likely to develop.[8] Then, Drummond informed the commissioners: 'the employment of the surrounding population, their connection with the town or with the country, their municipal or rural character, may become proper objects of inquiry and consideration'. Drummond also established that the commissioners did not need to use the boundaries of ancient administrative divisions (such as parishes, townships and chapelries) to establish new borough limits – although he did recommend their use where possible. Instead, the commissioners were given the power to design boundaries using arbitrary lines (that might cut through a parish or township) to ensure that the most suitable population grouping within seven miles of a deficient borough could be added to its boundary.[9]

Of the 146 ancient boroughs initially visited by the commissioners, 51 contained fewer than 300 £10 householders. Only 6 of these were found to contain more than 300 £10 householders when their boundaries were extended to encompass their modern town (Truro, Totnes, Sudbury, Tavistock, Lymington and Chipping Wycombe). In eleven instances the commissioners discovered that a borough's surrounding parish, or its adjoining parish, provided an obvious means of extension. The populations of Ashburton, Horsham, Honiton and Liskeard were found to have a similar socio-economic profile to those living in their surrounding parish.[10] The boroughs of Shaftesbury, Huntingdon, Bewdley, Bridgnorth, Malton, Richmond and Cockermouth were all found to have an adjoining administrative division that contained a population with a similar economic or social interest and sufficient £10 householders. For instance, commissioners Sheepshanks and Tallents recommended that the parish of Godmanchester (which contained 129 £10 householders) be added to the ancient borough of Huntingdon (which contained 276 £10 householders). Both parishes shared a similar agricultural profile. Godmanchester's other neighbouring parish, Brampton, was unsuitable, however, as it was 'liable to be overflowed and wholly unfit for sites of houses'.[11]

In the remaining thirty-four cases the commissioners were unable to identify such conveniently matched, adjoining, administrative divisions. This problem had become increasingly apparent by the end of September 1831, by which point the commissioners in Districts A, B and E had encountered difficult cases in Reigate, Christchurch and Droitwich. The number of £10 houses associated with the modern town in each of these boroughs was considerably fewer than 300, and in each case an appropriate nearby town within seven miles was identified with which to augment the original borough's electorate. However, the commissioners reported that these towns were separated from their respective boroughs by large swathes of countryside, whose scattered populations appeared to have a different social and economic profile. Although the commissioners had been granted permission to draw arbitrary lines to connect comparative areas, their original instructions required they connect any area to an original borough using 'continuous lines'. This meant that in order to extend the original borough to include its nearby similarly profiled town, some portion of the intervening non-matching countryside had to be included. The example of Droitwich (for which a full run of correspondence survives in the working papers of the boundary commission) provides an illustrative case study of how the commission attempted to deal with these boroughs.

Droitwich, grouping and the subtleties of interest representation

When commissioners Ord and Chapman visited Droitwich in September 1831, they reported to Drummond that the entire population associated with the town consisted of 128 £10 householders and that its local economy was based on salt production.[12] By contrast, the nine parishes and 20,000 acres of countryside that surrounded the borough were found to contain 123 'wholly rural' £10 voters. Based on their interpretation of Drummond's instructions, the commissioners felt that the most appropriate population within seven miles with which they could increase Droitwich's electorate was Bromsgrove (Map 6.1). The town contained over 200 £10 householders, its population was engaged chiefly in nail-making and the inhabitants of both towns, when asked, had suggested 'Bromsgrove as the only source' of similarly interested voters with which to increase Droitwich's electorate.[13] The difficulty that the commissioners discovered was that in order to unite the two towns, their instructions recommended they do so via arbitrary, continuous lines that required the inclusion of some of the intervening agricultural district. For the commissioners, this appeared to defeat the object of creating borough electorates with broadly similar social and economic interests. They also expressed concern that an arbitrary boundary would remove freeholders in Droitwich's surrounding agricultural districts from the county franchise. They advised Drummond that such a recommendation would:

> ... be liable to much objection, because the interposed agricultural population will find themselves overwhelmed by their more powerful

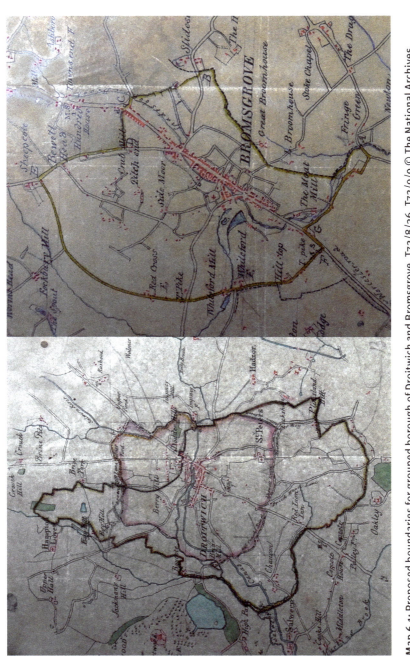

Map 6.1: Proposed boundaries for grouped borough of Droitwich and Bromsgrove, T72/8/36, T72/9/9 © The National Archives.

and numerous neighbours in the election of a <u>single</u> member [in the borough of Droitwich] – and will be deprived of their privilege of voting for <u>two</u> members in the county [of Worcester].[14]

Although it was not clear whether they had the power to do so, the commissioners suggested that it might be more appropriate to assign distinct boundaries around Droitwich and Bromsgrove, and group both towns in the franchise, as was commonplace in Welsh boroughs and Scottish burghs (Map 6.1).[15]

When Drummond received this report in late September, the same commissioners had already enquired into the viability of grouping Evesham with nearby Pershore.[16] Drummond had also received a similar report from commissioners Drinkwater and Saunders, who had suggested grouping Reigate with Dorking.[17] Although the government had not sanctioned grouping, Drummond discovered that both pairs of commissioners had made their own interpretation of the 7 September draft of the reform bill, since its publication in the national press. This version of the bill stated that in boroughs with fewer than 300 £10 householders, the commissioners were empowered to include 'any part of any one or more parishes, townships or other places ... within seven statute miles of such city or borough'.[18] After clarifying the issue with the government, Drummond advised Ord and Chapman that:

> It is not required by the [reform] Act [sic] that the line connecting the two places should be continuous ... it is not the intention of government to introduce any restriction into the clause – and all admit that as it now stands we have the power [to propose grouping].[19]

Drummond's discussions with the government revealed that, while grouping was allowed, there had to be clear economic and social similarities between the two towns being connected, and some evidence that the boundary changes would be accepted in the locality. On the matter of Droitwich, he advised:

> is this town of the same description as Bromsgrove? Are its inhabitants more connected with manufactures than with agriculture; are the interests of both these towns essentially the same; if you reply in the affirmative, then your recommendation will most probably be approved of.

Drummond expressed concern that the salt producers of Droitwich might actually be more closely associated with their surrounding agricultural parishes than the nail-makers of Bromsgrove. He warned both commissioners to be cautious not to 'injure the <u>interest</u> to which that constituency

[Droitwich] is attached [in the Commons]', advising against simplistic definitions of interest that conflated 'town' with 'manufacturing', and 'agricultural' with 'rural'.[20] Setting boundaries, in Drummond's mind, required a subtle conception of interest representation – one that accepted that as much difference of interest could exist between two town populations, as between a town and an agricultural district, and that scattered rural populations could also be connected to town settlements.

The commissioners revisited Droitwich in November, but only found further complications. Following their original visit, rumours had spread locally that Droitwich might be grouped with Bromsgrove or expanded into its surrounding countryside. Both options, it transpired, were equally unpopular. The inhabitants of Droitwich feared being overwhelmed in future elections by the interests of voters in the larger town of Bromsgrove. Meanwhile, county voters around Droitwich were unhappy about the prospect of sacrificing their two county votes, only to be overpowered by Droitwich's inhabitants in the election of a single borough member who was unlikely to represent their interests.[21] Both complaints were considered to be legitimate grievances. Whatever decision the commission made, one population's legitimate interest had to be marginalised to create a borough that contained 300 £10 householders.

The guidance provided by Drummond over grouping was not published in the official boundary commission reports. However, it was distributed to the commissioners, who by late November had proposed grouping as an option in at least twenty-six boroughs (Table 6.1). The commissioners took two distinct approaches when interpreting this guidance. The first was best exemplified by commissioners Drinkwater and Saunders in District A. They exhibited the same subtlety in their conception of interest representation as Drummond and were unwilling to propose the grouping of two towns without good reason. New Winchelsea, for instance, was felt to be a suitable addition to Rye as both towns were ports. Likewise, Arundel and Littlehampton were felt to have a natural connection due to a connecting river and the manner in which coal distribution in Sussex was managed between both towns.[22] By contrast, they opposed grouping Maldon and Heybridge, due to an ongoing rivalry that existed between the two towns following the recent development of a canal that had diverted trade past the latter at the expense of the former.[23] They also advised against grouping Lyme Regis with Axminster as they were in separate counties and had no obvious economic or social connection.[24] In general the commissioners in Districts C, D and E approached grouping on this basis.

By contrast, Gawler and Ansley in District B had interpreted their ability to propose grouping simply as a requirement that all future borough constituencies contained 300 predominantly town-based £10 householders

Table 6.1: Boroughs for which grouping options were identified prior to 20 December 1832.[1]

Constituency	Grouping proposal
Amersham	Beaconsfield (disfranchised by third reform bill)
Arundel	Littlehampton
Bodmin	Lostwithiel
Buckingham	Multiple nearby towns identified, but none deemed ideal
Calne	Melksham
Chippenham	Corsham
Christchurch	Ringwood
Droitwich	Bromsgrove
Great Grimsby	Caistor
Great Marlow	Maidenhead
Hythe	Folkestone
Lyme Regis	Axminster (identified, but not deemed an ideal match)
Maldon	Heybridge (identified, but not deemed an ideal match)
Malmesbury	Tetbury
Marlborough	Ramsbury and Aldborough
Morpeth	Bedlington
Northallerton	Thirsk
Penryn	Falmouth
Reigate	Dorking
Rye	New Winchelsea
Thetford	Brandon (identified, but not deemed an ideal match)
Thirsk	Northallerton and Sowerby
Wallingford	Several nearby villages proposed as optional
Wareham	Corfe Castle
Westbury	Warminster and Trowbridge
Wilton	Fisherton

[1] Compiled from TNA, T72.

– even if there was no obvious economic or social connection between the two towns proposed for association. Their recommendations also had a more overtly reformist bent, in so much as they saw grouping as a necessary means of increasing the political respectability of the small, often economically depressed towns that were associated with small boroughs. For instance, Tetbury was identified as the most suitable place to be grouped with Malmesbury because it was the largest, most respectable town within seven miles. They described Malmesbury itself as 'a place of no trade whatever, and not a great thoroughfare, [with] no stage-coach of any kind running to or through the town',[25] and lamented privately to Drummond that the town's inhabitants were generally 'indifferent about having members to represent them'.[26] They paid little attention to the socio-economic profile of the two towns, and even acknowledged that Tetbury was in a different county to Malmesbury. Nevertheless, they felt that the size and respectability of Tetbury marked it out as the most suitable grouping option. All nine of Ansley and Gawler's grouping proposals were identified in a similar manner, according to the size and respectability of eligible towns, with little attention being paid to the actual interests those towns purported to represent.[27] Even though Wrottesley and Tancred in District G were more thorough in terms of reporting on the social and economic profile of the towns they visited, their approach bore more resemblance to that of Ansley and Gawler than of the other commissioners.[28]

Of the eight remaining boroughs that were due to remain enfranchised prior to December 1831 and contained fewer than 300 £10 householders, it is impossible to confirm whether grouping was considered, as the commissioners' original reports have not survived. In five boroughs (St. Ives, Launceston, Helston, Clitheroe and Saltash) it is likely grouping was considered, but in three (Aldborough, East Grinstead and Okehampton, all of which were later disfranchised), no eligible place within seven miles of the borough was identified.[29] Until 20 December 1831 the commissioners had considered grouping as the government's preferred option for ensuring that every reformed borough contained 300 £10 householders. In some boroughs, however, the options available for grouping were far from ideal. Not only did grouping seem potentially unpopular, but in some cases, it threatened to marginalise the interest that an ancient borough had traditionally represented in the Commons. Following the receipt of the commissioners' individual proposals, it was left to the sitting committee of the commission and the cabinet to agree on how to proceed.

The sitting committee, the cabinet and the Waverers

When Drummond, Littleton and Beaufort, as the sitting committee of the boundary commission, commenced its review of the commissioners' proposals in late October 1831, their largest source of apprehension derived from the thirty-four proposals in which grouping had been considered.[30] Droitwich was one of the first cases considered and became an important test case. On reviewing the commissioners' report, Beaufort was wary that the commission did not have sufficient authority to recommend grouping Droitwich with Bromsgrove: 'the policy of associating two distant and independent towns appears to involve considerations of far too great importance to be left to the discretion of the commissioners. Government or the legislature should decide the point'.[31]

For Littleton, grouping threw up important political questions, which, in contrast to Beaufort's bureaucratic deference, he felt compelled to steer the cabinet towards answering to his satisfaction. First, Littleton feared that grouping would throw the government's rationale for disfranchisement into disarray. If Droitwich (in Schedule B) was allowed to retain the franchise through grouping, the principle, he remarked, could reasonably be claimed for Schedule A boroughs, which because of their insufficient populations had been scheduled to be completely disfranchised.[32] Littleton's primary concern, however, was that all available options for extending Droitwich's boundaries were likely to have a significant impact on electoral politics in Worcestershire. He feared that extending Droitwich into 20,000 acres of surrounding countryside would remove hundreds of voters from the county, and also that extending the borough to Bromsgrove (through either continuous lines or grouping) would remove an important town influence from Worcestershire's county elections.[33] These problems were compounded for Littleton by the fact Worcestershire was proposed to be divided; Dudley and Kidderminster were due to be enfranchised; and Evesham and Bewdley also appeared to require large boundary extensions. He wrote in his diary on 31 October: 'Bewdley will swallow Stourport, Evesham, Pershore, Droitwich, Bromsgrove, Kidderminster to be enfranchised – There will not be a <u>town</u> left [in Worcestershire] except Stourbridge'.[34]

For Littleton, the question of extending borough boundaries to obtain 300 £10 householders required careful thought. He feared that the blanket removal of town voters from England's counties, through either boundary or franchise changes, would lead to a reformed Commons divided between 'a town party and a county party – and jealousy and hatred would thus be engendered, and would endure till one party destroyed the other'.[35] His preferred option was to not divide the counties. Or, if the counties were to be divided, disfranchise Droitwich altogether so as to ensure that some town influence remained in the county division in which both Droitwich and Bromsgrove fell. Similar considerations, Littleton felt, would be required in other counties that contained a high number of boroughs in need of extensive boundary change.[36]

Littleton maintained close contact with the cabinet throughout November and December in an attempt to address his concerns. His first port of call was Russell, whom he met on 8 November. From this initial meeting Littleton discovered that the cabinet had not considered the question of these boundaries in detail and had not intended to do so until additional cabinet members, particularly Brougham, had returned to Westminster following parliament's recent prorogation.[37] Littleton continued to discuss the ongoing work of the boundary commission with Russell over the following days, and on 15 November, Russell, Grey and Althorp met the sitting committee at the Privy Council office.[38] Unfortunately for Littleton, the primary purpose of this meeting was not, as he had presumed, to provide clarity over boroughs such as Droitwich. Rather, Grey had spotted an opportunity to use the information already collected by the commission to put him one step ahead in his negotiations with the 'Waverers' – a group of peers who sought to moderate the reform bill in return for its safe passage through the Lords.[39]

One concession that Grey was willing to make to the Waverers was the removal of plans for single-member boroughs from the reform bill (those in Schedule B and Schedule D).[40] In the unreformed electoral system, the English double-member constituency was widely celebrated for its ability to allow for compromise agreements between parties, reduce the need for contested elections and ensure a level of minority representation.[41] It transpired that Grey and Althorp had seized on grouping as a means of retaining the double-member borough principle across England's reformed electoral map. They enquired into the viability of an elaborate scheme that disfranchised some Schedule B boroughs; grouped some Schedule B boroughs with each other; grouped some Schedule D boroughs with each other; and extended the number of £10 householders in others in order that all boroughs could return two members.[42] Such a scheme would have inadvertently addressed the sitting committee's misgivings over boroughs like Droitwich, as twenty-one of the twenty-nine boroughs in which grouping had already been proposed were in Schedule B.[43] In such a proposal, Droitwich could have been grouped with Evesham (which also stood in Schedule B), leaving Bromsgrove and Pershore to participate in Worcestershire's county elections.

Even though this scheme satisfied one of Littleton's concerns, both he and Russell expressed reservations over its impact. They feared that anti-reformers would claim the right of grouping for Schedule A boroughs, as well as the electoral consequence of indiscriminately forcing together boroughs with conflicting interests. Russell suggested an alternative arrangement, which proposed to abolish Schedule B but increase the amount of total disfranchisement from fifty-seven to seventy-two boroughs; reduce the number of enfranchisements from forty to thirty but allow all new boroughs to return two MPs; and reduce the borough franchise to all rated houses. This latter option appeared preferable to Littleton, as it removed the need for extensive boundary change in the remaining Schedule B boroughs and double-member boroughs that contained fewer than 300 £10 householders.[44]

Ultimately, Grey and Althorp's grouping scheme was proposed to the Waverers the following day.[45] By early November 1831, then, as far as Littleton was aware, the government's plan to appease the Waverers by abandoning Schedule B was genuine. Furthermore, although the solution may not have been to his liking, it appeared to have settled the question of boundaries in boroughs such as Droitwich. Over the following days, the increased participation of the Waverers' chief cabinet allies, Lansdowne and Palmerston, in discussions over boundary changes at the Privy Council office seemed to confirm this view.[46] Unknown to Littleton, however, these negotiations had stalled by the end of November, following the cabinet's growing concerns over the political unions, the Waverers' increasingly impractical demands and Brougham's return to London.[47] The cabinet decided on 29 November to retain Schedule B, but offer the Waverers a slight reduction in the amount of boroughs to be partially disfranchised – news that did not reach Littleton until 2 December, and returned the sitting committee to its original impasse.[48]

The cabinet agrees a way forward

In the three weeks prior to the government's introduction of their third reform bill on 12 December, the priorities of the boundary commission shifted to the remodelling of the disfranchisement schedules (see Chapter 4). Following this, Littleton renewed discussions with Russell and Althorp in an attempt to clarify the government's intentions over boroughs with fewer than 300 £10 householders. Littleton now preferred that the sitting committee be granted authority to consider each of these boroughs on a case-by-case basis (with grouping allowed when appropriate) in order that boundaries could be based on local circumstance.[49] Such a decision would have allowed the commission to draw from its vast amount of socioeconomic investigation, while also allowing Littleton the power to design boundaries, to his liking, in the midlands. Such a decision was not forthcoming, however, and following cabinet discussions on 20 December 1831 an alternative solution was identified.

In one final concession to the Waverers, the cabinet agreed to a boundary scheme that, it transpired, Lansdowne and Palmerston had been advocating since late November.[50] Both wanted to extend every ancient borough that contained fewer than 300 £10 householders into its surrounding agricultural district in order to provide a blanket increase in the influence of voters associated with the 'landed interest' in the boroughs.[51] In effect, they wanted to revive proposals for a slightly tamer version of what had happened in the four corrupt boroughs that had been thrown into their surrounding hundreds since the late eighteenth century – and which, as discussed above, had been proposed as a solution to these boroughs since February 1831. Palmerston and Lansdowne hoped such reforms would appeal to moderates as they promised to counterbalance the increased influence of resident, but not necessarily property-owning, voters in newly enfranchised boroughs, but also provide greater opportunities for candidates supportive of political issues connected with the landed interest at future elections. The reform bill had already sought to provide for an increased representation of these interests by giving additional seats to the counties and extending the county franchise to copyholders and £50 occupiers, and, as discussed in Chapter 2, by dividing the counties and removing large portions of town populations from the county franchise by enfranchising new boroughs.[52]

In November, Lansdowne had proposed that the commissioners draw a two-mile radius around each borough containing fewer than 300 £10 householders.[53] However, the data already gathered by the commission suggested that in most cases this would not supply 300 £10 voters. After consulting the commissioners' draft reports during December, Lansdowne and Palmerston instead proposed that these boroughs should be extended up to four miles into their neighbouring parishes or townships until the requisite number of £10 householders was achieved.[54] On 20 December the cabinet agreed to Lansdowne's scheme (with the support of Grey and Goderich), which they hoped would 'ensure' the reform bill's success.[55] As a result, they provided new instructions to the commissioners that were backdated to 24 November when published, so as to prevent parliament from discovering that they had agreed to this plan after the introduction of their third reform bill.[56] Following news of the cabinet's decision, Littleton discovered that his attempts since November to influence the cabinet through Russell had been futile. Russell, according to Melbourne, had been less than forceful in raising the issue at cabinet during November and December, or advocating on Littleton's behalf when he did.[57]

The cabinet's new instruction was not received well by the boundary commission. Having just completed a last-minute survey of England's smallest boroughs for the purpose of remodelling the disfranchisement schedules, the commissioners were now required to complete an immediate visit to every borough that contained fewer than 300 £10 householders, and for which their proposed boundaries did not meet the new criteria. Littleton wrote in his diary on 21 December: 'poor Drummond [is] at work trying to coax the commissioners into good humour with the government instructions. Many of their reports must be torn, and reconstructed, and many of them must revisit their boroughs in the frost and snow'.[58]

The commissioners were now required to shelve their proposal to group Bromsgrove and Droitwich. Instead, they drew a circle with a four-mile radius on top of their map of the borough and gathered new £10 householder data for each of the parishes within this circle (Map 6.2). This provided an addition of 130 £10 householders to the existing borough of Droitwich's 128 £10 householders. As this was still below the desired level of 300, the commissioners extended their search into three adjoining parishes (parts of which were within four miles of the borough), where they discovered an additional 53 £10 householders. In stark contrast to the commissioners' initial report in September, which had discounted Droitwich's surrounding parishes as inappropriate for extension on the basis of the size of the boundary and the fact that the surrounding population was 'wholly rural', their final proposed boundary now covered 37.4 square miles and contained a majority of rural, previously county freehold, voters.[59]

The 20 December instructions led to wholesale changes in the commissioners' recommendations ahead of the publication of their proposals in

Map 6.2: Four-mile radius around Droitwich for identifying reformed boundary, T72/9/9 © The National Archives.

February 1832. Instead of proposing to extend Tavistock and Chipping Wycombe to encompass their modern town, the sitting committee now felt no qualms in extending both boroughs into their extensive surrounding parish due to doubts over the number of £10 householders in both boroughs.[60] Similar doubts about the number of £10 householders in Shaftesbury led to the borough's extension into thirteen parishes.[61] The sitting committee also had little hesitation in now recommending that five boroughs (Banbury, Peterborough, Tamworth, Grantham and Tewkesbury) whose ancient boundaries had included just over 300 £10 householders should be extended into their surrounding parish. Four further boroughs (New Woodstock, Midhurst, Eye and Petersfield) that had recently escaped disfranchisement due to the remodelling of the disfranchisement schedules were extended into multiple surrounding parishes.[62] And, as was the case with Droitwich, the commissioners' final reports recommended large extensions to twenty-six of the thirty-four boroughs where grouping had originally been considered. Of the seven that were not, five were disfranchised (Aldborough, Amersham, East Grinstead, Okehampton and Saltash) as a result of the remodelled disfranchisement schedules, and the remaining three (Thetford, Penryn and Hythe) were all considered anomalies. It was agreed to leave Thetford's existing boundary (which already encompassed three parishes) unchanged, as the addition of every parish within four miles of the borough (an area that cut across two counties) only contained an additional thirty-nine £10 houses.[63] As parliament had already agreed to associate the borough of Penryn with nearby Falmouth during debates on the second reform bill, and both towns combined contained over 300 £10 householders, they were connected by an arbitrary line that the commissioners reported allowed for future growth between the two towns.[64] And, the commission proposed that Hythe be connected to Folkestone (which was five miles from the borough) by arbitrary lines on the basis that the former was on the coast, half of the area included in a four-mile radius around the town included the sea, and its surrounding parishes on land contained insufficient £10 householders.[65]

Hythe was one of eight of the commissioners' published proposals that were subsequently overruled by parliament during debates over the boundary bill. In June 1832 parliament agreed to extend the four-mile limit for expanding Hythe, in order that the parish that contained Folkestone could be included in the borough without drawing arbitrary lines.[66] Following a close reading of the commission's reports by anti-reformers, particularly Croker, the government also agreed to extend Cirencester and Leominster into their surrounding parish to maintain consistency with boroughs that contained just over 300 £10 householders, and which the sitting committee had agreed to throw into their parish. Similarly, the government agreed to extend Rye, Helston and St. Ives into even more surrounding parishes than originally proposed, on the basis that the number of £10 houses in the commissioners' original published recommendations were on the cusp of 300.[67] Wareham was also extended even further than initially recommended, after the government eventually decided to risk offending several MPs who had a personal interest in the borough by moving a Lords amendment that lifted the four-mile limit for borough extension in order to ensure the borough contained over 300 £10 householders – creating a reformed borough that spread over 50 square miles.[68]

The only other modification that took place to the commissioners' boundary proposals for boroughs with fewer than 300 £10 householders was in Arundel. Commissioners Drinkwater and Saunders's proposal to extend the borough into the parish of Leominster (Lyminster) and Littlehampton unwittingly invoked the anger of local inhabitants, and, unfairly prompted accusations from anti-reformers that the commissioners had identified their boundary in order to give the Whig Duke of Norfolk control of the borough.[69] In reality, Littlehampton had initially been identified as a suitable socio-economic partner for grouping with Arundel, and following the 20 December instruction the sitting committee had agreed to include Littlehampton and two further parishes in the borough to ensure it contained 300 £10 householders.[70] As the dispute over the commission's recommendations threatened to disrupt the relatively smooth discussions that had taken place over the boundary bill up to that point, a select committee was established to consider the borough's boundaries and a surveyor was sent to Arundel to re-count the number of £10 houses in the ancient borough. Somewhat conveniently for the government, who were willing to compromise if it meant passing the boundary bill quickly, the surveyor reported that there were over 300 £10 householders within Arundel's ancient limits, negating any need to extend the borough's boundary.[71] This appears to be one of the few examples where the government actively doctored figures provided by the commissioners (who had originally reported that after 'very minute discussion' with local officials the maximum number of £10 houses in the ancient borough was 254) in order to ensure the passage of the boundary bill.[72]

'Deference communities' and political impact

After the various modifications to the commissioners' original proposals following the 20 December instruction, as well as parliamentary negotiations over the boundary bill, the 1832 Boundary Act extended fifty ancient English boroughs into their surrounding parish or parishes. Following 1832,

Table 6.2: Area of boroughs extended into their parish or parishes following 1832.[1]

Constituency	Pre-1832 (sq. miles)	Post-1832 (sq. miles)
Ashburton	Not known	10.82
Banbury	0.20	7.31
Bewdley	3.20	11.47
Bodmin	4.50	24.73
Bridgnorth	1.80	17.44
Buckingham	8.00	28.64
Calne	1.60	13.46
Chippenham	0.10	17.19
Christchurch	0.70	37.04
Cirencester	0.10	7.27
Clitheroe	3.60	25.09
Cockermouth	3.90	13.02
Droitwich	2.70	37.41
Eye	6.40	32.27
Grantham	0.20	9.29
Great Marlow	0.10	22.65
Grimsby	2.60	28.65
Helston	0.20	8.23
Honiton	0.10	5.04
Horsham	0.30	16.99
Huntingdon	1.90	9.68
Hythe	2.50	21.93
Launceston	2.60	23.61
Leominster	1.40	12.56
Liskeard	3.70	13.83
Lyme Regis	0.20	2.89
Maldon	5.40	8.91
Malmesbury	0.20	34.11
Malton	0.10	11.02
Marlborough	0.30	6.86
Midhurst	0.90	42.39
Morpeth	0.40	28.13
New Woodstock	0.10	32.04
Northallerton	Not known	16.41
Peterborough	2.50	9.47
Petersfield	0.40	36.80
Reigate	0.10	9.73
Richmond	2.97	12.69
Rye	1.60	34.57
Shaftesbury	0.30	36.95
St. Ives	2.80	13.75
Tamworth	0.30	18.14

Lyme Regis was the smallest of these boroughs by area at 2.9 square miles, while Wilton at 50.8 square miles was the largest. The median area of these fifty boroughs prior to 1832 was 0.55 square miles; after 1832 it was 17.31 square miles (Table 6.2). Such extensive boundary changes had not been envisaged by the government until the end of December 1831, and were inconsistent with the principles by which the boundary commission had redrawn the rest of England's reformed borough map. However, the government had been forced into making these boundary changes as a result of the commission, whose work revealed that England's small boroughs and their surrounds contained considerably fewer £10 householders than had ever been envisaged when the £10 franchise level was agreed in February 1831. Drummond and his commissioners had initially sought to address this problem by proposing the introduction of the grouping principle into England's borough representation – a process that previous histories of the 1832 reform legislation have not acknowledged. They did so in the hope that boroughs with fewer than 300 £10 householders might remain as consistent as was possible with their ancient socio-economic profile and associated parliamentary interest after 1832. The rejection of the second reform bill in October 1831, and the government's negotiations with the Waverers during November led

Table 6.2 continued

Constituency	Pre-1832 (sq. miles)	Post-1832 (sq. miles)
Tavistock	0.50	17.90
Tewkesbury	0.08	3.86
Thirsk	0.11	18.24
Wallingford	0.60	27.48
Wareham	0.70	50.53
Westbury	0.04	18.42
Wilton	0.20	50.76
Wycombe	0.20	9.99

[1] PP1831–2 (92) (126) (493), xxxvi. 31, 91, 479; PP1859 (166), xxiii. 121, PP1867–8 (3972), xx. 1; Great Britain Historical GIS Project, University of Portsmouth (2012). The use of the GIS dataset accounts for the difference between figures in Gash, *Age of Peel*, 432–33; Salmon, 'English Reform Legislation, 395–401.

to a considerable delay in establishing whether these boundary designs would be sanctioned. Ultimately, the commission's efforts were disregarded in favour of arbitrary boundary changes that caused indiscriminate alterations to the socio-economic profile of these boroughs, and were intended to appease wavering parliamentarians over the reform bill by increasing the influence of the landed, agricultural interest in borough elections.

Two questions arise from this episode. First, what does it tell us about the intention of the reform bill's architects, and second, what impact did these boroughs have on the reformed electoral system? In 1966 D. C. Moore suggested that the creation of these fifty extensive boroughs had been a constituent part of a Whig plan to transform England's parliamentary constituencies, via socio-economic investigation, into 'deference communities'. Namely, communities that consisted of 'men who lived in close contact with one another, who had the same occupation or were connected by the same "interest", and – most important of all – who recognised the same individual as their social, economic and ideological leader'.[73] Moore made use of the commissioners' August 1831 instructions to contend that in boroughs containing fewer than 300 £10 householders the government had intended to create electoral communities that were deferential to leaders associated with a 'rural-agricultural-aristocratic complex'.[74] A key aspect of this, Moore argued, had been the process through which the boundary commission designed boundaries that ensured these boroughs represented 'one interest, and … one interest only'.[75] Doing so allegedly provided local elites in each of these reformed boroughs with a deferential electorate – as long as those elites took steps to identify themselves with 'the interests their constituencies symbolized'.[76]

On one level, the working papers of the commission reveal that Moore was correct to identify that geographic, economic and social investigation, as well as a consideration of interest representation, underpinned the work of the boundary commission. However, Moore's suggestion that the desired end of this investigative method was the creation of deference communities is less defensible. At a basic level, Moore incorrectly supposed that the boroughs discussed in this chapter were created as a result of the commissioners' original instructions, when in fact they were agreed to in late December 1831 as a last-minute concession to the Waverers. Furthermore, in stark contrast to what Moore claimed, the ultimate extension of (for example) Droitwich into its rural surrounds created a borough that the boundary commission knew contained a mixture of commercial and agricultural interests – not a rural-agricultural-aristocratic complex. Even if Moore's theory regarding how the government intended that elites should control deferential communities was correct, in reformed Droitwich a multiplicity of local interests existed with which prospective local elites had to align themselves in the reformed system. Far from simplifying the electoral conditions of boroughs for prospective local candidates and their agents as Moore supposed, these changes complicated them.

It might be contended that the government's original intention for deference communities manifested itself in the commissioners' proposals for grouped constituencies – due to the fact that these more closely resembled single-interest boroughs. However, even if the commission's proposals for grouping had been implemented, the geographic position of England's ancient boroughs was more likely to have led to the creation of an assortment of mixed-interest commercial or mixed-interest agricultural boroughs. For instance, Droitwich's salt-makers would have been united with Bromsgrove's nail-makers. Even though both together could have been held to represent the commercial interest, broadly defined, it is unlikely that prospective candidates would have found the ensuing electorates easy to manage. The commission's work more often than not discovered subtle complexities in the economic and social make-up of the population groupings that surrounded England's deficient boroughs. Given this, the commission would have quickly realised that any governmental ambition to create deference communities (even accepting the anachronism of such a concept) would have been unrealistic.[77]

If their ambition had not been to create deference communities, why did the commission base their investigation around socio-economic investigation? Furthermore, why was the commission so eager to conceptualise the boroughs and towns they investigated by interest? As discussed in the previous three chapters, resort to geographic and socio-economic investigation had provided the commission with a bureaucratic framework with which they could rationalise their investigation into England's constituency structure, and which avoided a direct consideration of the political and electoral consequences of their boundary changes. The second question is perhaps best answered by a rephrasing of the question. Why would the commission *not* have conceptualised boroughs by interest? As the first chapter of this book demonstrated, for contemporaries, interest representation was integral to understanding how constituencies operated, and a rebalancing of the representation of interests underpinned the Grey ministry's ambitions for parliamentary reform.

As far as the boroughs discussed in this chapter were concerned, what eventually trumped this focus on interests was a need to ensure that every reformed borough contained over 300 £10 householders. The boundary commission, Grey and Althorp, Russell and Littleton, and then Palmerston and Lansdowne all developed different schemes that they hoped would ensure these conditions. Each scheme, if accepted, would have introduced its own set of electoral variables into a small number of England's reformed boroughs and was based on its own conception of an ideal balance of interest representation. An advanced and all-encompassing desire to create deference communities, as Moore posits, did not underpin any of these schemes. In reality, the scheme that was finally agreed to had been conceived as a means of tempering the electoral influence of the non-property-owning £10 householder in small boroughs with voters who had historically proved their constitutional worth as freeholders in the counties. While this makes Moore's deference thesis less plausible, it does reveal that the Grey ministry was open to the kind of constitutionally curative thinking that he has argued influenced the 1832 reform legislation.[78]

Even if Moore's deference thesis is unconvincing, it is clear that the extension of constituency boundaries in these fifty boroughs ensured that landed proprietors continued to wield significant electoral influence in reformed borough politics. In at least twenty-one cases, patrons maintained, or re-established, a preponderating influence over a constituency for most, if not all, of the reformed period.[79] In thirteen boroughs power was diffused between two or more landlords.[80] And in a further nine, new landed proprietors assumed a major influence over constituency politics after 1832.[81]

The path to establishing, or re-establishing influence was rarely straightforward, however. And while these boroughs – many of which were included in Gash's enduring categorisation of post-1832 'proprietary boroughs' – retained their pre-reform names, the drastic changes to their electoral geographies and electorates meant the reality of local proprietorial influence and electoral politics was much more complex after 1832 than it had been before.[82] Building on Edwin Jaggard's reappraisal of the nature of politics in England's small boroughs, the retention of proprietorial influence required one, or several, of the following electoral strategies: close attention to the electoral register; the cultivation of local parties; continual patronage of a borough between elections; ensuring candidates were broadly in line with shifts in local opinion; the provision of pecuniary benefits to electors and non-electors; and more dubious corrupt practices such as vote creation.[83] Furthermore, securing influence was not always immediate and, in many instances, took several years of constituency nursing to achieve. In most of these boroughs too, the influence of a known patron was regularly susceptible to challenges from 'independent' Liberal or Conservative interests and could be lost if continual attention was not paid to the electorate, or if a new landed, financial or commercial interest emerged in a constituency's limits.

Of the twenty-one boroughs that remained under an established interest, even the most blatant pocket boroughs such as Calne (under the Whig marquess of Lansdowne), Wilton (under the Conservative, and later Peelite, Pembroke interest) and Huntingdon (under the Conservative Sandwich interest) experienced occasional, if not doomed, challenges to proprietorial control between 1832 and 1868.[84] On paper, the former burgage borough of Eye, which had been controlled by the Conservative Kerrison interest prior to 1832 and returned a Kerrison unopposed at each election following 1832, appears as one of the most obvious examples of Gash's proprietary boroughs.[85] Under the surface, however, the Kerrison family worked consistently to maintain their influence, via continued local philanthropy, assuming a prominent position in Conservative county politics and keeping close ties with Eye's Conservative Association in this sprawling agricultural borough.[86] Securing influence was less straightforward for successive dukes of Northumberland in the previously restricted freeman borough of Launceston, which required massive levels of organisation and expenditure during the 1830s to manage registration and the provision of pecuniary rewards for voters.[87]

Once in control, proprietors could not rest on their laurels. Even though the local Conservative party was able to claim a majority in the parishes added to Peterborough in 1832, the established Whig Fitzwilliam interest was able to maintain control of the borough's two seats through to the 1850s, via a tacit alliance with the borough's numerically significant 'independent' Liberals. However, when the fifth Earl Fitzwilliam overplayed his hand in forcing a moderate second candidate on the constituency in 1852, a coalition of independent Liberals and Conservatives united over a seven-year period of frenzied electoral activity (with all sides employing a range of corrupt practices) to finally capitalise on the borough's reformed electoral geography and secure one of the borough's seats by 1859.[88] Unexpected shifts in a borough's economy could also spell the end for a proprietor who had maintained control of a borough after 1832. In Reigate the 'Somers interest' quickly assumed electoral control after purchasing the property of the borough's other pre-reform patron, the earl of Hardwicke. This allowed successive earls of Somers to control the seat until 1857, when new railways, the town's proximity to London, its small electorate and the Somers's decision to let out sizeable portions of land for building over the previous decades, transformed the borough into a battleground for competing prospective Liberal MPs with deep pockets and business interests in London.[89]

In the thirteen boroughs that saw influence divided between multiple landlords, the forms that electoral power assumed also varied hugely. The massive disfranchisement of non-resident freemen in Bridgnorth in 1832 destroyed the pre-existing independent reforming-Whig interest, and allowed the old Tory interests of the Pigot and Whitmore families, whose estates dominated the borough's new boundaries, to cultivate extensive power bases and defeat Liberal challenges at most elections prior to 1868.[90] By contrast, the expansion of Clitheroe's boundaries and the introduction of the £10 franchise destroyed the power of the borough's former 'aristocratic overlords' who had controlled the constituency's historic burgage properties. Instead, after 1832 organisation of Clitheroe's vibrant, often corrupt, party politics and the battle for its single seat and small electorate fell under the oversight of multiple Conservative and Liberal families within the constituency's boundaries.[91] Tensions between landed proprietors of the same political faith could also come to the fore, as in St Ives, which saw multiple contests during the period between rival Conservative landowners who sought control of the borough's single seat.[92] And in Christchurch and Hythe, the sheer size of the 1832 boundary extensions led to unforeseen power struggles between established proprietors and those associated with the newly thriving towns of Bournemouth and Folkestone, which developed within each borough's limits, respectively, after 1832.[93]

One of the nine cases where boundary extension led to a power shift to a new landed interest was Droitwich. By the 1837 election, the extensive changes to the borough's boundaries had thrown the constituency out of the control of the Whig corporation, and into the power of the Conservative, Sir John Pakington, whose Westwood Park estate was the major property within the borough's new limits. Pakington gradually asserted himself as the leader of the local Conservatives after 1832, by supporting the party to maintain the borough's register of majority Conservative, rural voters, staying in tune with local protectionist opinion after 1846 and deftly shifting to a more moderate Conservatism as the risk of Liberal challenges increased during the 1850s.[94] By contrast, the influence of property within the parishes of Charlton and Brokenborough within Malmesbury's new boundaries was sufficient for the Whig earl of Suffolk to seize control of the former Tory corporation in the borough after 1832. However, consistent attention to, and funding of, registration and electoral organisation were required to stave off constant Conservative electoral challenges.[95] Shifts in influence to new landowners could take time, as was the case in the householder borough of Honiton, whose reputation for 'shameless venality' continued throughout the period.[96] After 1832 the majority of Honiton's £10 properties within its extended boundaries were in the manor of Honiton, whose ownership was tied up in a legal dispute until 1846 when the Liberal engineer Joseph Locke purchased the property. Locke's primary reason for purchasing the manor had been to facilitate the building of the South Western Railway, but his patronage of the borough (which was helped by his power over railway employment) also meant he was elected as one of the borough's MPs.[97]

In the remaining cases the control of landed proprietors was less significant to post-1832 electoral dynamics. Liskeard was thrown out of the control of the Tory Earl St Germans after 1832 and into the hands of the local Liberal Association which easily fended off the borough's largest landed proprietor, and chief Conservative electoral interest, Samuel Kekewich.[98] By the end of the period, however, the Liberal *Daily News* warned that employment in the customs department had become a major factor at Liskeard's elections, regretting that government influence had destroyed a previously 'pure' Liberal electorate.[99] Banbury did not fall under the sway of the marquess of Bute as had been predicted (see Chapter 4), and a thriving independent radical and Liberal culture ensured the return of one of the boundary commissioners, Henry Tancred, until 1859.[100] And in Ashburton, Hythe, Lyme Regis, Maldon and Tewkesbury the power of money, via consistent and flagrant practices of treating, bribery, patronage and voter creation during, and between, elections proved the ultimate influence over the return of candidates. This certainly required the participation, and deep pockets, of local landowners. However, none of these boroughs could be considered to have remained, or fallen, under the power of the landed interest after 1832.

At the 1832 election the extension of borough boundaries into their surrounding parishes, the introduction of the £10 franchise and the reduction of thirty of these boroughs to single-member seats appeared to have paid off for the Grey ministry. Having returned a slight majority of MPs willing to support a Tory administration at the 1831 election (when these boroughs returned 108 MPs), at the 1832 election (when these boroughs returned 78 MPs) the party labels of 59 per cent of MPs indicated they were willing to support a Whig administration (Table 6.3).[101] As in the English counties this pro-Whig-Liberal majority proved short-lived. At every subsequent general election until the Second Reform Act, the party labels of MPs representing these boroughs indicated majority support for Conservative administrations or, as in 1835 and 1857, was split 50:50. The generally pro-Conservative bias of these MPs was borne out by their behaviour at Westminster in confidence and policy divisions between 1832 and 1868. As well as usually voting against Whig-Liberal administrations, MPs representing these boroughs were consistent in offering the lowest levels of support among borough MPs to free trade, the ballot and the abolition of church rates (Graphs C.1, C.3, C.5 and C.7 and Tables C.3, C.5, C.7 and C.9).

These boroughs provided majorities in favour of the short-lived Peel ministry in 1835. And in 1846, 48 per cent of Conservative MPs representing these boroughs signalled their continued commitment to protectionism by voting against the Peel ministry or abstaining on corn law repeal (the same figure for boroughs with unchanged boroughs was 19 per cent, and 33 per cent for boroughs extended to their modern town). There were some instances of majority Whig-Liberal voting activity – a single-seat majority in support of the Russell administration in 1850, and a two-seat majority against Disraeli's Conservative budget of 1852. The latter vote was thanks to four Peelite MPs, however, who subsequently voted against the Aberdeen coalition's management of the Crimean War in 1855.[102] And during the 1859 Parliament, six of the eight Liberal-Conservatives returned for these boroughs at the 1859 general election ensured a slim majority for the

Table 6.3: Whig-Liberal support by party label in English boroughs, 1832–68 (seat count and percentage support).

	1832	1835	1837	1841	1847	1852	1857	1859	1865
Multiple parish	14	0	−4	−12	−8	−10	0	−2	−6
Unchanged borough	24	−2	6	−14	10	2	28	30	14
Modern town	61	19	5	−5	9	22	43	15	25
New borough	47	33	29	37	31	35	39	37	34
All English boroughs	140	50	34	6	42	49	110	80	67
Multiple parish	58.97%	50.00%	47.44%	42.31%	44.87%	43.59%	50.00%	48.72%	46.15%
Unchanged borough	68.18%	48.48%	54.55%	39.39%	57.58%	51.52%	71.21%	56.76%	60.61%
Modern town	76.52%	58.26%	52.17%	47.83%	53.98%	59.82%	69.37%	57.14%	61.26%
New borough	87.30%	76.19%	73.02%	79.37%	74.60%	77.78%	80.95%	79.37%	76.56%
All English boroughs	71.74%	57.76%	55.28%	50.93%	56.56%	57.68%	67.30%	62.58%	60.50%

Palmerston administration. Several subsequent Liberal by-election victories ensured that by 1864 a majority of five MPs representing these boroughs supported Palmerston in the vote of censure over Denmark. The 1865 election saw a decisive swing back to Conservative majorities, following which these constituencies were the only type of English borough to vote against the Liberal government's reform legislation, the ballot, the abolition of church rates and the disestablishment of the Irish Church.

What lay behind this pro-Conservative bias among MPs returned for these boroughs? While it is wise not to over-emphasise the electoral power of public opinion, given the clear levels of proprietorial influence in the selection, and election, of candidates, the mixture of rural and town voters in these constituencies does appear to have tempered MP behaviour at Westminster. It was also generally the case that where Whig landed proprietors maintained influence, representatives veered towards the moderate side of the Liberal political spectrum. As well as the declining popularity of Whig governance and the increasingly ruthless organisation of Conservative interests during the 1830s (which were factors evident in the Conservative surge by 1841 across England), it was significant that by 1841 the Conservatives had become the party of agricultural protection. Electoral support for Whigs and reformers in these boroughs was much higher when the corn laws remained a cross-party issue. At the 1832 election only 20 per cent of Whigs and reformers returned for these boroughs were willing to support alterations to the corn laws. The comparative figure was 42 per cent in the rest of the ancient boroughs and 72 per cent in the new boroughs. By 1841 in boroughs that contained a sizeable minority, and sometimes majority of agricultural constituents, candidates had to take the rallying cry of protectionism seriously. This was reflected in the consistently high levels of protectionist opposition to the Peel ministry among MPs in boroughs extended into their surrounding parishes by 1846. Even after the repeal of the corn laws, the need to accommodate political opinion in these mixed constituencies led to a decline in MPs willing to support free trade between 1846 and 1850. The need for MPs to straddle divergent constituency opinion over free trade also meant that at the 1847 election Grimsby, Shaftesbury, Thirsk and Wareham were the only boroughs in the UK to return MPs that ascribed to the now apparently contradictory party labels of 'protectionist' Liberals, Reformers or Whigs.[103]

As protectionism was replaced with the defence of the established Church as a Conservative rallying call after 1852, the abolition of church rates remained a divisive issue. In Tamworth, for instance, discontent with support for abolition from one of its Liberal MPs during the 1850s was not seen to 'fairly represent the view of the borough' and by 1865 its Liberal and Liberal-Conservative MPs both voted against abolition.[104] The issue of electoral reform, for often self-serving reasons, also served to unite these constituents and MPs from the 1850s. These boroughs consistently exhibited the highest level of opposition to the ballot among Liberal MPs in the English borough system. In 1861 only 44 per cent of Liberal MPs returned for these boroughs were willing to vote for the ballot, the equivalent figure for other ancient boroughs was 80 per cent and for the new boroughs it was 97 per cent. In boroughs with generally small electorates, where proprietors and agents realised the benefit of open voting in terms of knowing how their tenants were voting, and electors and non-electors were able to fully capitalise on the pecuniary benefits of a household's vote being public knowledge, it is perhaps unsurprising that the introduction of secret voting held little positive prospect.

On a wider level, by the 1850s Liberal proposals for parliamentary reform posed a very real threat to the survival of these boroughs, due to the combination of their continually small electorates and Conservative bias. By the 1865 election, 39 of the 50 boroughs discussed in this chapter still contained fewer than 500 registered electors, and 8 of these contained fewer than 300. Historians have previously observed the importance of these 'small boroughs' to the Conservative electoral interest after 1832. They have, however, failed to note that the majority of boroughs with fewer than 500 voters were actually some of the largest in geographic terms.[105] Successive Liberal reform proposals from 1852, which primarily emanated from Lord John Russell, sought to neuter the influence of these boroughs at Westminster by either disfranchisement, or grouping them together on the basis of their limited electorates. By contrast, Conservative reform proposals from 1859 discarded Liberal proposals for disfranchisement or grouping and proposed to keep these boroughs intact.[106] It did not escape Disraeli's attention that the combination of small electorates and large boundaries had proved important to the forces of Conservatism in the reformed electoral system. In 1866 he understood that both factors had been crucial in allowing 'about ninety borough seats' to be 'appended to the landed interest' since 1832.[107] This was significant in ensuring the survival of all but four of these boroughs in the 1867–8 Conservative reform legislation, when the partial disfranchisement of most of the double-member boroughs in this group was the preferred means of redistributing seats to the counties and new boroughs.[108] When the electoral system was reformed again in 1884–5, the experience of these rural boroughs for the past-half century was surely crucial in prompting the Conservative administration to consent to a transformative move to single-member county divisions across England.[109] These constituencies proved, and continue to prove, the bedrock of Conservative power in the English electoral map.

Notes

1. N. Gash, *Politics in the Age of Peel: A Study in the Technique of Parliamentary Representation* (London, 1971), 68–72; T. Crosby, *English Farmers and the Politics of Protection 1815–1852* (Hassocks, 1977), 81, 105.
2. P. Salmon, 'The English Reform Legislation, 1831–32', in D. Fisher (ed.), *The House of Commons, 1820–32*, i. (Cambridge, 2009), 397.
3. D. C. Moore, 'Concession or Cure: The Sociological Premises of the First Reform Act', *Historical Journal*, 9, 1 (1966), 54; D. C. Moore, *Politics of Deference: A Study of the Mid-Nineteenth Century Political System* (New York, 1976), 174–5.
4. B. Hilton, *A Mad, Bad, & Dangerous People?: England 1783–1846* (Oxford, 2006), 436, 501–2.
5. DSC, Grey, B46/1/33. 'Paper ... based on Lord J. Russell's plan of reform', clause iv. 1.
6. DSC, Grey, B46/2/36, Russell to Durham, 13 Feb. 1831, 5; PP1830–31 (247), ii. 5–6.
7. PP1831-2 (232), iii. 85.
8. Hansard, 3, vi. (1 Sept. 1831), 986–1009.
9. PP1831-2 (141), xxxviii. 6–7.
10. TNA, T72/9/39, 'Honiton'; TNA, T72/8/11, 'Ashburton'; TNA, T72/9/38, 'Horsham'; PP1831-2 (141), xxxviii. 72–4.
11. TNA, T72/9/41, 'Huntingdon', 'Report for Huntingdon', Sheepshanks and Tallents to Drummond, 20 Sept. 1831, Drummond to Sheepshanks, 1 Oct. 1831; TNA, T72/8/19, 'Bedford', Drummond to Sheepshanks and Tallents, 21 Sept. 1831.
12. TNA, T72/11/41, 'Tewkesbury', Ord to Drummond, 18 Sept. 1831.
13. TNA, T72/9/9, 'Droitwich', 'Report on Droitwich', Ord and Chapman to Drummond, undated (before 20 Sept. 1831).
14. TNA, T72/9/9, Ord and Chapman to Drummond, 25 Sept. 1831.
15. TNA, T72/9/9, 'Report on Droitwich'.
16. TNA, T72/9/12, 'Evesham', 'Report on Evesham', Ord and Chapman to Drummond, 16 Sept. 1831.
17. TNA, T72/11/3, 'Reigate', 'Report on Reigate', Drinkwater and Saunders to Drummond, undated (before 29 Sept. 1831).
18. PP1831 (232), iii. 11.
19. TNA, T72/9/12, 'Evesham', Drummond to Ord and Chapman, 17 Sept. 1831; T72/11/46, 'Truro', Drummond to Birch, 27 Sept. 1831; T72/11/34 'Sudbury', Drummond to Sheepshanks, 30 Sept. 1831.
20. TNA, T72/9/9, 'Droitwich', Drummond to Chapman, 29 Sept. 1831.
21. TNA, T72/9/9, Chapman to Drummond, 19 Nov. 1831.
22. TNA, T72/11/11, 'Rye', 'Report on Rye', Drinkwater and Saunders to Drummond, 11 Oct. 1831; TNA, T72/8/10, 'Arundel', 'Report on Arundel', Drinkwater and Saunders to Drummond, 29 Sept. 1831.
23. TNA, T72/10/25, 'Maldon', 'Report on Maldon', Drinkwater and Saunders to Drummond, undated.
24. TNA, T72/10/20, 'Lyme Regis'.
25. TNA, T72/10/27, 'Malmesbury', 'Report on Malmesbury', Ansley and Gawler to Drummond, 5 Nov. 1831.

26. TNA, T72/10/27, 'Malmesbury', Drummond to Ansley and Gawler, 14 Nov. 1831.
27. See respective TNA, T72 folders; PP1831 (141), xxxviii–xli.
28. TNA, T72/10/51, 'Northallerton'; TNA, T72/11/6, 'Richmond'; TNA, T72/11/43, 'Thirsk'.
29. See respective TNA, T72 folders; TNA T72/10/63, 'Plymouth', Drummond to Birch and Brandreth, 7 Nov. 1831; PP1831 (141), xxxviii–xli.
30. For details on the sitting committee see Chronology and voting data.
31. TNA, T72/9/9, 'Droitwich', Note by Beaufort, undated (before 31 Oct. 1831); SRO, Hatherton, D260/M/F/5/26/7, 31 Oct. 1831, 195.
32. TNA, T72/9/9, 'Droitwich', Note by Littleton.
33. SRO, Hatherton, D260/M/F/5/26/7, 12 Nov. 1831, 205.
34. SRO, Hatherton, D260/M/F/5/26/7, 31 Oct. 1831, 195, 8 Nov. 1831, 200.
35. SRO, Hatherton, D260/M/F/5/26/7, 7 Dec. 1831, 253.
36. TNA, T72/9/9, 'Droitwich', undated note by Littleton.
37. SRO, Hatherton, D260/M/F/5/26/7, 8 Nov. 1831, 200.
38. SRO, Hatherton, D260/M/F/5/26/7, 11–15 Nov. 1831, 204–9.
39. M. Brock, *The Great Reform Act* (London, 1973), 247; J. Cannon, *Parliamentary Reform 1640–1832* (Cambridge, 1973), 225–6; I. Newbould, *Whiggery and Reform, 1830–41: The Politics of Government* (London, 1990), 72.
40. DSC, Grey, B46/1/45, 'Memorandum on Reform Bill, by Russell, 20 Oct. 1831', 1–8; SRO, Hatherton, D260/M/F/5/26/7, 12 Nov. 1831, 205.
41. Salmon, 'English Reform Legislation'.
42. SRO, Hatherton, D260/M/F/5/26/7, 15 Nov. 1831, 205, 209; PRO, Russell Papers, 30/22/1B, 'Althorp to Grey re: "Russell's plan as to Reform Nov.1831"', 64–7; TNA, T72/11/45, 'Totnes', note by Littleton, Beaufort and Russell, undated.
43. This figure includes Helston, Clitheroe, St. Ives and Launceston.
44. SRO, Hatherton, D260/M/F/5/26/7, 18 Nov. 1831, 220.
45. DSC, Grey, B46/2/46, 'Memorandum by 2nd Earl Grey on a conversation with Lord Wharncliffe', 16 Nov. 1831, 1–8.
46. SRO, Hatherton, D260/M/F/5/26/7, 20 Nov. 1831, 23 Nov., 28 Nov. 1831, 224, 231, 241; Kriegel, *Holland House*, 83–84.
47. A. Kriegel, *The Holland House Diaries, 1831–1840* (London, 1977), 84; SRO, Hatherton, D260/M/F/5/26/7, 27 Nov. 1831, 227; Brock, *Reform Act*, 257–63; Cannon, *Parliamentary Reform*, 226.
48. Kriegel, *Holland House*, 85–6; SRO, Hatherton, D260/M/F/5/26/7, 2 Dec. 1831, 250.
49. SRO, Hatherton, D260/M/F/5/26/7, 15 Dec., 17 Dec. 1831, 271, 279.
50. SRO, Hatherton, D260/M/F/5/26/7, 23 Nov., 28 Nov., 20 Dec. 1831, 231, 241, 281; Kriegel, *Holland House*, xxxi, 83–4.
51. Kriegel, *Holland House*, 99–100.
52. Also see, D. C. Moore, 'The Other Face of Reform', *Victorian Studies*, 5, 1 (1961), 7–34; Hilton, *Mad, Bad*, 434–7; Salmon 'English Reform Legislation'.
53. Kriegel, *Holland House*, 83–4.
54. Kriegel, *Holland House*, 99–100; SRO, Hatherton, D260/M/F/5/26/7, 23 Nov. 1831, 231.

55. SRO, Hatherton, D260/M/F/5/26/7, 27 Dec. 1831, 291.

56. SRO, Hatherton, D260/M/F/5/26/7, 27 Dec. 1831, 291; PP1831–2 (141), xxxviii. 14.

57. SRO, Hatherton, D260/M/F/5/26/7, 21 Dec. 1831, 285–7.

58. SRO, Hatherton, D260/M/F/5/26/7, 21 Dec. 1831, 285–7.

59. TNA, T72/9/9, 'Droitwich', 'Report on Droitwich', Ord and Chapman to Drummond, undated but prior to 20 Sept. 1831; PP1831–2 (141), xl. 141–2.

60. TNA, T72/11/39, 'Tavistock'; TNA, T72/11/74, 'Chipping Wycombe'.

61. TNA, T72/11/18, 'Shaftesbury'.

62. See reports, PP1831 (141), xxxviii–xli.

63. TNA, T72/11/42, 'Thetford'.

64. TNA, T72/10/60, 'Penryn and Falmouth'; PP1831–2 (141) xxxix. 12–13.

65. TNA, T72/9/42, 'Hythe'.

66. *HCJ*, 87 (8 June 1832), 390; PP1831–2 (521), iii. 355; SRO, Hatherton, D260/M/F/5/26/8, 14 June 1832, 63–5.

67. PP1831–2 (488), iii. 311; Hansard, 3, xiii. (7 June 1832), 513–33; *HCJ*, 87 (8 June 1832), 390, (22 June 1832), 427.

68. Hansard, 3, xiii. (22 June 1832), 965–8, (3 July 1832), 1300, xiv. (4 July 1832), 73; S. Farrell, 'Wareham', in Fisher, *Commons*, ii. 344–45; Gash, *Age of Peel*, 71–2.

69. H. Spencer, 'Arundel', in Fisher, *Commons*, ii. 102.

70. TNA, T72/8/10, 'Arundel', Initial Report, 29 Sept. 1831; PP1831–2 (141) xl. 63–4.

71. PP1831–2 (537), v. 1–2.

72. TNA, T72/8/10 'Arundel', Initial Report, 29 Sept. 1831.

73. Moore, 'Concession or Cure', 56.

74. Moore, 'Concession or Cure', 54.

75. Moore, 'Concession or Cure', 44.

76. Moore, 'Concession or Cure', 44; Moore, *Politics of Deference*, 174–5.

77. R. W. Davis, 'Deference and Aristocracy in the Time of the Great Reform Act', *American Historical Review*, 81, 3 (1976), 532–9.

78. Moore, 'Other Face', 7–34.

79. Buckingham, Calne, Chippenham, Eye, Great Marlow, Huntingdon, Launceston, Malton, Marlborough, Morpeth, New Woodstock, Peterborough, Petersfield, Reigate, Richmond, Shaftesbury, Tamworth, Tavistock, Westbury, Wilton, Wycombe.

80. Bewdley, Bodmin, Bridgnorth, Christchurch, Cirencester, Clitheroe, Cockermouth, Grantham, Helston, Northallerton, St. Ives, Thirsk, Wareham.

81. Droitwich, Grimsby, Honiton, Horsham, Leominster, Malmesbury, Midhurst, Rye, Wallingford.

82. Gash, *Age of Peel*, 438–9.

83. E. Jaggard, 'Small Town Politics in Mid-Victorian Britain', *History*, 89, 1 (2004), 3–29.

84. *Cambridge Chronicle and Journal*, 2 Jan. 1835; *Cambridge Independent Press*, 17 July 1847, 2 Mar. 1867; *The Times*, 13 Feb. 1852; *South Durham & Cleveland Mercury*, 24 Feb. 1877; *Liverpool Echo*, 24 Mar. 1884.

85. Gash, *Age of Peel*, 438–9.

86. J. Owen, 'Eye', in Salmon and Rix, *Commons 1832–1868*.

87. T. Jenkins, 'Launceston', in Fisher, *Commons*, ii. 161–2; E. Jaggard, *Cornwall Politics in the Age of Reform, 1790–1885* (London, 1999), 117–19, 177–8.

88. M. Spychal, 'Five elections in seven years: Peterborough, Whalley and the Fitzwilliam interest', *Victorian Commons*, https://victoriancommons.wordpress.com/2017/04/28/five-elections-in-seven-years-peterborough-whalley-and-the-fitzwilliam-interest/ [accessed 19 Aug. 2022]; T. Bromund, '"A Complete Fool's Paradise": The Attack on the Fitzwilliam Interest in Peterborough, 1852', *Parliamentary History*, 12, 1 (1993), 47–67.

89. *Berkshire Chronicle*, 14 Mar 1857; *Illustrated London News*, 16 May 1857; *British Standard*, 15 Jan. 1858; *Morning Advertiser*, 16 Jan. 1858.

90. *Daily News*, 24 Sept. 1868; M. Escott, 'Bridgnorth', in Fisher, *Commons*, ii. 869–70.

91. K. Rix, 'Clitheroe', in Salmon and Rix, *Commons 1832–1868*.

92. T. Jenkins, 'St. Ives', in Fisher, *Commons*, ii. 190–91; Jaggard, *Cornwall Politics*, 121–2.

93. P. Salmon, 'Christchurch', in Salmon and Rix, *Commons 1832–1868*; H. Spencer and P. Salmon, 'Christchurch', in Fisher, *Commons*, ii. 429–30; *Daily News*, 24 Aug. 1868.

94. S. Ball, 'Droitwich', in Salmon and Rix, *Commons 1832–1868*.

95. C. Dod, *Electoral Facts, from 1832 to 1853, Impartially Stated* (London, 1853), 204; S. Farrell, 'Malmesbury', in Fisher, *Commons*, iii. 205; *Salisbury and Winchester Journal*, 4 Apr. 1857; *Wilts and Gloucestershire Standard*, 15, 22 July 1865.

96. T. Jenkins, 'Honiton', in Fisher, *Commons*, ii. 276–7.

97. M. Spychal, 'Honiton', in Salmon and Rix, *Commons 1832–1868*.

98. Jaggard, *Cornwall Politics*, 124–5.

99. *Daily News*, 10 Sept. 1868.

100. B. Trinder, *Victorian Banbury* (Chichester, 1982), 50–64, 205; M. Spychal, 'Banbury', in Salmon and Rix, *Commons 1832–1868*.

101. This figure includes the four Clause 4 boroughs extended into their surrounding hundreds prior to 1832.

102. Lord Bruce, Henry Baring (Marlborough), Jonathan Peel (Huntingdon) and James Hogg (Honiton).

103. K. Rix, 'Bell, John (1809–1851)', and M. Spychal, 'Sheridan, Richard Brinsley (1806–1888)', in Salmon and Rix, *Commons 1832–1868*; John Drax (Liberal, Wareham) and Edward Heneage (Whig, Grimsby) voted for a reinstatement of protection in 1850.

104. H. Miller, 'Tamworth', in Salmon and Rix, *Commons 1832–1868*.

105. B. Coleman, *Conservatism and the Conservative Party in Nineteenth-Century Britain* (London, 1988), 102–5; R. Stewart, *The Foundation of the Conservative Party, 1830–1867* (London, 1978), 215–16; J. Parry, *The Rise and Fall of Liberal Government in Victorian Britain* (London, 1993), 338–41; A. Hawkins, *Victorian Political Culture: Habits of Heart and Mind* (Oxford, 2015), 181–2, 189–94.

106. R. Saunders, *Democracy and the Vote in British Politics, 1848–1867: The Making of the Second Reform Act* (Farnham, 2011).

107. Disraeli to third Earl Grey, 2 July 1866: *Benjamin Disraeli Letters, 1865–1867*, ed. M. Wiebe et al. (Toronto, 2009), ix. 91–2.

108. D. Rossiter, R. Johnston and C. Pattie, *The Boundary Commissions: Redrawing the United Kingdom's Map of Parliamentary Constituencies* (Manchester, 1999), 27–49.

109. M. Chadwick, 'The Role of Redistribution in the Making of the Third Reform Act', *HJ*, 19, 3 (1976), 665–83.

Chapter 7

'All the kindred interests of the town and neighbourhood': New borough limits

In June 1831 the parish officers of Royton, Chadderton and Crompton submitted a memorial to the Grey ministry requesting that their respective townships be included in the recently proposed parliamentary borough of Oldham. Earlier that April the government had announced their intention to enfranchise the Lancashire town as a single-member borough, but had not included the three townships within the constituency's preliminary boundaries. The memorialists pleaded their case by drawing attention to the 'thirty large cotton manufactories', 'seventeen collieries' and 'great numbers of hat-making establishments' in their respective townships, which they contended formed an integral part of Oldham's economy; the over £1,000 a year they had been contributing collectively to Oldham Parish Church in the township of Oldham; and the 'activity, industry and intelligence' of the upwards of 500 voters the townships were likely to contribute to Oldham's electorate. Later that June the government acceded to the request, adding all three townships to Oldham's preliminary parliamentary limits.[1]

Oldham was one of forty-one English parliamentary boroughs enfranchised in 1832. Located primarily in England's northern and midland industrial heartlands, these constituencies returned sixty-three MPs to the reformed Commons. They were conceived broadly as a means of providing representation to the newly emergent manufacturing and commercial interests of the post-Napoleonic political nation, and infusing the constitution with popular, but not democratic, legitimacy.[2] The constituencies were the first major additions to England's borough map since the seventeenth century, and alongside the dismantling of the notorious 'rotten borough system' formed the centrepiece of the Grey ministry's electoral reforms of 1832. As the activity of Oldham's parish officers suggests, when the 1831–2 boundary commission commenced their work in England's new boroughs in August 1831 they did so following several months of active lobbying and parliamentary discussion about the parliamentary boundaries they had been appointed to propose. This stood in stark contrast to England's existing boroughs, whose reformed boundaries had been subject to minimal parliamentary intervention prior to the commission's work. As well as ensuring the process by which boundaries were established in the new boroughs was more complex than elsewhere, the activities of the parish officers at Oldham formed part of a wider, previously underappreciated, episode of engagement between the centre and the localities over the fine details of the 1832 reform legislation. This central-local interaction introduced a significant new variable into the boundary commission's decision-making process. If parliament had already offered its approval to a local boundary, could Drummond and his commissioners override this decision if it proved inconsistent with their boundary-setting principles elsewhere?

This chapter explores how the boundaries of England's new boroughs were established by the 1832 Boundary Act, before providing an analysis of their electoral and political impact. It outlines four stages in their design process: parliamentary and local lobbying prior to the commencement of the 1831–2 boundary commission; the commission's attempts to define new borough limits via Drummond's 'scientific' framework; ministerial interference with the commission's proposals prior to their publication; and parliamentary and local lobbying as the 1832 Boundary Act progressed through parliament between February and July 1832. As well as providing a case study of central and local interaction in the late-Hanoverian state, this chapter complicates D. C. Moore's contention that the boundary commission sought to create 'deference communities' in the new boroughs, by isolating urban electorates from their rural counterparts in the counties.[3] Importantly, the commission's ability to draw boundaries consistently across every new borough was restricted by ministerial, parliamentary and public engagement with the issue throughout 1831 and 1832, which contrary to Moore's arguments tempered the extent to which urban and rural communities were separated in England's new boroughs. Ultimately the establishment of fixed electoral boundaries in a group of predominantly northern and midland industrial towns combined with the introduction of an elite £10 franchise and a remarkably partisan registration system in 1832 to provide the ideal conditions for the manufacturing and commercial-focused electoral interest communities that the Whig government had hoped would flourish after 1832.[4] Politically, these constituencies became the bulwarks of the free trade and Nonconformist interest prior to 1846, and of the emerging Liberal party at Westminster in the years that followed.

The identification of preliminary boundaries

The 1831–2 boundary commission identified boundaries for England's new parliamentary boroughs in a manner similar to that for existing boroughs – by defining the modern extent of the town associated with the borough and allowing space for its future growth (see Chapter 5). However, unlike in England's existing boroughs, this process was complicated by Schedules C and D of the reform bill, which since March 1831 had provided every new borough with a preliminary boundary. The 15 September version of the government's second reform bill (the details of which had been agreed to as the commission commenced its work) identified a specific boundary for twenty-four new boroughs based around particular parishes or townships, and a non-specific boundary for the remaining boroughs, which stipulated that the 'town' of the borough should form its parliamentary limits.[5] These preliminary boundaries had been under discussion since December 1830, when the committee of four began drafting the reform bill, and were identified for three reasons. First, to provide the opportunity to those within the vicinity of a new borough – like the parish officers of Oldham's townships – to make a claim for inclusion within its limits. Second, in order that elections could take place in the event of a reform bill passing through parliament, and a privy council committee (as it had initially been planned) not being able to identify parliamentary boundaries. And third, when the reform bill was announced on 1 March, eight boroughs identified for enfranchisement were amalgamations of towns or administrative divisions, rather than a single place.[6]

These amalgamations of districts, in particular, revealed the limits of the 1821 census data initially used to identify potential new boroughs, the committee of four's limited geographic knowledge (or ready access to maps) of the boroughs they proposed to enfranchise, and the fluid, if not haphazard, nature of cabinet negotiations over the reform bill ahead of its publication. The Staffordshire boroughs of Wolverhampton and Walsall are cases in point. In March 1831 the first public version of the reform bill stipulated that the borough of Wolverhampton should consist of the townships of Wolverhampton and Bilston and the parish of Sedgley. In January 1831 the committee of four had initially proposed to enfranchise all three towns as separate single-member boroughs, as each had a population of over 10,000 according to the 1821 census.[7] Concurrently, in late January, Littleton lobbied the cabinet for the 'equal claim of Walsall', after he had heard that Gateshead was to be enfranchised due to its importance to the manufacturing interest.[8] Neither Gateshead nor Walsall had been included in the committee of four's initial list of unrepresented towns with a population above 10,000, but when their entire respective parishes were taken into consideration they met this threshold.[9] The only difficulty was that there was no spare seat to be assigned to Walsall, prompting a compromise solution based on Littleton's local knowledge of Staffordshire. By February he had informed the cabinet that, as Wolverhampton, Bilston and Sedgely adjoined each other, they could be combined into a double-member borough, freeing up a seat for Walsall.[10]

Following this, the government identified preliminary boundaries for as many boroughs as possible ahead of the publication of its first reform bill, by resort to local knowledge, census data, published maps and, probably, topographical dictionaries.[11] As a result, twenty-two new boroughs were provided with a specific preliminary boundary in the first reform bill, and nine were given unspecific boundaries, stating that 'the town of' the borough should form its limits. The reliance on census data, in particular, led to the assignment of very wide preliminary boundaries to Blackburn and Bradford, initially defined by their parish.[12] The frenzied manner in which these preliminary boundaries had been compiled, and an acceptance among ministers of their geographic ignorance about the fine details of England's new boroughs, meant they were more than willing to take on board suggestions from the localities to fine-tune their proposals.

As a result of this consultation between Westminster and the localities, between March and September 1831 parliament modified the preliminary boundaries of twenty boroughs.[13] In seven cases, specific preliminary definitions were changed to unspecific definitions. On 5 August, for instance, Bury was changed from 'the township of Bury' to 'the town of Bury'.[14] In the remaining thirteen cases, townships or parishes were added to, or removed, from a borough's preliminary definition. These changes took place following parliamentary debate, petitions from local inhabitants and private representations to cabinet members. Parliamentary debate was integral to the shifting definition of Bradford's preliminary boundary, originally defined in March 1831 as the 'parish of Bradford'. This was reduced in April to the 'township of Bradford', following a parliamentary return that revealed the government's misinterpretation of the 1821 census (this return prompted similar changes to Blackburn, Dudley and Tynemouth).[15] Bradford's preliminary boundary was amended again on 5 August, after the MP for Hedon, Robert Farrand, and the Whig MP for Yorkshire, Viscount Morpeth, complained that Bradford stretched across three townships, but not the entire parish of the same name.[16] Following this, Bradford's preliminary boundary was changed to the unspecific 'town of Bradford'. As Morpeth advised the Commons, this allowed Bradford's definition to be 'left to the [boundary] commissioners'.[17] The specific preliminary boundaries of Blackburn, Brighton, Bury, Tynemouth and Wakefield were removed for the same reason.[18]

Petitioning and private representations were central to the alteration of Manchester's preliminary boundaries and Salford's eventual enfranchisement as a separate borough. The urban settlement associated with Manchester lay in the parish of Manchester, which comprised twenty-nine townships.[19] The government's first reform bill proposed that eight of these townships (including Manchester and Salford) should form the parliamentary borough of Manchester, based on the 1821 census.[20] However, in April 1831 the government agreed to enfranchise Salford as a separate single-member borough, along with two of its neighbouring townships of Pendleton and Broughton. This followed private representations to the cabinet from the inhabitants of the township of Salford, who contended that their interests were distinct from those of the neighbouring township of Manchester and that their population of over 50,000 entitled them to separate representation.[21] The preliminary definition of Manchester was then further amended in May 1831, following a petition from the township of Bradford, Lancashire. These petitioners successfully requested that Bradford be included in Manchester's boundaries, as its inhabitants were employed either in the collieries that powered Manchester's cotton factories, or in Manchester itself.[22]

Petitions relating to the boundaries of five further boroughs – Bury, Halifax, Oldham, Rochdale and Whitehaven – were submitted to parliament. Those from Bury and Whitehaven were motivated by concerns with local landed proprietors, the earls of Derby and Lonsdale respectively, assuming control of politics in their future boroughs.[23] The petitions from Halifax, Oldham and Rochdale were prompted by a mixture of protest at the government's confused employment of census definitions, internal political manoeuvring and a civic desire for enfranchisement.[24] Of these only one petition (that from the townships of Chadderton, Crompton and Royton, discussed above, asking to be included in the limits of Oldham) was entirely successful. The other four prompted the government to provide unspecific preliminary definitions for each borough in order that the commissioners could settle the issue.[25]

In addition to Salford, private representations to MPs or the cabinet prompted changes to the preliminary boundaries of Birmingham, Cheltenham, Huddersfield, Lambeth, Stoke-on-Trent, Whitby and Wolverhampton. Most of these requests appear to have been motivated by the genuine civic desire of a town's inhabitants to be included in a borough.[26]

This was evident in Birmingham (Map 7.1), whose preliminary boundaries underwent a series of amendments between March and August 1831. When the reform bill was first announced, the omission of the parish of Edgbaston from Birmingham's preliminary boundaries was raised by the moderate *Birmingham Journal*, which suggested that the government's 'ignorance of the population' of Birmingham threatened to exclude a 'very great proportion of the respectable merchants and manufacturers' from the borough. In the context of the Birmingham Political Union's petitioning efforts in favour of the reform bill (which did not specifically mention the town's boundaries but brought several key figures in the town into contact with the cabinet), the editor of the paper urged 'representations' to ministers on the issue, which by April had led to the addition of Edgbaston as well as the townships of Deritend, Duddeston and Nechells to the borough's preliminary limits, and the exclusion of the parish of Aston.[27]

While electioneering was already in full swing in the proposed borough, these amendments do not appear to have prompted any political controversy locally. Neither did a subsequent amendment in August, following a private representation from the inhabitants of the township of Bordesley to Francis Lawley, Whig MP for Warwickshire. The independent *Aris's Birmingham Gazette* provided an intriguing insight into how this request led to an immediate amendment to the reform bill:

> A communication on the subject [of Bordesley] was in consequence made last week to Mr. Lawley, by whom, ... the case was immediately brought under the consideration of Lords Althorp and Russell; and by return of post, an assurance was received ... that Bordesley now forms part of the bill.[28]

By contrast to Birmingham, partisan motivations clearly lay behind alterations to Whitby, where Richard Moorsom, the borough's future Liberal candidate, successfully lobbied Lord John Russell to add the townships of Whitby, Ruswarp and Hawsker to its preliminary boundary. As will be discussed below, Russell was aware that such a boundary favoured the 'liberal interest' in the constituency and did all in his power to ensure it remained in place.[29]

This consultation between the localities and Westminster over the boundaries of new boroughs meant that by the third Commons reading of the government's second reform bill on 15 September, parliament had settled on specific boundaries for twenty-four new boroughs. As it was not originally intended to subject the boundary commission's proposals to full parliamentary scrutiny, it was not clear whether the commission had the legal authority to overturn these boundaries. Although the government had refused to publicly commit to their finality, they were only initially willing to allow the commission to overturn specific preliminary boundaries if they contained an 'obvious omission or error'.[30] By October 1831, however, Drummond had successfully advocated for more extensive powers. He had discovered that extensive, usually agricultural, districts, unconnected with a town's immediate population, had been included in a number of preliminary boundaries. In a small number of cases, such as Whitby, it was also confirmed that the impetus behind the identification of preliminary boundaries had been political. The presence of inconsistent boundary proposals, as well as a fear that partisan considerations had been allowed to influence the boundary-setting process, underlined the necessity, for Drummond, of a consistent application of his 'scientific' framework for identifying boundaries.

Proposing boundaries for the new boroughs

The majority of England's new boroughs were in the north, west midlands or the south-east of England, meaning the commissioners in districts H, G, E and A visited a disproportionate number in comparison to their colleagues (see Table 7.1). As in the existing boroughs, the commissioners and their surveyors made their boundary recommendations following a cartographic and socio-economic survey, and the collection of £10 householder and boundary data in each new borough (see Chapter 4). Most new boroughs had undergone a period of rapid socio-economic growth during the previous decade, and on average, had increased in population by 29 per cent since 1821. This compared to an average increase of 8 per cent across England's existing boroughs, and 4 per cent across boroughs scheduled to be disfranchised in 1832.[31] These averages mask some extremes, such as Bradford whose population had increased by 78 per cent since 1821, as well as four new boroughs whose populations had actually decreased since 1821 – Whitby, Whitehaven, Frome and Tynemouth. The increased rate of demographic growth across the new boroughs was reflected in the

Table 7.1: Location of new boroughs by boundary commission district.

District	Region	Total boroughs
A (including Metropolitan boroughs)	South-east	7
B	South	1
C	South-west	1
E	West midlands	10
G	North-east	7
H	North-west	15
Total		41

commissioners' reports and willingness to propose extensive boundaries that allowed for future population growth.[32] In Bradford, commissioners Romilly and Allen reported that:

> ... the population in the last ten years has nearly doubled, and factories and buildings are fast increasing ... the rapid spread that the town seems to be making in all directions, presents a considerable difficulty in laying down a boundary as would take in every thing that is desirable, without giving to it an unusually wide extent.[33]

The commissioners' attempts at predicting future growth in the new boroughs were also complicated by newly built, or proposed, railways, which had already become a significant factor in the urban landscape of England's northern manufacturing economies by 1831.[34] The commission's final published map of the aforementioned Bradford is notable for its spider-like tentacles in the south-east of the borough, marking the recently built, private railroad network of the Bowling Ironworks.[35] In north-east England, the proposed development of railways and the expectation of exponential future economic and demographic growth led to the proposal of some very wide boundaries. Commissioners Tancred and Wrottesley proposed an extensive boundary for Sunderland that allowed for the planned development of coal mines to the south of the town – the development of which had only been made viable by the ability of rail to transport large amounts of coal through the 'rural townships' to the south of Sunderland.[36] On the south of the Tyne, the new borough of Gateshead was found to contain a wide variety of thriving industries: '... great grindstone quarries are situated in the midst of the parish; and within it are extensive manufactories of chain-cables, heavy iron work and steel, and also of glass and other valuable commodities'. This, combined with the discovery that 'a railroad is in contemplation, for which a survey has been made, and subscriptions entered into', prompted the commissioners to affix an additional area to the government's already wide preliminary boundary for the borough, which the town had already expanded beyond.[37]

Where new boroughs were in a less flourishing state, the space allowed for future growth tended to be reduced accordingly. The commissioners discovered that the decrease in Whitehaven's population since 1821 had resulted from Liverpool supplanting the town as the chief exporter of coal to Ireland during the 1820s.[38] In Frome, the commissioners reported that the 'employment of powerful machinery' had 'superseded human labour', and that as a result many of the inhabitants had emigrated to America and Canada. With little prospects for future expansion, a tight boundary was proposed around both boroughs.[39] The recently opened Liverpool to Manchester railroad was found to have depressed the economies of two new boroughs. Warrington had lost the daily business of 'seventy public carriages', which had previously travelled through the town between Liverpool and Manchester.[40] And commissioner Romilly was sceptical about Bolton's prospects for future growth, which had 'probably been injured, and will continue to be so, by the greater advantage which the new rail road has given to Manchester'. Even though Bolton had 'a large trade', he reported, it 'is suffering a considerable depression … the place has not a thriving appearance, and its unequal supply of foot pavements, the number of its narrow streets, and lanes, and the want of drainage generally give to it an air of discomfort at every turn'.[41] As a result, Romilly recommended a smaller space for Bolton's future expansion than he had been in the habit of doing elsewhere.

Wherever possible, the commissioners made use of existing administrative divisions when designing new borough boundaries – either ancient townships or parishes, or recently created boundaries for municipal purposes. Doing so had several practical and legal advantages. It obviated the need for the commissioners to draw a new boundary; pre-existing limits tended to be well known within localities; avoiding the creation of additional boundaries reduced the potential for confusion or legal dispute within a locality; and the practice was consistent with some preliminary boundaries identified in the reform bill. Drummond commended Allen and Romilly's decision to use the existing circular boundary provided to Rochdale by its 1825 Lighting, Cleansing and Watching Act. 'A multiplicity of boundaries', he reminded them, 'is so great an evil'.[42]

Existing ancient boundaries, particularly townships in the north of England, were also convenient as they tended to allow ready-made space for future expansion. Although North Shields' population had decreased slightly since 1821, a considerable amount of building was found to be in progress, particularly in the township of Chirton where a new railroad to Newcastle upon Tyne was in development. The commissioners initially considered cutting off a portion of the township from their proposed boundary, but reported that: 'on considering [Chirton's] commercial character, its great and rapid increase in population, and the small comparative breadth of its northern portion, it seemed … better to abide by the old established boundary'.[43] A preference for the use of ancient boundaries, as well as the time constraints that the commissioners were under, also led to the provision, in some instances, of too much space for future expansion. This was the case in both Blackburn and Warrington, which were not predicted to expand at the same rate as Bradford, Sheffield or Sunderland. In both cases, however, Romilly and Allen preferred to abide by established boundaries, instead of acting on Drummond's advice to consider a reduced, arbitrary boundary.[44]

Arbitrary boundaries were only proposed when boroughs exhibited little propensity for future expansion, or if existing ancient boundaries were found to extend too far from a borough's immediate population. When these scenarios occurred, the commissioners defined the immediate populations of new boroughs by contrasting manufacturing, commercial or town-based populations with their rural or agricultural surrounds. At Wakefield, commissioners Wrottesley and Tancred proposed a boundary that encompassed the entire township of Wakefield as well as parts of the surrounding townships of Alverthorpe, Stanley and Thornes, which they reported were 'intimately connected' with the prospective borough.[45] When in Wakefield, the commissioners discovered from an 'old man (whom seemed a staunch reformer)' that the inhabitants of the remaining parts of Alverthorpe, Stanley and Thornes had expressed a desire to be included in the parliamentary borough due to their regular attendance at Wakefield's weekly market.[46] After investigation, however, they deemed that these outlying areas were 'chiefly agricultural district[s] ... very little connected' with the town of Wakefield.[47] As Wakefield was deemed unlikely to expand much further, the commissioners used an arbitrary boundary to define the borough by its immediate community, which excluded its secondary, more agricultural, community (even though Wakefield was a market town for the surrounding townships). This report, which was held up by Drummond as an exemplar, was printed and distributed to the other teams of commissioners to help ensure their work was 'as perfect and as uniform' as possible.[48] Similar explanations were provided for arbitrary boundaries in the equally dormant boroughs of Kidderminster, Kendal, Frome and Whitehaven.[49]

Arbitrary boundaries were also proposed in the more flourishing boroughs of Gateshead, Bury, Macclesfield and Halifax. In each instance parts of an ancient parish or township were excluded from a borough due to their 'rural' or 'agricultural' nature, or because the immediate population associated with a borough was deemed unlikely to expand into these areas.[50] Agricultural populations were not always discounted, however. In Wolverhampton, Walsall, Stoke-on-Trent (which was in reality a collection of six towns) and Stroud, the commissioners discovered that the farming and manufacturing populations of each locale were intermixed. These cases required more extensive boundaries that were not focused on a single urban conurbation. For instance, commissioner Chapman reported that Stroud's clothing mills were focused around a web of streams that spread across multiple parishes but which also contained large sections of 'purely agricultural' land. Despite this, he recommended an extensive boundary for the borough that took in all of Stroud's mills, as he discovered that 'parts of the families employed in agriculture generally find occupation in the manufactories and are thus interested in them'.[51]

The question of whether agricultural populations should be included in the new boroughs was also raised by eleven cases where the reform bill had stipulated extensive specific preliminary boundaries. When they commenced their work in September 1831, the commissioners were informed that they were only allowed to amend a preliminary boundary if it excluded part of the town associated with a borough. This meant the commissioners were initially obliged to abide by the excessively wide boundaries provided for Whitby, Sunderland, Huddersfield and Birmingham in the 15 September draft of the reform bill. In their initial report on Sunderland, Wrottesley and Tancred informed Drummond that had their instructions not required them to do so, 'we cannot affirm that we should have been disposed to recommend so ... extensive an incorporation of rural districts'.[52] Drummond became particularly wary of the extensive preliminary limits provided for Whitby, Huddersfield and Birmingham. Each boundary, he discovered, had been created on the basis of local representations to the government after the introduction of their reform bill. While it transpired that the local requests from Birmingham discussed above had been the result of ignorance over the remit of the boundary commission, the preliminary definitions of both Huddersfield and Whitby were found to have been the product of political scheming by local parties already in the full throes of electioneering.[53] The discovery that politics had influenced the definition of these preliminary boundaries made it all the more apparent to Drummond that boundaries needed to be based on the 'particular application of general principles', which disregarded local opinion and were applied equally to all cases.[54]

Following the receipt of their report on Whitby, Drummond informed Tancred and Wrottesley that the borough was 'one of those cases which I should like [to] bring forward [to the government] as an example of the unfitness of the Schedule [C & D] boundaries ... defining the boundaries of [certain] towns by townships – or parishes'.[55] The reform bill had stipulated that the townships of Whitby, Ruswarp and Hawsker should constitute the borough of Whitby (Map 7.2). Despite this, the commissioners discovered that the 'wealthy', but 'declining' sea-port town of Whitby only extended partly into Ruswarp and Hawsker, was unlikely to expand much further and the outlying houses in these townships were 'far removed' from the town of Whitby and 'entirely agricultural'.[56] Although they were not formally allowed to do so, the commissioners proposed a tentative boundary for Whitby that was in keeping with their proposals elsewhere. This boundary cut off the outlying parts of Ruswarp and

Hawsker and was met with approval by Drummond, who agreed that it included all of the 'small portions of Ruswarp and Hawsker [that] could contribute essentially to the constituency of the town'.[57]

Drummond presented the case of Whitby to the cabinet, which accepted his rationale and gave him permission to submit a supplementary set of instructions to the commissioners. In late October 1831 he advised the commissioners that if they had:

> reason to believe that the description given in the schedule [of a borough] either does not embrace what is truly connected, by similarity of interest with the town or district, or that it includes portions of an opposite character, or ... that it is not consistent with the intentions of the framers of the late bill, then it would be desirable to ... propose for the consideration of government what you consider an improved boundary.[58]

In addition to Whitby, this instruction led to the proposal of contracted boundaries for Sunderland, Huddersfield, Oldham, Stoke-on-Trent, Sheffield, Birmingham, Tower Hamlets, Finsbury, Marylebone and Lambeth (Maps 7.1 and 7.2). As a demonstration of what the commissioners, and Drummond, understood as the 'intentions of the framers of the late bill', their reports for these boroughs recommended the exclusion of 'rural' or 'agricultural' portions of land that were unconnected with the immediate populations associated with these boroughs, and not deemed likely to see future development.[59]

Political interference on the sitting committee

Following the October amendment to their instructions, Drummond ensured that the commissioners identified consistent boundary proposals for all forty-one new boroughs. Later in the month, the sitting committee of the boundary commission (Drummond, Littleton and Beaufort) commenced a review of these proposals, which concluded in the publication of the boundary bill in February 1832. Throughout, channels of communication were kept open with the cabinet, with Russell acting as the primary conduit. The sitting committee approved thirty-nine of the commissioners' recommendations but overturned their proposals for Birmingham and Whitby. In both cases, Littleton and Russell, respectively, secured alterations that they perceived to be favourable to their electoral interests.

Birmingham (Map 7.1) had been provided with extensive preliminary limits by the 15 September version of the reform bill, but following

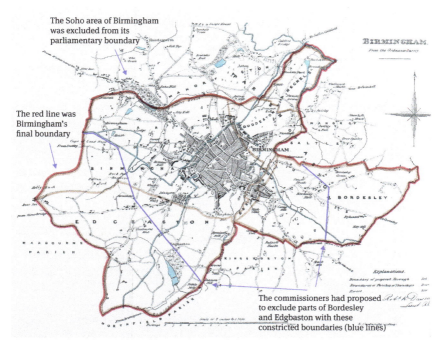

Map 7.1: Birmingham, Soho, its proposed and final boundary, PP1831–2 (141), xl
© National Library of Scotland; digital additions by author.

Drummond's October instruction, an alternative boundary was proposed that separated 'the town [of Birmingham] from the rural districts' of Edgbaston and Bordesley (the parishes of which had been included in the borough's preliminary description).[60] Beaufort, Littleton and Russell approved this aspect of the proposal. Littleton termed it 'desirable', Beaufort stated that 'to include the whole of them [the parishes of Bordesley and Edgbaston] seems contrary to the spirit of the bill', and Russell observed 'I confess my own inclination points … to excluding the … rural districts mentioned in the report'.[61]

Birmingham's proposal was complicated by the presence of the Boulton and Watt steam engine manufactory to the north of the town, in the Soho area of the parish of Aston. Although it appeared to form an extension of Birmingham, the commissioners had not proposed to include Soho in their boundary as it was in Staffordshire. The rest of Birmingham was in Warwickshire. This rationale baffled Beaufort and Russell, as it was well known that the Boulton and Watt manufactory formed an integral part of Birmingham's identity. Beaufort asserted that, 'Soho, which is intimately connected with the town, and which stands at the head of its great establishments, should surely be a constituent part of the borough' and Russell stated that he was for 'taking in Soho'.[62] Littleton dissented on the basis that Soho was in Staffordshire and that he had 'reason to think Messers Boulton and Watt would not desire the junction'.[63] Although Littleton claimed to 'have no private wish about excluding Soho', as MP for Staffordshire he had a longstanding electoral connection with Soho, as well as a personal connection with Matthew Boulton.[64] Furthermore, as discussed in the previous two chapters, Littleton had privately expressed a preference for ensuring that some manufacturing populations (excluding borough freeholders) remained in the midland counties.[65] The issue of Soho's inclusion in Birmingham had a backstory, as the parish of Aston had been included in the preliminary boundary of Birmingham identified by the March 1831 draft of the reform bill. By April 1831, however, Aston had been removed from Birmingham's preliminary boundaries, probably at the behest of Littleton who, as discussed above, influenced the preliminary boundaries of the Staffordshire boroughs of Wolverhampton and Walsall.[66]

Due to the disagreement, Russell proposed that Drummond should decide whether to include Soho in the borough and advised him to 'send a surveyor down [to Birmingham] next week to fix any [boundary] points'. This visit did not take place, as Littleton, sufficiently alarmed that Drummond would take in Soho, contacted his constituent, long-term correspondent and manager of the Soho foundry, Matthew Boulton. Littleton informed Boulton: it is desired by some parties ... to include Soho within the boundary [of Birmingham]. What is your wish about it? It shall be as you like'.[67] Boulton advised Littleton of his preference that Soho remain in Staffordshire but asked him if he should consult Soho's inhabitants over the matter and defer to their wishes. Littleton, seeking to avoid public pressure for Soho to form part of Birmingham, informed Boulton that it was 'better not to consult your parishioners'.[68] Littleton then used his correspondence from Boulton to plead with Russell that Soho should not form part of Birmingham, to which Russell acceded, 'your letter respecting Soho is quite satisfactory, so be it'.[69] With Soho's manufacturers to be excluded from Birmingham, the commissioners', Beaufort, Russell and Littleton's earlier expressed desire that they should 'draw such a line [around Birmingham] to generally comprehend the manufacturers and exclude the farmers [of Bordesley and Edgbaston]' now appeared highly contradictory. Thus, to avoid questions in parliament over why the rural parts of Bordesley and Edgbaston, as well as the Soho manufactory, had been excluded, the boundary bill recommended no alteration to the specific preliminary boundaries for Birmingham identified by the 15 September version of the reform bill.

That something suspicious had taken place in the proposal of Birmingham's boundary did not fail to escape Croker. When discussing the boundary bill in the Commons in June 1832, he exclaimed his disbelief that 'the father of the arts in Birmingham, the great manufacturer, the man who had done more for the industry and trade of that great town than almost any individual that ever lived – Matthew Boulton, was excluded from a vote for Birmingham'. This observation was shamelessly rebuffed by Littleton on the basis that it had been deemed too difficult to draw a boundary that included the Soho area – even though Littleton had prevented Drummond from sending a surveyor there specifically for this purpose. Littleton then assured the Commons that Soho's exclusion was not an issue, as he had consulted Boulton, who had consented to Soho remaining in Staffordshire.[70] Ultimately Littleton got his way. Croker's complaints were discounted, and Soho was excluded from the boundaries of Birmingham as stipulated by the 1832 Boundary Act.

Two further cases prompted disagreement among the sitting committee: Whitby and Sunderland. Following Drummond's October instruction, commissioners Wrottesley and Tancred had recommended an extensive exclusion of unconnected rural districts from the preliminary boundaries of both boroughs in order to bring their proposals in line with elsewhere (Map 7.2). Beaufort and Littleton approved of both proposals. On Sunderland they wrote:

> We concur with the commissioners' view of the fitter boundary – it includes all the kindred interests of the town and neighbourhood, and still leaves an ample margin [for future growth]. The very extensive district comprised with the description contained in the schedule to the late bill would have included an unnecessarily extensive portion of rural district.[71]

By contrast, Russell objected to both proposals. His attention was drawn to them in January 1832, when he was contacted by the prospective pro-reform candidate for Whitby, Richard Moorsom. Moorsom had heard a rumour that the commissioners planned to exclude the township of Hawsker from the borough, which he warned Russell, would be 'a decided blow to the liberal interest here [in Whitby] and would ... highly gratify the opposite party: men who are not only adverse to the present government on questions of reform, but who oppose them on every other'.[72] Moorsom also informed Russell that the earl of Mulgrave, a Whig peer and local proprietor, agreed with him and would be contacting him over the matter. Following this, Russell conducted a review of the boundaries proposed for the new north-eastern boroughs and expressed his objection to the

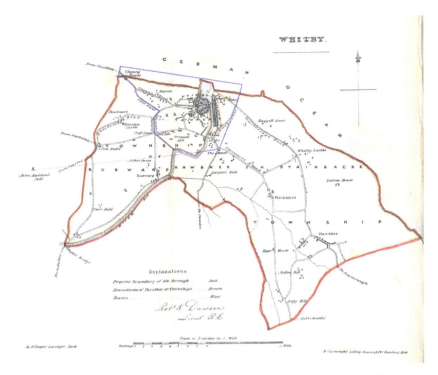

Map 7.2: Whitby and its proposed boundaries, PP1831 (141), xl. Author's collection; digital additions by author.
Key: final boundary (red); commission's proposed arbitrary boundary (blue) [digital addition].

commissioners' practice of reducing the specific preliminary boundaries of Sunderland and Whitby.

Russell highlighted several objections to the cases of Whitby and Sunderland that he had not made for other new boroughs whose specific preliminary boundaries had been modified in a similar manner. First, he stated that given that Whitby and Sunderland's preliminary boundaries had been found to be legally correct, and had not been objected to by local inhabitants, there had been no need to amend them. Furthermore, he objected to the commissioners' application of 'general notions regarding town and country' to divide the immediate populations associated with a borough from their surrounding rural populations. He observed:

> With respect to the assumption that a rural parish is certainly unconnected with a shipping town it seems to me too easily adopted. The interest of the producers of corn, butter and cheese is that the great town in their neighbourhood should flourish and whatever tends to that end will be agreeable to them.

In the same note, Russell provided his seemingly contradictory approval to the commissioners' proposal to exclude Huddersfield's surrounding secondary rural population from its preliminary boundaries, and approved of excluding the agricultural districts surrounding Birmingham.

Russell insisted that Whitby and Sunderland's boundaries be reviewed by Althorp and Grey.[73] Following this, Drummond wrote, 'Lord John Russell has since expressed a decided opinion that the boundaries of Whitby and Sunderland given in the first [reform] bill should be adhered to'. Interestingly, Russell's opinion was ignored in the case of Sunderland, as Beaufort and Littleton insisted on the commissioners' proposed reduction of its preliminary boundaries.[74] In Whitby, however, the commissioners' proposals were overruled in favour of the more extensive boundary favoured by Russell and Moorsom. Given that only Whitby was modified to allow for Russell's wider conception of a shipping borough's 'connected population', as well as his contradictory preference for a narrower conception of connected populations in other cases, it appears he used Sunderland as a stalking horse to ensure Whitby's boundaries were amended to his liking. Once Whitby's boundaries had been amended, he relented on altering Sunderland's in order that they fell in line with the principles used to identify new borough boundaries elsewhere. Ironically, Russell's attempts at gerrymandering were unsuccessful, as Moorsom failed to beat his Conservative opponent in Whitby's first reformed election. Although Moorsom had completed a favourable canvass of Hawsker, he had failed to realise the township only contained five £10 householders.[75]

The new boroughs and the boundary bill

The government amended a further seven of the commissioners' new borough proposals following the boundary bill's introduction to parliament – Finsbury, Marylebone, Tower Hamlets, Stoke-on-Trent, Sheffield, Oldham and Bradford. In each case the government reinstated a specific preliminary boundary that had been agreed to by the Commons prior to the commission commencing its work. By doing so, the government acknowledged (following complaints from petitioners or parliamentarians), that the commission had been too zealous in their attempts to segregate urban and rural areas. In every other case, however, the government defended the commissioners' proposals on the basis that their application of Drummond's principles had been proportionate. These changes demonstrated that when it suited them, the government, unlike Drummond, was willing to allow local opinion a limited role in the boundary-setting process. Given that for every government modification, a contradictory case remained, the changes to these seven boroughs are best considered a product of the realpolitik of negotiations over the boundary bill during February and July 1832, rather than a rejection of the commission's general approach to boundary setting.

In their recommendation for the metropolitan borough of Marylebone, the commission had proposed to exclude the northern 'rural district' of the parish of St. Pancras, even though the entire parish had been included in the borough's preliminary boundary.[76] Following a petition from the inhabitants of St. Pancras on 8 May 1832, which had asked that the entire parish be included in the borough, the government overturned the commissioners' recommendation in the brief Commons committee stage that took place over the boundary bill on 25 May.[77] The reinstatement of the entire parish of St. Pancras into Marylebone was accompanied by the reinstatement of several rural parishes that the commission had proposed to exclude from the boroughs of Finsbury and Tower Hamlets, to ensure consistency between north London's adjoining metropolitan boundaries.[78] As the government had been working behind the scenes at Westminster to identify changes that would allow the bill to be 'committed proforma'[79] at the committee stage, it appears this decision was made to appease Middlesex's radical MP, Joseph Hume, who had presented the petition from St. Pancras's inhabitants.[80] The government's consent to these amendments did not signal a complete reversal of their support for excluding rural districts from every metropolitan borough, as the boundary proposed by the same commissioners for Lambeth, which excluded the 'purely agricultural' parts of the parishes of Lambeth and Camberwell, remained intact.[81] Significantly, the government had secured the support of Surrey's two representatives for their plans to divide that county, which was probably predicated on including as many agricultural voters in the eastern division of the county as possible.[82]

The commission's recommendations for arbitrary boundaries that excluded the rural parts of townships from Stoke-on-Trent and Sheffield were also overturned. However, it is unclear why these changes took place as they were not debated in parliament, and no petitions were recorded against them. In both cases, the preliminary boundaries that had been approved by parliament prior to the commission commencing their work were reinstated. The most plausible explanation for the rejection of the commission's proposals in these instances is that their arbitrary boundaries were too complex, and that the rural land excluded from both boroughs contained very few voters. Abiding by an existing legal boundary, in both cases, not only avoided the creation of a new boundary, but also had little material impact on either constituency.[83]

The changes made to the commissioner's recommendations for Bradford and Oldham provide the only instances where the government publicly acknowledged that the commission had made too narrow an assessment of a new borough's connected population (the metropolitan boroughs had been amended without debate).[84] To the surprise of the parish officers of Chadderton, Crompton and Royton, whose successful June 1831 memorial for their inclusion in Oldham started this chapter, the boundary commission recommended their exclusion from Oldham's boundaries. The commissioners had overturned this preliminary boundary on the basis that 'everything which can ... be considered as the town [of Oldham]' was included in its township, and that the land in its surrounding townships was 'without exception pasture, used for the keeping of cows'. Although the commissioners had acknowledged that the inhabitants of these townships were engaged in weaving, giving the population a 'mixed character, which is peculiar and unusual', they did not deem this sufficient for their inclusion.[85] Within days of this announcement, the inhabitants of Oldham and its surrounding townships submitted a cross-party memorial to parliament complaining of the 'injustice' of the latter's exclusion from the borough.[86] The Lancashire MP, Benjamin Heywood, and the Preston MP, John Wood, presented the memorial in late May 1832, which was successful in overturning the commissioners' recommendation. The cross-party nature of the memorial was clearly significant in affecting this change. However, reports of pro-reform activity in the township of Royton earlier that month were probably also influential in convincing the Grey ministry of the political benefits of an extended boundary.[87]

Similarly, on 7 June, a fortnight after Oldham's alteration, Bradford's boundaries were extended to its entire parish, in order that it included its more extended connected population (it had been proposed to only include three of the parish of Bradford's five townships in the borough). Significantly, the commissioners' proposed boundary had excluded the parish of Manningham, the location of the seat of Ellis Cunliffe Lister, one of Bradford's prominent mill-owners who had already announced his candidacy for the borough and had actively supported Morpeth and Brougham at the 1830 Yorkshire election.[88] The government had previously bowed to pressure from Morpeth to include Manningham in the borough's preliminary boundary in August 1831, and did so again in June 1832.

The changes to both Bradford and Oldham appeared to confirm to the pro-reform Yorkshire MP, George Strickland, that by early June the government preferred wider boundaries in the new boroughs, which took in both a town's immediate and secondary population. On this basis, he argued on 8 June for the extension of Halifax and Huddersfield's boundaries into their respective parishes. Following the introduction of the boundary bill, six petitions had been submitted to parliament from Halifax's surrounding townships, whose 'interests' Strickland confirmed were 'closely identified with those of Halifax'.[89] A petition had also been sent from Huddersfield, requesting that its parish, not its township, become its parliamentary boundary.[90] Strickland reasoned that Huddersfield and Halifax's boundaries should be extended on the same basis as Bradford and Oldham's. In Huddersfield, doing so also promised to reduce the power of the Whig proprietor and Yorkshire MP, John Charles Ramsden, who by the commissioners' own admission owned 'every house but one' within their proposed boundary.[91]

By contrast to Oldham and Bradford, Russell informed Strickland, and the petitioners from both towns, that the commissioners had come 'to a proper decision' over both boroughs.[92] In doing so, Russell reaffirmed his agreement with the commission's application of its principles, which acknowledged that parliamentary boundaries could not be designed to mitigate the 'natural influence' of property.[93] The cases of Huddersfield and Halifax were taken up by the anti-reform first Baron Wynford when the boundary bill reached the Lords in July 1832. However, the government refused to change either boundary, as the Duke of Richmond (who stewarded the boundary bill through the Lords) maintained his support for the commission's application of its principles to both boroughs.[94] As Strickland and Wynford found, and the case of the metropolitan boroughs suggests, the government's decision to overrule the commissioners' recommendations in some cases, but maintain them in others, defied simple explanation. It is likely that the government reasoned that giving in to Strickland and Wynford over Halifax and Huddersfield would have taken their concessionary stance too far, and simply encouraged further objections to the commissioners' proposals.

Electoral and political legacy

The identification of preliminary boundaries, Littleton and Russell's interventions on the sitting committee and parliamentary negotiations meant the new boroughs were the most contradictory class of boundaries enacted by the 1832 Boundary Act. After clarifying their ability to overturn the preliminary boundary schedules in the reform bill, the commission eventually proposed new borough boundaries according to Drummond's 'scientific' framework that included the immediate – but in most cases non-agricultural – populations associated with a borough and allowed space for its future growth. Nine of these forty-one proposals were modified in order that a more extensive space (which the commissioners had deemed too rural) was included in a borough's limits. Whitby and Birmingham, and probably Bradford, were modified by the government for overtly partisan ends. The remaining changes were made to appease certain parliamentarians and their conceptions of the interested populations associated with a borough. The government's deviation from Drummond's principles in these cases revealed they were not as attached as the commission had supposed to the exclusion of rural districts from the new boroughs, particularly if adding areas to a boundary aided parliamentary negotiations. This severely muddies Moore's claim that the government's primary intention in the new boroughs was to create 'deference communities' via the isolation of urban and rural electorates.[95] Furthermore, while the commissioners had clearly sought to achieve a separation of urban and rural populations with their proposals, they were not operating at the somewhat abstract level of 'deference community' creation as Moore has suggested. Rather they were combining their understanding of the government's public legitimisation for the new boroughs – to provide representation to particular manufacturing or commercial interests – with the legal, economic and social considerations that they had been using to redraw ancient borough boundaries in an apparently disinterested manner – by defining the entire community associated with a borough and allowing space for its future growth.

Of all the constituency types in England's reformed electoral landscape, the new boroughs proved the most supportive of Whig-Liberal governments and radical political issues between 1832 and 1868. New borough MPs delivered consistent majorities in favour of Whig and Liberal administrations, unless those administrations were seen to be acting in too moderate a manner, and offered continuous support to liberal economic, religious and political reforms. At the 1832 election, the party labels of fifty-five of the sixty-three new borough MPs suggested they were willing to support a Whig government (Graph C.1 and Table C.3), and of those fifty-five MPs, thirty-three (60 per cent) stood in advance of the Grey ministry as either radicals or reformers.[96] In England's existing boroughs the equivalent figure was 43 per cent and in England's counties it was 35 per cent.[97] Their radical leanings meant new borough MPs were the only type of English constituency to oppose the government's proposed church rates compromise in April 1834. While the new boroughs never reached the same heights of radicalism again, at least 73 per cent of their seats were filled by Liberal MPs for the rest of the period. This was reflected in major confidence divisions between 1835 and 1868, where between 70 and 80 per cent of MPs representing new boroughs supported Whig or Liberal administrations (or oppositions) over the Conservative alternative. The only times these levels of support shifted were in the major confidence votes with high levels of radical dissent during the 1850s.

The radical bias of new borough MPs was confirmed by their consistent support for free trade, the abolition of church rates and the ballot, in comparison to their English counterparts representing existing boroughs and counties (Graphs C.3, C.5 and C.7 and Tables C.5, C.7 and C.9). As Tories and protectionists had feared throughout the 1820s, the new boroughs proved a breeding ground for the parliamentary and extra-parliamentary movement for the repeal of the corn laws. A minimum of 75 per cent of new borough MPs supported corn law reform from 1832. By contrast, until 1846, support for the same issue in the English counties remained below 10 per cent, hovered around the 20 per cent mark for English boroughs extended to their surrounding parishes and remained around 40 per cent for every other ancient borough. It was a similar story in terms of support for the abolition of church rates and the ballot. The Whig government's compromise solution on church rates in 1834 led to the first major radical rebellion of the post-reform period, and by the 1850s around nine in ten new borough MPs supported their total abolition. Support for the ballot grew quickly among new borough MPs during the 1830s, when it became an electorally profitable means of signalling to radical constituents that they stood in advance of the Whig government and supported further electoral reform. This meant that at least seven in ten new borough MPs supported secret voting from the 1840s, compared to one in ten county MPs, two in ten MPs representing multiple parish boroughs and five in ten MPs representing every other ancient borough.

It would be rash to suggest that the boundaries provided to the new boroughs in 1832 were the primary reason for the Liberal and radical bias of the new boroughs. To an extent the commission's preference for excluding rural and agricultural districts from new borough boundaries proved favourable to Liberal and radical interests, although due to a lack of polling data this can only be deduced with any specificity in the handful of cases that were given extended boundaries against the commission's wishes. In Birmingham (whose parliamentary boundaries were adopted at a municipal level in 1838) the rural parishes of Edgbaston and Bordesley, which had been included in the boundary to deflect from Soho's exclusion to the north of the town, provided a clear power base for the local Conservative party – although their electoral success was limited and party identity in the borough was severely complicated by the enduring popularity of currency reform.[98] In Oldham two of the three townships that the commissioners had originally deemed too agricultural for inclusion in the borough (Chadderton and Crompton), and whose lobbying efforts for inclusion in the borough started this chapter, became a significant electoral base for local Conservatives after 1832, ensuring the return of their candidates at two elections and a by-election prior to 1868.[99] These experiences were consistent with the new borough of Leeds, where the commissioners agreed to retain parliament's wide preliminary definition of the borough in the expectation of urban expansion and to avoid the creation of arbitrary boundaries. The suburban areas in the borough's outskirts provided the foundation for the election of one Conservative member at six of nine general elections during the period – a power base that was gradually complicated by an influx of 'villa liberals' to the suburbs of Leeds prior to the Second Reform Act.[100]

The agricultural outskirts of new boroughs were not always advantageous to local Conservatives, however. The extension of Bradford into Manningham, which the commission had recommended against, benefitted the Whig manufacturer, Lister, who secured one of the borough's two seats for the next decade.[101] Likewise, the wider boundaries for London's northern metropolitan boroughs held little advantage for Conservative candidates, and the inclusion of Hackney in Tower Hamlets actually provided a significant electoral base from the 1850s for the locally born advanced Liberal MP Charles Butler.[102] Stoke and Sheffield's wider boundaries had little direct electoral impact either, due to the small number of voters these rural areas contributed to the constituency.[103] The latter two cases in particular suggest that even if wider boundaries had been proposed by the commission, the limited number of voters that might have been added to new borough boundaries would have had a limited impact on electoral outcomes.

A more fertile means of understanding the significance of the boundaries assigned to the new boroughs in 1832 is to consider their impact alongside the other major structural conditions that defined reformed constituency politics – the elite £10 franchise and the need to create complex systems of party organisation to oversee annual registration. When doing so, it becomes apparent that the fixed, generally urban, industrial electoral geographies defined by the 1832 Boundary Act created the ideal conditions in which the representation of commercial and manufacturing interests, and the politics of liberalism, flourished. Significantly, a lack of ancient franchise rights in the new boroughs meant that voters could only be enfranchised if they owned or rented property within its boundaries, focusing the organisation of electoral politics entirely on the electoral interest communities defined by the 1832 Boundary Act.[104] This created the ideal conditions for a type of constituency politics to flourish between 1832 and 1868, which in line with the findings of Taylor, led to the consistent return of MPs with close affiliations to the socio-economic interests of their localities.[105]

As reformers such as Russell had hoped prior to 1832, this meant that most new boroughs became associated with discernible interest groups in parliament. The largest group was the northern textile-interest boroughs, which if Manchester and Leeds are included in this categorisation, totalled fifteen constituencies.[106] They were followed by the shipping interest boroughs of the north-east (Sunderland, South Shields, Tynemouth and Whitby), the midland iron interest boroughs (Birmingham, Walsall and Wolverhampton) and the naval interest boroughs in the south (Devonport, Chatham and to a certain extent Greenwich). Sheffield was probably the only borough representing the steel – or cutlery – interest, Gateshead and Dudley fell broadly under the coal interests and Stoke-on-Trent under the pottery interest. The southern textile interest gained representation from Stroud and to a lesser degree, Frome. In addition, there were the metropolitan boroughs (Finsbury, Lambeth, Marylebone, Tower Hamlets and also Greenwich) whose interest representation was diffused among the variety of enterprises and varied socio-economic concerns of London.[107] By contrast, there was a small group of new boroughs – Brighton, Wakefield, Cheltenham, Whitehaven, Kidderminster and Kendal – whose dominant social and economic identities proved less clear. Brighton, in particular, saw its political identity transformed by the railways, as an influx of London commuters and middle and working-class holiday makers ended the borough's initial reputation during the 1830s as a pocket of royal influence and winter destination for London's elite.[108]

The success of the Whig interest representation model occurred because the organisation of politics in the new boroughs was generally overseen by the leading manufacturing and commercial figures, and sometimes landed elites, within a borough's boundaries, usually with the co-operation of local chapels and churches. In this respect, the electoral reforms of 1832 overtly politicised the economic and social interests within new borough limits, as their leading textile and metal manufacturers, ship-owners, mine-owners and potters, with the support of religious ministers, local bankers, lawyers and merchants, assumed responsibility for the leadership, funding and oversight of emerging local party machines.

In Macclesfield, John Brocklehurst, a Unitarian who owned the town's, and Britain's, largest silk manufactory enjoyed sufficient political influence in his local party hierarchy to be returned as a moderate Liberal for one of the borough's seats at every election between 1832 and 1868.[109] A complex network of 'small masters working in their own workshops' in Sheffield successfully co-operated with the town's Dissenting radical-Liberals to maintain electoral hegemony over a Conservative alliance among the town's financial and banking sectors, as well as its Anglicans and Wesleyan Methodists.[110] And in Rochdale, the 'Liberal Nonconformist manufacturing elite' were able to 'wield influence through party organisation' despite the proliferation of smaller textile manufacturers, a lack of £10 householders with direct connections to manufacturing and the borough's thriving radical culture.[111] The commercial elite that tended to sit at the top of these local party hierarchies were not necessarily Liberal, and in Blackburn, three of the town's five major cotton-spinning families provided the focal point for Conservatism in the borough, and were generally able to return at least one member throughout the period.[112] While they formed a minority of new boroughs, the influence of a Tory commercial elite combined with a strong Anglican vote to usually allow one Conservative to be returned for the double-member seats of Bolton, Oldham, Stoke, Sunderland and Macclesfield.[113]

It was not just a borough's economic and social elites whose politicisation was hastened by the electoral conditions established by the 1832 Boundary and Reform Acts. Living within a boundary legitimised the political participation of electors and non-electors, who found creative, if not always successful, means of engaging in electoral politics and challenging local party authority. Voters in the new boroughs, whose politicisation via the new registration system in 1832 has been convincingly documented by historians, were generally able to demonstrate their independence from local party machinery when its leaders acted against public opinion.[114] And, while the elite nature of the franchise, especially in the north, meant most working-class constituents, and all women, could not vote, it did not stop the unenfranchised within a borough's boundaries exhibiting some influence over electoral outcomes. As O'Gorman and Vernon have observed, the eliteness of the £10 franchise was significant in ensuring the adoption of canvassing, hustings and election day rituals in the new boroughs that had predominated in the unreformed borough system prior to 1832, in order that the voices of the unenfranchised could be heard by those who were voting on their behalf.[115] These electoral customs were not just window-dressing, they had real influence on electoral outcomes, and helped to ensure that politics in the new boroughs reflected the unique interests and political tensions of their electoral geographies. During the 1850s, for instance, Stroud, Bury and Dudley all witnessed coalitions between non-electors and independent electors that led to the defeat of incumbent MPs with the backing of established local party organisations.[116] While the political influence of non-electors, in particular, should not be overstated, inclusion in a borough's electoral geography had an enduring impact on the communities enfranchised in 1832. The implementation of boundary reform had an equally marked impact on England's counties. Its political outcomes, however, proved very different.

Notes

1. PP1831 (64) (112), xvi. 64–5; E. Butterworth, *Historical Sketches of Oldham* (Oldham, 1856), 197; PP1830–31 (0.37), ii. 28–31; PP1831 (22), iii. 32.
2. See Chapter 1.
3. D. C. Moore, *The Politics of Deference: A Study of the Mid-Nineteenth Century Political System* (New York, 1976), 176–77.
4. See Chapter 1. See also, Miles Taylor, 'Interests, Parties and the State: The Urban Electorate in England, c. 1820–72', in J. Lawrence and Miles Taylor (eds.), *Party, State and Society: Electoral Behaviour in Britain since 1820* (Aldershot, 1997), 50–78; A. Hawkins, *Victorian Political Culture: Habits of Heart and Mind* (Oxford, 2015), 162–3.
5. PP1831 (244), iii. 37–41.
6. 'Manchester and Salford', 'Birmingham and Aston', 'Greenwich, Deptford and Woolwich', 'Wolverhampton, Bilston, and Sedgeley', 'Sunderland and the Wearmouths', 'South Shields and Westoe', 'Whitehaven, Workington, Harrington', and 'Tynemouth and North Shields', *Morning Post*, 2 Mar. 1831; Hansard, 3, ii. (1 Mar. 1831), 1072.
7. DSC, Grey, GRE/B46/1/27, 'Reform Committee ... Dec. 11 & 14 1830', 1–2; DSC, Grey, GRE/B46/1/35, 'List of the Great Towns', 1; PP1830–31 (201), x. 5.
8. P. Salmon, 'Littleton, Edward John (1791–1863)', in D. Fisher (ed.), *The House of Commons, 1820–1832* (Cambridge, 2009), vi. 136.
9. PP1822 (502), xv, 84. 305.
10. PP1830–31 (247), ii. 16–18.
11. *Newcastle Chronicle*, 8 Jan. 1831, 4; M. Escott, 'Durham County', in Fisher, *Commons*, ii. 359; PP1831 (64) (112), xvi. 7–8.
12. PP1830–31 (247), ii. 16–18.
13. PP1830–31 (247), ii. 16–18; PP1831 (244), iii. 37–41; PP1831–2 (11), iii. 42.
14. *HCJ*, 86 (5 Aug. 1831), 731.
15. PP1830–31 (0.37), ii. 28–31; Hansard, 13, iii. (30 Mar. 1831), 1171.
16. PP1830–31 (247), ii. 17; PP1830–31 (0.37), ii. 30; Hansard, 3, v. (5 Aug. 1831), 838–9.
17. Hansard, 3, v. (5 Aug. 1831), 839.
18. *HCJ*, 86 (5 Aug. 1831), 731, (15 Sept. 1831), 845.
19. PP1822 (502), xv. 156–7.
20. PP1830–31 (247), ii. 16; PP1822 (502), xv. 195–9; PP1831–2 (141), xxxviii. 8.
21. Hansard, 3, iii. (18 Apr. 1831), 1519.
22. PP1831 (64) (112), xvi. 9.

23. K. Rix, 'Bury', and 'Whitehaven', in P. Salmon and K. Rix (eds.), *The House of Commons 1832–1868* (forthcoming).

24. K. Rix, 'Oldham', and 'Rochdale', in Salmon and Rix, *Commons 1832–1868*; PP1831 (64) (112), xvi. 35, 49, 65.

25. PP1831 (64) (112), xvi. 35–40, 49–62, 64, 70; Hansard, 3, v. (6 Aug. 1831), 893–902, vi. (24 Aug. 1831), 536; *HCJ*, 86 (5 Aug. 1831), 731, (15 Sept. 1831), 845.

26. Hansard, 3, v. (4 Aug. 1831), 746–51; TNA, T72/8/20, 'Birmingham'; TNA, T72/8/52, 'Cheltenham'; TNA, T72/11/51, 'Walsall'; PP1830–31 (247), ii. 17; PP1830–31 (0.37), ii. 30; PP1831 (22), iii. 33.

27. *Birmingham Journal*, 19 Mar. 1831. See also *Aris's Birmingham Gazette*, 7, 14 Mar. 1831

28. *Aris's Birmingham Gazette*, 15 Aug. 1831; *HCJ*, 86 (2 Aug. 1831), 720; PP1830–31 (0.37), ii. 28–31.

29. TNA, T72/11/60, 'Whitby', R. Moorsom to Russell, 3 Jan. 1832.

30. Hansard, 3, v. (5 Aug. 1831), 833–6.

31. Compiled from PP1831–2 (141), xxxviii–xli.

32. The existing boroughs of Liverpool, Derby, Southampton and Cambridge had seen similar increases.

33. PP1831–2 (141), xli. 183.

34. Railroads had also featured in predicting future growth in the existing boroughs of Poole, Hereford, Sandwich and Morpeth, PP1831–2 (141), xxxviii. 231; xxxix. 15, 143; xl. 169.

35. D. Pickles, 'The Bowling Tramways', Unspecified diss. held by Bradford Industrial Museum (1966).

36. PP1831–2 (141), xxxviii. 172.

37. TNA, T72/9/19, 'Gateshead', Report on Gateshead by John Wrottesley, 6 Oct. 1831.

38. PP1831–2 (141), xxxviii. 99.

39. TNA, T72/9/18, 'Frome', Gawler and Ansley to Drummond, 16 Oct. 1831.

40. TNA, T72/11/53, 'Warrington', 'Report on Warrington'; S. Lewis, *A Topographical Dictionary of England*, iv. (London, 1831), 393.

41. TNA, T72/8/26, 'Bolton', Romilly to Drummond, 28 Oct. 1831.

42. TNA, T72/11/8, 'Rochdale', Drummond to Allen, 7 Nov. 1831.

43. TNA, T72/11/47, 'Tynemouth', Report on Tynemouth by Wrottesley, 9 Oct. 1831.

44. TNA, T72/11/53, 'Warrington', Drummond to Romilly, 21 Sept. 1831; TNA, T72/8/24, 'Blackburn', 'Observations on Blackburn', 7 Nov. 1831.

45. PP1831–2 (141), xli. 209.

46. TNA, T72/11/49, 'Wakefield', Wrottesley to Drummond, 27 Sept. 1831.

47. TNA, T72/11/49, 'Report on the borough of Wakefield'.

48. TNA, T72/11/49, 'Report on the borough of Wakefield', Drummond to Wrottesley, undated.

49. TNA, T72/11/62, 'Whitehaven', Report on Whitehaven by Romilly, 1 Oct. 1831; TNA, T72/9/47, 'Kidderminster'; TNA, T72/9/45, 'Kendal'; TNA, T72/9/18, 'Frome'.

50. PP1831–2 (141), xxxviii. 55, 165, xxxix. 53, 143, xli. 185.

51. PP1831–2 (141), xxxviii. 198.

52. TNA, T72/11/35, 'Sunderland', Report on Sunderland by Wrottesley and Tancred, 5 Oct. 1831.

53. TNA, T72/10/56, 'Oldham', Chapman to Drummond, 3 Nov. 1831; TNA, T72/8/20, 'Birmingham', Ord to Drummond, 28 Sept. 1831; TNA, T72/9/39 'Huddersfield', Romilly to Drummond, 19 Oct. 1831; TNA, T72/11/60 'Whitby', Wrottesley to Drummond, 24 Oct. 1831.

54. TNA, T72/11/47, 'Tynemouth', Wrottesley to Drummond, 22 Nov. 1831; TNA, T72/9/39, 'Huddersfield', Romilly to Drummond, 19 Oct. 1831.

55. TNA, T72/11/60, 'Whitby', Drummond to Wrottesley, 15 Oct. 1831.

56. TNA, T72/11/60, 'Report on Whitby'.

57. TNA, T72/11/60, 'Report on Whitby', Drummond to Wrottesley, 15 Oct. 1831.

58. PP1831–2 (141), xxxviii. 13.

59. See individual reports in PP1831–2 (141), xxxviii–xli.

60. TNA, T72/8/20, 'Birmingham', Ord to Drummond, 28 Sept. 1831.

61. TNA, T72/8/20, 'Birmingham', undated note by Littleton, undated note by Beaufort, Russell and Littleton.

62. TNA, T72/8/20, 'Birmingham', undated note by Beaufort, Russell and Littleton.

63. TNA, T72/8/20, 'Birmingham', undated note by Littleton.

64. See Library of Birmingham, Boulton Papers [hereafter LB, Boulton], MS3782/13/22/1.

65. SRO, Hatherton, D260/M/F/5/26/7, 31 Oct. 1831, 195.

66. DSC, Grey, B46/1/35, 1, 'Appendix No. 3'; PP1830–31 (247), ii. 16–18.

67. LB, Boulton, MS3782/13/22/14, Littleton to Boulton, 30 Dec. 1831, 138.

68. LB, Boulton, MS3782/13/22/14, Littleton to Boulton, 6 Jan. 1831, 139.

69. SRO, Hatherton, D260.M.F.5.27.7, Russell to Littleton, 3 Jan. 1832, 3.

70. Hansard, 3, xiii. (7 June 1832), 535; *MOP*, iii. (7 June 1832), 2514–15.

71. TNA, T72/11/60, 'Whitby', note by Littleton and Beaufort.

72. TNA, T72/11/60, 'Whitby', R. Moorsom to Russell, 3 Jan. 1832; K. Rix, 'Whitby', in Salmon and Rix, *Commons 1832–1868*.

73. TNA, T72/11/60, 'Whitby', 'Sunderland and Whitby', note by Russell.

74. TNA, T72/11/60, 'Whitby', 'Sunderland and Whitby', note by Littleton and Beaufort.

75. TNA, T72/11/60, 'Whitby', 'Report on Whitby'.

76. PP1831–2 (141), xxxix. 118.

77. *Morning Post*, 9 May 1832, 2; *HCJ*, 87 (8 May 1832), 300.

78. PP1831–2 (488), iii. 53.

79. SRO, Hatherton, D260/M/F/5/26/8, 24 May 1832, 47.

80. PP1831–2 (141), xxxix. 108–30; D. Fisher, 'Hume, Joseph', in Fisher, *Commons*, v. 752–83.

81. PP1831–2 (141), xxxix. 125; 2 Gul. IV c.64 (11 July 1832).

82. *MOP*, iii. (7 June 1832), 2519, (22 June 1832), 2733.

83. PP1831–2 (141), xl. 7–9, xli. 205–07; PP1831–2 (174), iii. 47, 57; (488), iii. 71; *HCJ*, 87 (22 June 1832), 427.

84. Both boroughs were granted a second seat in the December 1831 expansion of Schedule C, but qualified to do so based on the population contained in the initial, smaller, boundaries proposed by the commission. See also, P. Salmon, 'English Reform Legislation, 1831-32', in Fisher, *Commons*, i. 385-8.

85. PP1831-2 (141), xxxix. 68.

86. *Manchester Times*, 3 Mar. 1832; *Manchester Courier*, 3 Mar. 1832; Butterworth, *Oldham*, 198-9.

87. K. Rix, 'Oldham', in Salmon and Rix, *Commons 1832-1868*; PP1831-2 (488), iii. 51; *Manchester Courier*, 12 May 1832; *Manchester Times*, 12, 26 May 1832.

88. *Leeds Mercury*, 8 Oct. 1831; *Leeds Intelligencer*, 24 Mar. 1831, 24 May 1832; J. James, *The History and Topography of Bradford* (London, 1841), 170; S. Lees, 'Lister, Ellis Cunliffe', and K. Rix, 'Bradford', in Salmon and Rix, *Commons 1832-1868*.

89. *MOP*, iii. (8 June 1832), 2533; *HCJ*, 87 (5 June 1832), 375.

90. *HCJ*, 87 (28 Feb. 1832), 153.

91. PP1831-2 (141), xli. 188; S. Richardson, 'Independence and Deference: A Study of the West Riding Electorate' (unpublished University of Leeds PhD thesis, 1995), 4.

92. *MOP*, iii. (8 June 1832), 2533.

93. TNA, T72/11/60, 'Whitby', 'Sunderland and Whitby' by Russell; TNA, T72/8/52, 'Cheltenham', Drummond to Chapman, 14 Sept. 1831.

94. *MOP*, iii. (3 July 1832), 2933-4, (4 July 1832), 2969; *HCJ*, 87 (14 June 1832), 398; *HLJ*, 64 (4 July 1832), 353.

95. Moore, *Politics of Deference*, 176-7.

96. Only Irish boroughs were more radical, with twenty-one of thirty-nine MPs standing in advance of the Whig government.

97. The figure in multiple parish boroughs was 37 per cent. For unchanged boroughs or those extended into their town it was 44 per cent.

98. *Aris's Birmingham Gazette*, 12 July 1841; *Birmingham Journal*, 7 May 1859; H. Miller, 'Birmingham', in Salmon and Rix, *Commons 1832-1868*; H. Miller, 'Radicals, Tories or Monomaniacs? The Birmingham Currency Reformers in the House of Commons, 1832-67', *Parliamentary History*, 31, 3 (2012), 354-77; D. Cannadine, 'The Calthorpe Family and Birmingham, 1810-1910: A "Conservative Interest" Examined', *HJ*, 18, 4 (1975), 737-9.

99. *Manchester Times*, 10 July 1852; *The Oldham Poll Book* (Oldham, 1852); J. Dodge, *The Poll Book* (Oldham, 1835); *The Remembrancer, Shewing how the electors of the borough of Oldham voted* (Oldham, 1847); K. Rix, 'Oldham', in Salmon and Rix, *Commons 1832-1868*.

100. *Leeds Mercury*, 2 June 1859; M. Roberts, '"Villa Toryism" and Popular Conservatism in Leeds, 1885-1902', *HJ*, 49, 1 (2006), 221-2; D. Fraser, *Urban Politics in Victorian England: The Structure of Politics in Victorian Cities* (Leicester, 1976), 215-7.

101. D. G. Wright, 'A Radical Borough: Parliamentary Politics in Bradford 1832-41', *Northern History*, 4, 1 (1969), 132-66.

102. M. Spychal, 'Butler, Charles Salisbury (1812-1870)', in Salmon and Rix, *Commons 1832-1868*.

103. *Sheffield Independent*, 4 April 1857.

104. In existing boroughs, ancient rights voters had to live within seven miles of the borough's main polling place, P. Salmon, *Electoral Reform at Work: Local Politics and National Parties, 1832-1841* (Woodbridge, 2002), 254-5.

105. Taylor, 'Interests, Parties and the State', 50–78.

106. Ashton-under-Lyne, Blackburn, Bolton, Bradford, Bury, Halifax, Huddersfield, Leeds, Macclesfield, Manchester, Oldham, Rochdale, Salford, Stockport and Warrington.

107. B. Weinstein, *Liberalism and Local Government in Early Victorian London* (Woodbridge, 2011), 43.

108. P. Salmon, 'Brighton', in Salmon and Rix, *Commons 1832–1868*.

109. K. Rix, 'Macclesfield', in Salmon and Rix, *Commons 1832–1868*.

110. S. Richardson, 'Independence and Deference', 136–55.

111. K. Rix, 'Rochdale', in Salmon and Rix, *Commons 1832–1868*; J. R. Vincent 'The Electoral Sociology of Rochdale', *Economic History Review*, 16, 1 (1963), 76–90.

112. K. Rix, 'Blackburn', in Salmon and Rix, *Commons 1832–1868*.

113. K. Rix, 'Blackburn', 'Bolton', 'Oldham', and 'Macclesfield', H. Miller, 'Stoke-on-Trent', and J. Owen, 'Sunderland', in Salmon and Rix, *Commons 1832–1868*; Hawkins, *Victorian Political Culture*, 183–6, 188–94.

114. Salmon, *Electoral Reform*.

115. F. O'Gorman, 'Campaign Rituals and Ceremonies: The Social Meaning of Elections in England 1780–1860', *Past and Present*, 135 (1992)', 79–115; J. Vernon, *Politics and the People: A Study in English Political Culture, 1815–1867* (Cambridge, 1993), 163–82.

116. K. Rix, 'Bury', in Salmon and Rix, *Commons 1832–1868*. On Dudley see G. Clark, *The Curiosities of Dudley and the Black Country* (Birmingham, 1881), 208; *Birmingham Daily Post*, 9 Mar. 1858, 28 Jan. 1863; *Birmingham Daily Gazette*, 22 Jan. 1864, 1 Feb. 1865. On Stroud see, *Sheffield Independent*, 8, 27 Jan. 1844; *Bristol Times*, 24 Apr. 1852; *Derby Mercury*, 25 Nov. 1863; *Stroud Journal*, 14 Mar. 1868; *Stroud News*, 12 Jan. 1877.

Chapter 8

Under the knife: Reconstructing the county map

In December 1832 over 3,000 voters polled in the first ever election for the constituency of Northamptonshire North. New electoral rolls were drawn up, the town of Kettering hosted its first ever nomination and the constituency's electors and non-electors – recently separated for electoral purposes from their neighbours in the south of the county – started the process of establishing new local party organisations and electoral traditions. Northamptonshire had returned two MPs to parliament since at least the thirteenth century. However, the 1832 Boundary Act broke this tradition, dividing the county into two double-member electoral districts. Northamptonshire was one of twenty-seven English counties divided by the 1832 reform legislation, which established fifty-five new double-member county constituencies. In addition, the Isle of Wight was separated from Hampshire and assigned a single MP, and seven counties were provided with a third member but remained undivided. This redrawing of long-established electoral boundaries and increase in England's county representation from 80 to 142 MPs was one of the most dramatic aspects in the reconstruction of England's electoral map in 1832.[1]

In March 1831, Grey's Whig government had proposed to redistribute over half of the seats made available by the disfranchisement of England's 'rotten boroughs' to newly divided counties. As discussed in Chapters 1 and 2, they hoped that doing so would provide for a balanced parliamentary representation of the landed and agricultural interests in the Commons, restore the esteemed historic status of the county MP and reduce the cost of county elections. To the cabinet's surprise, their drastic proposals provoked sustained criticism. The reform bill's opponents claimed county division would favour Whig electoral interests, eradicate ancient electoral communities and reduce the status of county MPs. Many of the reform bill's most vocal supporters also opposed the proposals, which they claimed would lead to aristocratic control of the counties. This opposition reached its peak in August 1831, when *The Times* threatened insurrection over what it viewed to be the reform bill's 'county-mongering' clause – a period of rebellion that was a major factor in the rejection of the second reform bill by the Lords in October 1831. This chapter resumes this narrative, as the Grey ministry put their plans for the division of counties into practice ahead of their proposed introduction of a third version of their reform bill in late 1831. It offers the first sustained analysis of how and why England's county map was reconstructed by the 1831–2 boundary commission, before considering its political and electoral impact.

Despite its clear significance to England's reformed electoral arithmetic, the division of counties has generally only received passing attention from historians of the 1832 reform legislation.[2] One exception is D. C. Moore, who combined a selective reading of the commission's published reports and the reform bill's borough freeholder clause to claim that the division of counties had been intended to separate urban and rural electors, as part of an all-encompassing scheme to transform England's electoral map into a system of 'deference communities'.[3] Less contentiously, Philip Salmon has identified the role of the rising proto-civil servant John George Shaw Lefevre in the initial design of county divisions, suggesting that his proposals formed the subject of ongoing parliamentary negotiations prior to the enactment of the Boundary Act. In contrast to Moore, Salmon has suggested that the commission's choice to design some counties according to their 'community of interest', rather than by equality of population, stemmed from a desire to pacify anti-reformers at Westminster, and that for every county division that appeared to provide a boon to the landed interest, there was one that contained an influential urban electorate.[4] As a further challenge to Moore's thesis, Salmon's wider analysis of post-1832 county politics and several constituency-level studies have moved historians towards an understanding of landed, aristocratic influence in the counties after 1832 within a participatory, rather than deferential framework.[5]

This chapter builds on Salmon's analysis, and further challenges Moore's assumptions, by exploring how John George Shaw Lefevre was hastily commissioned to divide the counties in November 1831. Like Drummond on the borough commission, Lefevre professed to have effected boundary change via several disinterested principles. A quantitative and qualitative analysis of Lefevre's initial proposals supports these claims but reveals that subsequent cabinet and parliamentary intervention led to some limited gerrymandering. This chapter also explores how Lefevre and Drummond oversaw the identification of nomination towns and polling places for England's reformed counties. The fiercely charged local and parliamentary debates that took place over these arrangements from February 1832 confirmed the wisdom of the boundary commission's wider ambition to redraw England's electoral map via a disinterested, 'scientific' framework. An analysis of England's reformed county map reveals how the division of counties combined with the introduction of electoral registration to provide the foundation for the Conservative political resurgence of the 1830s, as well as the structural conditions for the continuation of the Conservative party as an electoral force following the repeal of the corn laws in 1846.

Establishing the county commission

In contrast with the English borough commission, which had begun in August 1831, work did not start on dividing the counties until the end of November 1831, a fortnight before the planned introduction of the government's third reform bill. Following the rejection of the second reform bill by the Lords in October 1831, the division of counties had been identified by Grey, Althorp and Russell as a potential bargaining chip in their negotiations with the Waverers.[6] The Waverers, led by Lord Wharncliffe, were sceptical of the supposed aristocratic benefits of the measure, the mechanisms by which it was to be accomplished and the opportunity it provided for Whig gerrymandering.[7] Their position was strengthened by opposition to the division of counties during November in the City of London and at several county meetings from October.[8] By the middle of November, Littleton, a member of the borough boundary commission's sitting committee, had also applied pressure to the cabinet to abolish the division of counties. He feared that the borough commissioners' boundary proposals, and the potential the government might concede to the Waverers' separate demand to remove borough freeholders from the county franchise, would remove all town influence from reformed county elections.[9] It was not until a farcical breakdown in the City of London's attempts at agreeing to a final resolution in favour of reform on 22 November, Wharncliffe's sudden ambivalence to the issue on 23 November, and the return of the lord chancellor, Brougham, to London following the parliamentary recess on 25 November, that the government agreed not to 'sacrifice a tittle of our principle'.[10] Following this, the division of counties was delegated to Lefevre.

Lefevre was the second son of Charles Shaw Lefevre, a reforming MP for Reading between 1802 and 1820.[11] Lefevre was educated at Eton and graduated as senior wrangler from Cambridge in 1818. Less than enthused with life as a fellow at Trinity College, Cambridge, from 1819, he entered London's scientific and political intellectual circles as a fellow of the Royal Society in 1820 and was one of the first ten members elected to the Political Economy Club in 1821.[12] In 1822 he completed a grand tour with his boyhood friend George Spencer (Althorp's brother, and third son of the second Earl Spencer) before entering Inner Temple in 1822 and being called to the bar in 1825.[13] In 1826 he became the legal and financial auditor for the Spencer family's estates.[14] Lefevre had worked closely with the Spencer family from 1826 and also assumed an active role in the financial management of the family's constituencies, assisting Althorp when he was re-elected as a member for Northamptonshire in December 1830. His conveyancing commitments forced his resignation from the Political Economy Club in 1831, though he remained a member of the Society for the Diffusion of Useful Knowledge (which he had joined in 1828), and his own political ambitions were confirmed when he stood for election at Petersfield in 1832. His career as an MP was short-lived as he was unseated on petition in 1833. By contrast, his role as commissioner for dividing the counties in 1831 was the first in an extensive list of senior administrative positions that he assumed for the British state through to the late 1860s.[15]

The government had outlined the basic principles that they intended to guide the division of counties in August 1831, when Russell informed the Commons that most counties were to be divided into districts as equal in population and area as possible. These principles were to be discounted in cases where readily available 'recognised boundaries, separating one part of a county from another' existed.[16] This was consistent with the clauses in the government's reform bill that Yorkshire be provided with six seats, two for each of its three historic ridings, and that Lincolnshire be divided via its historic Lindsey, Kesteven and Holland districts.[17] As Salmon has observed, this pledge was intended to appease anti-reformers, who were wary that the division of counties would destroy historic county communities.[18]

When he commenced his work for the commission in late November 1831, Lefevre extended this latter principle, resolving that boundaries would not be drawn through pre-existing administrative divisions, such as hundreds or petty sessional divisions – a pragmatic decision given the surveying resources necessary to draw arbitrary boundaries across counties. These considerations, rather than a desire to divide counties into agricultural and manufacturing districts (as has been suggested by Moore), lay behind Lefevre's decision to discount equality of population and area when he discovered 'districts and places which, from their community of interest and feeling, manifestly ought to be placed in the same division of their county'.[19] As well as seeking to create county divisions that were equal in area and population, Lefevre also hoped to create divisions that were 'equal in the number of voters'. This was necessary as the presence of large borough electorates in some counties meant that population was not always an accurate indicator when trying to create broadly equal divisions. Within days of taking charge of the commission, then, Lefevre had established that the counties were to be divided, as far as was possible, into two equal districts according to size, population and voters, but that variation in equality was to be allowed to take into account any pre-existing geographic divisions or administrative units that existed in a county.[20]

In contrast to the borough commission, Lefevre did not have the time or resources to collect data via an individual inspection of each county, meaning that his proposals were based primarily on information collected from existing sources. In terms of demographic data, Lefevre obtained detailed population profiles of the counties from the census office, local records maintained by clerks of the peace relating to the number of persons qualified to serve on juries, and a tailor-made return from Drummond at the borough commission detailing the population of every parliamentary borough according to its most recent proposed boundary.[21] Although imperfect, Lefevre hoped these sources would allow him to estimate the geographic spread of voters in individual counties.

In terms of cartographic and geographic data, Lefevre had ready access via the borough boundary commission to precise ordnance survey or privately designed maps with hundred and parish boundaries detailed on them. These allowed him to predict the area of his proposed divisions to a tolerable degree of accuracy. He then worked with Robert K. Dawson, the head surveyor on the borough commission, and Richard Creighton, who had recently published small maps of every county for Samuel Lewis's 1831 edition of *A Topographical Dictionary of England*, to create illustrative maps for the commission's published report.[22] Lefevre, Dawson and Creighton used this process to create simple county maps with only towns, main roads and hundred divisions marked on them, which made electoral arrangements clear but also saved on production costs (Map 8.1). Lefevre also obtained details of petty sessional divisions (broken down by parish) that had been created in some counties following the passage of permissive legislation in 1828, and which were maintained by clerks of the peace.[23] The final type of data he gathered related to the 'communities of interest'

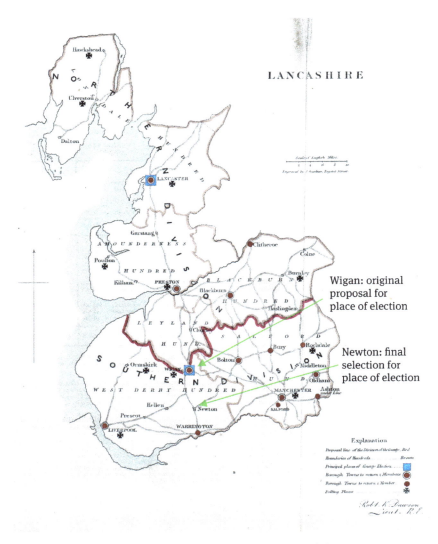

Map 8.1: Lancashire and its proposed divisions and places of election, PP1831–2 (141), xxxix © National Library of Scotland; digital additions by author.

that existed in a county. In two instances – Cumberland and Lancashire – Lefevre requested that the borough commissioners who had been working in the region complete an inspection of the economic and social conditions of both counties. For every other county it appears that Lefevre relied on data available in existing topographical dictionaries, and the knowledge of his friends, fellow boundary commissioners and political colleagues.[24]

Equality in population, area and voters?

Although Lefevre's data collection process demonstrated considerable initiative, it was hardly the ideal dataset with which to complete the task of 'statistical geography' (as he termed it) that had been assigned to him.[25] The following two sections analyse the extent to which he achieved his stated intention of proposing county divisions of roughly equal geographic, demographic and electoral extent (when ancient divisions were not readily available), or whether he erred from these principles in favour of a more partisan approach. With the reform bill having stipulated the divisions for Yorkshire and Lincolnshire, Lefevre proposed divisions for twenty-five of the twenty-seven counties divided by the English reform legislation. This section provides a statistical analysis of the equality of his published proposals, all of which were enacted by the Boundary Act. It is based on the population data provided by Lefevre in his published reports; acreage data for each county division from the 1831 census; a GIS analysis of county divisions whose size cannot be identified through the 1831 census; and records of registered electors at various intervals between 1832 and 1865.[26]

Lefevre considered each county on its own basis, seeking to divide it into two electoral districts of broadly equal geographic, demographic and electoral extent. He was provided with no formal guidance regarding the extent to which he was allowed to err from creating districts of an equal 50:50 ratio in terms of size, population and voters, and strict equality was not a possibility, given that pre-existing administrative divisions, such as hundreds, had to be used to divide each county. Lefevre also had the option to divide counties via their 'community of interest'. In order to identify some form of marker as to what can be considered 'equal', a variation of ±10 per cent from an entirely equal division has been settled on. So, if a county was divided into one district that contained 45 per cent of that county's population, and another that contained 55 per cent, then this could be considered equal – the same marker applies to a division's area and electors. This is an arbitrary marker, which Lefevre did not apply to his own work. However, it corresponds to the guidelines for constituency 'equality' proposed by the 2008 Venice Commission and the 2015 Political and Constitutional Reform Committee. The latter proposed that electoral districts in the UK should be considered equal if their populations were within ±10 per cent of the electoral quota (the total number of electors registered to vote, divided by the number of constituencies).[27]

When the populations of the twenty-five counties divided by Lefevre are considered, eight were divided into equal districts within a variance of ±10 per cent, and a further six within a variance of ±15 per cent. The

Table 8.1: Variation in population per county division for each county.

County	Population grouping that caused disparity	Variation in population
Norfolk		±1.04%
Worcestershire		±4.76%
Essex		±5.42%
Gloucestershire	Stroud	±6.78%
Staffordshire	Walsall, Wolverhampton and Dudley	±7.08%
Suffolk		±7.56%
Cumberland		±8.38%
Northamptonshire		±8.68%
Shropshire	Northern hundreds	±12.52%
Cheshire	Hundred of Macclesfield	±13.3%
Derbyshire		±13.8%
Cornwall	Hundred of Penwith	±14.36%
Wiltshire	Cricklade	±14.36%
Leicestershire	Leicester	±14.64%
Hampshire	Portsmouth	±17.34%
Somerset		±17.8%
Nottinghamshire	East Retford	±21.2%
Kent	Greenwich, Rochester/Chatham	±23.9%
Devon	Plymouth and Devonport	±24.22%
Sussex		±26.48%
Northumberland	Newcastle upon Tyne and Tynemouth	±32.28%
County Durham	Sunderland, Gateshead, Durham, South Shields	±35.1%
Lancashire	Salford hundred	±48.62%
Warwickshire	Birmingham	±51.88%
Surrey	Lambeth and Southwark	±64.56%

[+/− 10% equates to a 45:55 split]

most equal was Norfolk, whose east division contained 50.52 per cent of the county's population (Table 8.1). The remaining eleven counties were divided into districts with a population variance of over ±15 per cent. Surrey was divided into the two most unequal districts – Surrey East contained 83.29 per cent and Surrey West 17.72 per cent of the county's total population of 485,661. Such a discrepancy could not be avoided, however, as the hundred of Brixton – which contained the parliamentary boroughs of Lambeth and Southwark, and was situated in the very north-east of the county – contained 337,361 persons. Nine of the eleven counties that were divided with a variance of over ±15 per cent contained similar large town or city populations, which made inequality inescapable. The two remaining counties that contained a population discrepancy were Sussex and Somerset, and in these instances Lefevre recommended that existing administrative divisions, or 'communities of interest' that were in force at county level for Sussex, or had been in place 'from time immemorial' in Somerset were adopted.[28]

Lefevre was more successful in terms of creating county divisions of equal area, a consideration that was vital given that the division of counties had been justified as a means of reducing the expenses and time frames associated with county elections. Fourteen counties were divided into equal districts according to area. A further two counties were divided into areas with a variance between ±10 per cent and ±12.25 per cent. Devon was divided into the two most equal geographic districts – Devonshire North occupied 822,160 acres and Devonshire South 814,370 acres (Table 8.2). Geographic inequality acted as a counter to population inequality in seven of the eleven unequal divisions according to population. For instance, Devon's geographic equality was in stark contrast to its population inequality: its south division contained 62.11 per cent of the county's population, due to the positioning of Plymouth and Devonport in the south-west corner of the county. The most spatially unequal division was that proposed for Lancashire, whose population was distributed extremely unevenly in the south-west of the county (Map 8.1). This prevented any possibility of divisions equal in population or geographic extent. Lancashire South, which occupied 21.58 per cent of the county's area and contained Manchester, Salford, Liverpool and Bolton among other large manufacturing towns, also contained 60.32 per cent of the county's population. If the division had been extended any further north to make it more geographically equitable,

Table 8.2: Variation in area per county division for each county.

County	Variation in area
Devon	±0.48%
Suffolk	±1.10%
Essex	±3.02%
Northamptonshire	±3.58%
Wiltshire	±3.58%
Leicestershire	±4.88%
Somerset	±5.46%
Worcestershire	±5.96%
Kent	±6.04%
Warwickshire	±6.78%
Cornwall	±7.18%
Northumberland	±7.88%
Cumberland	±7.92%
Nottinghamshire	±9.88%
Sussex	±11.9%
Derbyshire	±12.22%
Norfolk	±16.56%
Shropshire	±19.14%
Gloucestershire	±20.2%
Cheshire	±20.46%
Staffordshire	±22.44%
County Durham	±22.52%
Hampshire	±24.72%
Surrey	±25.12%
Lancashire	±56.86%

it would have swallowed the hundreds of Leyland and Blackburn, creating an even more unequal division by population (the south division would have contained 1.2 million people, the north just 126,713). An alternative division of Lancashire into east and west districts would have been impractical due to its shape and the positioning of its hundreds.[29] Similar difficulties, although not to the same extent, were experienced in five of the remaining nine geographically uneven counties (Surrey, Shropshire, Hampshire, Durham and Cheshire), and in three of the further spatially uneven cases, the county divisions contained equal populations (Norfolk, Gloucestershire and Staffordshire).

Lefevre's third aim was to ensure that the counties were divided into districts with an equitable number of voters. Lefevre did not have access to an independent survey detailing the numbers of eligible freeholders, leaseholders, copyholders and tenants-at-will in each county. This meant that his published statements as to the future equitability of registered voters were the result of educated guesswork – based on a rough triangulation of population data inclusive and exclusive of boroughs, as well as the numbers of persons qualified to serve on juries in each county.[30] That said, the ready availability of post-1832 voter registration data does make it possible to evaluate the extent to which Lefevre created equitable county divisions according to voters. This data has been recorded in intervals from 1832; however, the following analysis is based on the annual registration data for 1836 (which was settled in November 1835), as it provides the most accurate indicator of the number of voters in each county in the immediate post-reform period. As well as allowing for a grace period for the reformed electoral system to bed in, as Salmon has demonstrated, the unexpected 1835 election (which had taken place in January and revealed deficiencies in that year's list of registered voters) prompted a mass of electoral administrative activity to ensure that registration data was maintained regularly and collected in a more methodical manner.[31]

When the 1836 registration data is considered, Lefevre's county divisions provided for an equal dispersion of voters in ten of the twenty-five counties that he divided, and six further counties were divided into districts with a voter equality of ±12.12 per cent (Table 8.3). The most even division of registered voters occurred in Nottinghamshire, where the south division contained 3,434 electors and the north 3,378. Of the nine counties that were divided into less equal voter districts, seven (Northumberland, Lancashire, Warwickshire, Hampshire, Shropshire, Surrey and Devon) contained dense population groupings, which had precluded the creation of equal divisions according to either, or both, population and area. Of these, Northumberland contained the greatest variation in voters at ±30.9 per cent. Although the county had been divided equally in spatial terms, the presence of Newcastle upon Tyne and Tynemouth meant that the southern division contained 65.45 per cent (5,121) of the county's electors, while the north contained 34.55 per cent (2,703). This was not the case for two counties, however – the aforementioned Sussex, which was divided unequally but in line with a pre-existing county administrative division, and Wiltshire, which had been divided very equally by area. As a whole, the average variation in the number of registered electors per division attests to the extent to which Lefevre's proposals delivered county constituencies containing a broadly equal electorate. In 1836 the average variation in electors between divisions was ±12.6 per cent, and when the entire period between 1832 and 1868 is considered, 1836 provided for the most equitable distribution of county voters. Over the following three decades the average variation of county voters between divisions increased gradually to ±16.24 per cent (Table 8.4).

When Lefevre's county divisions are evaluated on a purely statistical basis, no case failed to meet his stated criteria for equality of division

Table 8.3: Variation in registered voters per county division for each county in 1836.

County	Variation in electors 1836
Nottinghamshire	±0.84%
Somerset	±2.02%
Cumberland	±2.4%
County Durham	±3.42%
Essex	±4.92%
Gloucestershire	±5.02%
Leicestershire	±5.12%
Kent	±7.04%
Norfolk	±7.42%
Cheshire	±7.48%
Derbyshire	±10.14%
Northamptonshire	±10.5%
Suffolk	±10.78%
Cornwall	±11.86%
Worcestershire	±11.98%
Staffordshire	±12.12%
Devon	±16.24%
Shropshire	±16.9%
Surrey	±18.10%
Sussex	±10.71%
Hampshire	±21.9%
Warwickshire	±23.88%
Wiltshire	±24.64%
Lancashire	±28.32%
Northumberland	±30.9%

without an adequate explanation. In the cases that were unequal according to population and/or area, the distribution of population in a particular corner of a county genuinely prohibited the creation of equal divisions. And in the case of Sussex (which by 1865 had the most unequal divisions) Lefevre offered parliamentarians a choice of a more equal division or an uneven, historic administrative division. The latter was enacted by the Boundary Act.[32] Following 1832, Lefevre's divisions, unless the county district included a large town or city, contained a remarkably equitable number of registered electors – an achievement that may have had as much to do with luck on Lefevre's part as it did educated guesswork.

Table 8.4: Average variation in voters per county division between 1832 and 1865.

	1832	1836	1840	1846	1852	1859	1865
Mean	±13.42%	±12.6%	±12.68%	±13.9%	±13.78%	±14.34%	±16.24%
Median	±12.38%	±10.78%	±9.62%	±12.24%	±12.72%	±11.12%	±13.7%

This further refutes Moore's supposition that the Boundary Act sought to create county constituencies with an urban and rural divide, rather than on the basis of equality in numbers. Moore ignored the fact that equality in population had only formed one of Lefevre's criteria for equality, and that a division's area and its total number of voters were of equal, if not more, importance. Given that the division of counties was supposed to reduce canvassing costs (which were contingent on how many electors needed to be canvassed) as well as polling costs (a large proportion of which were spent on transporting electors and paying for accommodation and subsistence during nomination and polling), achieving equality in terms of area and voters was no doubt more important than equality in population, if election costs were to be similar in two county divisions.

County divisions and political influence

Although a quantitative analysis of the county divisions enacted by the 1832 Boundary Act reveals they were divided equitably, this does not preclude that their identification was influenced by political factors. A county might have been divided into both northern and southern divisions, or eastern and western divisions 'equally', but one of these may have suited a particular political interest. It is certainly the case that for interested parties, opportunities were presented, and sufficient intelligence was available, to gerrymander a county division. Lefevre's final recommendations, all of which were enacted by the 1832 Boundary Act, were printed on 16 February 1832.[33] The Cheshire MP, George Wilbraham, confirmed that these proposals had been shared with county members by 27 January, and Lefevre informed Earl Spencer on 28 January that 'the county members have in general approved of my carving'.[34] Following this, it is evident that county divisions were shared with interested borough MPs and peers ahead of their publication.[35] Most interested MPs or peers should have known their electoral strongholds in a particular county. Twelve of the twenty-five counties that Lefevre divided had held a contested election in 1826, 1830 or 1831, and in these instances detailed polling data, broken down by a county's electoral wards was readily available in manuscript or published poll books.[36] In the thirteen counties where contests had not taken place since 1820, intelligence derived from canvassing during the previous three elections should have provided county MPs with a good understanding of their electoral strongholds.

The primary difficulty in ascertaining the extent of political influence over the division of counties is the lack of working papers detailing Lefevre's activities. To counteract this, an evaluation of each of his published reports has been completed alongside poll books, constituency histories, parliamentary and local responses to the boundary bill, and surviving personal correspondence. This analysis needs to be read with one significant proviso regarding the nature of pre-reform partisanship. Although party labels were used in pre-reform electoral politics, party affiliation remained primarily local, rather than national. In large county districts, support for a Whig or Tory candidate in the north of a county did not necessarily translate to support for a similarly labelled candidate from the south. Furthermore, just because a hundred might have polled strongly for one Whig candidate, another candidate standing as a Whig in that same hundred would not necessarily have been able to secure the same level of support. The nature of contemporary electoral intelligence regarding partisan affiliation in the counties was understood primarily in personal, rather than party terms – and it is within this understanding of electoral politics that the extent of partisanship in Lefevre's proposals has been assessed.

After considering every option for division available to Lefevre in each county, there is only evidence to suggest that partisan considerations influenced his proposals in four cases. The mode and means of effecting boundary change in the counties – dividing an already prescribed existing area in two using pre-existing administrative divisions – provided the primary limiting factor in terms of identifying options for partisan division. Only five counties could have conceivably been divided into both north–south and east–west divisions, and these cases provided the most potential for partisan boundary setting.[37] Eighteen further counties could only be divided into either north–south or east–west divisions, meaning that any political negotiation in these cases would have rested on the inclusion of one or two hundreds (or sessional divisions, wards, rapes or wapentakes) positioned along an imaginary x or y axis in a county.[38] Due to the shape of their respective wards, two final cases (Cumberland and Durham) could only be divided in one way. And, although it was evident to interested parties at the time that these divisions favoured certain political interests, Lefevre's inability to draw arbitrary boundaries left no room for negotiation.[39] Prior to a discussion of the four instances that erred from Lefevre's principles, it will be instructive to provide an example of a county division judged to have not been influenced by partisan considerations.

The most obvious county for which a partisan division might have been drawn was Northamptonshire. Lefevre had managed Althorp's 1830 re-election for the constituency, and a contested election in 1831 – where the pro-reform candidates, Althorp and Viscount Milton, had beaten two anti-reformers, William Ralph Cartwright and Charles Knightley – had been followed by the publication of a poll book detailing individual candidate support in each of Northamptonshire's hundreds.[40] Northamptonshire's shape prohibited the creation of anything but a northern and southern division. Both anti-reform candidates had polled strongest in 1831 in the southern hundreds of the borough, and Althorp and Milton had polled strongest in the central hundreds. This meant that any division would have provided Cartwright and Knightley, whose estates were also in the south of the county, with a position of electoral strength in any southern division – as Lefevre's proposed boundary did.[41] Lefevre could have proposed an alternative, more partisan division, which would have dispersed Cartwright and Knightley's support more equally between the northern and southern divisions. However, this proposal would have provided a more unequal population distribution, and only a slightly more equal division according to area, in comparison to Lefevre's proposed division. This would suggest that if such a division had been a consideration, Lefevre preferred to adhere to his principle of equality in population, rather than create a division that might have marginalised Knightley and Cartwright's support in the south. An alternative interpretation of Lefevre's proposed division is that it created the conditions for an electoral stronghold for the Spencer and Cartwright families in the south, and the Milton and Tory Cardigan family in the north, thus splitting the county's four seats between its four established Whig and Tory families. Such an approach would have reaffirmed a consensus that had existed in the county between Whig and Tory proprietors since 1806, and which had ensured the uncontested return of Althorp and Cartwright at every election between 1807 and 1830.[42] However, given that the shape of Northampton required a north–south divide, any division of the county that Lefevre could have recommended, including the more partisan option, would also have led to a similar dispersion of power. With the options available to him, then, Lefevre divided Northamptonshire as evenly as possible.

A consideration of polling data, constituency histories and alternative options available for division produces similar conclusions for twenty-one of the twenty-five counties divided by the 1832 Boundary Act. By contrast, it is evident that political considerations undermined Lefevre's ability to adhere to his principles in four counties – Hampshire, Suffolk,

Worcestershire and Warwickshire. As with Northamptonshire, the shape of Hampshire precluded an obvious division of the county into east and west districts. Lefevre's brother (whose electoral strength lay in the very north of the county) had been elected as MP for Hampshire in 1831, and Grey's foreign secretary, Palmerston (whose Broadlands estate was in the parish of Romsey Extra), had long been involved in the county's electoral politics, particularly in the south. Hampshire was one of four cases where Lefevre's published reports provided two options for division – one based around ancient hundreds, the other around petty sessional divisions.[43] The proposal based around sessional divisions was enacted by the Boundary Act, yet it provided for a less equal division of the county according to both area and population. In his report, Lefevre legitimised this decision on the basis of 'careful investigation, and discussion' with 'persons acquainted with the county', following which he reported that the hundreds of Hampshire were 'practically inconvenient for the purposes for which they are now used'.[44] What he did not mention, however, was that the accepted, less equal, boundary placed Palmerston's Broadlands estate in the southern division, whereas the rejected, more equal boundary did not. Palmerston had strong ties with political families in the south of the county and needed to find a new constituency for when the reform bill passed, as he represented the pocket borough of Bletchingley.[45] He was subsequently returned for the southern division of Hampshire at the 1832 election, but then roundly defeated in 1835.

Suffolk provides another example of a somewhat anomalous proposal, which contradicted Lefevre's practice of using pre-existing divisions of a county where available, as in Kent, Somerset and Sussex.[46] Suffolk had traditionally been divided between the Liberty of Saint Edmund and the rest of the county. As in the case of Sussex, Lefevre provided parliamentarians with the option of two boundaries, one according to its ancient division and one that provided equality of population, area and voters. Whereas Sussex's ancient boundary was accepted by parliament, Suffolk's ancient boundary was rejected in favour of the more equal boundary. Suffolk's more equal division clearly favoured the electoral interests of the sitting MP Charles Tyrell as the ancient boundary divided his property interests. Tyrell had been one of the pro-reform MPs who voted against the division of counties in August 1831, and it is likely the government agreed to appease him ahead of the Commons' January 1832 vote over the division of counties clause in the third reform bill, by adopting the boundary most favourable to him.[47]

The final two divisions that appear to have been influenced by political considerations were Worcestershire and Warwickshire. Worcestershire's oddly shaped hundreds meant that sessional divisions were used to split the county into eastern and western divisions. Rather uncharacteristically, however, given that the county's shape also lent itself to a north–south divide, Lefevre's published report provided no alternative.[48] Significantly, Lefevre's final recommendation was in keeping with the preference of Littleton, the boundary commissioner who was active in parliamentary negotiations over the boundary bill, and the former Whig MP for Worcestershire, Lord Lyttelton. Both had expressed their preference for an east–west division in November 1831. Such a divide promised to contain the county's long-running aristocratic Whig–Tory seat-sharing arrangement in the western division, while providing Whig landowners with the best chance of challenging both seats in the east.[49]

Warwickshire also lent itself to both a north–south and east–west division, and in this instance Lefevre had outlined both options for parliamentarians (Map 8.2). While equitable in terms of area, the north–south division that Lefevre devised was considerably less equal in terms of population (±51.88 per cent vs ±32.26 per cent). Strictly speaking, he should have adopted this east–west division. However, the north–south division was formally recommended on the basis that it separated 'the agricultural from the manufacturing population of the county'.[50] This was in stark contrast to the very similar case of Leicestershire, where a division that separated the agricultural and manufacturing population had been rejected on the basis that a more equal division according to population and area was available.[51] In contradiction to the broad assertion of Moore, Warwickshire appears to be the only case where a desire to separate agricultural and manufacturing populations took precedence over considerations of equality in population, area and voters.[52] As with Worcestershire, the decision over Warwickshire was influenced by Littleton, who sought to appease the Warwickshire MP, Francis Lawley. Lawley's support for the division of counties since July 1831 had been contingent on a southern, agricultural division of the county that favoured the 'landed interest', free from the influence of the town electorates of Birmingham, Coventry and Nuneaton in the north – a demand that Lefevre's less equal north–south divide delivered.[53]

The four cases that erred from Lefevre's professed principles suggest a level of partisan pragmatism from the government in their negotiations with county members ahead of the publication of their boundary bill. This approach was largely successful, as the only county division that was actively challenged in parliament was Lefevre's proposal for Surrey. The government's response demonstrated how Lefevre's consistent approach in the majority of cases provided a convenient rhetorical defence for the boundary bill, as well as the fact that there were limits to the extent to which his proposals were open to negotiation. On separate occasions during June 1832,

RECONSTRUCTING THE COUNTY MAP   279

Map 8.2: Warwickshire and its proposed divisions and places of election, PP1831–2 (141), xl © National Library of Scotland; digital additions by author.
Key: Final boundary (red line). Alternate, more equal, east-west division provided by Lefevre (green line) [digital addition].

Henry Goulburn, the anti-reform MP for Cambridge University and resident of Reigate in Surrey, and John Somers Cocks, the anti-reform MP for Hereford and also resident of Reigate, requested that the government amend Surrey's division so as to segregate the agricultural population of the county from that associated with the metropolis.[54] On both occasions, Althorp objected to these grievances on the basis that the same principles had been applied elsewhere and neither of Surrey's members had raised an objection. He also contended that the proposed division provided for 'a fair mixture of the rural with the town population',[55] which was consistent with the government's wish to 'have at least some mixture of both interests' in each new county division.[56] Althorp's final statement was true in so much as that, while Lefevre's approach to the division of counties did not actively set out to mix the agricultural and manufacturing interests, it never actively sought to divide them – the only exception being Warwickshire.

Aside from the four cases that were subject to parliamentary interference, Lefevre ensured that where available, a county was divided according to its historic division, and when not, pre-existing administrative areas were used to divide each county as equally as possible according to population, area and voters. These principles allowed him to ignore party politics and the landholdings of individual landowners when completing his proposals, and it was only once the government started negotiating with parliamentarians that some partisan influence came to bear on a minority of his proposals. While Lefevre's divisions did impact the balance of power in counties after 1832, to suggest that he masterminded this impact would be to conflate intention with consequence. Rather, in keeping with the borough commission, Lefevre's adherence to consistent principles helped to diffuse a politically contentious issue. If during debates a county division was discovered to favour a certain political interest, the government argued that it had not been due to an active attempt to do so. Rather, it had been as a result of trying to provide as equal a division of a county according to population, voters and area as possible. In this sense the division of counties was as functional in its approach as the government had suggested when they introduced their reform bill – equally sized county constituencies, it was hoped, would make elections cheaper and more manageable for landed proprietors, whom the Whigs had always presumed would play an active role in reformed county politics.

Places of election and polling places

Prior to 1832 the nomination and polling for county elections took place at one location. If a candidate demanded a contest, several polling booths were erected at that location and polling was allowed to remain open for fifteen days – at considerable expense to candidates who were expected to fund the transportation, accommodation and refreshment of their supporters.[57] Along with the division of counties, the Grey ministry sought to reduce election expenses by allowing up to fifteen polling places in every county and limiting polling to two days. The nomination and declaration were still to take place in a constituency's 'principal place of election' (or nomination town), but electors were not to be required to travel any further than fifteen miles to vote.[58] Lefevre proposed a principal place of election for every county he divided, and only three of these recommendations were modified prior to the passage of the 1832 Boundary Act. Lefevre played no role in the subsequent identification of polling places, as the government had only agreed that its boundary bill would stipulate these on 11 February 1832.[59] An initial list of polling places was compiled by Drummond and the borough commission and was published on 25 May 1832.[60] These lists were amended for twenty-nine of the sixty-nine reformed English counties prior to the passage of the Boundary Act.[61]

Apart from three cases, the fifty principal places of election recommended by Lefevre were identified for historic, legal and functional reasons. A county's traditional election venue was recommended for the new division that it fell into in all but four instances. While these towns were not always centrally located, they tended to have good pre-existing transport links, and Lefevre was reluctant to deprive existing county towns of their historic 'species of privilege'. Of the four existing county towns that he recommended should be deprived of this privilege, plausible reasons were provided in three cases. The limited jurisdiction of county law officers in the towns of Chester and Nottingham prompted Lefevre to identify alternative locations for Cheshire South and Nottinghamshire North (Chester would later be reinstated by the Commons). Taunton was identified over Somerset's existing place of election, Ilchester, due to its location and status as an assize venue (and although not stated, probably due to Ilchester's pending disfranchisement).[62]

By contrast, Lefevre's recommendation that the iron manufacturing district of Walsall should supplant Lichfield as Staffordshire South's place of election received no explanation. The subsequent dispute over Walsall's recommendation revealed that contemporaries ascribed considerable importance to the electoral influence of a county's nomination town. Lefevre had originally intended to identify Lichfield (the county's traditional election venue) as Staffordshire South's nomination town until Littleton, the county's MP, had convinced him, for self-serving reasons, to recommend Walsall in the first draft of the boundary bill. Littleton had been preoccupied since November with ensuring some manufacturing influence in the midland counties, and intended to stand for the southern division of the county at the first reformed election, having recently championed Walsall's separate claims for borough enfranchisement.[63] Following the boundary bill's publication, the government received private objections to Walsall's selection due to Lichfield's historic status as a place of election and concern for the maintenance of law and order during elections, given that nearby Birmingham, Wolverhampton and Dudley were to be enfranchised. Complaints were also made that the presence of Walsall's non-county voting inhabitants at the nomination would be likely to secure the uncontested election of manufacturing candidates for the county.[64]

Littleton backtracked following these protests and coalesced with Peel, the Tamworth MP whose Drayton Hall estate was in the Staffordshire South division, to replace Walsall with Lichfield during the third Commons reading of the boundary bill on 22 June. When proposing this amendment, Peel stated that he still expected the 'southern iron districts' to sway Staffordshire South's future elections, but that 'if we can, by changing the place of nomination, add some little influence to the agricultural interests, I think that we ought to do so'.[65] Peel's amendment prompted a furious response from Staffordshire's southern iron districts, and on 27 June, a meeting called at Walsall's town hall to petition against the change 'was crowded to excess'. Over the following days, the towns of Wolverhampton, Bilston, Willenhall and Darlaston joined the protest, and by early July five petitions had been submitted to the Lords requesting that Walsall be reinstated.[66] However, as no-one in the Lords took up the petitioners' cause, Lichfield became Staffordshire South's principal place of election.

The identification of places of election for the remaining divided counties was completed in a similarly historico-legal manner. Lefevre's first preference was to assign the principal place of election to an assize venue, and if one of these was not available, a quarter sessions venue – both had the advantage of being established centres in a county, with established transport links. Twelve counties were assigned places of election in this manner, and in only two instances was a quarter sessions or assize town not chosen if available – both of which were probably the result of parliamentary interference. In Derbyshire North, Bakewell was proposed over Chesterfield, and the local Tory press were probably correct in their speculation that the recommendation favoured the attorney general and prospective candidate, Thomas Denman, whose property was in Bakewell.[67] In Warwickshire North (Map 8.2), the market town of Coleshill was chosen over Coventry (an assize and quarter sessions venue). As was the case with the design of Warwickshire's boundaries, the selection of Coleshill over Coventry, or even Birmingham (which was not centrally located), was probably intended to appease the MP for Warwickshire, Francis Lawley, as well as the agricultural interest in the county. In the eleven remaining cases, where no established county venue was available, Lefevre used his discretion to propose the most central and well-connected town as that division's place of election. These proposals proved particularly susceptible to challenge, and the two cases discussed below – Lancashire South and Gloucestershire West – further demonstrate the import placed on nomination towns by contemporaries.[68]

Although multiple venues were available, Wigan had originally been recommended as Lancashire South's place of election due to its centrality and transport connections.[69] This recommendation was overturned on 7 June 1832 in favour of Newton – a 'former market town' and parliamentary borough due to be disfranchised by the reform bill (Map 8.1).[70] Russell had proposed this amendment on behalf of the government, much to the disbelief of the radical MP for Wigan, Ralph Thicknesse, who described Newton as a 'mere village', with no town hall and little accommodation.[71] Unbeknown to Thicknesse, the government's amendment had been made to appease the county's MP, Lord Stanley, who had expressed concern that dividing Lancashire would throw it 'too much out of the landed scale'.[72] This rationale was kept private and Stanley publicly defended Newton's selection on the basis that it was more central to the division than Wigan; the newly opened Warrington–Newton railway ran through the town; places of election in reformed counties did not require accommodation due to the new two-day limit for elections; and the town had demonstrated its ability to host large crowds at its regular race-meets. The government's concession was popular, and in a late night Commons sitting only five members, including Thicknesse, voted against it.[73] While Stanley's functional argument had grounds, the government's willingness to appease the agricultural lobby, as they had with Warwickshire and Staffordshire, is telling when it is considered that electors from Liverpool, Manchester, Bolton, Wigan, Warrington, Oldham, Bury and Rochdale all had to travel to Newton to participate in the nomination and declaration in England's most manufacturing-centric county division.

The proposal that Dursley should be the principal place of election for Gloucestershire West provoked the kind of bitter local dispute, writ large over a parliamentary stage, that the boundary commission and the government had worked hard to avoid when settling the details of the boundary bill. Lefevre's initial recommendation of Dursley was amended four times by parliament, to Wotton-under-Edge on 25 May, to Thornbury on 7 June, back to Wotton-under-Edge on 22 June, and then back again to Dursley on 9 July.[74] These changes were prompted by a familial battle between Gloucestershire's major landowners, the Tory Beauforts and the Whig Berkeleys. Although it is unclear what prompted the government's decision to amend Lefevre's initial recommendation to Wotton-under-Edge, Lord Granville Somerset, son of the sixth Duke of Beaufort, successfully advocated for Thornbury on 7 June, arguing that the town had better transport links, and that its agricultural character would allow for more 'freedom of discussion' at the nomination.[75] While he publicly declared that his recommendation had been made for functional reasons, in private he conceded the selection of Thornbury was beneficial to the Beaufort interest.[76] After Somerset had successfully amended Gloucestershire West's polling place to Thornbury, parliamentary advocates of the Beaufort and Berkeley families exchanged claim and counterclaim over ferry services across the Severn, accommodation, horse stalls, town hall sizes, roads and beer shops, before the Commons divided 83 to 54 in favour of reverting back to Wotton-under-Edge on 22 June.[77] With the issue seemingly settled, the Lords received three petitions from the inhabitants 'of the Western Side of the Severn', the hundred of Berkeley and the entire 'Western division' of Gloucestershire, opposing the change to Wotton-under-Edge, and requesting that Dursley, Lefevre's initial recommendation, be reinstated.[78] In response, the government sent a commissioner to investigate the towns in early July. His recommendation that Dursley was the most suitable town 'in point of geographical position, population, and accommodation' was adopted.[79] In this instance, the government skilfully used the independence of the commissioners to resolve a local feud that had occupied several hours of parliamentary time.

With the principal election towns mostly settled, Drummond and his borough commissioners identified satellite polling towns for each reformed county between February and May 1832. They did so in a similarly functional manner, by seeking to ensure that no county elector had to travel further than fifteen miles to vote. Locations were selected due to their accessibility by road and their placement within the topography of a county, to ensure electors were not required to travel over hills, or across rivers.[80] An initial list of polling places was published for all sixty-nine of England's reformed county constituencies on 25 May 1832, and by the time the Boundary Act passed into law on 11 July, twenty-nine amendments had been made to these lists. Although a large number of additions (and some subtractions) were made to the commissioners' selections, parliamentary debate over the issue occupied little time. This was because each reformed county was allowed up to fifteen polling places, enabling most requests for inclusion to be accommodated. The government did not concede to every request, however, and some suspicious appeals for the transfer of polling places from one location to another were rejected.[81]

As with the selection of the principal places of election, the identification of polling places prompted some local animosity, since it was perceived that the partisan allegiance of a polling town might influence the votes of electors and provide opportunities for patronage during elections. A letter in the Whig *Morning Chronicle* complained that 'a *hocus pocus* manoeuvre' by the anti-reform Berkshire MP, Robert Palmer, had led to the pro-Tory town of Wokingham replacing nearby Bracknell, and the addition of three further pro-Tory towns as polling places for the county.[82] In another instance, the postmaster general, the Duke of Richmond, advised the Lords that he had received a threat from the mayor of Arundel that 'his brother [Lord John Lennox, MP for Sussex] should hear of it at the next election' if Arundel was not selected as a polling place for Sussex West. In response, Richmond summed up the government's conciliatory position by agreeing to the amendment, not because of the mayor of Arundel's threat, but because 'he thought it a matter of no importance whether there were four polling places or five' in the division.[83] This conciliatory, almost indifferent, approach to parliamentary negotiations over polling places helped to ensure their parliamentary enactment with little trouble.

While parliamentary discussion over principal places of election and polling places was inherently parochial, it was significant for two reasons. First, the government's acceptance of agricultural nomination towns in the manufacturing-centric constituencies of Warwickshire North, Staffordshire South and Lancashire South demonstrated their willingness to appease the landed interest as they had also done with the creation of rural boroughs (see Chapter 6). These cases were consistent with the parliamentary statements made by Althorp, discussed above, regarding the government's intention to mix the agricultural with the manufacturing interests in reformed county constituencies wherever possible. Second, the debates demonstrated a level of local interaction, and tension over the fine details of the reformed constituency system, which have generally been ignored by historians of the 1832 reform legislation.[84] Contemporaries placed great stead on the cities, towns and villages selected to host the events of their reformed county elections, as they believed these selections were integral to their county's electoral identities. That the government successfully utilised the commission to distance itself from these local disputes revealed the value of legitimising, and implementing, reform within a framework of bureaucratic disinterestedness.

Parliamentary, electoral and political outcomes

The 1832 Boundary Act, for the most part, reconstructed England's reformed county map in an equitable and indiscriminate manner. Aside from in four cases, the counties were divided consistently with the principle of adhering to either historic divisions, or equality in population, area and voters. Similarly, the vast majority of nomination towns for England's divided counties were identified for historico-legal and functional reasons, and the selection of polling places genuinely sought to ensure that every elector could poll at a convenient location. The generally unpartisan manner in which England's reformed county map had been redrawn in 1832 was underlined by its electoral outcomes (Tables 8.5 and 8.6). The 1831 election had represented a high watermark in terms of pro-Whig or pro-reform county representation. However, by 1841 the counties were dominated by Conservative, protectionist representatives. In 1831, fifty-one (91 per cent) of the fifty-six MPs elected to the twenty-seven counties divided in 1832 had termed themselves as either Whig, liberal-Whig or radical, and a further two termed themselves liberal-Tory.[85] In 1832, the same counties returned 110 MPs, 74 per cent of whom were identified as either Whigs, reformers or radicals. Remarkably, by 1841 86 per cent of MPs returned for these divided counties classified themselves as Conservatives or moderate reformers. Conservative candidates continued to maintain their electoral hegemony over the divided counties from 1847, but support for Whig or Liberal candidates increased to 38 per cent by 1857, before reducing to 29 per cent in 1859 and recovering to 37 per cent in 1865. These electoral shifts were generally consistent with county constituencies that were not divided or became three-member counties in 1832 (Tables C.12 and 8.5).

The party labelling ascribed to county MPs was consistent with their behaviour in major parliamentary votes through to 1868 (Graph C.2 and Table C.4). After providing slim majorities in favour of the Peel administration in 1835, support among county MPs for Conservative oppositions or governments increased gradually to nine in ten MPs by 1842, when the second Peel ministry introduced its key proposal to introduce the income tax. County MPs split evenly in the division over the Irish coercion bill that brought down the Peel ministry in 1846, before gradually regrouping around the Derby–Disraeli leadership during the 1852 Parliament, when at least eight in ten supported the short-lived 1852 Conservative government and voted against the Aberdeen ministry's management of the Crimean War in 1855. The impact of increasing county urbanisation and Liberal registration drives during the 1850s, as discussed below, meant that county MPs became slightly more tolerant of Liberal governments during the 1859 and 1865 Parliaments, when support for Conservative oppositions and administrations had declined to around seven in ten county MPs. This still represented a marked contrast to English borough MPs who provided an almost inverse level of support for Liberal governments by 1868.

On policy (Graphs C.4, C.6 and C.8 and Tables C.6, C.8 and C.10), county MPs consistently opposed free trade during the first decade of the reformed Parliament, reaching a climax in 1843 when only one county MP was

Table 8.5: Election results in the twenty-seven divided counties, 1832–65.

	1832	1835	1837	1841	1847	1852	1857	1859	1865
Whig/reformer/radical	73.87%	50.45%	28.83%	13.51%	26.12%	18.02%	38.74%	29.73%	37.72%
Moderate reformer/Liberal-Conservative	6.31%	5.41%	1.80%	0.9%	0.00%	2.7%	7.21%	8.11%	6.14%
Conservative (free trade)	0.00%	0.00%	0.00%	0.00%	6.31%	4.5%	0.00%	0.00%	0.00%
Conservative	19.82%	42.34%	65.77%	84.69%	0.9%	26.13%	54.05%	62.16%	56.14%
Conservative (protectionist)	0.00%	0.00%	0.00%	0.00%	65.77%	47.75%	0.00%	0.00%	0.00%
No label	0.00%	1.80%	3.6%	0.9%	0.91%	0.9%	0.00%	0.00%	0.00%

Table 8.6: Election results in every county, 1832–65.

	1832	1835	1837	1841	1847	1852	1857	1859	1865
Whig/reformer/radical	68.31%	46.47%	27.46%	12.68%	25.35%	16.90%	37.32%	30.99%	35.17%
Moderate reformer/Liberal-Conservative	8.45%	7.75%	4.23%	0.70%	0.70%	2.82%	7.75%	7.75%	4.83%
Conservative (free trade)	0.00%	0.00%	0.00%	0.00%	4.93%	3.52%	0.00%	0.00%	0.00%
Conservative	23.24%	44.37%	64.79%	85.21%	1.41%	22.54%	54.93%	61.26%	60.00%
Conservative (protectionist)	0.00%	0.00%	0.00%	0.00%	66.91%	52.81%	0.00%	0.00%	0.00%
No label	0.00%	1.41%	3.52%	1.41%	0.70%	1.41%	0.00%	0.00%	0.00%

willing to consider a repeal of the corn laws. Only two in ten MPs representing divided counties supported repealing the corn laws in 1846, which increased marginally to three in ten MPs by 1850. It was only after the 1852 election, when the Conservative leadership jettisoned its support for protection in favour of a policy of agricultural relief, that a majority of county MPs were willing to endorse free trade. County MPs proved even more consistent in their opposition to further parliamentary reform, and from the 1840s fewer than one in ten were willing to support proposals for secret voting at parliamentary elections. Support for the abolition of church rates fared only slightly better, with support for the issue among all county MPs fluctuating between 20 and 30 per cent from the mid-1850s. This consistent opposition to the ballot and church reform was bolstered by the fact that county MPs using the Liberal label were more likely to sit on the small 'c' conservative side of the political spectrum than their borough counterparts. For instance, in 1861, 61 per cent of county MPs using the Liberal label opposed the ballot. The same figure for Liberal MPs representing English boroughs was 22 per cent.

The short-term electoral experiences of the four MPs who had successfully engineered a preferable county division revealed that an increased focus on electoral organisation following 1832 was necessary to retain any of the initial benefits that a favourable county division provided. Palmerston was elected to Hampshire South with a moderate reformer in 1832, but both were unseated by a resurgent Conservative interest by 1835.[86] In Suffolk West, Charles Tyrell retained his seat in 1832, but retired prior to the 1835 election, and by 1837, Henry Bunbury, Tyrell's former Whig ally, failed to prevent the election of two Conservatives.[87] Two Whig candidates were returned with the support of Lord Lyttelton and his allies for Worcestershire East in 1832 and 1835, but by 1837 their influence had failed to prevent the election of two Conservatives.[88] And, Francis Lawley's desire to secure representation for the agricultural interest in Warwickshire South was temporarily stalled by the return of an anti-corn law campaigner, the Lancashire cotton manufacturer and local landowner George Philips, in 1832. It took until the 1836 by-election for the county, perhaps not as the Whig Lawley had quite intended, for the county to fall under the control of the highly organised pro-agricultural, Conservative interest, where it would remain until 1880.[89]

As voter registration, the corn laws and the 'church in danger' cry took centre-stage in English politics between 1832 and 1852, the division of counties provided the ideal conditions for the co-ordinated efforts of locally organised Conservative associations to thrive across England's reformed county map. The removal of many of the discrepancies that had existed between the unreformed counties, in terms of voter numbers and geographic size, were also crucial in placing these new structures of reformed county politics within the financial reach of the country gentry. This type of politics would not have been sustainable in larger, four-member constituencies – as had briefly been the case in the undivided, four-member constituency of Yorkshire from 1826.[90] The government's decision in November 1831 to persevere with the division of counties, rather than create four-member counties, was crucial in terms of stalling the development of cheaper means of caucus-like party organisation, reliant on national frameworks, central party organisation and based around a national press. Instead, divided counties ensured that the development of locally based registration societies and party associations became the most practicable, and financially effective, means of securing electoral success.[91]

Suffolk East, and the aforementioned Western division, witnessed some of the earliest division-based organisational efforts of the period, which were quickly replicated across the country. By 1837 all four of Suffolk's seats were in Conservative hands, a huge turnaround from 1831 when the undivided county had returned two reformers. Prominent Conservative landowners led their respective East and West Suffolk Agricultural Societies from 1832, whose division-focused registration drives and promotion of agricultural issues, such as the corn laws and the malt tax, secured control of both counties for the next two decades.[92] The spread of similar division-based associations across England during the 1830s was also significant in establishing a new generation of Conservative country gentlemen, as figures within the local gentry used the opportunities provided by constituency dinners, hustings speeches and committee meetings to establish themselves within local party hierarchies. For example, John Yarde Buller sat as a Conservative MP for Devonshire South between 1835 and 1858, and Lewis William Buck represented Devonshire North between 1839 and 1857. While both had started their political careers during the 1820s, the opportunities provided by co-ordinating local registration drives, and delivering repeated, staunch anti-Whig, pro-Anglican and pro-agricultural public speeches during the 1830s placed them at the head of their division's respective parties and ensured their seats in the Commons for the next two decades.[93]

While the Conservative revival was the most striking aspect of county politics during the 1830s, political organisation did not evolve evenly. In rare cases such as Somerset East, Staffordshire South and Cornwall West, well organised Whig-Liberal registration efforts proved that seats were winnable, even when agricultural issues dominated politics throughout the 1830s and 1840s.⁹⁴ This contrasted with the internal divisions, and a distaste for organising county politics, that tended to define Whig-Liberal efforts elsewhere. Essex South's Whig and radical factions, for instance, took over three decades to fully recover from their internal divisions at the 1832 election.⁹⁵ And in Northamptonshire South, Conservative candidates thrived due to the unwillingness of the county's Whig leaders to imitate their opponents' 'unfeeling and ungentlemanly' approach to registration.⁹⁶

This contributed to a growing sense of defeatism about Whig-Liberal county prospects, and in the aftermath of the 1835 election John Bull was already being pictured by the pro-reform *McLean's Monthly Sheet of Caricatures* as being 'poisoned' by the division of counties and £50 tenants-at-will (Figure 8.1). Whig-Liberals tended to blame Conservative deployment of illegitimate influence, bribery, the creation of fictional voters and voter intimidation, rather than themselves. While such practices did take place (on both sides of the political spectrum), to accept these excuses as the primary explanation for the Conservative revival in the counties during the 1830s would be to believe contemporary Liberal propaganda. Importantly, it ignores the fact that, as well as their organisational efforts, the Conservatives were helped by the electoral popularity of protection and Protestantism during the 1830s and 1840s.⁹⁷ One poll book analysis of Norfolk East during the 1830s has revealed a Conservative-supporting 'rural electorate that was relatively free of [landlord] controls'.⁹⁸ And despite the clear territorial influence of major landlords in Shropshire South and North, support for the corn laws and the established Church ensured both divisions in this primarily agricultural and Anglican county remained 'persistently tory' for most of the period.⁹⁹

Local economies were also influential in defining a county's party politics, but they should not be understood within a simple urban-Liberal, rural-Conservative binary. The ruthlessness of organisation, and the genuine popularity of the Conservative message, helped ensure Conservative success in divisions with huge urban electorates during the 1830s, such as Lancashire South, Sussex East, Warwickshire North and Yorkshire's West Riding.¹⁰⁰ It was only during the 1850s that Whig-Liberal candidates enjoyed wider-spread success, following the decline of protection as a defining political issue, an element of 'Conservative apathy', increasing urbanisation in some counties and the revival of Liberal registration efforts.¹⁰¹ This built on some of the county registration efforts of Anti-Corn Law League campaigners during the 1840s, but was also thanks to a new generation of Whig-Liberal leaders, who were not as squeamish about organising electoral politics, and by the early

Figure 8.1: Thomas McLean, 'Doctoring', *The Looking Glass*, 2 February 1835. Author's collection.

1860s, were willing to cede local influence to the formative, national Liberal Registration Society.[102]

The legacy of D. C. Moore's provocative analysis of nineteenth-century electoral politics means that the issue of proprietorial control, and voter deference, needs to be considered in any analyses of reformed county politics, particularly when the impact of the division of counties is considered. However, the extent of aristocratic and gentry landowner influence over county politics after 1832 has to be understood subtly, as intersecting with questions of registration and organisation. Proprietorial influence over a county's representation was most evident when family pacts or generational changes in aristocratic leadership led to changes in the operation of electoral politics. In Sussex West the conversion of the fifth Duke of Richmond to Conservatism by the late 1830s was crucial in ensuring the division returned two Conservatives by 1841.[103] And in Staffordshire South an election compromise between the leading Whig and Conservative families following the expensive 1837 election remained in place until Liberal registration efforts successfully challenged the pact at an 1854 by-election.[104]

Despite its much-promised cost-cutting benefits, the continued expense of organising politics in some divided counties gave major landowners, such as the Conservative Londonderrys and the Whig-Liberal Lambtons in Durham South, the ability to over-rule the candidate choices of their respective local associations.[105] However, in most counties proprietorial influence needed to be co-ordinated with local party activities, and if MPs did not move in lockstep with registration efforts and increasing levels of partisanship during the 1830s, their influence diminished. This proved to be the case with Gilbert John Heathcote, the largest landed proprietor in Lincolnshire South and the division's MP since 1832. His insistence on standing as an independent and refusal to engage with the South Lincolnshire Conservative Association or appease the division's Dissenting Liberal vote by supporting the abolition of church rates forced his retirement by 1841 in the face of an electorate polarised 'along clear party, rather than proprietorial lines'.[106] Proprietorial influence could also be challenged from within, and by the early 1850s in Cornwall East frequent petitioning and meetings among a range of farmers' organisations meant 'it was farmers rather than gentry whose opinions counted' during the division's 1852 election.[107] Similar instances of such 'farmers' revolts' against landlord influence were seen in the three-member county of Herefordshire, and the divided counties of Nottinghamshire North and South, and Leicestershire South.[108]

The combination of new systems of voter registration after 1832, the division of counties and a proliferation of towns associated with the electoral politics of a county, either as new places of election or polling places, had a clear impact on the wider identity and culture of England's counties. As the *Morning Post* had predicted in September 1831, reform politicised localities that had previously been able to escape constant electioneering due to their geographic and institutional distance from their county's electoral centre:

> ... every little hamlet is to be the home of electioneering excitement. Parties will gradually form, quarrel will grow upon quarrel, and all the confusion, and ill blood, and angry feeling which now characterise the county town only during the election, will be domesticated with tenfold violence in every peaceful and retired village throughout the United Kingdom.[109]

As historians have recognised, parliamentary and local voter registration, as well as the development of poor law administration, led to something of a realisation of the *Morning Post*'s fears during the 1830s.[110] The division of counties, as well as the introduction of new places of election and polling places, contributed to a similar politicisation of county life. Both reforms were also significant in ensuring the survival, proliferation and evolution of pre-reform electoral customs in existing and new county locations.[111]

This was particularly marked in county divisions that were not assigned a county's historic nomination town and had to develop their own electoral culture in new settings. While Northamptonshire South got to keep the county's historic nomination town, the unincorporated Kettering became the election town for Northamptonshire North. The reality of county politics shocked Kettering's unprepared local officials when a violent by-election nomination in 1835 revealed the need for co-ordinated planning of election events, following which the town's public houses and meeting rooms gradually superseded the parliamentary borough of Peterborough as the central venue for the division's electoral activity. The town's increasing political significance meant that by the late 1830s the division's Chartists made it the focal point for their county-wide activities, and as the period wore on internal divisions within Kettering's Baptist politics assumed county-wide significance, as their exaggerated influence over county politics split the division's Liberals into warring factions of respectable and radical Dissenters.[112] New polling towns could also be transformed by their formal association with electoral politics. As the Victorian Election Violence project has revealed, the vast majority of recorded instances of violent election incidents in the counties, ranging from fights to riots and deaths, tended to take place in newly established polling towns after 1832. These could be isolated incidents, such as when a local reverend was 'thrown down and rolled in the mud' by a crowd during polling for Hampshire North at Basingstoke in December 1832.[113] Or they could relate to widespread violence that spread across an entire county, as happened in Hertfordshire's polling towns of Hertford, Hitchin, Hemel Hempstead, Hoddesdon, Watford and Great Berkhamsted in 1852.[114]

The continued relevance of the division of counties in 1832 must also be acknowledged, given that the considerations which guided boundary reform in the counties in 1832 remain remarkably similar to those that guide boundary reform in the United Kingdom today. Most of Lefevre's county divisions remained in place for over half a century – ten of the counties that Lefevre divided were allocated additional seats and re-divided by the 1868 Boundary Act, but fifteen of his divisions remained in place until the 1885 Redistribution of Seats Act, which divided the counties into 231 single-member districts. The differentiation between the county and borough franchise remained in place until 1918, and the basic means of subdividing the counties used by Lefevre in 1832 was replicated in 1868, 1885 and 1918. On each occasion, boundary commissioners were required to base county divisions around existing administrative areas – hundreds and petty sessional divisions in 1868, and sessional divisions and aggregates of parishes from 1885. The instructions for division in 1868 were very similar to that of 1832 (incidentally, Lefevre's brother, and former speaker of the Commons, Charles Shaw Lefevre, chaired the 1868 enquiry), but in 1885 and 1918 the boundary commissions were asked to discount equality in area in favour of an explicit request to segregate urban and rural portions of counties.[115] On all occasions, as had been the case in 1832, a need to juggle these requirements led to a considerable variety in terms of equality in population between the subdivisions of England's counties – even when population had become an accepted unit of representation by 1918. Similarly, the redefinition of the United Kingdom's entire electoral map since 1944, when seat redistribution became based on an electoral quota, has been completed using existing local governmental subdivisions to create as equal a voter distribution as possible while also paying attention to existing community identities. Since 1944, balancing these considerations has continued, and continues, to prevent the creation of truly equal parliamentary districts within the United Kingdom.

Notes

1. Monmouthshire, with its two MPs, has been considered part of Wales in line with M. Cragoe, *Culture, Politics and National Identity in Wales 1832–1886* (Oxford, 2004).

2. M. Brock, *The Great Reform Act* (London, 1973), 222–3, 264; J. Cannon, *Parliamentary Reform 1640–1832* (Cambridge, 1973), 247; J. Parry, *The Rise and Fall of Liberal Government in Victorian Britain* (London, 1993), 81.

3. D. C. Moore, *The Politics of Deference: A Study of the Mid-Nineteenth Century Political System* (New York, 1976), 177–79; D. C. Moore, 'Concession or Cure: The

Sociological Premises of the First Reform Act', *Historical Journal*, 9, 1 (1966)', 39–59; D. C. Moore, 'The Other Face of Reform', *Victorian Studies*, 5, 1 (1961), 7–34; E. P. Hennock and D. C. Moore, 'The First Reform Act: A Discussion', *Victorian Studies*, 14, 3 (1971), 337.

4. P. Salmon, 'English Reform Legislation, 1831–32', in D. Fisher (ed.), *The House of Commons, 1820–1832*, i. (Cambridge, 2009), 407–12.

5. F. O'Gorman, *Voters, Patrons, and Parties: The Unreformed Electoral System of Hanoverian England 1734–1832* (Oxford, 1989), 225–44; D. Eastwood, 'Contesting the Politics of Deference: The Rural Electorate, 1820–60', in J. Lawrence and Miles Taylor (eds.), *Party, State and Society: Electoral Behaviour in Britain since 1820* (Aldershot, 1997), 27–49; D. Fisher, *The House of Commons, 1820–1832*, ii–iii. (Cambridge, 2009); A. Heesom, '"Legitimate" versus "Illegitimate" Influences: Aristocratic Electioneering in Mid-Victorian Britain', *Parliamentary History*, 7, 2 (1988), 282–305; T. Nossiter, *Influence, Opinion and Political Idioms in Reform England: Case Studies from the North-East, 1832–74* (Hassocks, 1975); Eastwood, 'Contesting the Politics of Deference', 42; P. Salmon, *Electoral Reform at Work: Local Politics and National Parties, 1832–1841* (Woodbridge, 2002), 119–82.

6. DSC, Grey, B46/1/45, 'Memorandum on Reform Bill, by Russell, 20 Oct. 1831', 1–8; DSC, Grey, B46/1/54, 'Paper endorsed by Lord Althorp "Mr Horsley Palmers proposals"', 1–2; B46/2/5, Wharncliffe to Grey, 24 Nov. 1831, f.1–2; DSC, Grey, B46/2/6, 'Copy of Paper by Lord Wharncliffe on modifications on Reform Bill', 10 Nov. 1831, f.1–10; H. Taylor (ed.), *The Reform Act, 1832: The Correspondence of the Late Earl Grey*, i. (London, 1867), 408; A. Kriegel, *The Holland House Diaries, 1831–1840* (London, 1977), 81.

7. Brock, *Reform Act*, 264; Salmon, 'English Reform Legislation', in Fisher, *Commons*, i. 407–410; Taylor, *Correspondence of the Late Earl Grey*, i. 474.

8. DSC, Grey. B46/2/8, 'Substance of what passed at the Bank on 9 Nov. between H.P. & P.G', 1–2; B46/2/10, 'Grenfell to Ellice', 11 Nov. 1831, 1–2; *The Times*, 12, 18 Nov. 1831.

9. SRO, Hatherton, D260/M/F/5/26/7, 31 Oct., 8 Nov., and 18 Nov. 1831, f.195, 200 and 220; SRO, Hatherton, D260/M/F/5/27/7, Lyttelton to Littleton, 10 Nov. 1831; see Chapters 5, 6 and 7.

10. *The Times*, 23, 24 and 25 Nov. 1831; *Courier*, 25 Nov. 1831; Taylor, *Correspondence of the Late Earl Grey*, i. 474; Kriegel, *Holland House*, 84; Brock, *Reform Act*, 260.

11. D. Fisher, 'Charles Shaw-Lefevre', in R. G. Thorne, *The House of Commons, 1790–1820*, iv. (Cambridge, 1986), 403.

12. F. Wilson, *A Strong Supporting Cast: The Shaw Lefevres 1789–1936* (London, 1993), 106.

13. Wilson, *Strong Supporting Cast*, 54, 63–4; M. Curthoys, 'Lefevre, Sir John George Shaw-(1797–1879)', *ODNB*, https://doi.org/10.1093/ref:odnb/25275 [accessed 6 Sept. 2016].

14. P. Mandler, *Aristocratic Government in the Age of Reform: Whigs and Liberals 1830–1852* (Oxford, 1990), 91.

15. Wilson, *Strong Supporting Cast*, 62, 90–218; Curthoys, 'Lefevre'.

16. Hansard, 3, v. (11 Aug. 1831), 1222.

17. PP1830–31 (247), ii. 4.

18. Salmon, 'English Reform Legislation', in Fisher, *Commons*, i. 409.

19. Moore, *Politics of Deference*, 178; PP1831–2 (357), xli. 4.

20. PP1831–2 (357), xli. 3.

21. PP1831 (348), xviii. 410–17.

22. TNA, T72/43, 'Ledger of the Commissioners', f. 140; Lewis, *Topographical Dictionary* (1831).

23. PP1831–2 (357), xli. 23–6, 57–60; 9 Geo IV, c.43 (15 July 1828).

24. PA, Lefevre Papers, SLF/15/46, Lefevre to Spencer, 2 Dec. 1831, 146; PP1831–2 (357), xli. 11–12, 16–17, 23, 29–30; SRO, Hatherton, D260/M/F/5/27/7, Lyttelton to Littleton, 10 Nov. 1831.

25. PA, Lefevre Papers, SLF/15/46, Lefevre to Spencer, 2 Dec. 1831. 146.

26. See Introduction for data sources.

27. PP2014–15, HC 600, *What Next on the Redrawing of Parliamentary Constituency Boundaries?*, 3, 16, 19–20; The 2023 Review of Parliamentary Constituencies was completed on a stricter +/-5 per cent variance, Boundary Commission for England, 'Guide to the 2023 Review of Parliamentary constituencies' (2021), 8.

28. PP1831–2 (357), xli. 43, 51.

29. PP1831–2 (357), xli. 28–30.

30. PP1831–2 (357), xli. 3.

31. Salmon, *Electoral Reform at Work*, 146–82.

32. PP1831–2 (357), xli. 51.

33. PP1831–2 (174), iii. 173.

34. Hansard, 3, ix. (27 Jan. 1832), 993; PA, Lefevre, SLF/15/47, Lefevre to Spencer, 28 Jan. 1832, 3

35. SRO, Hatherton, D260/M/F/5/26/7, 7 Feb. 1832, 336; SRO, Hatherton, D260/M/F/5/27/8, Lansdowne to Littleton, undated, catalogued after 6 Feb., 9.

36. J. Gibson and C. Rogers, *Poll Books 1696–1872: A Directory to Holdings in Great Britain* (Bury, 2008).

37. Gloucestershire, Leicestershire, Nottinghamshire, Warwickshire and Worcestershire.

38. Cheshire, Cornwall, Derbyshire, Devonshire, Essex, Hampshire, Kent, Lancashire, Norfolk, Nottinghamshire, Northumberland, Shropshire, Somerset, Staffordshire, Suffolk, Surrey, Sussex and Wiltshire.

39. BL, Add. MS. 79714, Browne to Graham, 4 Apr. 1831, 192; BL, Add. MS. 79715, Blamire to Graham, undated, 25–9; M. Escott, 'Cumberland', in Fisher, *Commons*, ii. 213–17; H. Spencer, 'Russell, William, 1798–1850', in Fisher, *Commons*, vi. 1077–9.

40. Wilson, *Strong Supporting Cast*, 76; Anonymous, *A Copy of the Poll for Two Knights of the Shire for the County of Northamptonshire* (Northampton, 1831).

41. PP1831–2 (357), xli. 34–5.

42. H. Spencer, 'Northamptonshire', in Fisher, *Commons*, ii. 752–61.

43. PP1831–2 (357), xli. 22–6.

44. PP1831–2 (357), xli. 23.

45. H. Spencer and P. Salmon, 'Hampshire', in Fisher, *Commons*, ii. 418–25; R. Foster, *Politics of County Power: Wellington and the Hampshire Gentlemen 1820–1852* (Hemel Hempstead, 1990), 11, 105–50.

46. J. H. Andrews, 'Political Issues in the County of Kent, 1820–1846' (University of London MPhil. dissertation, 1967), 11–12.

47. Hansard, 3, v. (11 Aug. 1831), 1221–48, ix. (27 Jan. 1832), 890–1020.

48. PP1831–2 (357), xli. 57–60.

49. SRO, Hatherton, D260/M/F/5/27/7, Lyttelton to Littleton, 10 Nov. 1831; P. Salmon, 'Worcestershire', in Fisher, *Commons*, iii. 225-9; D. Fisher, 'Ward, Hon John (1781-1833)', in Fisher, *Commons*, vii. 637-42.

50. PP1831-2 (357), xli. 54.

51. PP1831-2 (357), xli. 31.

52. Moore, *Politics of Deference*, 178; Hennock and Moore, 'Sociological Premises of the First Reform Act', 337.

53. SRO, Hatherton, D260/M/F/5/26/7, 25 July 1831, 84-6.

54. *MOP* (7 June 1832), iii. 2519.

55. *MOP* (22 June 1832), iii. 2733

56. *MOP* (7 June 1832), iii. 2519.

57. O'Gorman, *Voters, Patrons*, 135.

58. Hansard, 3, ii. (1 Mar. 1831), 1075.

59. Hansard, 3, x. (11 Feb. 1832), 247-8.

60. SRO, Hatherton, D260/M/F/5/26/7, 16 Feb. 1832, 347-8; *MOP* (8 June 1832), iii. 2529; PP1831-2 (488), iii. 27-34.

61. 2 William IV c.64 (11 July 1832).

62. PP1831-2 (357), xli. 4, 7, 39, 43.

63. SRO, Hatherton, D260/M/F/5/26/7, 4 Aug. 1831, 107; P. Salmon, 'Staffordshire', in Fisher, *Commons*, iii. 10.

64. SRO, Hatherton, D260/M/F/5/26/7, 7 Feb. 1832, 336, D260/M/F/5/26/8, 14 June 1832, 63-5; BL, Add. MS. 79717, Graham to Russell, undated, 66 (incorrectly attributed to Durham).

65. *MOP* (22 June 1832), iii. 2732-3.

66. *Staffordshire Advertiser*, 30 June 1832; *HLJ* (1831-2), lxiv. 330, 336, 342, 365.

67. *Derby Mercury*, 4 July 1832; PP1831-2 (357), xli. 13; Lewis, *Topographical Dictionary* (1831), ii. 28.

68. *HCJ* (1831-2), lxxxvii. 387, 425.

69. PP1831-2 (357), xli. 29; Lewis, *Topographical Dictionary* (1831), iii. 19.

70. Lewis, *Topographical Dictionary* (1831), iii. 377.

71. Hansard, 3, xiii. (7 June 1832), 543.

72. BL, Add. MS. 79717, Graham to Russell, undated, 66; M. Escott, 'Smith, Stanley Edward, 1775-1851', in Fisher, *Commons*, vii. 158.

73. *MOP* (7 June 1832), iii. 2518; *Lancaster Gazette*, 16 June 1832.

74. PP1831-2 (357), xli. 20-21; PP1831-2 (488), iii. 7; PP1831-2 (521), iii. 7; *HCJ* (1831-2), lxxxvii. 425; 2 Gul. IV, c.64 (11 July 1832).

75. *MOP* (8 June 1832), iii. 2518.

76. T. Jenkins, 'Gloucestershire', in Fisher, *Commons*, ii. 393.

77. *MOP* (22 June 1832), iii. 2731-2.

78. *LJ* (1831-2), lxiv. 353.

79. BL, Add. MS. 79717, Graham to Russell, undated, 66; *MOP* (9 July 1832), iv. 3052.

80. *MOP* (8 June 1832), iii. 2529.

81. *LJ* (1831-2), lxiv. 342, 348.

82. *Morning Chronicle*, 30 June 1832.

83. Hansard, 3, xiv. (9 July 1832), 170–72.

84. The exceptions being Salmon, 'English Reform Legislation', in Fisher, *Commons*, 411; H. Miller, *Nation of Petitioners: Petitions and Petitioning in the United Kingdom, 1780–1918* (Cambridge, 2023), 60–61.

85. Compiled from Fisher, *Commons*, iv–vii.

86. H. Spencer and P. Salmon, 'Hampshire', in Fisher, *Commons*, i. 424; Foster, *Politics of County Power*, 130–50.

87. J. Owen, 'Suffolk West', in P. Salmon and K. Rix, *The House of Commons 1832–1868* (forthcoming).

88. C. Dod, *Electoral Facts, from 1832 to 1853, Impartially Stated* (London, 1853), 353.

89. H. Miller, 'Warwickshire South', in Salmon and Rix, *Commons 1832–1868*.

90. M. Casey, 'Yorkshire', in Fisher, *Commons*, iii. 236–53.

91. Salmon. *Electoral Reform*, 146–82; M. Cragoe, 'The Great Reform Act and the Modernization of British Politics: The Impact of Conservative Associations, 1835–1841', *Journal of British Studies*, 47, 3 (2008), 581–603.

92. J. Owen, 'Suffolk East', and 'Suffolk West', in Salmon and Rix, *Commons 1832–1868*.

93. M. Spychal, 'Buck, Lewis William', and 'Buller, John Buller Yarde', in Salmon and Rix, *Commons 1832–1868*.

94. P. Salmon, 'Somerset East', and H. Miller, 'Staffordshire South', in Salmon and Rix, *Commons 1832–1868*; E. Jaggard, *Cornwall Politics in the Age of Reform, 1790–1885* (London, 1999), 94–5.

95. J. Owen, 'Essex North', in Salmon and Rix, *Commons 1832–1868*.

96. M. Spychal, 'Northamptonshire South', in Salmon and Rix, *Commons 1832–1868*.

97. A. Gambles, *Protection and Politics: Conservative Economic Discourse, 1815–1852* (Woodbridge, 1999), 176–229; T. Crosby, *English Farmers and the Politics of Protection 1815–1852* (Hassocks, 1977), 81–186.

98. Salmon, *Electoral Reform*, 139–40.

99. *Birmingham Daily Post*, 22 July 1865. See also, *West Kent Guardian*, 6 Feb. 1836; *Daily News*, 24 Sept. 1868; Dod, *Electoral Facts, from 1832 to 1853*, 274–6; M. Spychal, 'Botfield, Beriah', in Salmon and Rix, *Commons 1832–1868*.

100. *Daily News*, 29 Sept. 1851; Salmon, *Electoral Reform*, 61–2, 129–31, 138–9, 174–82; H. Miller, 'Warwickshire North', in Salmon and Rix, *Commons 1832–1868*.

101. *John Bull*, 18 Mar. 1865.

102. *South Eastern Gazette*, 8 June 1847; *Daily News*, 29 Sept. 1851; *Evening Mail*, 14 Feb. 1859; *Worcester Journal*, 26 Feb. 1859; *Wiltshire Independent*, 16 July 1863, 4 Aug. 1864; *Nonconformist*, 14 Oct. 1863; *Devizes and Wiltshire Gazette*, 8 Dec. 1864; *John Bull*, 18 Mar. 1865; H. Miller, 'Leicestershire South', and 'Staffordshire South', M. Spychal, 'Northamptonshire North', in Salmon and Rix, *Commons 1832–1868*.

103. *Brighton Gazette*, 11 June, 2 July 1835; *Standard*, 11 Oct. 1837; *Sun*, 20 Nov. 1839; *Daily News*, 28 Aug. 1868.

104. H. Miller, 'Staffordshire South' in Salmon and Rix, *Commons 1832–1868*.

105. J. Owen, 'Durham South', in Salmon and Rix, *Commons 1832–1868*.

106. Salmon, *Electoral Reform*, 160.

107. Jaggard, *Cornwall Politics*, 155.

108. J. Owen, 'Nottinghamshire North', and 'Nottinghamshire South', H. Miller, 'Herefordshire', and 'Leicestershire South', in Salmon and Rix, *Commons 1832–1868*; Crosby, *Politics of Protection*, 161–71.

109. *Morning Post*, 15 Sept. 1831.

110. Salmon, *Electoral Reform*, 185–200, 224–32; P. Salmon, 'Local Politics and Partisanship: The Electoral Impact of Municipal Reform, 1835', *Parliamentary History*, 19, 3 (2000), 357–76; J. Phillips and C. Wetherall, 'The Great Reform Act of 1832 and the Political Modernization of England', *American Historical Review*, 100, 2 (1995), 411–36; D. Fraser, 'The Poor Law as a Political Institution', in D. Fraser (ed.), *The New Poor Law in the Nineteenth Century* (London, 1976), 111–27; D. Fraser, *Urban Politics in Victorian England: The Structure of Politics in Victorian Cities* (Leicester, 1976), 55–90.

111. On this phenomenon see, O'Gorman, *Voters, Patrons, Parties*, 392–3; F. O'Gorman, 'Campaign Rituals and Ceremonies: The Social Meaning of Elections in England 1780–1860', *Past and Present*, 135 (1992), 79–115; J. Vernon, *Politics and the People: A Study in English Political Culture, 1815–1867* (Cambridge, 1993), 207–50.

112. M. Spychal, 'Northamptonshire North', in Salmon and Rix, *Commons 1832–1868*.

113. *Sussex Advertiser*, 24 Dec. 1832.

114. Patrick M. Kuhn; Luke Blaxill; Gidon Cohen; Gary Hutchison; Nick Vivyan (2022), 'Interactive Map of Election Violence Events in England and Wales, 1832–1914', Causes and Consequences of Electoral Violence: Evidence from England and Wales, http://victorianelectionviolence.uk/interactive-map/ [accessed 29 Nov. 2022].

115. D. Rossiter, R. Johnston, and C. Pattie, *The Boundary Commissions: Redrawing the United Kingdom's Map of Parliamentary Constituencies* (Manchester, 1999), 39–42, 53, 60–74; M. Cowling, *1867, Disraeli, Gladstone and Revolution: The Passing of the Second Reform Bill* (Cambridge, 1967), 52–3; M. Chadwick, 'The Role of Redistribution in the Making of the Third Reform Act', *HJ*, 19, 3 (1976), 680; M. Roberts, 'Resisting 'Arithmocracy': Parliament, Community and the Third Reform Act', *JBS*, 50, 2 (2011), 381–409.

Conclusion

As electioneering commenced across England's reformed electoral map in September 1832, Thomas Drummond remained at the boundary commission headquarters in London. 'Still at the council office', he informed Littleton, 'our end approaches, and there are now strong symptoms of departure: bales of boundary reports and plans ready for delivery, and our rooms looking very much like a warehouse'. Drummond wrote in the hope of obtaining 'subordinate situations in a government office' for his clerks, Malcolm Douglas Crosbie and George Sheldrick. Both, he regretted, looked 'adrift in the world … like a secretary of state going out of office'. He was also writing to confirm the commission's final accounts, stating that in addition to 1,850 copies of the commission's twelve-volume initial report, thirty copies on 'large paper' and 'corrected according to the [1832 Boundary] Act[s]' had just been completed.[1] Even with the commissioners only claiming expenses, Drummond reported that for the English, Welsh, Irish and Scottish boundary commissions, the overall labour cost of 'placing the information on the table of the House of Commons' was £11,320. In relative labour values in 2024 that equates to around £10,600,000.[2] Engraving and printing the commission's maps and reports proved more expensive, costing £15,297. In total, the commission produced 2,000 copies of its initial boundary maps – of which there were 454 in each full report. Staggeringly, this amounted to over 900,000 maps. The commission's official reports and plans were circulated to MPs and peers, distributed to local municipal offices and reference libraries, and sold by booksellers for up to £6 6s. a set.[3]

Drummond's personal recommendations ensured both Crosbie and Sheldrick enjoyed long civil service careers.[4] Drummond remained at Westminster for the following two years, serving as private secretary to the chancellor of the exchequer, Viscount Althorp. In 1835 he was appointed under-secretary of Ireland. As Jay Roszman has observed, Drummond 'assumed a central position in the machinery of Dublin Castle, where he touched nearly every paper that entered or exited the building'.[5] Alongside his enforcement and defence of Whig coercive policies, he pursued an 'unprecedented' concessionary policy of amelioration that sought to introduce Catholics to every level of judicial and law enforcement.[6] He also opposed the forced payment of the Anglican Church tithe by the majority Catholic population, and sparked controversy at Westminster for his contentious warning to Irish landlords in 1838 that 'property has its duties as well as its rights'.[7] During the home rule debates in 1886, William Gladstone cited this statement as a formative moment in Liberal Irish policy.[8] Drummond also found an avenue for his surveying and statistical skills, via his increasingly complex analysis and public exposition of the Outrage Reports and as chairman of the 1836–8 Irish railway commission. The latter produced two remarkably wide-ranging reports. However, Drummond's proposals for massive state intervention to develop Ireland's railways were rejected by an increasingly hostile Westminster, as the Whig majority in the Commons dwindled by the end of the decade. With his thoughts turning towards a parliamentary career, Drummond died of erysipelas in April 1840, aged forty-two. Having worked day and night for the previous five years, he was in effect killed by his tireless commitment to administration and bureaucracy.[9]

The boundary commission proved equally formative for Drummond's fellow commissioners, most of whom remained active in Westminster life for the following four decades. Five became MPs, including Henry Tancred, who represented Banbury for over two decades as a radical Whig between 1832 and 1858, and John Romilly, who during his second stint as a Whig MP was appointed attorney general in the 1847 Russell administration, before serving as master of the rolls for the rest of his career.[10] After sitting briefly for Petersfield as a reformer in 1832, John Shaw Lefevre served as under-secretary for the colonies from 1833, where he was appointed to the slavery compensation commission before securing full-time employment as a poor law commissioner between 1834 and 1841.[11] He later acted as deputy clerk, and then clerk of the parliaments from 1848 until his retirement in 1875.[12] By September 1832, John Chapman, William Wylde and John Wrottesley had transferred to the 1832–4 commission on the poor laws.[13] John Drinkwater worked as a factory commissioner from 1833, following which he was appointed to the 1833–5 municipal corporations commission alongside Thomas Flower Ellis.[14] Robert Saunders served as a factory inspector between 1833 and his death in 1852.[15] Robert Kearsley Dawson reassembled the boundary commission's network of surveyors and map-makers for the municipal corporations commission and the 1836 tithes commission.[16] While Dawson's ambitions for a cadastral survey of Britain were rejected by parliament, his oversight of the tithe commission over the following decade led to the production of over 11,000 tithe district maps, which provide a remarkably accurate picture of mid-nineteenth-century land ownership in England and Wales.[17] Henry Bellenden Ker was appointed to successive royal commissions on the criminal law between 1833 and 1849, where he channelled Drummond's influence as a 'tireless organizer' of 'data, papers, articles, reports, and draft legislation'.[18] And the outspoken Sheepshanks, who found his way to the 1838 and 1843 commissions on weights and measures, spent 'eleven laborious years' from 1844 in a basement in Somerset House, where he registered 'nearly 90,000 micrometrical readings' during his oversight of the commission for standards of length and weight.[19]

Mapping the State has established that as well as acting as a nursery for a new generation of bureaucrats, the boundary commission, guided by Drummond, was pivotal in establishing the governing techniques and methods that underpinned the increasingly ambitious domestic social policy of the nineteenth-century British state. Conspicuous for his absence from previous accounts of late Hanoverian and early Victorian governance, Drummond's development and successful application of a 'scientific' framework for the boundary commission initiated a major rhetorical and practical shift in the ambition of Whig and Liberal legislators and their expanding arsenal of administrators in the decades that followed. Within years, 'system, method [and] science' had been applied to the reform of local government, the poor law, factory employment, policing, public health and education via an array of commissions, committees and permanent inspectorates.[20] Over 220 commissions of inquiry alone were established between 1833 and 1868, leaving few areas of domestic or colonial policy untouched by legislative investigation.[21] Commissions and commissioners quickly became synonymous with Whig rule among Conservative and radical critics. In 1835 a young Disraeli characterised commissioners as 'unsavoury fungi' polluting the country, the social commentator Sydney Smith remarked in 1838 that 'the whole earth, is in fact, in commission', and in 1849 the radical self-government advocate, Joshua Toulmin Smith, railed against the seemingly all-pervasive 'illegal and pernicious' system of 'government by commissions'.[22] While historians have been more forgiving in their analysis of this new generation of bureaucrats and their reforming endeavours, what started as a novel Whig attempt at applying scientific methods as a means of instituting reform, for many quickly morphed into a new form of unwarranted centralised intrusion and corruption.

In addition to revealing the long-term significance of the 'Great Reform Act' to the development of British domestic governance, prioritising the issue of boundary reform has shifted our understanding of the 1832 reform legislation in several key areas. Firstly, it has confirmed the fruitlessness of seeking to understand the electoral reforms of 1832 through an anachronistic lens of democratisation that prioritises franchise reform.[23] Instead, the 1832 reform legislation is better understood as an attempt to legitimise parliament's claims to represent the political nation via the establishment of a diverse network of electoral interest communities.[24] A varied franchise across England's electoral map was only one component of how this electoral ideal was expected to function. It also required boundary reform and seat redistribution that retained a massive variation in constituency sizes and types, alongside open voting, public hustings, double-member seats and a rigorous registration system. Far from democratic in any modern sense of the term, this parliamentary and electoral model was deeply rooted in contemporary understandings of political community, the Commons' historic function as a representative body and a desire to ensure the electoral map reflected the social and economic reality of late Hanoverian England.

Secondly, *Mapping the State* has demonstrated that the 1831–2 boundary commission was central to how and why electoral reform was enacted by 1832. The previously unexplored working papers of the boundary commission have revealed how Drummond and his fellow commissioners worked behind the scenes at Westminster to create an innovative, technical framework for electoral reform that on one level became increasingly acceptable to parliament's various stakeholders at Westminster and in the localities, and on another so intricate that few parliamentarians, if any, had the capacity to challenge it. The commission initiated a major shift in the reform legislation, which was entirely remodelled from August 1831 following an in-depth national survey of the electoral system. Their multi-volume reports provided the basis for a separate boundary bill that received parliamentary scrutiny; an innovative remodelling of the disfranchisement schedules via Drummond's list; and a data-led defence of a newly refined £10 borough franchise. By early 1832 discussion over proposals for England's reformed electoral map was no longer an abstract debate over parliamentary process or an imagined democratic, gerrymandered electoral system. Parliamentarians had been provided with boundary proposals based on a cartographic, demographic and socioeconomic profile of their reformed constituencies, which for all but the most ardent of anti-reformers revealed that the reform legislation struck a comfortable balance between innovation and restoration in England's electoral system. For the vast majority of boroughs and counties, parliament and the localities proved remarkably accommodating of Drummond and Lefevre's claims to have defined England's reformed electoral communities via an objective framework. And, when concerns were raised with individual proposals, the government's concessionary stance ensured the passage of the 1832 Boundary Act after only a few hours of debate.

Next, the work of the commission led to a vastly improved central understanding of England's localities and electoral communities, which strengthened parliament's authority and legitimised the House of Commons' role as a representative body following 1832.[25] Along with the introduction of a £10 householder franchise across the boroughs, and a new system of voter registration, the work of the boundary commission and the 1832 Boundary Act for England and Wales introduced a level of structural uniformity to the electoral system that had not previously existed. For the first time every constituency had a boundary, and its details were publicly available – knowledge that was widely disseminated by the printing of election handbooks and gazetteers, such as Samuel Lewis's *A Topographical Dictionary of England*.[26] This transfer of locally held knowledge was one step in a slow (but not inevitable) process that saw Westminster assume an increasing role in constituency politics in the years to come. In this respect, boundaries and bureaucracy are a new element in the story of what some historians have termed the political 'modernisation', or the standardisation of the nineteenth-century British state, which was technocratic, relied on demographic data and required a wide knowledge of the social, economic and geographic realities of England's towns and counties.[27] With the exception of the boundary changes that accompanied the redistribution of seats to Lancashire and Yorkshire in 1861, every boundary identified by the 1832 Boundary Act remained in place until at least 1867.[28] Although calls for equal electoral districts formed part of the Chartist demands, the overarching structure of England's electoral map faced little serious parliamentary challenge until the shift to predominantly single-member seats initiated by the electoral reforms of 1884–5.

Fourthly, an unprecedented, and previously underappreciated, engagement at all levels of the state in the processes of reform was integral to the longevity (and general acceptance) of England's boundary reform settlement in 1832. It was not just MPs in interminable committee debates and behind the scenes high political manoeuvring that decided the details of reform, but the commissioners, parish officers, tax collectors, surveyors, returning officers and local petitioners who engaged with the boundary reform process during 1831 and 1832. This affirms, and allows for an extension of, Salmon's interpretation of the 1832 reform legislation as a 'consultation'. It is also in line with Miller's recent claim that mass petitioning during 1831 and 1832 revealed a 'dynamic interaction' between politicians, bureaucrats and constituents at a central and local level over the wider reform process.[29] It is important to observe, however, that the consultation process that influenced the boundary settlement was not open to all. The terms of engagement were set by the executive which realised the necessity for consultation with electoral officials in the localities to implement the basic aspects of reform, following which information sharing took place via the formal channels of a boundary commission, parliamentary returns and petitioning, as well as private representations to ministers. Unlike future boundary reforms from 1867, non-official constituency involvement was limited to the latter two forms of engagement, rather than a more openly public 'consultation' via boundary commission hearings.

Fifthly, in contrast to theories of liberal governmentality that view the state within a top-down model, this book has confirmed the necessity of conceptualising the evolving nineteenth-century British state as a genuine nation state, that was as reliant on the local churchwarden to function as it was the civil servant or politician at Whitehall.[30] *Mapping the State* does indicate that aspects of the liberal governmentality interpretation hold weight, particularly Joyce's contention that the collection of data and the production of maps and statistics served to support and reinforce reform and governmental institutions. In this regard, boundary reform, and its successful implementation and settlement for thirty-six years, demonstrated how the redefinition of public space could reinforce the institutional authority of parliament within a locality. However, simply 'knowing' what a space was did not allow an administrator or politician to control it.[31] On one level, the electoral statistics and cartographic data generated by the boundary commission, and the masses of parliamentary returns that followed in their wake, were also available to the non-official public, who were able to utilise this improved knowledge about a constituency's political geography to make their own political claims and challenges to the electoral status quo. On another, a locality's continued acceptance of the institution of parliament (at the level of electoral politics) was always reliant on actors outside of formal officialdom. Even in the most electorally dormant of post-1832 constituencies, politicians, parties, patrons and agents had to work within the electoral communities identified by the 1832 reform legislation to develop some consensus about who represented those places at Westminster. And, if established elites or party organisations did not adapt, new sites of influence and power quickly developed.[32] Contrary to Joyce's suggestion that liberal governmentality led to an increased elite control of public space, 'knowing the governed' with new technologies and data such as maps and statistics actually encouraged the contestation of such space by helping to generate new political communities and providing the means for old political communities to adapt to challenge authority.[33]

Moving to the political implications of the 1832 boundary reforms at Westminster, *Mapping the State* has revealed that England's reformed electoral map accentuated the urban–rural divide in the electoral system and entrenched political division over the corn laws and religion in the decades that followed. England's reformed constituency structure provided a significant foothold for the forces of protectionism prior to 1846, and for the emerging Conservative party under the subsequent direction of Derby and Disraeli. If the commission's plans for the grouping of English boroughs with fewer than 300 £10 householders had been favoured over the eventual proposal to throw those boroughs into their surrounding parishes, and the division of counties had not gone ahead (as was so nearly the case during November 1831), it is probable that Whig-Liberal candidates would have secured at least an additional thirty English seats at elections during the first reform era. Such small margins would have ensured three unbroken decades of Whig-Liberal governance after 1832, and relegated non-liberal Conservatives, and protectionists, to a position of long-term opposition. The boundary settlement elsewhere, which socio-economically defined the vast majority of England's reformed boroughs around their associated town populations and reasserted the centrality of community to borough politics, proved remarkably beneficial to an emerging Liberal party that coalesced around free trade, Dissent and industry – particularly in the new boroughs and as the £10 householder started to completely dominate ancient franchise holders in the old boroughs.[34]

The irony of this was that Russell and his emerging case for moderate Whig reform during the 1820s had sought to stop a combative Commons divided along such lines. To an extent it was unfortunate for Russell (but also short-sighted of him) that those attached to the landed, agricultural interest found their natural home under Peel, Derby and Disraeli in the years prior to, and following, 1846. Granted, if such a balance had not been maintained in 1832, it is hard to conceive that Conservative candidates would have been as eager to accept the finality of the reform settlement ahead of the 1835 election. However, by the 1850s the motivations behind Russell and Disraeli's ambitions for further reform were telling. Disraeli professed in 1859 that the Derby government's reform bill sought to 'adapt the settlement of 1832 to the England of 1859' through boundary changes and by seeking to accentuate the divide between urban and rural electorates.[35] Russell's failed reform bills from 1849 sought to leave boundaries untouched so that large town electorates penetrated the counties, while disfranchising small boroughs. He hoped this would mitigate his great regret concerning 1832 – namely the distinct divide that the 1832 reform legislation had produced in the representation of rural and urban interests in the reformed Commons.[36] In fact, it was Disraeli's close attention to the boundary issue during debate over the Liberal reform bill of 1866, and his presentation in the Commons of privately commissioned boundary maps, that one contemporary blamed for the downfall of the second Russell ministry.[37]

Finally, the long-term legacy, and continued relevance, of the redrawing of England's electoral map in 1832 needs to be recognised. The 1867, 1884 and 1918 Reform Acts were all accompanied by boundary commissions whose recommendations were enacted by separate acts of parliament. Each commission had to contend with preserving the representation of communities, while also having to ensure that constituencies represented an increasingly equitable number of electors. On each occasion the boundary commission's initial report and proposals provided a vital opportunity for informal and formal negotiations between parties over the extent of reform.[38] While this precedent was broken in 1944, when a permanent independent boundary commission was established, parliamentary boundaries have continued to provide the primary means by which the electoral system has been, and continues to be, reformed. The efficiency of the 1831–2 commission's work, and the speed of its enactment, is best demonstrated by contrasting it with the most recently completed review of English boundaries, which commenced in 2011 and following three separate reviews was not approved by parliament until 2023. As well as contending with a proposed reduction of Commons seats (as the Grey ministry had also initially done in 1831), the failure of the 2013 and 2018 reviews revealed the continued relevance of Drummond's insistence that the boundary-setting process be based on the most up-to-date electoral data and anchored in a disinterested means of defining electoral communities. These debates were reopened in response to the 2023 boundary review, but failed to halt a review whose parameters were changed to allow for the retention of 650 MPs.[39] That twenty-first-century Westminster continues to reform itself in the shadow of, and according to the methods established by, the Grey ministry, Drummond and Lefevre is testament to the enduring significance and legacy of the 1831–2 boundary commission.

Notes

1. SRO, Hatherton, D260/M/F/5/27/8, Drummond to Littleton, 4 Sept. 1832, 40–41.
2. MeasuringWorth, 'Five Ways to Compute the Relative Value of a U.K. Pound Amount, 1270 to present' (2022), https://www.measuringworth.com/calculators/ukcompare/ [accessed 12 Jan. 2024].

3. *Morning Herald*, 11 Dec. 1832; *Gentleman's Magazine* (1835), xxxix. 828.

4. *Sun*, 7 Jan. 1851; *Morning Herald*, 31 Oct. 1857; *Week's News*, 23 Mar. 1872; *Shipping and Mercantile Gazette*, 26 Apr. 1883.

5. J. Roszman, *Outrage in the Age of Reform: Irish Agrarian Violence, Imperial Insecurity, and British Governing Policy, 1830–1845* (Cambridge, 2022), 248.

6. S. Palmer, 'Drummond, Thomas', *ODNB*, https://doi.org/10.1093/ref:odnb/8084 [accessed 8 Dec. 2022].

7. PP1837–8 (735), xlvi. 574; Roszman, *Outrage in the Age of Reform*, 76–7, 94–6, 104, 128–9, 131–2, 136, 156–7, 163, 231–4, 237–8, 248–54.

8. *Hansard*, 3, ccciv. (13 Apr. 1886) 1542.

9. Roszman, *Outrage in the Age of Reform*, 179–84, 231–4, 248–54; Palmer, 'Drummond, Thomas'; J. Mclennan, *Memoir of Thomas Drummond* (Edinburgh, 1867); R. B. O'Brien, *Thomas Drummond: Under-Secretary in Ireland 1835–40; Life and Letters* (London, 1889); M. A. G. Ó Tuathaigh, *Thomas Drummond and the Government of Ireland, 1835–41* (Dublin, 1978); T. Jordan, 'An Enlightened Utilitarian: Thomas Drummond (1797–1840)', *New Hibernia Review*, 7, 3 (2003), 127–35; T. Jordan, 'Two Thomases: Dublin Castle and the Quality of Life in Victorian Ireland', *Social Indicators Research*, 64 (2003), 257–91.

10. J. Hamilton and P. Polden, 'Romilly, John, first Baron Romilly (1802–1874)', *ODNB*, https://doi.org/10.1093/ref:odnb/24048 [accessed 8 Dec. 2022]; M. Spychal, 'Tancred, Henry', and S. Lees, 'Ord, William Henry', in P. Salmon and K. Rix (eds.), *The House of Commons, 1832–1868* (forthcoming).

11. F. Wilson, *A Strong Supporting Cast: The Shaw Lefevres 1789–1936* (London, 1993), 86–9; N. Draper, *The Price of Emancipation: Slave-Ownership, Compensation and British Society at the End of Slavery* (Cambridge, 2009), 115; *Liverpool Echo*, 5 Mar. 1880.

12. M. Curthoys, 'Lefevre, Sir John George Shaw-(1797–1879)', *ODNB*, https://doi.org/10.1093/ref:odnb/25275 [accessed 6 Sept. 2016].

13. J. M. Collinge, *Office Holders in Modern Britain, Volume 9, Officials of Royal Commissions of Inquiry 1815–1870* (London, 1984), 16–28.

14. K. Prior, 'Bethune, John Elliot Drinkwater (1801–1851)', *ODNB*, https://doi.org/10.1093/ref:odnb/2310 [accessed 9 Dec. 2022]; M. Lobban, 'Ellis, Thomas Flower (1796–1861)', *ODNB*, https://doi.org/10.1093/ref:odnb/8713 [accessed 9 Dec. 2022].

15. I. Cawood, 'Corruption and the Public Service Ethos in Mid-Victorian Administration: The Case of Leonard Horner and the Factory Office', *English Historical Review*, 135 (2020), 860–91; P. Clamp, 'Robert J. Saunders, Factory Inspector, and his National Factory Schools Experiment 1841–1843', *Journal of Educational Administration and History*, 18, 1 (1986), 23–33.

16. HOP, Unpublished Parkes Transcripts, J. Parkes to E. Littleton, 12 Feb. 1835, Parkes to Brougham, 17 Nov. 1835.

17. E. Baigent, 'Dawson, Robert Kearsley (1798–1861)', *ODNB*, https://doi.org/10.1093/ref:odnb/7355 [accessed 9 Dec. 2022]; D. Gatehouse, 'Estrangement at the Church Door: Silas Marner and the Projection of New English Spaces', *European Journal of English Studies*, 27, 2 (2023), 258–71; R. Kain and R. Oliver, *The Tithe Maps of England and Wales* (Cambridge, 1995); R. Oliver, *The Ordnance Survey in the Nineteenth Century: Maps, Money and the Growth of Government* (London, 2014), 108–30.

18. W. Cornish and D. Cairns, 'Ker, (Charles) Henry Bellenden (c. 1785–1871)', *ODNB*, https://doi.org/10.1093/ref:odnb/15447 [accessed 9 Dec. 2022].

19. Clerke and Hoskin, 'Sheepshanks, Richard', *ODNB*, https://doi.org/10.1093/ref:odnb/25290 [accessed 9 Dec. 2022].

20. B. Hilton, *A Mad, Bad, & Dangerous People?: England 1783–1846* (Oxford, 2006), 599–602; D. Eastwood, '"Amplifying the Province of the Legislature": The Flow of Information and the English State in the Early Nineteenth Century', *Historical Research*, 62, 149 (1989), 276–94; U. R. W. Henriques, *Before the Welfare State: Social Administration in Early Industrial Britain* (London, 1979), 26; P. Mandler, *Aristocratic Government in the Age of Reform: Whigs and Liberals 1830–1852* (Oxford, 1990), 35–6; J. Parry, *The Rise and Fall of Liberal Government in Victorian Britain* (London, 1993), 113–26.

21. PP1834 (291), xli. 349; PP1836 (528), xxxvii. 491; PP1837 (290), xxxix. 205; PP1840 (237), xxix. 323; PP1847–8 (669), xxxix. 295; PP1850 (720), xxxiii. 25; PP1856 (415), xxxviii. 395; PP1859 (196), ii; PP1862 (317), xxx. 615; PP1867 (261), xl. 361; PP1888 (426), lxxxi. 491. Z. Laidlaw, *Colonial Connections, 1815–45: Patronage, the Information Revolution and Colonial Government* (Manchester, 2005), 169–99; Draper, *Price of Emancipation*, 114–37.

22. *Cambridge Chronicle*, 9 June 1838, 4; W. Hutcheon (ed.), *Whigs and Whiggism: Political Writings by Benjamin Disraeli* (London, 1913), 92; J. Toulmin Smith, *Government by Commissions: Illegal and Pernicious* (London, 1849), 22–30; B. Weinstein, '"Local Self-Government Is True Socialism": Joshua Toulmin Smith, the State and Character Formation', *EHR*, 123 (2008), 1193–228.

23. Miles Taylor, 'Parliamentary Representation in Modern Britain: Past, Present and Future', *Historical Journal*, 65, 4 (2022), 1145–73; A. Hawkins, *Victorians and Modernity* (Oxford, 2023), 74–87.

24. A. Hawkins, *Victorian Political Culture: Habits of Heart and Mind* (Oxford, 2015), 156–7; Parry, *Rise and Fall*, 87–9.

25. See also, H. Miller, *A Nation of Petitioners: Petitions and Petitioning in the United Kingdom, 1780–1918* (Cambridge, 2023), 280.

26. Anonymous, *The Maxima Charta of 1832 for England, Ireland and Scotland* (London, 1832); *Atlas*, 6 Jan., 3 Feb. 1833; S. Lewis, *A Topographical Dictionary of England* (London, 1835).

27. J. Phillips and C. Wetherall, 'The Great Reform Act of 1832 and the Political Modernization of England', *American Historical Review*, 100, 2 (1995), 411–36.; M. Cragoe, 'The Great Reform Act and the Modernization of British Politics: The Impact of Conservative Associations, 1835–1841', *Journal of British Studies*, 47, 3 (2008), 581–603; P. Salmon, 'Electoral Reform and the Political Modernization of England, 1832–1841', *Parliaments, Estates and Representation*, 23, 1 (2003), 49–67.

28. Vict. 24 & 25, c. 112 (1861).

29. Miller, *Nation of Petitioners*, 276.

30. See also, T. Crook, *Governing Systems: Modernity and the Making of Public Health in England, 1830–1910* (2020), 63–105; T. Crook, 'Sanitary Inspection and the Public Sphere in Late Victorian and Edwardian Britain: A Case Study in Liberal Governance', *Social History*, 32, 4 (2007), 369–93.

31. P. Joyce, *The Rule of Freedom: Liberalism and the Modern City* (London, 2003), 13, 35–61.

32. See also, K. Navickas, *Protest and the Politics of Space and Place 1789–1848* (Manchester, 2016), 154–76.

33. Joyce, *Rule of Freedom*, 13.

34. P. Salmon, *Electoral Reform at Work: Local Politics and National Parties, 1832–1841* (Woodbridge, 2002), 203–4, 254; Miles Taylor, 'Interests, Parties and the State: The Urban Electorate in England, c. 1820–72', in J. Lawrence and Miles Taylor (eds.), *Party, State and Society: Electoral Behaviour in Britain since 1820* (Aldershot, 1997), 55–61.

35. D. C. Moore, *The Politics of Deference: A Study of the Mid-Nineteenth Century Political System* (New York, 1976), 383–4.

36. D. C. Moore, 'Social Structure, Political Structure and Public Opinion in Mid-Victorian England', in Robson, R. (ed.), *Ideas and Institutions of Victorian Britain* (1967), 50–55; Moore, *Politics of Deference*, 380–97; R. Saunders, *Democracy and the Vote in British Politics, 1848–1867* (Farnham, 2011), 45–6.

37. M. Baxter, *In Memoriam, R. Dudley Baxter, MA* (London, 1878); R. Woodberry, 'Redistribution and the Second Reform Act: The Intended, and Unintended, Electoral Effects on the Balance of the Political Parties' (PhD diss. Bristol, 2007); M. Spychal, 'The 1868 Boundary Act: Disraeli's attempt to control his "leap in the dark"?' *History of Parliament Blog* (2018) https://thehistoryofparliament.wordpress.com/2018/05/10/the-1868-boundary-act-disraelis-attempt-to-control-his-leap-in-the-dark/ [accessed 9 Dec. 2022].

38. D. Rossiter, et al. *Boundary Commissions: Redrawing the United Kingdom's Map of Parliamentary Constituencies* (Manchester, 1999); Woodberry, 'Redistribution'; M. Chadwick, 'Role of Redistribution in the Making of the Third Reform Act', *Historical Journal*, 19, 3 (1976), 665–83; M. Roberts, 'Resisting "Arithmocracy": Parliament, Community and the Third Reform Act', *Journal of British Studies*, 50, 2 (April 2011), 381–409.

39. PP2014–15, HC 600, *What Next?*, 10–15; R. Johnston, D. Rossiter and C. Pattie, *Equality, Community and Continuity: Reviewing the UK Rules for Constituency Redistributions* (London, 2014); C. Pattie and D. Rossiter, 'Another nail – but whose coffin? Redrawing Britain's constituency map (again) and the future of the UK's voting system', *Constitution Unit*, https://constitution-unit.com/2021/07/12/another-nail-but-whose-coffin-redrawing-britains-constituency-map-again-and-the-future-of-the-uks-voting-system/ [accessed 9 Dec. 2022]; M. Spychal, 'Some parallels: The 1832 and 2018 boundary reviews', *Victorian Commons* (2017), https://victoriancommons.wordpress.com/2017/07/03/some-parallels-the-1832-and-2018-boundary-reviews/ [accessed 9 Dec. 2022]; *The Times*, 13 Sept. 2011, 6 Dec. 2013, 11 May 2015, 12 Feb., 29 Aug. 2016, 19 Feb., 11 Sept. 2018; *Telegraph*, 8 June 2021, 8 Nov. 2022; *Gloucestershire Echo*, 10 Nov. 2022; *Aberdeen Press and Journal*, 18 Nov. 2022; *Birmingham Post*, 24 Nov. 2022.

Bibliography

Unpublished primary sources

Birmingham Library, Special Collections
    Boulton Papers
Dublin, National Library of Ireland
    Drummond Papers
Durham University, Special Collections
    Grey Papers
London, British Library
    Althorp Papers
    Graham Papers
    Iddesleigh Papers
    Place Papers
    Liverpool Papers
London, History of Parliament
    Unpublished Parkes transcripts
    Unpublished facsimile 'Autobiography of five hundred members of Parliament'
London, National Archives, Kew
    T72 –Municipal and Parliamentary Boundaries Commission: Draft Maps and Plans
    PC 2 –Records of the Privy Council –Privy Council: Registers
    PRO 30/22 –Russell Papers
    CO43 –Goderich Papers
    WO47 –Board of Ordnance: Minutes
London, News International Archives
    Barnes Papers
London, Parliamentary Archives
    Le Marchant Papers
    Lefevre Papers
London, Royal Society
    Herschel Papers
Stafford, Staffordshire Record Office
    Hatherton MSS
London, UCL Special Collections
    SDUK Papers
    Brougham Papers

Published primary sources

Parliamentary pollbooks

I have used a wide range of constituency pollbooks for the period before and after 1832. Election results in individual constituencies broken down into voting district were also printed in the contemporary press. The best guide to published pollbooks is Gibson, J., and Rogers, C., *Poll Books 1696–1872: A Directory to Holdings in Great Britain* (Bury, 2008).

Contemporary newspapers and periodicals

I have used a number of physical and online newspaper archives, primarily those held by the British Library, British Library Nineteenth Century Newspapers, British Newspaper Archive, Newspaperarchive.com and the Gale Newsgroup archives. The primary titles used were:

Birmingham Gazette
Birmingham Journal
Cobbett's Political Register
County Chronicle
Edinburgh Review
Essex Standard
Examiner
Globe
Guardian
Hampshire Telegraph
Jackson's Oxford Journal
John Bull
Leamington Spa Courier
Leeds Intelligencer
Leeds Mercury
London and Edinburgh Philosophical Magazine and Journal of Science
Looking Glass
Morning Chronicle
Morning Herald
Morning Post
Newcastle Courant
Northampton Mercury
Penny Magazine
Philosophical Magazine

Quarterly Review
Stamford Mercury
Standard
Sun
The Times
Weekly Dispatch
Westmorland Gazette
Worcester Herald

Official papers and published documents

Cobbett's Parliamentary History of England
Hansard's Parliamentary Debates
House of Commons Divisions Lists, 1836–1910
House of Commons Journals
House of Lords Journals
Mirror of Parliament

Parliamentary papers

The major collections that I have used are:

Report from the Select Committee on the Survey and Valuation of Ireland, PP1824 (445), vii. 79
Parliamentary Representation (multiple volumes published between 1830 and 1832, including published reports of the boundary commission and returns relating to the electoral system), PP1830–1, x., PP1831, xvi., PP1831–2, xxxvi–xliii
Census Returns, 1831–71, PP1833 (149) xxxvi., PP1843 (496) xxii., PP1852–3 (1691) lxxxviii., PP1863 (3221) liii., PP1873 (872) lxxi
Various returns relating to electoral registration, published between 1833 and 1867, primarily, PP1833 (189) xxxvii. 21; PP1836 (190) xliii. 363; PP1837–8 (329), xliv. 553; PP1840 (579) xxxix. 187; PP1846 (284) xxxiii. 145; PP1852 (4) xlii. 303; PP1854 (280) liii. 211; PP1859 (140) xxiii. 139; PP1862 (410) xliv. 703; PP1865 (448), xliv. 549
Various returns relating to members of commissions of inquiry during the 1830s, *Boards or Commissions*, PP1834 (291), xli. 349; *Commissions*, PP1836 (528), xxxvii. 491; PP1837 (290), xxxix. 205; PP1837–8 (346), xxxvi. 191; PP1840 (237), xxix. 323; *Commissions of Inquiry*, PP1847–8 (669), xxxix. 295
Boundaries of Boroughs, PP1859 Session 1 (166), xxiii. 121

HMSO, *Guide to the Contents of the Public Record Office: State Papers and Departmental Records* (1963)
Tenth Report of the Deputy Keeper of the Public Records, C 1046 (1849)
What Next on the Redrawing of Parliamentary Constituency Boundaries?, PP2014–5, HC 600

Bills

A bill to amend the representation of the people in England and Wales (multiple versions between 1830 and 1832, PP1830–31 (247, .37, .36, .37), ii; PP1831 (22, 232, 244), iii.; PP1831–2 (11, 265, 277, 507), iii.
A bill to settle and describe the divisions of counties, and the limits of cities and boroughs in England and Wales, in so far as respects the election of members to serve in Parliament, PP1831–2 (174, 488, 521), iii.

Statutes

An act for the better regulation of divisions in the several counties of England and Wales, 1828, 9 George IV c. 43
An act to amend the representation of the people in England and Wales, 1832, 2 William IV c. 45
An act to settle and describe the divisions of counties, and the limits of cities and boroughs in England and Wales, in so far as respects the election of members to serve in parliament, 1832, 2 & 3 William IV c.64
An act to settle and describe the limits of certain boroughs and the divisions of certain counties in England and Wales, in so far as respects the election of members to serve in parliament, 1868, 31 and 32 Victoria c.46
An act for the redistribution of seats at parliamentary elections, and for other Purposes, 1885, 48 and 49 Victoria c.23
An act to amend the law with respect to parliamentary and local government franchises, and the registration of parliamentary and local government electors, and the conduct of elections, and to provide for the redistribution of seats at parliamentary elections, and for other purposes connected therewith, 1918, 8 George. V. c.64

Contemporary articles, pamphlets and printed books

Anonymous, *The Assembled Commons* (London, 1836–1838)
Anonymous, *A Copy of the Poll for Two Knights of the Shire for the County of Northamptonshire* (Northampton, 1831)

Anonymous, *The Maxima Charta of 1832 for England, Ireland and Scotland* (London, 1832)
Anonymous, *Parliamentary Test Book for 1835* (London, 1835)
Anonymous, *Political Economy Club, Names of Members 1821–1860* (London, 1860)
Anonymous, *Report of the First and Second Meetings of the British Association for the Advancement of Science* (London, 1833)
Anonymous, *Thoughts on County Elections Addressed to the Landed Interest of the Country* (London, 1812)
Anonymous, *Two Letters to the Right Honourable Lord John Russell on the Classification of Boroughs* (London, 1832)
Babbage, C., *Reflections on the Decline of Science* (London, 1829)
Bassett, F., *Free Parliaments: or a Vindication of the Parliamentary Constitution of England; in Answer to Certain Visionary Plans of Modern Reformers* (London, 1783)
Baxter, M., *In Memoriam, R. Dudley Baxter, MA* (London 1878)
Blackstone, W., *Commentaries on the Laws of England* (1832)
Brougham, H., *The Life and Times of Henry Lord Brougham* (London, 1871)
Brougham, H., *The Objects, Advantages, and Pleasures of Science* (London, 1827)
Butterworth, E., *Historical Sketches of Oldham* (Oldham, 1856)
Cartwright, J., *The People's Barrier Against Undue Influence and Corruption* (London, 1780)
Child, J., *A New Discourse of Trade* (London, 1804)
Dod, C., *Electoral Facts, from 1832 to 1853, Impartially Stated* (London, 1853)
Dod, C., *Electoral Facts, from 1832 to 1866, Impartially Stated* (London, 1866)
Dod, C., *The Parliamentary Companion* (London, 1832–68)
Drummond, T., 'On the Illumination of Lighthouses', *Philosophical Transactions of the Royal Society of London*, 120 (London, 1830)
Gooch, R., *The Book of the Reformed Parliament* (London, 1834)
James, J., *The History and Topography of Bradford* (London, 1841)
Jenyns, S., *Thoughts on a Parliamentary Reform* (London, 1784)
Knight, C., *Passages of a Working Life during Half a Century* (London, 1864)
Lewis, S., *A Topographical Dictionary of England* (London, 1835)
Mackintosh, J., 'Universal Suffrage', *Edinburgh Review*, 31 (1818), 165–208
Oldfield, T. H. B., *An Entire and Complete History, Political and Personal of the Boroughs of Great Britain* (London, 1792)
Oldfield, T. H. B., *The Representative History of Great Britain and Ireland* (London, 1816)
Olivier, J., *Parliamentary and Political Director for the Session 1848* (London, 1848)

Ord, W. H., *A Dialogue on Election by Ballot* (London, 1831)
Page, F., *The Principle of the English Poor Laws* (London, 1830)
Park, J. J., *The Dogmas of the Constitution* (London, 1832)
Russell, Lord, *An Essay on the History of the English Government and Constitution from the Reign of Henry VII to the Present Time* (London, 1821)
Russell, Lord, *An Essay on the History of the English Government and Constitution from the Reign of Henry VII to the Present Time* (London, 1823)
Scott, R., *A Topographical and Historical Account of Hayling Island, Hants* (Skelton, 1826)
Toulmin Smith, J., *Government by Commissions: Illegal and Pernicious* (London, 1849)
Trevelyan, G. O., *The Life and Letters of Lord Macaulay* (London, 1876)

Published diaries and correspondence

Arnould, J. (ed.), *Memoir of Lord Denman* (London, 1873)
Ashley, E. A., *The Life and Correspondence of Henry John Temple Viscount Palmerston* (London, 1879)
Aspinall, A. (ed.), *Three Early Nineteenth Century Diaries* (London, 1952)
Baring, F. T., *Journals and Correspondence of Sir Francis Thornhill Baring, Afterwards Lord Northbrook* (London, 1905)
Bamford, F. and Wellington, Duke (eds.), *The Journal of Mrs Arbuthnot, 1820–1832* (London, 1950)
Brandreth, M. E., *Some Family and Friendly Recollections of 70 years, of Mary Elizabeth Brandreth* (1888, Privately Printed)
Carr, C., *A Victorian Law Reformers Correspondence* (London, 1955)
Colchester, Lord (ed.), *A Political Diary 1820–1830, by Edward Law Lord Ellenborough* (London, 1881)
Hutcheon, W. (ed.), *Whigs and Whiggism: Political Writings by Benjamin Disraeli* (London, 1913)
Jennings, L. (ed.), *The Correspondence and Diaries of the late Right Honourable John Wilson Croker, LL.D., F.R.S., Secretary to the Admiralty from 1809 to 1830* (London, 1885)
Kriegel, A. (ed.), *The Holland House Diaries, 1831–1840* (London, 1977)
Marchant D. L. (ed.), *Memoir of John Charles Viscount Althorp, Third Earl Spencer* (London, 1876)
Mclennan, J., *Memoir of Thomas Drummond* (Edinburgh, 1867)
O'Brien, R. B., *Thomas Drummond: Under-Secretary in Ireland 1835–40; Life and Letters* (London, 1889)

Parker, C. S., *Life and Letters of Sir James Graham* (London, 1907)
Seymour, Lady (ed.), *The Pope of Holland House, Selections from the Correspondence of John Whishaw and his Friends, 1813–1840* (London, 1906)
Taylor, H. (ed.), *The Reform Act, 1832: The Correspondence of the Late Earl Grey with His Majesty King William IV* (London, 1867)
Wellington, Duke (ed.), *Despatches, Correspondence, and Memoranda of Field Marshall Arthur Duke Wellington* (London, 1878)
Wiebe, M. G., et al., *Benjamin Disraeli Letters 1815–1868* (Toronto, 1982–2014)

Art

Doyle, J., *Political Sketches* (London, 1829–41)
Grant, C. J., *Every Body's Album & Caricature Magazine* (London, 1834–5)
Heath, W., *March of Intellect* (British Museum, London, 1828–30)
Maclean, T., *The Looking Glass: or, Caricature Annual* (London, 1830–36)
Maclise, D., *The Editor of "The Times"* (British Museum, London, 1830)
Pickersgill, H., *Thomas Drummond* (University of Edinburgh, Scotland, 1832)

Secondary sources

Works of reference

Fisher, D. (ed.), *The House of Commons, 1820–1832* (Cambridge, 2009)
Gibson, J., and Rogers, C., *Poll Books 1696–1872: A Directory to Holdings in Great Britain* (Bury, 2008)
Hanham, H (ed.), *Electoral Facts, from 1832 to 1853, Impartially Stated* (Brighton, 1972)
Namier, L., and Brooke, J. (eds.), *The House of Commons, 1754–1790* (Cambridge, 1985)
Oxford Dictionary of National Biography
Salmon, P. and Rix, K. (eds.), *The House of Commons, 1832–1868* (forthcoming)
Thorne, R. G. (ed.), *The House of Commons, 1790–1820* (Cambridge, 1986)
Victoria County History
Vincent, J., and Stenton, M. (eds.), *McCalmont's Parliamentary Poll Book, British Election Results, 1832–1918* (Brighton, 1971)

Books and articles

Aidt, T. S., and Franck, R., 'Democratization under the Threat of Revolution: Evidence from the Great Reform Act of 1832', *Econometrica*, 83 (2015), 505–47

Anonymous, *The History of The Times: "The Thunderer" in the Making 1785–1841* (London, 1935)

Ashton, R., *Victorian Bloomsbury* (London, 2012)

Aspinall, A., *Lord Brougham and the Whig Party* (Stroud, 2005)

Aspinall, A., *Politics and the Press* (London, 1949)

Aydelotte, W. O., 'Constituency Influence on the British House of Commons', in W. Aydelotte (ed.), *The History of Parliamentary Behaviour* (New Jersey, 1977)

Aydelotte, W. O., 'The House of Commons in the 1840's', *Comparative Studies in History and Society*, 5 (1962–3), 134–63

Aydelotte, W. O., 'Voting Patterns in the British House of Commons in the 1840s', *Comparative Studies in Society and History*, 5 (1963), 134–63

Baer, M., *The Rise and Fall of Radical Westminster, 1780–1890* (Basingstoke, 2012)

Barnes, D., *A History of the English Corn Laws from 1660–1846* (London, 1930)

Beales, D., 'The Electorate Before and After 1832: The Right to Vote and the Opportunity', *Parliamentary History*, 12, 2 (1992), 139–50

Beales, D., 'The Idea of Reform in British Politics, 1829–1850', in T. Blanning and P. Wende (eds.), *Reform in Great Britain and Germany, 1750–1850* (Oxford, 1999), 159–74

Beales, D., 'Parliamentary Parties and the Independent Member', 1810–1860', in Robson, R. (ed.), *Ideas and Institutions of Victorian Britain* (London, 1967), 1–19

Beer, S., 'The Representation of Interests in British Government: Historical Background', *American Political Science Review*, 51, 3 (1957), 613–50

Berrington, H., 'Partisanship and Dissidence in the Nineteenth-Century House of Commons', *Parliamentary Affairs*, 21 (1968), 338–74

Birch, A. H., *Representation* (London, 1971)

Blaxill, L., 'Quantifying the Language of British Politics', *Historical Research*, 86 (2013), 313–41

Blaxill, L., *The War of Words: The Language of British Elections, 1880–1914* (London, 2020)

Blaxill, L., 'Why Do Historians Ignore Digital Analysis? Bring on the Luddites', *Political Quarterly*, 94, 2 (2023), 279–89

Bord, J., *Science and Whig Manners: Science and Political Style in Britain, c. 1790–1850* (Basingstoke, 2009)

Brent, R., *Liberal Anglican Politics: Whiggery, Religion, and Reform, 1830–1841* (Oxford, 1987)
Brewer, J., *Party Ideology and Popular Politics at the Accession of George III* (Cambridge, 1976)
Briggs, A., *Victorian Cities* (London, 1990)
Brock, M., *The Great Reform Act* (London, 1973)
Brockington, F., 'Public Health at the Privy Council 1831–34', *Journal of the History of Medicine and Allied Sciences*, 16, 2 (1961), 161–85
Bromund, T., '"A Complete Fool's Paradise": The Attack on the Fitzwilliam Interest in Peterborough, 1852', *Parliamentary History*, 12, 1 (1993), 47–67
Brooke, J., 'The Members', in L. Namier and J. Brooke (eds.), *The House of Commons 1754–1790* (Cambridge, 1985), i. 97–176
Brown, D., Crowcroft, R. and Pentland, G., *The Oxford Handbook of Modern British Political History, 1800–2000* (Oxford, 2018)
Brown, M., 'How Not to "Regain Paradise": Henry Bellenden Ker, F.R.S. from 1819 to 1831', *Notes and Records of the Royal Society of London*, 50, 2 (1996), 211–15
Brundage, A., *England's Prussian Minister: Edwin Chadwick and the Politics of Government Growth, 1832–54* (London, 1988)
Brundage, A., *The Making of the New Poor Law: The Politics of Inquiry, Enactment and Implementation* (London, 1978)
Butler, J. R. M., *The Passing of the Great Reform Bill* (London, 1914)
Bylsma, J., 'Party Structure in the 1852–1857 House of Commons: A Scalogram Analysis', *Journal of Interdisciplinary History*, 7, 4 (1977), 617–35
Cain, M., 'The Maps of the Society of the Diffusion of Useful Knowledge: A Publishing History', *Imago Mundi*, 46 (1994), 151–67
Cannadine, D., 'The Calthorpe Family and Birmingham, 1810–1910: A "Conservative Interest" Examined', *Historical Journal*, 18, 4 (1975), 725–60
Cannadine, D., *Victorious Century: The United Kingdom, 1800–1906* (London, 2017)
Cannon, J., *Parliamentary Reform 1640–1832* (Cambridge, 1973)
Cannon, S., *Science in Culture: The Early Victorian Period* (New York, 1978)
Carr, C., *A Victorian Law Reformers Correspondence* (London, 1955).
Cawood I., 'Corruption and the Public Service Ethos in Mid-Victorian Administration: The Case of Leonard Horner and the Factory Office', *English Historical Review*, 135 (2020), 860–91
Chadwick, M., 'The Role of Redistribution in the Making of the Third Reform Act', *Historical Journal*, 19, 3 (1976), 665–83
Chester, N., *The English Administrative System* (Oxford, 1981)

Christie, I., 'The Yorkshire Association, 1780–4: A Study in Political Organization', *Historical Journal*, 3, 2 (1960), 144–61

Clamp, P., 'Robert J. Saunders, Factory Inspector, and his National Factory Schools Experiment 1841–1843', *Journal of Educational Administration and History*, 18, 1 (1986), 23–33

Clark, A., 'Gender, Class and the Nation: Franchise Reform in England, 1832–1928', in J. Vernon (ed.), *Rereading the Constitution* (Cambridge, 1996), 230–53

Clark, A., *Scandal: The Sexual Politics of the British Constitution* (Princeton, 2004)

Clark, G., *The Curiosities of Dudley and the Black Country* (Birmingham, 1881)

Clokie, H., and Robinson, J., *Royal Commissions of Inquiry* (New York, 1937)

Close, C., *The Early Years of the Ordnance Survey* (Newton Abbot, 1969)

Close, D. H., 'The Formation of a Two-Party Alignment in the House of Commons between 1830 and 1841', *English Historical Review*, 84 (1969), 257–77

Coleman, B., *Conservatism and the Conservative Party in Nineteenth-Century Britain* (London, 1988)

Collinge, J. M., *Office Holders in Modern Britain, Volume 9, Officials of Royal Commissions of Inquiry 1815–1870* (London, 1984)

Collini, S., Winch, D. and Burrow, J., *That Noble Science of Politics: A Study in Nineteenth-Century Intellectual History* (Cambridge, 1983)

Conti, G., *Parliament the Mirror of the Nation: Representation, Deliberation, and Democracy in Victorian Britain* (Cambridge, 2019)

Coohill, J., *Ideas of the Liberal Party: Perceptions, Agendas and Liberal Politics in the House of Commons, 1832–52* (Chichester, 2011)

Cowling, M., *1867, Disraeli, Gladstone and Revolution: The Passing of the Second Reform Bill* (Cambridge, 1967)

Cox, G., *The Efficient Secret: the Cabinet and the Development of Political Parties in Victorian England* (Cambridge, 1987)

Cragoe, M., *Culture, Politics and National Identity in Wales 1832–1886* (Oxford, 2004)

Cragoe, M., 'The Great Reform Act and the Modernization of British Politics: The Impact of Conservative Associations, 1835–1841', *Journal of British Studies*, 47, 3 (2008), 581–603

Cragoe, M., and Readman, P. (eds.), *The Land Question in Britain, 1750–1950* (Eastbourne, 2010)

Cromwell, V., 'Mapping the Political World of 1861: A Multidimensional Analysis of the House of Commons', *Legislative Studies Quarterly*, 7, 2 (1982), 281–97

Crook, T., *Governing Systems: Modernity and the Making of Public Health in England, 1830–1910* (Oakland, CA, 2020)

Crook, T., 'Sanitary Inspection and the Public Sphere in Late Victorian and Edwardian Britain: A Case Study in Liberal Governance', *Social History*, 32, 4 (2007), 369–93

Crosby, T., *English Farmers and the Politics of Protection 1815–1852* (Hassocks, 1977)

Cullen, M. J., *The Statistical Movement in Victorian Britain* (Hassocks, 1976)

Davis, R. W., 'Buckingham, 1832–1846: A Study of a "Pocket Borough"', *Huntingdon Library Quarterly*, 34, 2 (1971), 159–81

Davis, R. W., 'Deference and Aristocracy in the Time of the Great Reform Act', *American Historical Review*, 81, 3 (1976), 532–9

Davis, R. W., *Political Change and Continuity, 1760–1885: A Buckinghamshire Study* (Newton Abbot, 1972)

Dawson, L., *Memoirs of Hydrography Part One 1750–1830* (Eastbourne, 1883)

Delano-Smith, C., and Kain, R., *English Maps: A History* (London, 1999)

Dickinson, H. T., *Liberty and Property: Political Ideology in Eighteenth-century Britain* (London, 1977)

Draper, N., *The Price of Emancipation: Slave-Ownership, Compensation and British Society at the End of Slavery* (Cambridge, 2009)

Draper, N., 'The Rise of a New Planter Class? Some Countercurrents from British Guiana and Trinidad, 1807–33', *Atlantic Studies*, 9, 1 (2012), 65–83

Dumas, P., *Proslavery Britain: Fighting for Slavery in an Era of Abolition* (New York, 2016)

Dyer, M., *Men of Property and Intelligence: Scottish Electoral System Prior to 1884* (Aberdeen, 1996)

Eastwood, D., '"Amplifying the Province of the Legislature": The Flow of Information and the English State in the Early Nineteenth Century', *Historical Research*, 62, 149 (1989), 276–94

Eastwood, D., 'Contesting the Politics of Deference: The Rural Electorate, 1820–60', in J. Lawrence and Miles Taylor (eds.), *Party, State and Society: Electoral Behaviour in Britain since 1820* (Aldershot, 1997), 27–49

Eastwood, D., *Government and Community in the English Provinces, 1700–1870* (Basingstoke, 1997)

Eastwood, D., 'Parliament and Locality: Representation and Responsibility in Late-Hanoverian England', *Parliamentary History* 17, 1 (1998), 68–81

Eastwood, D., 'Robert Southey and the Intellectual Origins of Romantic Conservatism', *English Historical Review*, 104, 411 (1989), 308–31

Eggers, A. C., and Spirling, A., 'Electoral Security as a Determinant of Legislator Activity, 1832–1918: New Data and Methods for Analyzing

British Political Development', *Legislative Studies Quarterly*, 39 (2014), 593–620
Eggers, A. C., and Spirling, A., 'Party Cohesion in Westminster Systems: Inducements, Replacement and Discipline in the House of Commons, 1836–1910', *British Journal of Political Science*, 46, 3 (2014), 567–89
Ellens, J. P., *Religious Routes to Gladstonian Liberalism* (University Park, PA, 1994)
Ertman, R., 'The Great Reform Act of 1832 and British Democratization', *Comparative Political Studies*, 43,8 (2010), 1000–1022
Evans, E. J., *The Great Reform Act of 1832* (London, 1983)
Ferguson, W., 'The Reform Act (Scotland) of 1832 – Intention and Effect', *Scottish Historical Review*, 45, 139, (1966), 105–14
Fontana, B., *Rethinking the Politics of Commercial Society: The Edinburgh Review 1802–1832* (Cambridge, 1985)
Foote, G., 'The Place of Science in the British Reform Movement 1830–1840', *ISIS*, 42, 3 (1951), 192–208
Foster, R., *The Politics of County Power: Wellington and the Hampshire Gentlemen 1820–1852* (Hemel Hempstead, 1990)
Fraser, A., *Perilous Question: The Drama of the Great Reform Bill 1832* (London, 2014)
Fraser, D., *Urban Politics in Victorian England: The Structure of Politics in Victorian Cities* (Leicester, 1976)
Fraser, D. (ed.), *The New Poor Law in the Nineteenth Century* (London, 1976)
Fraser, P., 'The Growth of Ministerial Control in the Nineteenth-Century House of Commons', *English Historical Review*, 75, 296 (1960), 444–63
Friendly, A., *Beaufort of the Admiralty* (London, 1977)
Gambles, A., *Protection and Politics: Conservative Economic Discourse, 1815–1852* (Woodbridge, 1999)
Garrard, J., *Democratisation in Britain: Elites, Civil Society and Reform* (Hampshire, 2002)
Gash, N., *Politics in the Age of Peel: A Study in the Technique of Parliamentary Representation* (London, 1971)
Gatehouse, D., 'Estrangement at the Church Door: Silas Marner and the Projection of New English Spaces', *European Journal of English Studies*, 27, 2 (2023), 258–71
Gauci, P., 'The Clash of Interests: Commerce and the Politics of Trade in the Age of Anne', *Parliamentary History*, 28, 1 (2009), 115–25
Gaunt, R., *Politics, Law and Society in Nottinghamshire: The Diaries of Godfrey Tallents of Newark 1829–1839* (Nottingham, 2010)
Gaunt, R., *Unhappy Reactionary: The Diaries of the Fourth Duke of Newcastle-under-Lyne* (Nottingham, 2003)

Gaunt, R., *Unrepentant Tory: Political Selections from the Diaries of the Fourth Duke of Newcastle-under-Lyne, 1827–38* (Woodbridge, 2006)
Gibbs, R., *A History of Aylesbury* (Aylesbury, 1885)
Gillin, E. J., *The Victorian Palace of Science: Scientific Knowledge and the Building of the Houses of Parliament* (Cambridge, 2017)
Gleadle, K., *Borderline Citizens: Women, Gender, and Political Culture in Britain 1815–1867* (Oxford, 2009)
Gleadle, K. (ed.), *Women and British Politics, 1760–1860: The Power of the Petticoat* (Macmillan, 2000)
Goldman, L., 'The Origins of British Social Science: Political Economy, Natural Science and Statistics, 1830–1835', *Historical Journal*, 26, 3 (1983), 587–616
Goldman, L., *Victorians & Numbers: Statistics and Society in Nineteenth Century Britain* (Oxford, 2022)
Gordon, B., *Economic Doctrine and Tory Liberalism, 1824–1830* (London, 1979)
Gordon, B., *Political Economy in Parliament, 1819–1823* (London, 1976)
Gray, V., *Charles Knight: Educator, Publisher and Writer* (Aldershot, 2006)
Gunn, J. A. W., '"Interests Will Not Lie": A Seventeenth-Century Political Maxim, *Journal of the History of Ideas*, 29, 4, 551–64
Gunn, S., *The Public Culture of the Victorian Middle Class* (Manchester, 2000)
Gurowich, P. M., 'The Continuation of War by Other Means: Party and Politics, 1855–1865', *Historical Journal*, 27, 3 (1984), 603–31
Hall, C., Draper, N., McClelland K., Donington, K. and Lang, R. (eds.), *Legacies of British Slave-Ownership* (Cambridge, 2014)
Hamlin, C., *Public Health and Social Justice in the Age of Chadwick* (Cambridge, 1998)
Hargreaves, E., *The National Debt* (London, 1930)
Harley, J. B., 'Cartography, Ethics and Social Theory', *Cartographica*, 27, 2 (1990), 1–23
Harley, J, B., 'Deconstructing the Map', *Cartographica*, 26, 2 (1989), 1–20
Harley, J. B., *Maps for the Local Historian* (London, 1972)
Harley, J. B., *The New Nature of Maps* (Baltimore, 2001)
Harling, P., 'Parliament, the State, and "Old Corruption": Conceptualizing Reform, c. 1790–1832', in A. Burns and J. Innes (eds.), *Rethinking the Age of Reform* (Cambridge, 2003), 98–113
Harling, P., *The Waning of 'Old Corruption': The Politics of Economical Reform in Britain, 1779–1846* (Oxford, 1996)
Harling, P., 'The Power of Persuasion: Central Authority, Local Bureaucracy and the New Poor Law', *English Historical Review*, 107, 422 (1992), 30–53

Harling, P., 'The Powers of the Victorian State', in P. Mandler (ed.), *Liberty and Authority in Victorian Britain* (Oxford, 2006), 25–50
Harvie, C., and Matthew, H. C. G., '"Villa Tories": The Conservative Resurgence', *Nineteenth-Century Britain: A Very Short Introduction* (Oxford, 2008), 107–17
Hawkins, A., *British Party Politics, 1852–1886* (Basingstoke, 1998)
Hawkins, A., *Modernity and the Victorians* (Oxford, 2023)
Hawkins, A., '"Parliamentary Government" and Victorian Political Parties, c. 1830–c. 1880', *English Historical Review*, 104 (1989), 638–69
Hawkins, A., *Victorian Political Culture: Habits of Heart and Mind* (Oxford, 2015)
Hayton, D., 'The "Country" Interest in the Party System, 1689–c.1720', in C. Jones (ed.), *Party and Management in Parliament, 1660–1784* (Leicester, 1984), 37–85
Hearder, H., and Lyon, H. R. (eds.), *British government and administration: studies presented to S.B. Chrimes* (Cardiff, 1974)
Heesom, A., '"Legitimate" versus "Illegitimate" Influences: Aristocratic Electioneering in Mid-Victorian Britain', *Parliamentary History*, 7, 2 (1988) 282–305
Hennock, E. P., and Moore, D. C., 'The First Reform Act: A Discussion', *Victorian Studies*, 14, 3 (1971), 321–37
Henriques, U. R. W., 'An Early Factory Inspector: James Stuart of Dunearn', *Scottish Historical Review*, 50, 149 (1971), 18–46
Henriques, U. R. W., *Before the Welfare State: Social Administration in Early Industrial Britain* (London, 1979)
Hewitt, R., *Map of a Nation: A Biography of the Ordnance Survey* (London, 2010)
Higgs, E., *Before The Information State: The Central Collection of Information on Citizens since 1500* (Basingstoke, 2004)
Higman, B. W., 'The West India "Interest" in Parliament, 1807–1833', *Historical Studies* (Australia and New Zealand), 13, 49 (1967), 1–19
Hilton, B., *Corn, Cash, Commerce: Economic Policies of the Tory Governments, 1815–30* (Oxford, 1977)
Hilton, B., *A Mad, Bad, & Dangerous People?: England 1783–1846* (Oxford, 2006)
Hilton, B., 'Peel: A Reappraisal', *HJ*, 22 (1979), 585–614
Hilton, B., 'The Political Arts of Lord Liverpool', *TRHS*, 38 (1998), 147–70
Hirst, D., Keith-Lucas, B. and Redlich, J., *The History of Local Government in England* (London, 1970)
Holmes, G., *British Politics in the Age of Anne* (London, 1987)
Hoppen, K. T., *Elections, Politics, and Society in Ireland 1832–1885* (Oxford, 1984)

Hoppen, K. T., 'An Incorporating Union? British Politicians and Ireland 1800–1830', *English Historical Review*, 123, 501 (2008), 328–50
Hoppen, K. T., *Ireland since 1800: Conflict and Conformity* (Harlow, 1999)
Hoppen, K. T., *The Mid-Victorian Generation, 1840–1886* (Oxford, 1998)
Hoppit, J., 'The Landed Interest and the National Interest, 1660–1800', in J. Hoppit (ed.), *Parliaments, Nations and Identities in Britain and Ireland, 1660–1850* (Manchester, 2003)
Hoppit, J., 'Petitions, Economic Legislation and Interest Groups in Britain, 1660–1800', *Parliamentary History*, 37, 1 (2018), 52–71
Hoskin, M., 'Astronomers at War: South v. Sheepshanks', *Journal for the History of Astronomy*, 20, 3 (1989), 175–212
Hoskin, M., et al., 'More on "South v. Sheepshanks"', *Journal for the History of Astronomy*, 22, 2 (1991), 174–9
Howe, A., *The Cotton Masters, 1830–1860* (Oxford, 1984)
Hume, L., 'Jeremy Bentham and the Nineteenth-Century Revolution in Government', *Historical Journal*, 10, 3 (1967), 361–75
Hyde, R., 'Mapping Urban Britain 1831–2: The Compilation of the Reform Bill Plans', *Bulletin of the Society of University Cartographers*, 9, 2 (1978), 1–9
Innes, J., 'Forms of "Government Growth", 1780–1830', in D. Feldman and J. Lawrence (eds.), *Structures and Transformations in Modern British History* (Cambridge, 2011), 74–99
Innes, J., *Inferior Politics: Social Problems and Social Policies in Eighteenth-Century Britain* (Oxford, 2009)
Innes, J., 'Seeing Like a Surveyor: Imagining Rural Reform in the Early Nineteenth-Century UK', in B. Kinzer, M. B. Kramer and R. Trainor (eds.), *Reform and Its Complexities in Modern Britain: Essays Inspired by Sir Brian Harrison* (Oxford, 2022), 57–76
Jaggard, E., *Cornwall Politics in the Age of Reform, 1790–1885* (London, 1999)
Jaggard, E., 'Small Town Politics in Mid-Victorian Britain', *History*, 89, 1 (2004), 3–29
Jenkins, T., *The Liberal Ascendancy, 1830–1886* (Basingstoke, 1994)
Jenkins, T., *Sir Robert Peel* (Basingstoke, 1999)
Johnson, H, J., and Pooley, C. G. (eds.), *The Structure of Nineteenth Century Cities* (London, 1982)
Johnston, R., Rossiter, D. and Pattie, C., *Equality, Community and Continuity: Reviewing the UK Rules for Constituency Redistributions* (London, 2014)
Jordan, T., 'An Enlightened Utilitarian: Thomas Drummond (1797–1840)', *New Hibernia Review*, 7, 3 (2003), 127–35

Jordan, T., 'Two Thomases: Dublin Castle and the Quality of Life in Victorian Ireland', *Social Indicators Research*, 64 (2003), 257–91

Joyce, P., *Democratic Subjects: The Self and the Social in Nineteenth-Century England* (Cambridge, 1994)

Joyce, P., *The Rule of Freedom: Liberalism and the Modern City* (London, 2003)

Joyce, P., *The State of Freedom: A Social History of the British State since 1800* (Cambridge, 2014)

Joyce, P., *Visions of the People: Industrial England and the Question of Class 1848–1914* (Cambridge, 1991)

Joyce, P., *Work, Society and Politics: The Culture of the Factory in Later Victorian England* (Brighton, 1980)

Judd, G. P., *Members of Parliament, 1734–1832* (New Haven, 1955)

Jupp, P., *British Politics on the Eve of Reform: The Duke of Wellington's Administration, 1828–30* (Basingstoke, 1998)

Jupp, P., *The Governing of Britain 1688–1848* (Abingdon, 2006)

Kain, R., and Baigent, E., *The Cadastral Map in the Service of the State* (Chicago, 1992)

Kain R., and Oliver, R., *The Tithe Maps of England and Wales* (Cambridge, 1995)

Kain, R., Chapman, J. and Oliver, R., *The Enclosure Maps of England and Wales, 1595–1918* (Cambridge, 2004)

Keller, L., *Triumph of Order, Democracy and Public Space in New York and London* (New York, 2009)

Kinzer, B., *The Ballot Question in Nineteenth-Century English Politics* (1982)

Kriegel, A., 'Whiggery in the Age of Reform', *Journal of British Studies*, 32, 3 (1993) 290–98

Laidlaw, Z., *Colonial Connections, 1815–45: Patronage, the Information Revolution and Colonial Government* (Manchester, 2005)

Langford, P., *A Polite and Commercial People, England 1727–1783* (Oxford, 1989)

Langford, P., 'Property and "Virtual Representation" in Eighteenth-Century England', *Historical Journal*, 31, 1 (1998), 83–115

Larcom, Captain, 'Memoir of the Professional Life of the Late Captain Drummond', *Royal Engineers Professional Papers*, 4 (1841), xviii–xxii

Lewis, G., 'Memoir of Henry Rowland Brandreth', *Papers on Subjects Connected with the Duties of the Corps of Royal Engineers*, 10 (1849), 1–36

Lipscomp, P., 'Party Politics, 1801–1802: George Canning and the Trinidad Question', *Historical Journal*, 12, 3 (1969), 442–66

Lloyd-Jones N., and Scull, M. (ed.), *Four Nations Approaches to Modern 'British' History: A (Dis)United Kingdom?* (London, 2019)

Loft, P., 'Involving the Public: Parliament, Petitioning, and the Language of Interest, 1688–1720', *Journal of British Studies*, 55, 1 (2016), 1–23

Loft, P., 'Petitioning and Petitioners to the Westminster Parliament, 1660–1788', *Parliamentary History*, 38, 3 (2019), 342–61

LoPatin, N. D., *Political Unions, Popular Politics and the Great Reform Act of 1832* (Basingstoke, 1999)

Lopatin-Lummis, N., 'The 1832 Reform Act Debate: Should the Suffrage Be Based on Property or Taxpaying?', *JBS*, 46, 2 (2007), 320–45

Lowell, J., 'The Influence of Party on Legislation in England and America', *Annual Report for the American Historical Association* (1901), i. 321–544

Lubenow, W., *The Politics of Government Growth* (Plymouth, 1971)

MacDonagh, O., *Early Victorian Government 1830–1870* (London, 1977)

MacDonagh, O., 'The Nineteenth-Century Revolution in Government: A Reappraisal', *Historical Journal*, 1, 1 (1958), 52–67

McLean, I., 'Interests and Ideology in the United Kingdom Parliament of 1841–7: An Analysis of Roll Call Voting', *Contemporary Political Studies*, 1 (1995), 1–20

Mandler, P., *Aristocratic Government in the Age of Reform: Whigs and Liberals 1830–1852* (Oxford, 1990)

Mandler, P., (ed.), *Liberty and Authority in Victorian Britain* (Oxford, 2006)

Mandler, P., 'Tories and Paupers: Christian Political Economy and the Making of the New Poor Law', *Historical Journal*, 33, 1 (1990), 81–103

Marx, K., 'The Elections – Tories and Whigs', *New York Daily Tribune*, 3540 (1852)

Marx, K., 'Lord Russell', *Neue Oder-Zeitung*, 359 (1855)

McClelland, K., 'Redefining the West India Interest: Politics and the Legacies of Slave-Ownership', in C. Hall et al. (eds.), *Legacies of British Slave-Ownership* (Cambridge, 2014), 127–62, 288–97

McCord, N., 'Some Difficulties of Parliamentary Reform', *Historical Journal*, 10, 4 (1967), 376–90

Mclennan, J., *Memoir of Thomas Drummond* (Edinburgh, 1867)

Middleton, A., '"High Politics" and its Intellectual Contexts', *Parliamentary History*, 40, 1 (2021), 168–91

Miller, H., *A Nation of Petitioners: Petitions and Petitioning in the United Kingdom, 1780–1918* (Cambridge, 2023)

Miller, H., 'Radicals, Tories or Monomaniacs? The Birmingham Currency Reformers in the House of Commons, 1832–67', *Parliamentary History*, 31, 3 (2012), 354–77

Miller, P., *Defining the Common Good: Empire, Religion and Philosophy in Eighteenth-Century Britain* (Cambridge, 1994)

Milton-Smith, J., 'Earl Grey's Cabinet and the Objects of Parliamentary Reform', *Historical Journal*, 15,1 (1972), 55–74

Mitchell, A., 'The Whigs and Parliamentary Reform Before 1830',
 Historical Studies (Australia and New Zealand), 12 (1965) 22–42
Mitchell, L. G., 'Foxite Politics and the Great Reform Bill', *English
 Historical Review*, 108, 427 (1993), 338–64
Molesworth, W. N., *The History of the Reform Bill of 1832* (London, 1865)
Moore, D. C., 'Concession or Cure: The Sociological Premises of the First
 Reform Act', *Historical Journal*, 9, 1 (1966), 39–59
Moore, D. C., 'The Matter of the Missing Contests: Towards a Theory of
 the Mid-19th Century British Political System', *Albion*, 6,2 (1974),
 93–119
Moore, D. C., 'The Other Face of Reform', *Victorian Studies*, 5, 1 (1961),
 7–34
Moore, D. C., 'Political Morality in Mid Nineteenth Century England:
 Concepts Norms, Violations', *Victorian Studies*, 13, 1 (1969)
Moore, D. C., *The Politics of Deference: A Study of the Mid-Nineteenth
 Century Political System* (New York, 1976)
Moore, D. C., 'Social Structure, Political Structure and Public Opinion in
 Mid-Victorian England', in Robson, R. (ed.), *Ideas and Institutions of
 Victorian Britain* (1967), 20–57
Morrell, J., and Thackray, A., *Gentlemen of Science: Early Years of the
 British Association for the Advancement of Science* (New York, 1981)
Mullen, S., 'Henry Dundas: A "Great Delayer" of the Abolition of the
 Transatlantic Slave Trade', *Scottish Historical Review*, 100, 2 (2021),
 218–48
Murphy, C., 'The Future of British Political History', *Political Quarterly*,
 94, 2 (2023), 201–7
Namier, L., *The Structure of Politics at the Accession of George III*
 (London, 1970)
Navickas, K., *Protest and the Politics of Space and Place 1789–1848*
 (Manchester, 2016)
Nechtman, T., *Nabobs: Empire and Identity in Eighteenth-Century Britain*
 (Cambridge, 2010)
New, C. W., *Lord Durham* (Oxford, 1929)
Newbould, I., 'The Emergence of a Two-Party System in England from
 1830 to 1841: Roll Call and Reconsideration', *Parliaments, Estates and
 Representation*, 5, 1 (1985), 25–31
Newbould, I., 'Whiggery and the Growth of Party 1830–1841: Organisation
 and the Challenge of Reform', *Parliamentary History*, 4 (1985)
Newbould, I., *Whiggery and Reform, 1830–41: The Politics of Government*
 (London, 1990)
Nossiter, T., *Influence, Opinion and Political Idioms in Reform England:
 Case Studies from the North-East, 1832–74* (Hassocks, 1975)

O'Brien, B., *Thomas Drummond: Life and Letters* (London, 1889)
O'Gorman, F., 'Campaign Rituals and Ceremonies: The Social Meaning of Elections in England 1780–1860', *Past and Present*, 135 (1992), 79–115
O'Gorman, F., 'The Electorate Before and After 1832', *Parliamentary History*, 12, 2 (1993), 171–83
O'Gorman, F., 'The Unreformed Electorate of Hanoverian England: The Mid-Eighteenth Century to the Reform Act of 1832', *Social History*, 11, 1 (1986), 33–52
O'Gorman, F., *Voters, Patrons, and Parties: The Unreformed Electoral System of Hanoverian England 1734–1832* (Oxford, 1989)
Oliver, R., *The Ordnance Survey in the Nineteenth Century: Maps, Money and the Growth of Government* (London, 2014)
Olney, R. J., *Lincolnshire Politics 1832–1885* (Oxford, 1973)
Ó Tuathaigh, M. A. G., *Thomas Drummond and the Government of Ireland, 1835–41* (Dublin, 1978)
Parris, H., *Constitutional Bureaucracy: The Development of British Central Administration since the Eighteenth Century* (Bristol, 1969)
Parris, H., 'The Nineteenth-Century Revolution in Government: A Reappraisal Reappraised', *Historical Journal*, 3, 1 (1960), 17–37
Parry, J., *The Rise and Fall of Liberal Government in Victorian Britain* (London, 1993)
Parsons, F., *Thomas Hare and Political Representation in Victorian Britain* (Basingstoke, 2009)
Pearce, E., *Reform!: The Fight for the 1832 Reform Act* (London, 2004)
Pentland, G., 'The Debate on Scottish Parliamentary Reform, 1830–32', *Scottish Historical Review*, 85, 1 (2006)
Pentland, G., *Radicalism, Reform and National Identity in Scotland 1820–1833* (Woodbridge, 2008)
Pentland, G., 'Scotland and the Creation of a National Reform Movement, 1830–32', *Historical Journal*, 48, 4 (2005), 999–1023
Phillips, J., *The Great Reform Bill in the Boroughs: English Electoral Behaviour 1818–1841* (Oxford, 1992)
Phillips, J., and Wetherall, C., 'The Great Reform Act of 1832 and the Political Modernization of England', *American Historical Review*, 100, 2 (1995), 411–36
Phillips, J., and Wetherall, C., 'The Great Reform Bill of 1832 and the Rise of Partisanship', *Journal of Modern History*, 63, 4 (1991), 621–46
Pole, J. R., *Political Representation in England and the Origins of the American Republic* (London, 1966), 385–404
Porter, T., *The Rise of Statistical Thinking, 1820–1900* (Princeton, 1986)
Porter, T., *Trust in Numbers: The Pursuit of Objectivity in Science and Public Life* (Princeton, 1995)

Quinault, R., 'The French Revolution of 1830 and Parliamentary Reform', *History*, 75, 297 (1994), 377–93

Quinault, R., 'The Industrial Revolution and Parliamentary Reform', in P. O'Brien and R. Quinault (eds.), *The Industrial Revolution and British Society* (Cambridge, 1993), 183–202

Rauch, A., *Useful Knowledge: The Victorians, Morality and the March of Intellect* (Durham, N.C., 2001)

Richardson, S., *The Political Worlds of Women: Gender and Political Culture in Nineteenth-Century Britain* (Routledge, 2013)

Rix, K., '"Whatever Passed in Parliament Ought to be Communicated to the Public": Reporting the Proceedings of the Reformed Commons, 1833–50', *Parliamentary History*, 33, 3 (2014), 453–74

Roberts, D., *Paternalism in Victorian England* (London, 1979)

Roberts, M., 'Resisting "Arithmocracy": Parliament, Community and the Third Reform Act', *Journal of British Studies*, 50, 2 (April 2011), 381–409

Roberts, M., '"Villa Toryism" and Popular Conservatism in Leeds, 1885–1902', *Historical Journal*, 49, 1 (2006), 221–2

Robson, B., 'Maps and Mathematics: Ranking the English boroughs for the 1832 Reform Act', *Journal of Historical Geography*, 46 (2014), 66–79

Robson, B., and Wyke, T., 'Surveying the surveyors: Richard Thornton and his Publishers', *Northern History*, 56, 1 (2019), 1–20

Rossiter, D., Johnston, R., and Pattie, C., *The Boundary Commissions: Redrawing the United Kingdom's Map of Parliamentary Constituencies* (Manchester, 1999)

Roszman, J., *Outrage in the Age of Reform: Irish Agrarian Violence, Imperial Insecurity, and British Governing Policy, 1830–1845* (Cambridge, 2022)

Salmon, P., 'Electoral Reform and the Political Modernization of England', *Parliaments, Estates, and Representation*, 23, 1 (2003), 49–67

Salmon, P., *Electoral Reform at Work: Local Politics and National Parties, 1832–1841* (Woodbridge, 2002)

Salmon, P., 'The English Reform Legislation, 1831–32', in D. Fisher (ed.), *The House of Commons, 1820–32*, i. (Cambridge, 2009), 374–412

Salmon, P., 'Local Politics and Partisanship: The Electoral Impact of Municipal Reform, 1835', *Parliamentary History*, 19, 3 (2000), 357–76

Salmon, P., '"Reform Should Begin at Home": English Municipal and Parliamentary Reform, 1818–32', in C. Jones, P. Salmon and R. Davis (eds.), *Partisan Politics, Principles and Reform in Parliament and the Constituencies, 1689–1880* (Edinburgh, 2004), 93–113

Saunders, R., *Democracy and the Vote in British Politics, 1848–1867: The Making of the Second Reform Act* (Farnham, 2011)

Saunders, R., 'God and the Great Reform Act: Preaching against Reform, 1831–32', *Journal of British Studies*, 53, 2 (2014), 378–99

Scholefield P., and Pease-Watkin, C. (eds.), *The Collected Works of Jeremy Bentham* (Oxford, 2002)

Schonhardt-Bailey, C., *From the Corn Laws to Free Trade: Interests, Ideas and Institutions in Historical Perspective* (London, 2006)

Schonhardt-Bailey, C., 'Ideology, Party and Interests in the British Parliament of 1841–47', *British Journal of Political Science*, 33, 4 (2003), 581–605

Scott, J., *Seeing Like a State: How Certain Schemes to Improve the Human Condition Have Failed* (Yale, 1998)

Searle, G., *A New England: Peace and War, 1886–1918* (Oxford, 2004)

Seymour, C., *Electoral Reform in England and Wales* (Oxford, 1970)

Skjönsberg, M., 'The History of Political Thought and Parliamentary History in the Eighteenth and Nineteenth Centuries', *Historical Journal*, 64, 2 (2021), 501–13

Skjönsberg, M., *The Persistence of Party: Ideas of Harmonious Discord in Eighteenth-Century Britain* (Cambridge, 2021)

Smith, D., *Victorian Maps of the British Isles* (London, 1985)

Smith, E., 'The Election Agent in English Politics, 1734–1832', *English Historical Review*, 134 (1969), 12–35

Smith, F., *The Making of the Second Reform Bill* (Cambridge, 1966)

Smith, R. J., *The Gothic Bequest: Medieval Institutions in British Thought, 1688–1863* (Cambridge 1987)

Southgate, D., *The Passing of the Whigs, 1832–1886* (London, 1962)

Stewart, R., *Party and Politics 1830–1852* (Houndsmills, 1989)

Stewart, R., *The Foundation of the Conservative Party, 1830–1867* (London, 1978)

Stockwell, W. D., 'Contributions of Henry Brougham to Classical Political Economy', *History of Political Economy*, 23, 4 (1991), 645–73

Sutherland, L., *The East India Company in Eighteenth-Century Politics* (Oxford, 1952)

Taylor, Michael, 'Conservative Political Economy and the Problem of Colonial Slavery, 1823–1833', *Historical Journal*, 57, 4 (2014), 973–95

Taylor, Michael, *The Interest: How the British Establishment Resisted the Abolition of Slavery* (London, 2020)

Taylor, Miles, *The Decline of British Radicalism, 1847–1860* (Oxford, 1995)

Taylor, Miles, 'Empire and Parliamentary Reform: The 1832 Reform Act Revisited', in A. Burns and J. Innes (eds.), *Rethinking the Age of Reform* (Cambridge, 2003), 295–311

Taylor, Miles, 'Interests, Parties and the State: The Urban Electorate in England, c. 1820–72', in J. Lawrence and Miles Taylor (eds.), *Party, State*

and Society: Electoral Behaviour in Britain since 1820 (Aldershot, 1997), 50–78
Taylor, Miles, 'Parliamentary Representation in Modern Britain: Past, Present and Future', *Historical Journal*, 65, 4 (2022), 1145–73
Taylor, P., *Popular Politics in Early Industrial Britain: Bolton 1825–1850* (Bodmin, 1995)
Tillott P., (ed.), *A History of the County of York: The City of York* (London, 1961)
Thane, P., 'Government and Society in England and Wales, 1750–1914', in F. M. L. Thompson., *The Cambridge Social History of Britain*, iii. (Cambridge, 1990)
Thompson, S. J., '"Population Combined with Wealth and Taxation": Statistics Representation and the Making of the 1832 Reform Act', in Tom Crook and Glen O'Hara (eds.), *Statistics and the Public Sphere, Numbers and the People in Modern Britain, c. 1800–2000* (New York, 2011), 205–23
Tompson, R., *The Charity Commission and the Age of Reform* (London, 1979)
Trevelyan, G. M., *Lord Grey of the Reform Bill* (London, 1920)
Trevelyan, G. M., *The Seven Years of William IV* (London, 1952)
Trinder, B., *Victorian Banbury* (Chichester, 1982)
Trinder, B., *A Victorian Member of Parliament and His Constituents: Correspondence, 1841–59* (Banbury, 1969)
Vaizey, J., 'No. 67 "Charles Henry Bellenden Ker", *The Institute: A Club of Conveyancing Counsel. Memoirs of Former Members*, i. (London, 1907)
Veitch, G. S., *The Genesis of Parliamentary Reform* (London, 1965)
Vernon, J., *Politics and the People: A Study in English Political Culture, 1815–1867* (Cambridge, 1993)
Vincent J., 'The Electoral Sociology of Rochdale', *Economic History Review*, 16, 1 (1963), 76–90
Vincent, J., *The Formation of the Liberal Party, 1857–1868* (London, 1966)
Vincent, J., *Pollbooks: How the Victorians Voted* (Cambridge, 1967)
Wadsworth, A., 'Newspaper Circulations 1800–1954', *Transactions Manchester Statistical Society*, 72 (1954–5), 1–41
Wahrman, D., 'Virtual Representation: Parliamentary Reporting and Languages of Class in the 1790s', *Past and Present*, 136, 1 (1992) 83–113
Wahrman, D., *Imagining the Middle Class: The Political Representation of Class in Britain, c.1780–1840* (Cambridge, 1995)
Wasson, E. A., 'The Great Whigs and Parliamentary Reform, 1809–1830', *Journal of British Studies*, 24, 4 (1985), 434–64
Wasson, E. A., 'The Whigs and the Press, 1800–50', *Parliamentary History*, 25, 1 (2006), 68–87

Wasson, E. A., *Whig Renaissance: Lord Althorp and the Whig Party* (New York, 1987)
Weinstein, B., *Liberalism and Local Government in Early Victorian London* (Woodbridge, 2011)
Weinstein, B., '"Local Self-Government Is True Socialism": Joshua Toulmin Smith, the State and Character Formation', *EHR*, 123 (2008), 1193–228
Wilson, F., *A Strong Supporting Cast: The Shaw Lefevres 1789–1936* (London, 1993)
Wright, D. G., 'A Radical Borough: Parliamentary Politics in Bradford 1832–41', *Northern History*, 4, 1 (1969), 132–66

Online secondary sources

Royal Society, 'List of Fellows of the Royal Society 1660–2007', https://web.archive.org/web/20160303210110/https://royalsociety.org/~/media/Royal_Society_Content/about-us/fellowship/Fellows1660-2007.pdf
Pattie, C., and Rossiter, D., 'Another nail – but whose coffin? Redrawing Britain's constituency map (again) and the future of the UK's voting system', *Constitution Unit Blog* (April, 2021), https://constitution-unit.com/2021/07/12/another-nail-but-whose-coffin-redrawing-britains-constituency-map-again-and-the-future-of-the-uks-voting-system/
Salmon, P., 'Boundary changes: the Victorian legacy', *The Victorian Commons* (December, 2012), https://victoriancommons.wordpress.com/2012/12/06/boundary-changes-the-victorian-legacy/
Spychal, M., 'The 1868 Boundary Act: Disraeli's attempt to control his 'leap in the dark'?', *History of Parliament Blog* (May, 2018), https://thehistoryofparliament.wordpress.com/2018/05/10/the-1868-boundary-act-disraelis-attempt-to-control-his-leap-in-the-dark/
Spychal, M., 'The geography of voting behaviour: towards a roll-call analysis of England's reformed electoral map, 1832–68', *The History of Parliament Blog* (March, 2021), https://thehistoryofparliament.wordpress.com/2021/03/09/the-geography-of-voting-behaviour-towards-a-roll-call-analysis-of-englands-reformed-electoral-map-1832-68/
Spychal, M., 'Five elections in seven years: Peterborough, Whalley and the Fitzwilliam interest', *The Victorian Commons* (April, 2017), https://victoriancommons.wordpress.com/2017/04/28/five-elections-in-seven-years-peterborough-whalley-and-the-fitzwilliam-interest/
Spychal, M., 'Some parallels: the 1832 and 2018 boundary reviews', *The Victorian Commons* (July, 2017), https://victoriancommons.wordpress.com/2017/07/03/some-parallels-the-1832-and-2018-boundary-reviews/

Spychal, M., 'Surveying the UK's parliamentary boroughs: map-making and the 1831–2 boundary commissions', *The Victorian Commons* (June, 2018), https://victoriancommons.wordpress.com/2021/06/28/surveying-the-uks-parliamentary-boroughs-map-making-and-the-1831-2-boundary-commissions/

Spychal, M., '"The power of returning our members will henceforth be in our own hands": parliamentary reform and its impact on Exeter, 1820–1868', *The Victorian Commons* (May, 2020), https://victoriancommons.wordpress.com/2020/05/30/the-power-of-returning-our-members-will-henceforth-be-in-our-own-hands-parliamentary-reform-and-its-impact-on-exeter-1820-1868/

Online reference sources

Causes and Consequences of Electoral Violence: Evidence from England and Wales, 1832–1914, https://victorianelectionviolence.uk/interactive-map/

Clergy of the Church of England Database, http://www.theclergydatabase.org.uk

Digging into Linked Parliamentary Data, https://web.archive.org/web/20160213065928/http://dilipad.history.ac.uk/

Eggers and Spirling Database, https://andy.egge.rs/eggers_spirling_database.html

Great Britain Historical GIS, http://www.visionofbritain.org.uk

Hansard @ Huddersfield, https://web.archive.org/web/20230326061515/https://hansard.hud.ac.uk/site/site.php

Legacies of British Slave Ownership, https://www.ucl.ac.uk/lbs

Measuring Worth, https://www.measuringworth.com

Salmon, P., and Rix, K. (eds.), The House of Commons, 1832–68, https://www.historyofparliamentonline.org/research/1832-1868

Unpublished theses

Andrews, J. H., 'Political Issues in the County of Kent, 1820–1846', MPhil. diss. London (1967)

Atton, K. J., 'Municipal and Parliamentary Politics in Ipswich, 1818–1847', PhD diss. London (1979)

Bylsma, J., 'Political Issues and Party Unity in the House of Commons, 1852–1857: A Scalogram Analysis', PhD diss. Iowa (1968)

Dwyer, J. A., 'An Enlightened Scot and English Reform: A Study of Henry Brougham', PhD diss. British Columbia (1975)

Fraser, D., 'Politics in Leeds', PhD diss. Leeds (1969)

Grobel, M. C., 'The Society for the Diffusion of Useful Knowledge, 1826–1846', MA diss., London (1933)
Hayes, B. D., 'Politics in Norfolk, 1750–1832', PhD diss. Cambridge (1957)
Lively, J. F., 'Ideas of Parliamentary Representation in England, 1815–32', PhD diss. Cambridge (1957)
Lloyd-Jones, N., 'A New British History of the Home Rule Crisis: Public Opinion, Representation and Organisation', PhD diss. London (2019)
Pickles, D., 'The Bowling Tramways', Unspecified diss. held by Bradford Industrial Museum (1966)
Radice, P. K. V., 'Identification, Interests, and Influence: Voting Behaviour in Four English Constituencies in the Decade after the Great Reform Act', PhD diss. Durham (1992)
Richardson, S., 'Independence and Deference: A Study of the West Riding Electorate', PhD diss, Leeds (1995)
Smith, J., 'Legislating for the Four Nations at Westminster in the Age of Reform, 1830–1852', PhD diss. York (2021)
Speight, M. E., 'Politics in the Borough of Colchester, 1812–1847', PhD diss. London (1969)
Thompson, S., 'Census-Taking, Political Economy and State Formation in Britain, c. 1790–1840', PhD diss. Cambridge (2010)
Watt, R. G., 'Parties and Politics in Mid-Victorian Britain, 1857–1859: A Study in Quantification', PhD diss. Minnesota (1975)
Woodberry, R., 'Redistribution and the Second Reform Act: The Intended, and Unintended, Electoral Effects on the Balance of the Political Parties', PhD diss. Bristol (2007)

Index

A

1831-2 boundary commission (England and Wales)
  ancient boroughs, 113-25, 173-91, 201-21
  anti-reform criticism, 101-3, 115, 127, 128-9, 134-40, 178-9, 188-90, 216-17, 247
  boundary bill, 86
  data gathering, 13, 111-43
  division of counties, 6, 13, 213, 263-85
  Drummond's list, 5-6, 13, 112-13, 128-40, 213, 304-5
  establishment, 13, 83-106
  four nations precedent, 11, 86
  gerrymandering (cabinet), 140, 217, 244-9, 238, 247-9, 251-3, 264, 274-80
  gerrymandering (commissioners), 187-9
  gerrymandering (Littleton), 184, 188-9, 210-14, 221, 236, 244-7, 252, 278, 281-2
  historiography, 5-6, 86, 103-4, 112-13, 173-4, 218, 264
  legacy, 142-3, 191, 294, 301-2, 303, 304-5, 308
  local opinion, 112-17, 176-9, 208
  new boroughs, 125-8, 233-52
  nomination towns and polling places, 265, 280-85, 292-4
  parliamentary committee, 68-70, 87-90, 101, 85-90, 116
  privy council committee, 62-6, 67-70, 234
  pro-reform response, 102-3, 110-11, 115-16, 142-3
  published reports, 1, 134-6, 142, 178-9, 188, 208, 216, 244, 269, 275-7, 301, 304-5
  royal commission, 64
  'scientific' approach, 6, 7, 83-5, 96-105, 111-13, 118-43, 151, 173-4, 175-9, 183-4, 190-1, 220-21 234, 239, 266-8, 278-80, 284-5
  significance to British state, 13, 83-5, 103-5, 113, 140-43, 303
  sitting committee, 124-5, 152, 174, 176, 183, 186, 188, 202, 210-13, 216-17, 244-52, 265
  working committee, 94-5, 99, 152, 173-91, 201-21, 232-52
  working papers (T72), 2, 11-12
Abercromby, James, 89-90
Abingdon, 190, 193
administrative geographies, 174-86, 191, 203-4, 241, 254, 266-7, 294

Airy, George Biddell, 135
Aldborough, 114, 209-10, 216
Allen, Launcelot Baugh, Tancred, Henry, 89, 99, 176, 182, 240-41
Althorp, Viscount, 33, 92, 266, 276, 301
  boundary commission, 97, 103, 128, 186, 211, 212-13, 221, 238, 249
  division of counties, 72-5, 280-81, 285
  language of science, 84, 101-2, 104
  SDUK, 91
America, 24-5, 37, 240
Amersham, 137-9, 209, 216
Andover, 120, 193
Ansley, Benjamin, 89, 94, 99, 123, 124-5, 178-9, 182, 208-9
anti-corporation reformers, 64, 112, 141
anti-reformers, 33-5, 44, 95-6
Appleby, 139-40
Aris's Birmingham Gazette, 238
Arundel, 122, 190, 208-9, 217, 285
Ashburton, 120, 204, 218, 224
Ashton, Rosemary, 92
Attwood, Thomas, 71
Aydelotte, William, 10
Aylesbury, 39, 45, 171, 195, 202-3

B

ballot (secret voting), 70, 72, 74, 153, 159, 162, 166-70, 191-2, 225-7, 254, 288
Baily, Francis, 94
Banbury, 116, 120, 216, 224, 302
Barlow, Peter, 134
Barnes, Thomas, 70-78
Barnstaple, 39-42, 190
Bassett, Francis, 28
Bath, 182, 193
beating the bounds, 111, 118
Beaufort, Francis, 88-9, 92-3, 134-5, 152, 184, 210, 244-9
Bedford, 192
Berkshire, 284-5
Berwick-upon-Tweed, 114, 178-9
Bewdley, 204, 211, 218, 230
big data. *See* methodology
Birch, Thomas, 89, 95, 99, 130, 176, 180
Birmingham
  boundaries, 115, 237-8, 243-9, 253, 254, 256
  Political Union (BPU), 71
  representation of, 27, 29, 40, 42-4, 47-9, 51, 278, 282
Birmingham Gazette, 115, 238

339

Birmingham Journal, 238
Black, Joseph, 90
Blackburn, 46, 126, 127, 236–7, 241, 257, 262, 272
Blaxill, Luke, 12, 22–3
Bletchingley, 47, 277
Bloomsbury, 85, 92, 127
Bolton, 241, 257, 262, 271, 283
boundaries. *See* 1831–2 boundary commission (England and Wales)
boundary reform
  anti-reform views, 66–70, 95–6, 100–103, 188–9, 216–17
  historiography, 5–6, 62
  government defence, 67–70, 70–8, 87, 142, 188–9, 252
  pro-reform views, 70–78, 95–6, 186–9
  reform bill clauses, 62–6
  See also 1831–2 boundary commission (England and Wales)
boroughs (boundaries)
  300 £10 householder threshold, 62, 64–6, 67–70, 98, 117, 123–5, 151, 200–17
  ancient boroughs, 64–5, 118–21, 151–2, 173–91, 201–21
  new boroughs, 64, 151–2, 232–52
Bord, Joe, 96–7
Boston, 186, 190
Boulton, Matthew, 12, 245–7
Bourne, William Sturges, 87–8
Brackley, 133, 138
Bradford, 236–7, 239–40, 241, 249, 251–2, 253, 255, 262
Brandreth, Henry Rowland, 89, 94, 99, 176, 180
Brand, Thomas, 40
Bridport, 138, 190
Brighton, 53, 237, 256
British Association for the Advancement of Science, 96–7
British state
  central-local relationships, 110–12, 111–40, 140–43, 234–52, 305, 306–7
  commissions of inquiry, 7–8, 13–14, 83–5
  historiography, 1, 7–8, 84–5, 103–4
  'revolution in government', 7, 84
  science, 83–5
  significance of 1831–2 boundary commission, 13, 83–5, 103–5, 113, 140–43, 303, 305–7
Bridgnorth, 115, 204, 218, 213, 230
Bridgwater, 120, 180–81
Bristol, 28, 140, 182
Brock, Michael, 5, 65
Bromsgrove, 205–14

Brooke, John, 27
Brougham, Henry Peter, first Baron Brougham and Vaux, Lord, 13, 33
  1831–2 boundary commission, 85, 90, 92–7, 102, 113
  representation of Yorkshire, 63–4, 251
  reform attempts, 64, 112
  significance to British state, 104–5
  SDUK, 90–1, 101
  The Times, 74, 76, 102
  Waverers, 211–12, 265–6
Bryant, Andrew, 99
Buck, Lewis William, 289
Buckingham, 133, 209, 218, 230
Buckingham, marquess of, 38–9
Buller, John Yarde, 289
Burdett, Francis, 33–4
Burke, Edmund, 28
Bury St. Edmunds, 192
Bury, 236–7, 242, 257–8, 262, 283
Bute, second marquess of, 117, 224

C
Calne, 111, 119, 123–4, 218, 222, 230
Calvert, Nicolson, 40–1, 48
Cambridge, 28, 259, 185–6, 192
Cambridge (University), 92, 94, 97, 134–7, 266, 279
Campbell, John, 70
Cannon, John, 39
Canning, George, 45–51
Canterbury, 28, 120
Carrington, George, 182
cartography and map-making, 7–8, 12
  boundary commission, 7, 13, 85, 97–100, 118–21, 130–40, 175–89, 202–17, 239–44, 267–8, 301, 304–5, 306–7
Cartwright, William, 87–8, 276
Catholic emancipation, 21, 38, 48–50, 51
Census data, 6, 64–6, 100, 118, 128–9, 134, 141, 235–9, 267, 269
Chadwick, Edwin, 83, 142–3
Chapman, John James, 89, 94, 99, 115–6, 119, 125, 186–9, 205–7, 242
Chartists, 293, 305
Cheltenham, 53, 237, 256
Cheshire, 290–93, 274, 281, 296
Christchurch, 114, 124, 204, 209, 218, 223, 230
church rates, abolition, 153–71, 191–2, 225–6, 253–4, 288, 292
Cirencester, 73, 120, 216, 218, 230
Clitheroe, 210, 218, 229, 230
Cockermouth, 204, 218, 230
Cocks, John Somers, 278–9
Colby, Thomas, 93, 101

commissions and committees,
  1816 select committee on education, 90
  charity commission, 85–6, 90, 92
  commissions of inquiry, 85–6
  'committee men', 87–8
  constitutional precedent, 65–6, 86, 103
  criminal law, 303
  factory reform, 7, 83, 84, 103, 302
  municipal corporations, 8, 83, 103, 191, 302
  poor laws, 7, 83, 84, 103, 142–3, 302
  public health, 83–4, 141–3, 303
  slavery compensation, 302
  tithes, 8, 83, 302–3
  weights and measures, 303
  See also 1831–2 boundary commission (England and Wales)
committee of four, 62–6, 235–6
Cobbett's Parliamentary Debates, 12, 29–30
Cobbett, William, 46
Colchester, 41, 115, 119
corn laws, 10, 25, 29, 35–7, 46–7, 49, 153–71, 191–2, 224–6, 234–5, 254, 286–8, 307
Cornwall, 180, 270–73, 289, 292, 296
corpus linguistics, 12–13, 29–38
constituency system, pre–1832
  boroughs, 21, 24, 26–9, 111–43
  boundary reform, 38–53
  counties, 21, 24–6, 280–81
  defence of, 21–9
  nomination boroughs, 28–9, 73, 233–4
  university boroughs, 21–2
constituency system, post–1832, 9, 13, 305–7
  boroughs, 128, 151
  counties, 151, 285–94
  divided counties, 13, 151–70, 263–94, 306
  double-member system, 211–12
  enfranchisement rates, 128–9
  modern town, 13, 151–70, 173–95, 306
  multiple parish, 13, 151–70, 186, 201–27, 306
  new boroughs, 13, 126, 128, 151–70, 232–58, 306
  nomination towns and polling places, 292–4
  proprietorial influence, 220–24, 280, 291–2
  unchanged boroughs, 13, 151–70, 173–95, 306
  unchanged counties, 13, 151–70, 285–94
  university boroughs, 151–70
Conservatives, 10–11, 13, 191–5, 221–7, 252–8, 288–94, 306–7

Conti, Gregory, 23
corruption, 22, 39–51, 159, 194–5, 221–4, 226–7, 290, 303
Courier, 134
Courtenay, William 88–9
Coventry, 115, 188, 192, 278, 282
Cragoe, Matthew, 7–8
Creighton, Richard, 267–8
Cricklade, 38, 45, 171, 195, 202–3
Cripps, Joseph, 73
Croker, John Wilson,
  boundary bill, 176–9, 216, 247
  division of counties, 73
  Drummond's list, 134–8
  minor reform, 44–5, 47
Crook, Tom, 141
Crosbie, Malcolm Douglas, 301
Cumberland, 270–73, 275
currency reform, 35, 37, 254

D

Daily News, 224
Dartmouth, 139, 193
Dawson, Robert Kearsley, 11, 89, 94, 98–9, 103, 130, 267, 302–3
democratisation (concept), 2–3, 4, 305
Denman, Thomas, 65, 91, 282
Derby, 188–9, 192, 259
Derby, fourteenth earl of (Edward Smith Stanley), 48, 70, 283
  governments of, 159, 286, 307
Derbyshire, 74, 270–73
Devizes, 119, 193
Devon, 130, 180, 270–73
Devonport, 270–71, 256
Dickinson, William, 87
disfranchisement schedules, (reform bill), 68, 121, 128–40, 210, 212
Disraeli, Benjamin, 227, 286, 303, 307
division of counties
  anti-reform criticism, 66–70, 267
  development of reform bill clauses, 62–4, 263–6
  government defence, 67, 266–7, 274, 278–80
  pro-reform criticism, 70–78, 267
  See also 1831–2 boundary commission (England and Wales)
Dod, Charles, 13
Dorchester, 175–6
Doyle, John, 77–8
Draper, Nicholas, 28
Drinkwater, John Elliot, 89, 94, 97, 99, 103, 121, 127, 175–6, 180, 207–8, 217, 302

Droitwich, 114, 201, 204, 205–17, 218, 220, 223
Drummond, Thomas, 92–4
    ancient boroughs, 173–189
    centrality to reform, 1, 3, 304–5
    division of counties, 267, 284–5
    Drummond's list, 5–6, 128–40, 141–3, 304–5
    establishing commission, 85, 89–90, 92–5
    legacy, 142–3, 191, 301–2, 303, 304–5, 308
    local opinion, 113–18
    multiple parish boroughs, 201–18
    new boroughs, 234, 239–52
    'scientific' approach, 96–105, 111–13, 118–43, 151, 173–4, 184, 190–91, 234, 239
    supervision of commission, 118–28, 152, 301
Duncannon, Viscount, 74
Dudley, 115, 211, 236, 256, 257, 270, 282
Durham (borough), 120, 178–9, 183
Durham (county), 112, 114, 270–73, 292
Durham, earl, 64, 112

E

economic distress, 23, 35–8
Edinburgh Review, 90–91
Edinburgh, University, 90, 93
Eggers, Andy, Spirling, Arthur, 9–10, 13
electoral culture, 9, 193–5, 221–7, 256–8, 292–3
Ellis, Thomas Flower, 89, 94, 99, 111, 176, 302
Eastwood, David, 9
East India Company, 37
Essex, 270–73, 290, 296
Essex Standard, 115
Evesham, 39, 122, 133, 207, 211–12
Examiner, 74
Exeter, 176–7, 194
expertise, 84, 86, 87, 92, 95, 98, 141, 182, 301–3
Eye, 133, 216, 218, 222, 230

F

Finsbury, 126, 127–8, 244, 249–50, 256
Fox, Charles James, 28
franchise
    £10 householders, 64–6, 75, 98, 100, 115, 121–8, 190, 192–5, 200, 255
    ancient boroughs, 65, 120–21, 128–9, 192–5, 221–7, 255, 304
    counties, 68, 75, 102, 187–9, 205–6, 213, 265, 272–4, 290

enfranchisement rates, 126, 128–9
types of, 28, 39, 48
French Revolution, 1830, 5
free trade, 10, 25, 29, 35–7, 46–7, 49, 153–71, 191–2, 224–6, 234–5, 254, 286–8, 307
Freshfield, James, 69
Frome, 239, 240, 242, 256

G

Gash, Norman, 2, 5, 201–2
Gateshead, 114, 236, 240, 242, 256, 270
Gawler, Henry, 89, 94, 99, 114, 123, 178–9, 182, 208–9
gender
    women and 1832 reform legislation, 4, 128, 257
general elections
    1826, 46–7, 63–4, 225, 274
    1830, 202, 225, 274
    1831, 61–2, 68–70, 86, 87, 202, 224, 225, 274, 286
    1832, 128–9, 224, 225, 226, 248, 253, 277, 290, 301
    1835, 129, 225, 272, 288, 290, 307
    1837, 129, 159–60, 223, 225, 292
    1841, 129, 225,
    1847, 129, 192, 225–6
    1852, 129, 159, 225, 288, 292
    1857, 129, 225
    1859, 129, 192, 224–5
    1865, 128–9, 192, 225–6, 227
Gilbert, Davies, 88–9, 138
Globe, 74
Gloucester, 115, 119, 188, 194
Gloucestershire, 187, 270–74, 283–4, 296
Goderich, Viscount, 214
Goulburn, Henry, 73, 279
Gordon, Sir James Willoughby, 88–9
Graham, Sir James, 92
Grampound, 39–45, 46, 63
Grantham, 216, 218, 230
Great Britain Historical GIS Project, 13
Greenwood, Christopher, 98, 119
Greenwood, Cox & Co., 98
Grenville, Lord, 38–9
Grey, second Earl, 34, 93
    boundary reform, 71, 86–7, 89, 112, 127, 128, 140, 211–12, 214, 221, 249, 265
    government of, 4, 7, 11, 22, 51, 61–2, 76, 78, 83–5, 86, 90, 95, 96, 104–5, 113, 141, 142, 195, 201–2, 221, 224, 233–4, 251, 253, 263–4, 280, 308
    unreformed electoral system, 26
Grimsby, Great, 184, 209, 218, 226, 230, 231
Grinstead, East, 120–21, 210, 216

H

Hallam, Henry, 88–9
Halifax, 43, 128, 237, 242, 251–2
Hampshire, 263, 270–73, 276–7, 288, 293, 296
Hansard's Parliamentary Debates, 12, 29–30
Hansard at Huddersfield, 30
Harvey, Daniel Whittle, 41
Harwich, 192
Hastings, 192, 197
hats, 233
Hawkins, Angus, 10, 174, 304–5
Heath, William, 91
Heathcote, Gilbert John, 292
Heesom, Alan, 9
Helston, 39–42, 137–9, 210, 217–18
Herefordshire, 292
Herschel, John, 12, 96, 134–5
Hertford, 40, 120, 191, 197, 294
Hertfordshire, 294
Heygate, Alderman, 41
Heywood, Benjamin, 251
Hilton, Boyd, 83, 202
History of Parliament, 6, 9, 13, 151
Honiton, 120, 204, 218, 224, 230
Hoppit, Julian, 25
Horner, Leonard, 142
Horsham, 124, 204, 218, 230
Huddersfield, 237, 243–4, 252, 262
Hughes Hughes, William, 72–4
Hull, 114, 123, 183
Hume, David, 90
Hume, Joseph, 33–4, 250
Hunt, Henry, 136
Huntingdon, 133, 137, 204, 218, 222, 231
Huskisson, William, 34, 47–51
Hythe, 209, 216, 218, 223, 224, 230

I

Ilchester, 281
India, 8, 28, 30, 31, 37, 52
Inglis, Robert, 21–2
Ireland, 4–5, 11, 21, 38–9 93, 301–2

J

Jaggard, Edwin, 221
Jardine, George, 93
John Bull, 68, 74, 115
Jolliffe, Colonel Hylton, 68–9
Jones, Richard, 97
Joyce, Patrick, 8, 306–7
Judd, Gerrit, 27

K

Keck, George Legh, 47
Kendal, 242, 256
Kent, 75, 99, 270–73, 277
Ker, Henry Bellenden, 92–5, 99, 101–02, 175, 182, 303
Kettering, 263, 293
Kidderminster, 115, 211, 242, 256
King's Lynn, 122, 186
Knaresborough, 42, 193
Knatchbull, Edward, 87–8
Knightley, Charles, 276

L

Lambeth, 237, 244, 250, 256, 270
Lancashire, 43, 51, 126, 232, 237, 251, 288
  division of, 268–73, 283, 285, 290, 305
Lancaster, 182–3
Langford, Paul, 25
Lansdowne, third marquess of, 64, 87–8, 96, 212, 213–14, 221–2
Launceston, 210, 218, 222, 230
Lawley, Francis, 238, 278, 282, 288
Leeds, 27, 29, 40, 42–4, 51, 183, 255, 256
Leeds Mercury, 74
Leeds Intelligencer, 115
Lefevre, John George Shaw, 13, 88, 92, 302
  division of counties, 264–80, 294, 305, 308
  nomination towns and polling places, 280–85
legislation
  1707 Act of Union, 65
  1765 Stamp Act, 24–5
  1828 Sacramental Test Act, 38
  1832 Boundary Act (England and Wales), 1, 11, 13, 86, 152, 174, 190–91, 193, 194, 201, 217, 234, 247, 249–55, 264, 269, 273–4, 276–80, 281, 284, 285, 294, 301, 304–6, 308
  1832 Boundary Act (Ireland), 4–5, 11
  1832 Reform Act (England and Wales), 11, 61–2, 152
  1832 Reform Act (Ireland), 4–5, 11
  1832 Reform Act (Scotland), 4–5, 11
  1832 reform legislation, 305–8
    contemporary debate, 3, 23–4, 45, 126, 127–8, 130–33, 134–140
    development of boundary clauses, 13, 61–78, 86, 234–9, 265–6, 304
    disfranchisement schedules, 5–6, 13, 112–13, 128–40, 210, 212, 304
    franchise clauses, 127–8
    historiography, 1, 4–6, 11, 22, 218, 234
    precedents, 13, 294

legislation (*continued*)
    1835 Municipal Corporations Act, 191, 193
    1867–8 reform legislation, 227
    1868 Boundary Act, 191, 294, 305–6
    1885 Redistribution of Seats Act, 191, 226, 294, 305–6
Leicester, 194, 270
Leicestershire, 47, 70, 75–6, 270–3, 278, 292
Lennard, George Barrett, 89, 94–5, 99, 101, 182
Leominster, 120, 133, 176, 216–18, 230
Leslie, John, 93
Lewis, Thomas Frankland, 87–8
liberal governmentality, 8, 306–7
liberal Tories, 7, 47–53, 83, 91, 96, 102, 286
Liberal Conservatives, 10
Liberal (party), 10–11, 13, 158–62, 191–5, 221–7, 252–8, 288–94, 306–7
Liberal Registration Society, 291
Lichfield, 192, 281–2
Lincoln, 120
Liverpool, 28, 126, 182, 194, 240–41, 259, 271, 283
Liverpool, second earl of (formerly Robert Jenkinson), 26, 27–8, 34, 44, 45, 47
Liskeard, 120, 204, 218, 224
Lister, Ellis Cunliffe, 251, 255
Littleton, Edward,
    boundary commission, 88, 301
    division of counties, 72, 277–9
    midland boundaries (gerrymandering), 188–9, 210–14, 221, 236, 244–7, 252, 277–2
    sitting committee, 152, 184, 210, 244, 247, 249, 265
Lloyd-Jones, Naomi, 12
local officials, 101–2
    information sharing, 62, 64–6, 100, 103, 111–34, 140–43, 178–9, 233–44, 305–7
London (city), 72, 120, 265
London University (later UCL), 85, 90–92, 94–5
Lostwithiel, 133, 138–9, 209
Ludlow, 120, 175
Luttrell, John, 26
Lyme Regis, 120, 208, 209, 218, 224
Lymington, 114, 204
Lyttelton, Lord, 278, 288

M

Macaulay, Thomas, 110–11, 140
Macclesfield, 242, 256, 257, 262, 270
Mackintosh, James, 42–3, 48
McIntyre, Eneas, 137
McLean's Monthly Sheet of Caricatures, 290–91

Maidstone, 180
Maldon, 208–9, 218, 224, 230
Malmesbury, 124, 133, 209, 218, 223, 230
Malton, 114, 204, 218, 230
Manchester, 27, 29, 40, 42–4, 47–8, 51, 126–7, 182–3, 237, 256, 258
Manchester Statistical Society, 97
Manners-Sutton, Charles, 64
mathematics, 90, 93, 128–30, 133–4, 133–8
maps. *See* cartography and map-making
'march of intellect', 91–2
Marlborough, 119, 209, 218, 230
Martin, Henry, 88–9
Marx, Karl, 4
Marylebone, 127, 244, 249–50, 256
mechanics' institutes, 90, 96
Melbourne, Viscount (William Lamb), 47–51, 75
    boundary reform, 95, 97, 214
    governments of, 83, 153
methodology
    corpus linguistics, 29–31
    digital methods, 3, 12–13, 22–3, 30–31
    roll-call analysis, 9–11, 13, 150–65
    traditional approach to political history, 11–12
merchants, 27
Midhurst, 133, 139, 216, 218, 230
Millar, John, 90
Miller, Henry, 12, 306
Milton, Viscount, 44–5, 96, 276
Minehead, 139
Mirror of Parliament, 12
Moore, D. C., 2, 5, 4, 50, 5, 173–4, 201, 219–21, 253, 264–5, 267, 274, 278
Moorsom, Richard, 238, 247–9
Morning Chronicle, 72, 74–5, 284–5
Morning Herald, 74
Morning Post
    criticism of boundary reform, 68–9, 74, 101, 134, 292–3
    reporting on interests, 41, 45
Morpeth, 114, 139, 209, 218, 230

N

Namier, Lewis, 4
Navickas, Katrina, 8, 174, 191, 306–7
navigation laws, 37
Newark, 90, 184, 192
Newbould, Ian, 10
Newcastle upon Tyne, 183, 241, 270, 272–3
Newton (Lancashire), 133, 283
Nonconformists, 38, 159, 235, 257
Norfolk, 270–73, 290, 296
North, Lord, 26
Northallerton, 114, 120, 124, 209, 218, 230

Northampton, 34, 186, 194
Northamptonshire, 96, 263, 266, 270–73, 276–7, 290, 293
Northumberland, 113–14,1 86, 270–73
Norwich Mercury, 70
Nottingham, 188–89, 190, 281
Nottinghamshire, 75, 188, 270–73, 281, 292

O

Okehampton, 210, 216
Oldham, 233–4, 237, 244, 249, 251–2, 254, 257, 262
Oliver, Richard, 7
Ord, William, 89, 94–5, 99, 101, 115–16, 119, 125, 186–9, 205–7, 242
Ordnance Survey, 6, 85, 90, 93–4, 98–9, 101, 115, 118, 130, 141, 184, 267
O'Gorman, Frank, 9, 257
Oxford University, 21, 22, 92

P

Page, Frederick, 94
Palmerston, Viscount, 74
  boundary reform, 213–14, 221, 277, 288
  governments of, 226
  parliamentary reform, 47–9, 51
Parliamentary Companion, 13
parliamentary government, 10
parliamentary returns, 62, 64–6, 118, 121, 136, 267, 306–7
Parkes, Joseph, 72, 78, 142–3, 190
Peel, Robert, 33, 92
  boundary reform, 67, 73, 102, 134, 136, 282
  governments of, 153, 159, 224, 226, 286, 307
  minor reform, 47–9, 51–2
Penryn, 28, 39–42, 46–8, 69, 209, 216
Peterborough, 186, 216, 218, 222
Peterloo Massacre, 41, 45
Petersfield, 69, 131, 133–5, 216, 218, 230, 266, 302
petitioning, 23, 29, 35–7, 46, 61, 71, 78, 100, 292
  boundaries, 153, 179, 186, 190, 236–39, 249–50, 252, 305–6
  election petitions, 266
  Drummond's list, 137, 140
  nomination towns and polling places, 282, 284
Pickersgill, Henry William, 1
Pitt, William (the Younger), 26, 28
Pitt, William (Lord Chatham), 28
Playfair, John, 90, 93
Plymouth, 120, 132, 270–71

Plympton Earle, 130–34, 139
Phillips, John, 7–8
political parties, 9
  labels, 9, 13, 274
  organisation, 9, 10, 193–5, 221–7, 256–8, 263, 288–94
political unions, 5, 61, 71, 75, 76, 212, 238
political economy, 3, 7, 47, 52, 90–2, 96, 101, 266
Pollock, Frederick, 137–8
Pontefract, 114, 133, 190
Poole, 190, 259
Porter, Theodore, 97
Portsmouth, 193, 270
Preston, 136, 176, 251
protectionism, 35–6

Q

Quarterly Review, 67
Queen Caroline affair, 45, 90
Quetelet, Adolphe, 97

R

radicals, 10, 33–4
Reading, 192, 193, 266
railways, 223, 224, 240–41, 256, 283, 302
redistribution of seats, 4–5, 38, 40, 46, 51–2, 62, 64, 76–7, 190, 203, 294, 304–5
reformers, 10, 33–4, 71, 76, 191, 193, 226, 253, 286–7, 289
registration of voters, 9, 128, 193–5, 221–7, 255–7, 288–93, 304–5
Reigate, 204, 207, 209, 218, 222, 230, 279
Rendel, James Meadows, 131, 132–3
representation of interests, 3, 12, 63, 174, 220–21, 256, 307–8
  agricultural interest, 13, 30–32, 35–7, 40–53, 63, 73, 202–3, 206–8, 218, 220, 223–7, 242–9, 253, 263, 278–80, 281–3, 285, 306–7
  aristocracy, 26, 41, 62, 72–6
  boundary commission, 174, 175–9, 201, 205–10, 213, 219–21, 233, 237, 247, 252, 263, 279–80, 285
  Catholic interest, 22, 30–32, 38
  Church interest, 22, 30–32, 38, 52
  colonial interest, 22, 27, 28, 30–32
  commercial interest, 22, 24, 26–8, 30–32, 35, 36–8, 40–53, 63, 203, 220, 233–5, 253, 255–8, 306–7
  crown, 26
  defence of unreformed electoral map, 21–9
  democracy, 26, 41

representation of interests (*continued*)
  East India interest, 22, 28, 30–32, 52–3
  iron interest, 256, 282
  landed interest, 13, 24–6, 30–32, 35–6, 39, 62–3, 202–3, 213, 218, 223–7, 263, 306–7
  language of, 13, 29–38
  legal interest, 52
  manufacturing interest, 22, 27, 30–32, 35, 40–53, 188, 207–8, 233–5, 238, 242–9, 253, 255–8, 278–280, 285, 306–7
  monied interest, 22, 24, 27, 30–32, 36, 53
  naval interest, 52, 256
  professional interest, 22, 27, 28–9, 52
  shipping interest, 22, 30–32, 36–7, 52–3, 248–9, 256
  textile interest, 256–7
  'watering–hole' interest, 52
  West India interest, 22, 28, 30–32, 36–8, 52–3, 56
  representative theory
  mirroring models, 23, 42–3
  virtual representation, 24–5
Retford, East, 38, 45, 46–53, 171, 195, 202–3
Ricardo, David, 97
Richmond, 114, 120, 204, 218, 230, 252, 285, 292
Richmond, duke of, 284
Ripon, 120, 139, 193
Robson, Brian, 6
Rochdale, 237, 241, 257, 262, 283
Rochester, 175, 270
roll–call analysis, 9–11, 13, 150–65
Romilly, John, 89, 94–5, 99, 126–7, 176, 182–3, 240–41, 302
Rosslyn, Lord, 87
Roszman, Jay, 301–2
Royal artillery, 89, 90, 94–5
Royal Astronomical Society, 92–4, 184
Royal engineers, 90, 93–5, 141
Royal Geographical Society, 92
Royal Society, 87–90, 93, 138, 266
Russell, Lord John,
  attempted gerrymandering, 244–9
  boundary commission, 97, 128, 133, 134, 203, 211–14
  boundary reform proposals, 85–92, 95, 238, 265
  critique of unreformed electoral map, 23–4, 41–53, 112, 307
  defence of boundary bill, 252, 266, 283
  defence of reform bill, 67
  defence of Whig reform agenda, 83, 104
  drafting reform bill, 64–5
  governments of, 225, 302
  reform proposals after 1832, 227, 307–8
Rye, 208–9, 216–17, 218, 230

S

Saltash, 210, 216
St. Albans, 194, 197
St. Ives, 210, 217, 218, 223, 230
St. James's Chronicle, 137
Salford, 126, 237, 258, 262, 270, 271
Salmon, Philip,
  boundary reform, 2, 6, 201–2, 264, 266
  'consultation' model, 62, 76, 113, 141, 236, 238, 305–6
  registration, 7–8, 128, 272
Sandwich, 120, 259
Saunders, Robert John, 89, 94–5, 99, 103, 121, 175–6, 180, 207, 217, 302
Scarborough, 193
Schonhardt–Bailey, Cheryl, 10
science, 12, 96–7
  anti–reform view, 101–3, 134–8
  boundary commission, 6, 7, 83–5, 96–105, 111–13, 118–43, 151, 173–4, 175–9, 183–4, 190–91, 220–21 234, 239, 266–8, 278–80
  disinterestedness and impartiality, 3, 84, 87, 96–101, 104, 112–13, 116–17, 125, 140–43, 174–5, 178–9, 188, 203, 220–21, 253, 264–5, 278–80, 284–5, 304–5
  social science movement, 7, 90–91, 97
  Whig governing ethos, 3, 7, 83–5, 95–7, 103–5
Scotland, 4, 21, 93, 98–9, 202
Scotsman, 136
Scottish Enlightenment, 83, 85, 96
Scott, Richard, 89, 94, 99
Seymour, Robert, 50
Shaftesbury, 119, 124, 204, 216, 218, 226, 230
Sheepshanks, Richard, 89, 94, 99, 101, 179, 184–6, 204, 303
Sheffield, 43, 44, 182, 241, 244, 249–50, 255–7
Sheldrick, George, 301
Shields, North (Tynemouth), 241, 258
Shields, South, 114, 256, 258, 270
Shoreham, New, 38, 45, 171, 195, 202–3
Shropshire, 270–73, 290, 296
Sidney, Algernon, 24–5
slavery, 28, 35, 37–8, 302
Smith, James, 12
Smith, Joshua Toulmin, 303
Smith, Sydney, 90, 303
Society for the Diffusion of Useful Knowledge (SDUK), 7, 12, 76, 85, 89–101, 184, 266

Somerset, 180, 270–73, 277, 283–4, 289–90, 296
Southwark, 270
Stafford, 194
Staffordshire, 44, 72, 132, 152, 184
  boroughs, 235–6
  division of, 270–73, 281–3, 285, 289, 292
  representation of, 115, 245–7
Stamford, 185–6, 190
Standard, 101, 102, 137
Statistical Society of London, 97
statistics, 3, 6
  boundary commission, 7, 13, 85, 96–7, 100–1, 118–21, 128–43, 269–73
  electoral system, 42–3
  inductive method, 83, 85, 97, 104
  legislative application, 104–5, 302–3, 305, 306–7
  social science, 96–7
Stewart, Dugald, 90
Stanley, Edward John, 70
Stoke-on-Trent, 124, 127, 188, 237, 242, 244, 249, 250, 255, 256, 257
Strickland, George, 71, 251–2
Stroud, 242–3, 256, 257, 270
Sudbury, 41, 194–5, 204
Suffolk, 270–73, 276–7, 288–9, 296
sugar duties, 37–8
Sugden, Edward, 33, 69–70
Sumner, John Holme, 43–4
Sun, 137
Sunderland, 114, 240, 241, 243–4, 247–9, 256, 257, 258, 270
surveyors, 1, 94, 98–100, 112, 118–19, 123, 130–34, 141, 174, 175–83, 203–4, 217, 239, 246, 302, 305
Sussex, 208, 270–73, 277, 285, 290, 292

T

Tallents, William, 89–90, 95, 101, 121, 179, 184–6, 204
Tamworth, 124, 216, 218, 226, 230, 282
Tancred, Henry, 9, 94, 99, 113–14, 122–4, 178–9, 183, 209, 224, 240, 242–3, 247, 302
tariffs and trade duties, 27, 35–9, 46–7
Taunton, 120, 281
Tavistock, 41, 124, 139, 216, 230
taxation
  compounding, 126–8
  house duty (assessed), 100, 115, 120, 122–3, 126, 129–30, 132–4, 137, 139, 202
  paving, watch and lighting, 122
  poor rate, 36, 122–3, 126–7

Taylor, Miles, 9, 12, 256
Tennyson, Charles, 47–9, 190
Tewkesbury, 116, 119, 187, 216, 219, 224
Thetford, 192, 209, 216
The Times,
  boundary commission, 102, 116, 134
  division of counties, 62, 70–78, 264
  reporting on interests, 40–41, 45
Thicknesse, Ralph, 283
Thornton, Robert, 182
Thirsk, 114, 120, 209, 219, 226, 230
Tithes, 8, 38, 83, 97, 302–3
Tiverton, 192–3
Tories
  country Tories, 24, 26, 27
  ministerialists, 33–4, 47–53, 87
  ultra-tories, 33–4, 50, 51–2, 87
Totnes, 137, 194, 204
Thompson, Stephen, 6, 7
Tower Hamlets, 244, 249–50, 255, 256
Truro, 120, 192, 204
Tynemouth, 114, 236–7, 239, 256, 270, 273
Tyrell, Charles, 277, 288

U

universal suffrage, 42, 71–2

V

Vernon, James, 257

W

Wakefield, 114, 237, 242, 256,
Wales, 4, 11, 21, 98–100, 111, 182, 202
Wall, Charles Baring, 102–3
Wallace, William, 135
Wallingford, 124–5, 209, 219, 230
Walsall, 115, 235–6, 242, 246, 256, 270, 281–2
Warburton, Henry, 138
Ward, John, earl of Dudley, 44–5, 47, 49
Wareham, 133, 209, 217, 219, 226, 231
Warrington, 240–41, 283
Warwick, 115, 191
Warwickshire, 43, 51, 188, 238, 245, 270–73, 277–80, 282–3, 285, 288, 290
Wasson, Ellis, 45, 78
Waverers, the, 128–9, 139, 202, 210–13, 218, 219–20, 265–6
Wellington, duke of, 22, 47, 71, 87
  government of, 48–52, 61, 87

INDEX

Wells, 120
Westbury, 120, 137, 139, 209, 219, 230
Westminster (constituency), 192, 193
Wetherell, Charles, 103, 138
Weymouth, 72, 120
Wharncliffe, Lord, 265
Whewell, William, 96
Whitehaven, 237, 239, 242, 256
Wigan, 192, 283
Windsor, 193
Whigs, 4, 10, 33–4, 51, 91–2, 191–5, 221–7, 252–8, 288–94
   country Whigs, 24, 26, 27
   court Whigs, 24, 27
   rationale for reform, 41–5, 46, 49–53, 218–19, 244
   science, 83–5, 95–7
   social reform, 84–5
Whitby, 53, 114, 237–9, 243–4, 247–9, 253, 256
Wilbraham, George, 274
William IV, 5, 61, 93
Wilton, 119, 133, 209, 219, 222, 230
Wiltshire, 70, 119, 270–73
Winchester, 120, 178, 193

Wolverhampton, 115, 235–6, 237, 242, 246, 256, 258, 270, 282
Wood, John, 251
Woodstock, New, 216, 218, 230
Worcester, 114, 116–17, 187–9
Worcester Herald, 115
Worcestershire, 44, 71, 115, 187, 201, 207, 212, 270–73, 277–8, 288
Wright, Robison, 118
Wrottesley, John, 89, 94–5, 99, 101, 113–14, 122–4, 178–9, 183, 209, 224, 240, 242–3, 247, 302
Wycombe, Chipping, 204, 216, 219, 230
Wylde, William, 89, 94, 99, 176, 302
Wynford, Baron, 252, 34

Y

Yarmouth, Great, 186
York, 96, 120, 183, 193
Yorkshire, 71, 113, 236, 252
   division of, 62–3, 266, 269, 289–90, 305
   representation of, 40, 43–51, 72, 90, 251
Yorkshire Association, 26
Young, Thomas, 75

Printed in the USA
CPSIA information can be obtained
at www.ICGtesting.com
CBHW060740270924
14914CB00006B/42